# Mothering TWINS

## From Hearing the News to Beyond the Terrible Twos

❧

LINDA ALBI, DONNA FLORIEN DEURLOO, DEBORAH JOHNSON,

DEBRA CATLIN, AND SHERYLL GREATWOOD

A FIRESIDE BOOK
Published by Simon & Schuster
New York • London • Toronto • Sydney • Tokyo • Singapore

**F**

FIRESIDE
Simon & Schuster Building
Rockefeller Center
1230 Avenue of the Americas
New York, New York 10020

Designed by Chris Welch
Manufactured in the United States of America
1   3   5   7   9   10   8   6   4   2
Library of Congress Cataloging-in-Publication Data
Mothering twins : from hearing the news to beyond the terrible
twos / Linda Albi . . . [et al.].
p.      cm.
"A Fireside book."
Includes bibliographical references and index.
1. Twins.   2. Child rearing.   I. Albi, Linda.
HQ777.35.M58   1993
649'.144—dc20                    93-10244   CIP
ISBN 0-671-72357-X

# Acknowledgments

Our deepest thanks go to our husbands, children, families, and friends for their steadfast love, support, and encouragement.

We would also like to thank:

Carole Abel, our agent, for her enthusiastic and professional support.

Sydny Miner, our editor, for her vision of our book and her many reassurances that we were doing a fine job as she helped us shape and ready our book for publication.

Margo Moore for her guidance and literary perspective on the initial drafts of this book.

Elizabeth Lyons for her helpful insights into the field of publishing.

The Birth to Three Organization, whose support groups for parents of twins brought us all together.

And of course, a special thanks to our twins: Ricky and Aislynn, Max and Otto, Maiah and Sarah, Keegan and Colin, Emmy and Tessa, and Michael and Joanna. They were our inspiration!

*For parents of twins everywhere*

# Contents

# Mothering TWINS

# Introduction

Five years ago, Linda Albi, Florien Deurloo, and Debra Catlin all had infant or toddler-aged twins and were members of the same support group for mothers of twins. The three talked about writing magazine articles about their experiences with their young twins. Soon that plan was replaced with the decision to write a book.

After a year of research and discussion, Linda, Florien, and Debra realized that three authors were not enough to offer the diversity of experience they wanted for their book. This is when Sheri Greatwood and Debbie Johnson were recruited to join the project. And so, the book group, as we affectionately called ourselves, was formed.

That was just four years ago. Since then, in between our scheduled book meetings, personal appointments, and work and family commitments, we snatched a few more hours every week to write and rewrite our portions of the chapters.

As our work together neared completion, we realized how much our friendship had grown. We started as five women who were drawn together out of commitment to the same project, and ended as five friends. We are all quite different, and yet like all mothers of twins we are bound together by the incredible (but wonderful) challenge of being pregnant with, giving birth to, and raising twins.

## Linda Albi

My friends and family frequently introduce me by saying, "This is Linda, the mother of two sets of twins."

I was born thirty-eight years ago into a typical military family. My childhood was a transient one, moving from one Air Force base to another. My parents provided me with a strong foundation of love that has extended into my own marriage and family. In 1963, our family was transferred to Spain for three years. The biggest challenge and cultural shock came when our family moved back to a United States caught up in the turmoil of the sixties: the Vietnam Era.

When my father retired, he settled us down "far from the madding crowd" on a cattle ranch in Idaho. Because of my love for animals, I was soon mothering every living thing on our ranch. I didn't dream these nurturing experiences would help me develop the patience and understanding I would later need to be a mother.

I received a degree in Animal Health Technology and was working in a veterinary clinic in San Diego when I met Todd in 1978. He was a handsome member of the navy's elite SEAL team and our friendship quickly blossomed into romance. When Todd asked me to marry him, he promised that our life together would be exciting. Neither one of us imagined how true that would be!

Before Todd and I married, we discussed having children and agreed to wait awhile and then have *one*. The only part of our plan that was on track was the waiting, because eight years passed before we started our family. We had our first set of fraternal twins, Sarah and Maiah in 1986. Three years later, twin boys, Keegan and Colin, took us by surprise.

Of course, being the mother of four young children has changed my life. Gone for now are the backpacking trips, bicycle touring, and traveling that Todd and I previously enjoyed. Most days, we travel no farther than our own backyard!

Being a mother has made my life fuller, but I'm still the same person I've always been. The children have simply helped me expand the qualities I have always had: tons of love, humor, and a spirit of adventure.

## *Donna Florien Deurloo*

I grew up in Waterford, Connecticut, as the middle child in a family with five children. I had a wonderful childhood on the New England shoreline as the daughter of a Dutch import bulb distributor and owner of a garden center. My British mother was responsible for raising the five of us while sharing many of the responsibilities of our family business.

I have many happy memories connected with our family business. The basement of our home was our garden shop and come Easter, there would be thousands of beautiful spring plants all sweetly in bloom, while outside occasional snowstorms raged. At Christmas, our front yard was full of people buying Christmas trees, fresh garlands, wreaths, and centerpieces, all of which I got to help make and decorate.

After high school, I left home for a year of college in New Hampshire, then transferred to the University of Oregon to obtain a degree in social work. I went from going by my first name, Donna, to my second name, Florien. I adjusted well to life in Oregon, but still planned to return home to live after graduation. Instead, during my last term in school, I met Devin.

Devin and I were both twenty-two years old when we married. He finished his degree and went on to do work as an audiovisual technician at a local social science research company. I worked at different jobs, but was having a difficult time finding a well-paying and satisfying job in social work because I only had a bachelor's degree in a town with an abundance of more highly qualified people in the same field.

While working in the local school district as a sign language interpreter/classroom assistant, I became pregnant. Although my pregnancy was not planned, Devin and I were excited by it and were even more thrilled to discover that we were having twins.

I was twenty-five years old when I gave birth to our identical sons, Otto and Max.

## Debbie Johnson
. . . . . . . . . . . . . . . .

There is so much to tell you about myself that I scarcely know where to begin. It isn't so much that my life has been filled with interesting and exciting events. It's more that my road to becoming the mother of twins is a bit more complicated than most. Like everyone else, my life story begins at my birth, which occurred thirty-eight years ago in Milwaukee, Wisconsin. I spent the first twenty-one years of my life in my parents' small home, which was also shared with three sisters, two brothers, and a dog. To say that we were a close-knit family is an understatement!

At age twenty-one, I graduated from college with a bachelor's degree in nursing, got married, and moved with my husband to Minnesota, where he was attending graduate school, and I was to begin working as a registered nurse. When my husband completed his education, he received a job offer in rural Oregon, which thrilled him. I was much less enthusiastic—in my view, one vacationed in the west, but one didn't live there. I agreed to the move, though, because I hoped it would provide our already troubled marriage with a fresh start.

Near the end of our first year in Oregon, I gave birth to our son Christopher, nicknamed Chris. When he was just a baby, my husband and I divorced amicably. I was a single parent for less than a year; then I fell in love and married my long-time friend Dale Johnson. Deciding to remarry so soon after my divorce seemed unwise to some of my family and friends, but it was the easiest and best decision I have ever made.

Dale, Chris, and I settled in Eugene, where Dale had work as an attorney and I found a job as a pediatric nurse. Chris, just two years old, settled nicely into the preschool scene. We were very happy. A desire to have more children grew out of this happiness, and within a year we were hoping to get pregnant. However, as the weeks and months passed without success, we consulted an infertility specialist.

In the midst of our infertility workup, I began to suspect that
I was pregnant. I had an ectopic pregnancy in one of my fallopian
tubes and severe inflammation in the other. As a result, both of
them were removed during emergency surgery; in a few short
hours I went from being pregnant to being sterile. Dale and I
felt devastated. Over a two-year period we worked through our
feelings of loss and made the decision to try in vitro fertilization
(IVF).

God must have been smiling on us, because I became pregnant
the first time we went through the IVF procedure. Our twins,
Michael and Joanna, were the miraculous result of this conception
and are constant reminders that life is unpredictable and love is
to be cherished.


## Debra Catlin
. . . . . . . . . . . . . .

I was born in 1951 into a traditional Catholic family; yes, I had
lots of brothers and sisters. My mom stayed home to care for us,
and my dad was a truck driver by day and a devoted father by
night. We lived comfortably in an inner city of the Los Angeles
area, but that didn't keep me and my siblings from exploring the
outdoors. I always felt that I belonged in the country; I was
fascinated with the natural world. I also had exceptional athletic
ability and preferred sports activities to playing house; being the
oldest child, I had real-life experience in that.

When I was sixteen, we moved to the suburbs. These were also
the socially liberating years of the sixties, which suited my open-
minded nature. I met the man who fathered my older son, Jason,
born in 1970. After a tumultuous relationship, Jason's father and
I decided not to marry, so I single-parented my son with the
support and acceptance of my family and friends.

I was working as a waitress and attending college part-time
when I met Rick in 1972. We fell passionately in love from the
start. We were complete opposites, but we felt that our differences
complemented each other nicely and that our values and goals
were compatible. Six years after we met, we bought our personal
piece of heaven in Oregon.

In the winter of 1978, Rick, Jason, and I came to Oregon, pulling a 35-foot travel trailer filled with all our earthly belongings, ready to start a new life. After purchasing our fifteen acres and parking the trailer for use as temporary living quarters, we settled down to the task of getting established. In 1982, our son Mehalic (whom we nicknamed Muggy) was born in our own bedroom with the assistance of a certified nurse-midwife.

The romantic illusions we had held about the country life were confronted by the harsh realities of hard work with little financial return. Rick and I worked various odd jobs to make ends meet, but none of these offered any security. Getting established took much longer than we had anticipated, and we had to fight to hold on to our property during the recessions in the early eighties. Though we adored living in Oregon and never thought of going back, the constant struggle, disillusionment, and lack of security and nearby family support eventually took its toll. It was during this unstable time that I became pregnant with our twins, Aislynn and Ricky.

## Sheri Greatwood

The only native Oregonian in this group of writers, I was born in 1958 and grew up as many Oregon girls do, the daughter of a lumber mill worker. My mother worked as the secretary at a plywood warehouse, and their combined incomes provided my three younger siblings and me with a very comfortable middle-class life-style. Both of my parents enjoyed their jobs but they always made time for family.

Growing up in the early sixties with a working mother was a bit unusual: I knew that Mom liked and needed to work to help support us, but I sure missed her after school. I'm sure that my strong feelings about staying home with my kids are motivated by my experiences as a child.

The positive side of my mother's ambition, however, was that she motivated me to set my goals high and follow my dreams. So, after graduating from high school and attending a local junior college for a year, I moved to San Francisco where I worked as a model. After a year of big-city life, I realized that Oregon was not only where my family and friends were, it was where my heart was.

When I returned to Eugene, my future husband, Steve, asked me out on a date; we were married in April of 1980. Steve was due to graduate from college that June, and I was also attending the university full-time. Afternoons and evenings, I worked as a nanny to a local doctor who was raising his three children alone. When Kallie was born in 1983, I decided to quit working so that I could stay home with her.

It was three years before Steve and I had any desire for more children. We had always been uncertain about whether we'd have two or three kids, so in 1983 when the ultrasound technician announced "It's twins!," our debate came to a screeching halt. When Emmy and Tessa arrived, they were the crowning glory that made our family complete.

# Chapter 1

# "You're having twins"

## Finding Out

Whether you find out months ahead of time or at the delivery, the news that "you're having twins" has to rate as one of life's more stressful events. The reactions we had when were presented with this news varies as much within each one of us as they did among us. A lot of plans go down the drain, leaving you with many questions and mixed emotions.

Learning about twins and the feelings that newly expectant mothers of twins can experience may help you to sort out your own feelings.

### Twin Facts

There are two types of twins: fraternal or dyzygotic (literally meaning *two cells*) and identical or monozygotic (one cell). Each is the result of a unique set of biological circumstances.

*Fraternal Twins:* Fraternal twins outnumber identical twins by more than 2 to 1. They occur when two separate eggs are fertilized by two different sperm. As a result, they are genetically no more alike than any set of siblings and can be two boys, two girls, or a boy and a girl.

During pregnancy, each fraternal twin grows within its own double-membraned bag of waters, the amniotic sac, and has his or her own placenta, although as pregnancy progresses, the placentas often grow together and appear to be one.

*Identical Twins:* Identical twins make up only about 30 percent of all twins. They are formed when one fertilized egg divides into two, resulting in two babies with identical genetic material; they are *always* the same sex and look alike. Developing in the uterus, each twin may have his or her own placenta and amniotic sac, just as fraternal twins do; but more often, they will share the placenta and the outer (chorion) membrane of the amniotic sac while still having their own inner (amnion) membrane. Very rarely, identical twins will share a placenta, chorion, and amnion. In this very unique situation, the developing twins lie skin-to-skin in the same oversized amniotic sac.

*Predisposition to Having Twins:* The occurrence of identical twinning is not well understood; it is considered to be a fluke of nature rather than the result of genetic predisposition or environmental factors. However, several factors are known to predispose women to having fraternal twins. The most common ones are: conceiving children after the age of thirty; conceiving with the help of fertility enhancing hormones or treatments such as in vitro fertilization (IVF); having a history of fraternal twins in the extended family; and having previously given birth to several other children, especially other sets of fraternal twins.

Those of us who gave birth to fraternal twins did fit at least one of the patterns of predisposition. Linda conceived both sets of her twins when she was over thirty. After having her first set of fraternals, she had an increased chance of having twins again, which she did three years later. Debra had three predisposing factors when she gave birth to her fraternal twins: She was over thirty years old, she had a history of twins in her family, and she had given birth to two other children before she got pregnant with her twins. For Debbie, who had another child and was also

over thirty when she gave birth to her twins, the deciding factor
was that she had conceived through IVF: Four fertilized eggs were
implanted in her uterus.

*Other Interesting Facts About Twins:*   Other factors may
affect twinning. A woman's diet, quality of health, level of sexual
activity, and timing of pregnancy following the cessation of birth
control pill usage may influence the likelihood of her having fraternal twins.

Black women have the highest fraternal twin birth rate, followed next by Caucasian women, with Asian women having the
lowest rate. On the other hand, identical twins are represented
in equal percentages among all races and cultures.

## Suspicions

Regardless of how twins are created, the discovery of a multiple
pregnancy can come about in many different ways. Some signs
and symptoms suggest the occurrence of twins, but an accurate
medical diagnosis is needed to rule out other possibilities.

Florien had a history of twins in her family and because of this,
she always believed that she would have twins: "I had every reason
in the world to think it would happen to me. My mother is a
fraternal twin. My father had fraternal twin sisters, and I am a
Gemini, the astrological sign of the twins. As a child, I drew
pictures of a mommy, a daddy, and twins, sometimes two sets!"

During her pregnancy, Debra also had an inkling that she was
carrying twins. "In my previous pregnancies, I had been able to
tap into some inner knowlege and know that each child was a
boy. So far in this pregnancy I had been unable to get a fix on
this baby, until one night, a thought bubbled to the surface.
'Maybe I was having a boy *and* a girl!' "

Perhaps these experiences seem a bit unusual, but when a
pregnant woman has premonitions and dreams about having
twins, she should not quickly dismiss them, especially if she has
other symptoms of a twin pregnancy. Some common symptoms
are: rapid weight gain not associated with overeating or retained

water, uterus size which is larger than expected for the stage of pregnancy, and the awareness by the pregnant woman of fetal movement in several areas of her abdomen at the same time.

All of us had symptoms such as these. Debbie, who conceived by in vitro fertilization, was suspicious of a twin pregnancy early in her first trimester. "I got much bigger so much faster than I had in my first pregnancy that I just knew I must be pregnant with twins! By eight weeks, I already needed to wear loose-fitting skirts and maternity pants."

For the rest of us, our suspicions grew over a longer period of time. Linda remembers her first pregnancy: "After three months of morning sickness and weight loss, my waistline began to expand at an incredible rate and I gained weight rapidly. My doctor mentioned that twins were one explanation for these rapid changes, but he was also concerned that he had miscalculated my due date or that a medical condition was complicating my pregnancy. He scheduled an ultrasound during my fourth month to check on the condition of my 'baby.'"

When Florien was about five months pregnant, her midwife scheduled an ultrasound because Florien was feeling flutters of movement all over her abdomen and her uterus was consistently measuring 4 to 5 centimeters larger than expected. With similar symptoms at six and a half months into her pregnancy, Debra's midwife grew suspicious. During the examination, the midwife believed that she heard two heartbeats and that she felt two babies. To be sure, she scheduled Debra for an ultrasound.

Twins, however, were not on Sheri's mind when she went to her prenatal appointments. So, even though her uterus measured larger than was expected, she didn't think much of it. It was the alpha fetal protein (AFP) test that eventually led to the discovery of her twins.

The AFP is a simple blood test done on the mother in the sixteenth to eighteenth week of pregnancy. It measures levels of alpha fetal protein, which is produced by the developing baby. Levels that fall above and below a specific range *may* indicate a problem with the pregnancy. The most common reason for very high levels of the protein is simply that the pregnancy is beyond the eighteenth week. But not to be overlooked is the possibility that the mother is carrying twins or that her baby has particular medical problems. Sheri recalls her reaction when she got news that her AFP level was high: "It was late on a Friday. The receptionist at my doctor's office tried to reassure me by saying that I was probably just farther along than we had thought. Or maybe I was having twins. She wanted to schedule an ultrasound to be sure the baby was okay, but it couldn't be done until Monday. That was the longest weekend of my life!"

## Confirmation

The most common method of confirming suspicions of a twin pregnancy is an ultrasound exam. Not too many years ago, obstetrical ultrasound procedures were used only in the most advanced medical practices to manage the most difficult pregnancies. Now they are routinely offered with many obstetrical services.

Ultrasound allows for early, noninvasive, accurate monitoring of the baby during pregnancy; to date no risk to the baby or mother has been detected. Although an accurate diagnostic tool, it is not foolproof: There are occasions of a baby's misdiagnosed sex, or the later discovery of a twin that wasn't seen on the first ultrasound.

Debbie describes her experience: "I was nine weeks pregnant when I had my first ultrasound. I was instructed to drink a quart of water one hour before the ultrasound and I was told not to urinate, so that I would have a full bladder for the test. I took my husband, Dale, and my seven-year-old son, Chris, with me when I went to have the ultrasound because I wanted them to be there to 'meet' our babies for the very first time. I remember how uncomfortable it was to lie on my back with a full bladder while the technician got me ready for the scan. She squirted a few teaspoons of gooey conducting jelly on my abdomen. The technician skidded a rodlike device, called a transducer, across my abdomen and pictures of my uterus were flashed onto the monitor. Everything looked gray-black and blotchy to me, but soon she pointed out a small shrimplike form surrounded by a dark gray circle. That was one of our babies in its amniotic sac!

She showed us the heartbeat, which at this stage just looked like small pulsations coming from the center of the baby. Moments later, she pointed out another baby. That heartbeat looked good, too. After continued searching, she found a third sac. Triplets? Looking from various angles, she could find no baby; the sac was empty, an 'almost' baby that never developed. She could find no evidence of the fourth egg that had been implanted. I was relieved and sad at the same time, but soon refocused on the fact that I was having twins! We all left the office on cloud nine."

Although ultrasound procedures are often routine, they can still be an emotional event for the woman who is full of wonder and worry. During Linda's first pregnancy, two technicians were scanning her abdomen and whispering to each other until one of them casually said to Linda, "Do twins run in your family?"

Linda sat straight up. "Why?"

She replied, "The only thing we are allowed to tell a patient is that she is going to have twins. Look, right here are two heads!"

As the technician summoned the doctor to verify the discovery, Linda couldn't help thinking, "How do they know it isn't one two-headed baby?"

Sheri, too, had her concerns. She and her husband, Steve, waited and worried over a weekend about the outcome of the ultrasound she would have: "I was so upset. I took long showers, crying and praying out loud. In my mind, I ruled out twins and thought the worst. When Monday morning finally came, with our hands clasped tightly, Steve and I watched the ultrasound screen intently. The technician said the baby looked all right. Then she said, 'Whoops! There goes another head.' We looked at each other with tears in our eyes and sighed in relief."

In Florien's case, the tables were turned. "I remember that the radiologist said the purpose of my ultrasound was to confirm a single pregnancy. When I told her of my absolute belief that I was carrying twins, the technician only shrugged, stating confidently that only one of out of a hundred ultrasounds confirmed multiples. She, not I, was surprised when the images revealed I was pregnant with twins. I was thrilled! She looked for the amniotic membranes and placenta. She found that they shared one placenta and the chorion, but not the amnion. They were destined to be identical. The technician was reluctant to say so, but it was obvious from the ultrasound that the twins were boys. I didn't mind knowing this ahead of time. What was most important to me was that they were both strong and healthy."

When Debra's ultrasound confirmed the midwife's suspicions, her reactions were mixed. "At first I didn't feel anything because I had been so upset and was hoping that the midwife was wrong. When the radiologist said I was definitely having twins, I just went emotionally numb, although intellectually I was intrigued by what I was seeing on the screen. The radiologist handed me pictures to keep. I felt like a robot until I reached the sanctuary of my car. As I sat there staring at the images, reality sank in. It was a 25-mile cry as I drove home."

"I, too, just started crying when I saw two heads on the ultrasound screen," Linda says about her second pregnancy. "For weeks, I had dreamed about how wonderful and easy it would be to take care of one baby after having twins. My husband and relatives had been teasing me about having two boys this time. I was so sure that the ultrasound would prove them wrong. My husband, Todd, was totally excited and I was totally hysterical!"

## Aftershocks

As the days passed and the idea of having twins became more real, new questions and feelings emerged. Debbie's reaction is a good example of this: "During my ultrasound procedure, the technician had casually mentioned that the second baby had a smaller amniotic sac than the first baby. I didn't think anything of this at the time, but then I started to wonder. Was the second baby's sac smaller because he was sick and going to die like the third and fourth ones that had been implanted? I worried about this, fought back the worries, and then worried some more. This would be my style throughout my whole pregnancy: worry, joy, worry, joy, worry, joy."

Sheri remembers, "We were so thrilled about having healthy babies that it took a week for the concept of twins to hit home. Then I began to feel overwhelmed. All the confidence and security I'd felt about parenting my second child went out the window. I felt like a first-time parent all over again."

Florien had little difficulty adjusting to the idea. "I became fully aware of my responsibility to the new lives I was carrying. I did not feel threatened or nervous about, perhaps, one of the most important challenges I would ever face. Of course, there were financial concerns. We needed a bigger house and a bigger car. But carrying two healthy babies to term became the goal my husband, Devin, and I worked toward together."

"Each of my experiences was so different," Linda comments. "The first time I found out I was having twins, Todd was out of town and I was dying to share the news with someone, so I called my mother. She said that a day before this, she had received a fortune cookie that read, 'A happy, blessed event will happen soon in your immediate family.' That made me feel so special. When Todd called later that evening, I teased him that the two children he desired to have were coming all at once. It was very festive around here for days. As the euphoria began to wear off, I grew concerned about the health of the babies. With my second pregnancy, this worry resurfaced even more strongly than before because I knew how difficult my first pregnancy had been. I cried for days, in spite of everyone else's excitement and consolation. Gradually, I came to realize that having two sets of twins was special and unique. But at first it was disappointing to lose the dream of being pregnant with and caring for one baby."

Debra had a different set of worries. "I had great confidence in my body's ability to produce healthy, full-term babies. It was all the other aspects of my life that felt so threatened; I didn't feel like celebrating at all. My marriage was going through rocky times; we were already having financial difficulties and living in a very small house. It was painful to think about the special closeness I shared with my three-year-old, Mehalic, having to change. And my older son, Jason, would have to take on so much more responsibility during his teen years. I wondered how I would possibly cope with my extended family living so far away. Then, thinking of them, I realized that I was the first in the generation of fifty-four grandchildren to have twins. With that, a little pride found its way into my inner turmoil. It took a few days to pull out of that initial hopelessness. I couldn't help feeling guilty for reacting so negatively to what others might have considered good news. It was just hard to feel fortunate about the timing."

## *Thoughts and Reflections*

Mixed feelings are a normal part of a woman's adjustment to learning she is pregnant with twins; unfortunately, not everyone is conscious of this. Friends, relatives, other mothers, even health care professionals may be unaware of how strongly, and at times negatively, a twin pregnancy impacts a family.

It is important to seek the support you need. Ask the questions that you need to have answered, and accept without shame any negative feelings you might have. If you need counseling to make sense of your life, get it! Taking good care of your emotional and physical self isn't selfish. It's sensible, and the best way to get yourself ready for the difficult, but rewarding, experience of having, giving birth to, and raising twins.

# "You must be due any day now!"

## The Pregnancy

Although it will be tempting to compare the progress of your twin pregnancy with that of a singleton, *don't*. You can expect that by the time you start your third trimester, you will probably look and feel as though you're ready to deliver.

We found that asking questions of others and reading everything we could about multiple birth and parenthood provided us with the information necessary to be active participants in our health care and to gather the resources we needed for ourselves and our families. More importantly, it bolstered our confidence and allowed us to enjoy our pregnancies as much as possible. And so, when we were six and seven months pregnant and approached for the umpteenth time by people who said, "You must be due any day now!" we were able to sigh pleasantly and say, "Not quite." Hang in there; you can do as well.

### Regaining Your Sense of Control

A twin pregnancy poses greater health risks to the expectant mother and developing babies than a singleton pregnancy. To reduce these risks, health care providers recommend a variety of precautions. Many of these directly affect the pregnant woman's life-style and may decrease her sense of control over her pregnancy and the birth of her twins. We first regained some of the control by becoming informed about the management of twin pregnancy and learning about the precautions we might take to balance out some of the risks.

Sheri read everything she could find. "There were wide varieties of opinion on how much weight to gain, the necessity of bedrest, and other relevant issues. Reading several books gave me information and ideas to discuss with my doctor. I wanted my husband and myself to play a truly informed role when decisions were made about the babies and me.

"Let's just say that growing a huge belly, leaking colostrum from my breasts, and having twenty-four-hour heartburn was not my idea of being in control, even though these things are common at the end of a pregnancy. To be outnumbered and literally taken over by two babies was very disconcerting. My books explained why these things were happening to my body and told me what to expect in the upcoming months."

Debbie started to keep a journal as a way to sort through her thoughts and concerns. "The journal gave me a nice diary of my pregnancy and helped me to organize the many thoughts and questions I had for my obstetrician. In this way, I was able to confront my fears of any potential problem that might come up and feel better about my pregnancy."

Each woman should realize that she is her own greatest resource. By tuning in to what she is thinking, feeling, and needing, she can integrate the information she acquires with her own personal changes throughout the pregnancy.

## A Twin Pregnancy Brings Changes

A twin pregnancy brings many hormonal changes in the expectant mother. These changes upset the equilibrium of her emotions. Moodiness and irritability may occur as the pregnant woman adjusts to them.

For Debbie, the early months were like riding a roller coaster.

"Hormones were surging through my body; I felt out of control. I couldn't help comparing this pregnancy to my previous one, and by comparison, it wasn't going well. The hormone surges, the nausea, the acne, the mood swings, the fatigue, and especially the worry were much worse than in my first pregnancy. At times, I felt victimized by my own body, yet at the same time, I felt incredibly blessed and special!"

Linda had similar reactions. "I was impossible to be with during the first few months. I remember lying on the couch one evening, feeling nauseated, as usual. Todd was in the kitchen, crunching tortilla chips and cooking dinner, and our poodle was chomping on dog food. I yelled at both my husband and the dog, 'If I hear another bite out of either of you, I'm going to throw up!' The noise stopped immediately."

Sometimes the mood swings and emotional outbursts that accompany early pregnancy are more than a reflection of hormonal changes and occasional irritability. We learned that our specific concerns or worries often revealed issues that needed to be resolved and that the intensity of the feeling indicated the significance of it to us as individuals. Sometimes it seemed easier or more comfortable to ignore these signals, but we realized that they were part of a healthy process that all parents work through to ready themselves for parenthood.

In the first trimester, expectant mothers and fathers are often concerned about the effects parenthood will have on them, their relationships, and their life-styles. Whether the pregnancy was planned or not, it is normal to have fears and ambivalent feelings, but the inner task for all expectant parents is to accept the reality that they will soon be mothers and fathers. When twins are expected, this may take a bit longer to occur, but when it does, a period of inner calm settles in and interest in healthy self-care, concern for the growing babies, and a desire to strengthen emotional bonds with others takes over.

In the second phase, the focus of thoughts and feelings turns inward and a shift in the parents' identities occurs as they make room in their hearts and lives for their babies. They begin to think of themselves and each other in the mothering and fathering roles. There is commonly a reflection of one's own childhood and a review of both positive and negative traits of their parents. As the mother centers on the baby, it is vital that she welcome and encourage the father to share this intimacy or he may feel left out.

This is a vulnerable time with strong feelings of love and protectiveness emerging and it is common to have strange dreams. If there are other children in the family, parents may be anxious about the sibling's adjustment and ability to love the new baby. These are all normal signs of a deepening attachment to the baby. When parents achieve attachment and are comfortable with their roles as parents, they become willing to assume the responsibilities of parenting their newborns.

While preparing the home and purchasing the equipment and supplies for the baby, parents have an opportunity to practice or fantasize the roles they will play. There is more dependency on the partner and concern about how the family will function as a unit, how the labor and birth will proceed, and if they have the skills needed to care for newborn babies. These worries are motivators to complete the tasks of pregnant parenting.

The phases just described are fairly universal and each one must be accomplished before moving on to the next. Individuals will pass through these stages at different rates and some may even get held up in one area or another. When a multiple pregnancy is discovered, parents may often go through many aspects of these phases more than once.

A high level of stress during pregnancy can interfere with the parents' abilities to work through these tasks before they take on the actual care of their infants, which compounds the adjustments that need to be made in the months following birth. Expectant parents who are feeling highly anxious or emotionally numb, and cannot resolve these issues regarding parenthood, may need help. For some, this may be as simple as talking out their feelings with a supportive family member or friend, while others may need professional help. We each had our own journeys through the emotional mountains and valleys of pregnancy.

Florien made the transition to parenthood with relative ease. "I loved being pregnant. Aside from the first four months of morning sickness, I felt healthy, glowing, full of pride, and always hungry. I was often the center of attention, which felt good. My husband, Devin, fully enjoyed the pregnancy as well. He was very proud to be the prospective father of twins, and he made sure I rested and ate well in order to stay healthy. It was a time of excitement and anticipation for both of us."

Linda adjusted quickly to her first twin pregnancy because she and Todd wanted to start a family and they felt that twins were an added bonus. But this wasn't the case with her second pregnancy. "After weeks of denying that I was once again carrying two babies, after many tears and long talks with Todd, myself, and God, I came to accept my second twin pregnancy. Only then could I start to look forward to and plan for two more additions to our family."

Debra comments that although she enjoyed being pregnant, she had a hard time emotionally. "I had little physical discomfort, except for becoming fatigued more easily. For me, it was my emotions that were such a mess. I had many days of crying, and would chastise myself for not getting myself together. I was plagued by fears of my inability to mother two more children at a time that the rest of my life and my marriage felt so insecure. My greatest fear was that I would become so buried in motherhood that I would lose a sense of myself; that had happened to my mother, who had nine children. It felt like I was standing on a hill of sand, trying to keep the ground underneath from caving in."

## Physical Changes in the First Trimester

The adaptations that a woman's body makes as it accommodates pregnancy and prepares for birth are unrivaled by any other biological process. Rapidly rising levels of hormones maintain the pregnant state and produce changes throughout the mother's body. Each symptom or discomfort in pregnancy can usually be related to a physical change within the body. When a woman is pregnant with twins, these changes are more often pronounced, and it is possible to get discouraged by the discomforts of these changes. However, when these bodily responses are seen as part of the babies' growth and the body's readiness to give birth, the aches and pains are easier to bear.

*Nausea:* Not all women experience nausea during pregnancy, but for those who do, it is often one of the first signs of pregnancy as the body responds to fluctuating hormone levels. Women carrying twins are more likely to experience nausea, and sometimes it will last longer or occur more frequently than with women pregnant with singletons. Morning sickness usually resolves or is greatly reduced after the fourth month of the pregnancy.

Although nausea is often called "morning sickness," it can be (and is!) felt at any time of the day. Some women are able to identify troublesome foods and can predict the worst time of day for them, while others are bothered all day no matter how they adjust their diets. Fatty, spicy, and gassy foods, anxiety, and increased hormone levels can all accentuate this feeling of queasiness. Try eating a well-balanced diet in smaller, more frequent portions, avoid an empty stomach by nibbling on low-salt crackers and avoid those foods that bother you most. Debra drank red raspberry leaf and mint teas and used nutritional brewer's yeast throughout her pregnancy and never experienced any nausea. Sometimes it is helpful to consult a prenatal nutrition specialist.

Florien and Devin were visiting friends in New York over the holidays and were unaware that she was pregnant when feelings of weakness and queasiness developed. "I couldn't go out and walk around much because I kept on getting dry heaves. As soon as Devin and I returned to my parents' house in Connecticut, we bought a home pregnancy test and discovered that I was, indeed, pregnant!

"The first two months I had a lot of dry heaves and often found myself feeling like I had to throw up, but I couldn't. The second two months I would vomit if I had an empty stomach or if I smelled certain foods. I found it most useful to eat frequent snacks such as crackers, cheese, celery with peanut butter, and nonacidic fruits. I put crackers and cheese by my bed each evening to snack on during the night if needed and to eat as soon as I woke up, so I could start my day with something in my stomach. Finally, at the end of my fourth month of pregnancy, the nausea simply disappeared."

While mild nausea is not medically serious, if persistent vomiting develops or nausea continues over a long period of time it can be debilitating and medical care should be sought. Although none of us developed this condition, known as hyperemesis gravidarum, Linda did have severe nausea which was complicated by a chronic health condition, Addison's disease.

Addison's disease is an adrenal gland insufficiency which, if unregulated by medication, can lead to problems in the body's electrolyte (sodium and potassium) balance, protein metabolism, and circulatory system. Fatigue, weakness, and loss of weight are all symptoms that can occur with Addison's disease; however, daily medications keep all physiological systems in balance. In Linda's situation, Addison's disease, in addition to the stress of pregnancy, resulted in a rapid onset of dehydration.

In both of her pregnancies, she began to feel awful almost from the start. "I felt sick morning, noon, and night. Every meal I ate had to be forced down. During the first months of pregnancy, I could hardly get any food down and steadily grew weaker. After eight weeks, I weighed 99 pounds, down from my normal 112 pounds. At this point, my doctor hospitalized me and began IV fluids to control dehydration.

"When I was released from the hospital, I felt much stronger and was determined to gain more weight. It wasn't easy. During the next few weeks, Todd cooked all my meals. My preferred diet was made up of bland food: potatoes, rice, scrambled eggs, toast, and steamed vegetables. Somehow I managed to regain the lost weight and was able to return to my job. Finally, after four months, the morning sickness abated and I was able to enjoy my pregnancy."

*Other Physical Changes in the First Trimester:* With the increased hormonal activity of a twin pregnancy, other physical changes that occur in a mild form in a singleton pregnancy may also be more exaggerated with twins. As the uterus increases in size, it presses on the bladder, resulting in a need to urinate frequently. In singleton pregnancies, usually this doesn't occur until well into the first trimester; with twins, it is likely to occur sooner as the uterus is expanding at a faster rate. By the beginning of the second trimester the uterus has enlarged to the point that it rises higher in the abdomen and no longer pushes on the bladder.

It is also common to feel slightly fatigued in the second and third months of pregnancy and many women find that they need to take a nap or go to bed early during this time. This fatigue is most likely due to the changes in the circulatory system as it increases the available blood supply.

For Debbie, the minor physical changes that accompanied the first trimester in her singleton pregnancy became moderate to severe, and lasted longer in her twin pregnancy. "When I was pregnant with my twins, my breasts ached the entire first trimester. In my first pregnancy I developed minor acne that lasted a few months; in my twin pregnancy, I had a real problem with acne that lasted the length of the pregnancy. It was bad enough having sore breasts, feeling nauseated, and being moody, but also feeling unattractive really dragged down my self-esteem. I was even more frustrated when my doctor recommended that I not use medication to treat my acne during pregnancy. I just bore up, avoided mirrors, and reminded myself the twins were worth it!"

## Physical Changes in the Second Trimester

The second trimester is physically the most comfortable part of a twin pregnancy. Of course, women still experience discomforts and physical changes during this time period, but they usually are more tolerable. By the second trimester, nausea lifts, moodiness decreases, and bladder irritation ceases. Breast tenderness may resolve, although breast size continues to increase and the nipple and the areola begin to darken. Those of us who had previously been pregnant with singleton babies found that the growth in breast tissue was greater in our twin pregnancies, undoubtedly one of nature's ways of preparing to feed two babies.

In the second trimester, the growing uterus pushes abdominal organs out of place and puts pressure on the veins. These factors, coupled with an increased circulatory load can cause swollen or varicose veins to develop. Some women report that this is more aggravated by a twin pregnancy.

During Debbie's fifth month of pregnancy, she developed varicose veins. "I tried not to stand still or sit for long periods of time. When I did sit, I never crossed my legs and I occasionally flexed my leg muscles to help increase circulation. I also put my legs up above the level of my heart for a few minutes during the day and always wore my maternity pantyhose—until I outgrew them in my third trimester!"

Greater discomfort from constipation, hemorrhoids, and gas in the second trimester are also frequent complaints in women expecting twins. The hormonal changes cause the digestive system to relax and slow down so that nutrients are better absorbed. Drinking lots of water or prune juice and eating prunes and other high fiber foods may help keep stools soft, reduce gas, and prevent or minimize the discomfort. Try to avoid fried foods, cabbage, beans, and carbonated sodas. Some women also find it useful to eat smaller amounts of food more frequently throughout the day. These suggestions relieve discomfort from hemorrhoids, which may also be prevented if a woman tries not to strain while having bowel movements and puts her feet on a stool while on the toilet. If a pregnant women does get hemorrhoids that become swollen or painful, she'll need to talk to her health care provider about how to deal with them.

Some women also begin to experience backaches during this trimester. Debbie explains, "By the time I was twenty weeks pregnant, I started getting nagging backaches. They weren't severe, but they were constant. I was especially uncomfortable when I sat. My discomfort was eased quite a bit by using a soft, small pillow for the small of my back whenever I sat down. Oddly, my backaches lessened when I reached the third trimester."

## Physical Changes in the Third Trimester

During the last trimester of a multiple birth pregnancy, most pregnant women are going to be at least a little uncomfortable.

These discomforts are related to the necessary changes in the pregnant woman's body as it gets ready for birth. When carrying twins, many of these changes will begin earlier than in a singleton pregnancy. Each of us had different problems and developed our own ways of handling them. Heartburn, bladder pressure, stretch marks, swelling of feet and legs, disrupted sleep, backaches, and an overall sense of physical discomfort were some of our common complaints of the third trimester.

As Debbie entered her third trimester, she looked and felt as though she were ready to deliver. "Walking became difficult and my abdomen literally felt as though it were going to fall off to the ground. By twenty-eight weeks I was working only one day a week, as I could feel my energy waning. Heartburn and shortness of breath became major problems. In order to get a good night's sleep (and avoid nighttime heartburn), I had to stop eating by 5:00 P.M. I found that drinking a glass of milk before bedtime and sleeping with my head elevated also helped. On the positive side, my asthma, which had bothered me earlier in my pregnancy, stopped being a problem. I ate well, rested often, and kept reminding my babies to 'Grow, babies, grow!' They must have been listening, because by the time I delivered them, I had gained 50 pounds and had a 44-inch waist!"

Sheri's level of comfort also changed at the beginning of her third trimester. "By the sixth month I was big enough that people constantly asked me when I was due. By now my abdomen looked almost square! I rubbed cocoa butter with vitamin E on my tummy several times a day to help stop the itching. I was still sleeping pretty well at night, as long as I had all five pillows in place. For best circulation, I was careful to lie on my left side, with three pillows under my head, one holding my tummy, and one between my knees. It took me a while to get comfortable, but eventually I could sleep in this position."

By the seventh month of Linda's second twin pregnancy, "Eating became a problem again; there was simply no more room left for food. Finding a comfortable position to sleep in was nearly impossible, although sleeping on my side with lots of pillows to support my tummy helped. Todd got almost as little sleep due to my numerous trips to the bathroom and my constant tossing and turning."

Florien, although small-framed, also grew huge in the last months of her pregnancy. "My uterus measured 44 centimeters, very large for someone as petite as myself. My entire 40-pound weight gain was carried in front, and my arms and legs looked skinny compared to my bulging belly. Luckily, I didn't retain water or gain excessive weight during my pregnancy until a few days prior to Otto and Max's births. I had a difficult time finding maternity clothes that actually fit me in a comfortable way. I found balloon type dresses to be the most comfortable and accommodating. The most discomfort I experienced was from sitting in one position too long; if I sat for over half an hour, I needed to shift my weight or change chairs.

"At six months my belly was so stretched out that it itched all over and was blue, shiny, and numb. The boys' body parts were easily discerned through the thin skin that covered them. Devin and I would sit in bed at night and wait for ten o'clock: the babies would roll and kick and squirm for about forty-five minutes of nonstop entertainment! Even now, our boys are both very active."

At the end of Debra's pregnancy, she spent as much time as possible relaxing outdoors to decrease her discomfort. "On hot days, I sat in Muggy's wading pool, feeling like a beached whale. By this time, I looked like one, too. Wherever I went, I attracted stares because of my 'overripeness' and the awkward way I walked.

"The only thing that really drove me crazy was that I itched all over, especially on my back. A hairbrush with round-tipped bristles worked great to relieve this."

## The Importance of Good Self-Care

Twin pregnancy puts a strain on the physical resources of even the healthiest women. Maintaining good health habits during pregnancy made us better able to enjoy our pregnancies and keep up our stamina.

*Nutrition:* Eating a well-balanced diet is something that every pregnant woman can do to maximize her and her babies' health and to reduce the risk factors, especially when carrying multiples. A healthy diet is the single most important factor in preventing or reducing problems and complications in twin pregnancy. Fifty-two nutrients are required to grow the babies and supply the mother with what her body needs to accommodate the pregnancy.

The nutritional requirements of twin pregnancy have been well researched and documented. From 100 to 150 grams of protein and 2,900 to 3,500 calories each day will ensure an adequate weight gain of 40 to 60 pounds or more for the mother and help the babies achieve good size (6 to 7 pounds or more) at full term. A general rule of thumb is that the mother should gain 25 to 35 pounds, the weight of a full-term singleton pregnancy, by the end of the second trimester—and then gain an additional 15 to 25 pounds in the last trimester.

It is crucial to avoid tobacco products, alcohol, caffeine, recreational drugs, and over-the-counter medications (unless approved by your health practitioner) as they may interfere with the absorption of nutrients or the functions of the placentas that feed your babies.

Debra knew that a healthy diet was important in preventing premature labor. "On a day-to-day basis, it was a real challenge to include all my nutritional requirements. It took quite an effort to prepare different foods to eat when I didn't have much room to force down meals I wasn't in the mood for. In spite of that, I gained 45 pounds and my babies went to term with the weights of singletons!"

Sheri felt that twin books were by far the best source of information on nutrition. "Nowhere else were the diet requirements for multiple pregnancies laid out so well. Don't expect anyone to tell you specifics about things like folic acid supplements, or about how important it is to keep stuffing that food in: especially potatoes, leafy green vegetables, grains, fruit, and lots of milk. My babies came early and were small, but they were strong and healthy from the start. I believe it was because I made every bite count. Not that I didn't indulge: I always made room for dessert. But I got the good stuff in first, and drank every last drop of milk!"

Florien also referred to books to see what types of nutritional needs a woman pregnant with twins has, but didn't feel the need to change her diet too drastically to accommodate the growth of her twins. "Devin came home at noon every day and made me lunch, and cooked dinner every night. The high protein drinks he concocted actually tasted good with fresh spring and summer fruits blended in. I made sure I drank eight glasses of water each day and drank more milk than I ever dreamed possible. I also took a double dosage of prenatal vitamins each day, on the recommendation of my midwives. I stayed clear of junk food and stopped drinking caffeinated tea and coffee. When I worked, I brought nutritious snack foods with me to my classroom and nibbled throughout the day."

*Exercise and Activity:* Exercise and activity are often restricted in a multiple pregnancy by the beginning of the second trimester. Still, exercise is an important part of staying fit. It helps maintain good metabolism and circulation, and keeps up muscle strength and tone. Although exercise in multiple pregnancy is often reduced, it can include basic prenatal exercises. Each woman should talk to her health care practitioner about exercise that is appropriate for her.

Early in her pregnancy, Sheri joined a prenatal deep-water aerobics class with a pregnant friend of hers. "The class was held in the deep end of the pool. We wore flotation packs on our ankles and wrists and floated upright doing slow, stretching exercises. It felt wonderful, as floating made me weightless. I always left the pool feeling relaxed and refreshed.

"When I reached twenty-seven weeks, though, my doctor told me to stop all exercise. I felt torn about quitting my class, but our goal for the third trimester was to 'keep those babies inside me for as long as possible!' The doctor didn't want my uterus to become irritated by exercise and go into labor."

Florien had to change her exercise routines. "Before my pregnancy I rode my bike everywhere and took exercise classes. I was very active and considered myself to be in pretty good shape.

This exercise was not restricted by my obstetrician until my thirtieth week, but when I was four months along, I choose to slow down the pace; I stopped riding my bike and decreased my volunteer and outside commitments. I tried to narrow my range of activities before the twins were born so the adjustment to motherhood from an active, independent life-style would not be so difficult later on."

When Linda began feeling better in the fourth month of her first pregnancy, she was able to resume a limited version of her exercise routine. "For years, I had been jogging five days a week; now I walked briskly. Pregnancy and exercise made me glow. Unfortunately, my walking only lasted a few weeks, for I started having problems that necessitated hospitalization and bed rest."

At thirty weeks along in her pregnancy, Debra was advised to discontinue strenuous activities but she chose to maintain her garden, feeling that she would let her body be her guide in determining how much she should do. "Besides being a source of organic vegetables and supplementing our food supply, something compelled me to nurture the life I had planted in the spring. Rick had constructed beautiful raised beds; I could sit on the edge and work. I didn't find it too taxing and the sunshine and fresh air did me more good than being inside would have. As summer wore on and my energy waned, I just settled for watering the plants. I think this was a good compromise between medical advice and my own needs."

## Medical Care and Concerns

Some twin pregnancies and deliveries are problem-free. However, the increased possibility that complications may occur which will affect either the mother or the babies puts mothers pregnant with twins into the "high risk" category. Midwives or family practitioners may provide care for a multiple pregnancy as long as problems don't come up. But if complications arise, they will refer care to an obstetrician who has the skills to manage high risk pregnancies and births. In either case, the choice of a medical care team is an important element in the outcome of your pregnancy and birth.

*Choosing a Health Care Provider:* When choosing our health care providers, we looked for someone with whom we were comfortable and whose medical skills and judgment we respected. Once our twin pregnancies were confirmed, some of us opted to be followed by an obstetrician who specialized in the management and delivery of multiples. Others of us preferred to stay with our regular obstetrician, general practitioner, or nurse midwife. In making our decisions, we all felt it was important to ask our provider how many twin births they had attended, what preventive measures they recommended to avoid medical complications and premature labor, what treatment options they used when complications did occur, and what options they were open to for the delivery of multiples.

In the initial phases of her pregnancy, Florien saw a midwife at a birthing clinic that offered a variety of options for the birth: at home, in their clinic, or in the hospital. They also had medical backup provided by respected obstetricians. One of the four doctors providing backup support to the midwives was an obstetrician with extensive experience in the birth of multiples.

"Devin and I understood that having twins usually necessitated frequent testing and the possibility of taking drugs to forestall premature labor, but we felt a strong need for a measure of control over our own birthing experience. We agreed to aim not only for excellent care, but also for an atmosphere of intimacy and warmth."

Debra chose the same certified nurse-midwife clinic that attended births in the home, birth center, or hospital with the backup of a team of obstetricians that Florien had chosen, but for different reasons. Once her twin pregnancy was confirmed, she chose one of the obstetricians for her primary care because he was skilled at breech delivery. "My doctor was comfortable delivering a second twin that was in breech position vaginally, if the first baby was head down. He also seemed to genuinely care about my concerns as well as being mildly pleased by my attitude of confidence and willingness to take responsibility for my health care. It was important to me that my preferences were honored. Together we would work on preventing a premature delivery. We negotiated agreements on the many possibilities of twin delivery, with emphasis on avoiding cesarean birth. My doctor responded positively to all my questions, respected my feelings, and even volunteered several times to attend my delivery even if he were not on call."

Sheri also went to a midwife when she became pregnant, hoping that she would deliver her second baby vaginally. "Kallie, our four-year-old daughter, had been delivered by cesarean section after a long labor and a failure to progress past 6 centimeters. But when we found out about the twins, my midwife recommended that I switch to an obstetrician. The chances of my having another cesarean were high because I hadn't ever delivered a baby vaginally, and my pelvis is small. I didn't argue with her decision; I learned with my first pregnancy that the long-awaited birthing process becomes ancient history as soon as the baby makes his or her appearance."

The doctor whom Sheri's midwife recommended turned out to be her own obstetrician, and twin pregnancies were his speciality. "His expertise and open-mindedness were wonderful. But it was a jolt to go from the calm and quiet atmosphere of the midwifery clinic to a busy doctor's office. I always left my midwife with a feeling of contentment. I often left my doctor's office feeling like I was just another patient to be seen."

Both Linda and Debbie stayed with their regular obstetricians. Debbie says, "I had been going to my doctor for years. Although multiple births weren't his speciality, I respected his abilities and I liked his nurse and the physicians who worked with him."

*What Is a "High-Risk Pregnancy?"*:   Multiple pregnancy is considered to be high-risk because there is an increased likelihood that the mother or babies may have medical problems or complications. While it does not necessarily mean that there *will* be problems, most health care providers want to monitor the pregnancy closely and suggest precautions that they believe will help minimize the risks involved. Our individual feelings about having the high-risk label and the extra medical tests and interventions varied greatly.

Because Linda had had a previous premature delivery with her twin girls, she was monitored even more closely during her second twin pregnancy. "If you have a history of delivering twins prematurely and become pregnant with twins for a second time, you are treated like a fragile eggshell! I had more frequent doctor appointments, more ultrasounds, and more non-stress tests, which measure the changes in the fetal heart rate following fetal activity. I was put on a home monitoring system and was on a maintenance dose of Terbutaline to control contractions for weeks.

"When I was twenty-six weeks along, I was having mild contractions off and on, and my doctor wanted to keep an eye on them. The home monitoring system I used required me to lie quietly on my side twice a day with a belt monitor strapped to my waist. After an hour, I would transmit my reading over the phone to a nursing service. Every time I shifted my weight around, fluffed up the pillows, or moved excessively, the monitor would stop recording. Many times the nurse on the phone would tell me to start over. In tears I listened to her instructions to lie quiet and not move around. I couldn't lie still when I was so big and so uncomfortable!"

Although Debra was made aware of the risks, she felt confident that she and her babies would do well. "The first time I met the backup doctor, I said, 'If my grandmother could do it, then I can, too! She birthed two seven-and-a-half-pound boys at forty years old with no problems!' I might have sounded a little cocky, but having faith in myself was the best counteraction to all the negative stuff I heard about having twins. Your pregnancy is no longer treated as a normal life function, but as a complication waiting to happen. I didn't buy it."

*Recommended Precautions:* Three precautions often recommended in multiple pregnancy are quitting work, getting bed rest, and abstaining from sexual intercourse. These are thought to be helpful in preventing the most common complications: preeclampsia, high blood pressure, and premature labor. There are areas of disagreement in the medical community about the effectiveness of these precautions. We each informed ourselves about the advantages and disadvantages of each precaution and then applied that information according to our own needs and feelings.

*Quitting Work:*   It is common practice these days for women to work outside the home. The need to reduce physical activity during a multiple pregnancy often requires that the pregnant woman stop working or significantly reduce her hours. This may create an added strain if the loss of employment brings financial hardship. Debbie, who worked part-time, cut back to one day of work per week when she was twenty-four weeks along. At twenty-eight weeks, she took a leave of absence which her doctor recommended and to which she heartily agreed!

Debra had quit her job prior to finding out she was carrying twins and was working part time as a waitress for the first few months of her pregnancy. "I worked at a dinner house. As my pregnancy advanced, it became difficult working on my feet and carrying heavy trays of food for so many hours. I only wish I could have worked longer to help out financially."

Florien continued working through the thirtieth week of her pregnancy as her doctor had recommended, although the last month she cut her hours from six to four per day. "I worked in a classroom as an interpreter/assistant with a deaf student. I felt able to continue to work because I had the physical stamina to do so and because my pregnancy was progressing well. Although it was not normally acceptable to eat in the classroom, I was permitted to do so because of my frequent need for small amounts of food.

"Also, during my second trimester, I prepared for a less stressful job that I could handle once the babies were born. I knew I would need to work just a little bit to help financially, but would be unable to look for a part-time, low-stress job once the babies were born. During my second trimester, I started arranging a therapeutic recreation program for teenagers who are deaf. I secured volunteers and organized one program during my pregnancy when I was resting at home. (I guess I've always been bored just sitting still!) In my mind I could envision a job that would allow me flexibility, take a minimum of time to do, and provide a way for me to reduce my stress level once the babies were born!"

*Bed Rest: "To Do or Not to Do?"* Bed rest is commonly used to prevent or delay premature labor. Two possibilities underlie this recommendation: one is the belief that the high rate of premature birth in multiple birth pregnancies is partly due to the pressure exerted on the cervix when a woman is in an upright position; the other is that physical activity stresses the mother's body and puts stress on the babies, which may initiate the hormonal changes that start labor. While either may be true in some cases, they do not apply to every woman. Premature labor can happen even with bed rest and is most likely due to a combination of variables.

In decisions about utilizing bed rest, the benefits should be weighed against the risks for each individual. Adaptations can be made in each case, taking into account a woman's needs and lifestyle.

It is important to clearly understand the doctor's specific instructions. Sometimes doctors recommend complete bed rest, but more often they recommend partial bed rest as a precaution against premature labor during the third trimester. The degree depends on whether or not contractions are occurring, whether the cervix is changing, or whether the pregnant woman has previously given birth prematurely. Complete bed rest is prescribed if high blood pressure or pre-eclampsia develops.

Once a decision is made for a woman to be on either partial or complete bed rest, the woman and her family need to adjust to the sudden change. Lack of support, loneliness, and loss of identity as wife, mother, or worker are all major problems for women on bed rest. A partner may feel worried and overwhelmed by the extra demands on him. If young children are at home, they may sense that something is wrong and need extra reassurance that Mommy still loves them and that she will be all right. Coping with prolonged bed rest is not easy, but it can be lived through with good spirits. Most important is the knowledge that you are doing something worthwhile for your babies.

Florien followed her doctor's routine orders for partial bed rest and restricted her activities. "I was supposed to begin partial bed rest at thirty weeks. I tried hard to comply with my doctor's directive, although my inner self felt certain that I would make it to term no matter what.

"I was up doing small things around the house or outside at least part of the day, but I stayed away from physical activities and let others take care of me as much as they wanted to. Devin kept an eye on me to be certain I didn't overdo anything. I had trouble staying flat in bed during the day and would often be found with my feet up in a recliner chair or sitting outside in the shade. I relaxed while I read books, mended clothes, chatted with friends on the phone, wrote letters, went through old photos, and watched old movies on TV."

Debra had a more difficult time. "Meeting the needs of my active two-and-a-half-year-old was obstacle enough, and I felt useless to the rest of my family. I was actually glad that Rick was unable to attend most of my checkups, so he couldn't hear all the things I wasn't supposed to be doing yet continued to do. This was an area of great conflict for me. I couldn't just lie around for twenty-four hours a day. I was careful to not overexert myself, and rested long periods throughout the day, but I chose to get up and down as frequently as I needed to. When I did rest, I read books on pregnancy and parenting and used visualization techniques to encourage myself and my babies to do well."

Sheri also struggled to balance bed rest with the rest of her active life. "Looking back, I can say that I should probably have stayed down more than I did. I'd go out Christmas shopping and then come home for a nap. I always kept going until my feet got puffy. I felt good, so it was easy to convince myself that things were just fine. We didn't realize that I was developing pre-eclampsia."

When Linda was ordered to have partial bed rest in her first twin pregnancy at twenty-six weeks, she knew it was necessary. "I tried hard to adhere to the doctor's orders. I continued to do paperwork at home while I was confined to bed and also found myself doing small chores around the house just to keep from going crazy. I was getting bigger all the time, and was extremely uncomfortable lying down for long periods. I would stay up for a brief period, then lie down for an hour, then up again for a short time, then back down.

"During my second twin pregnancy, complete bed rest was ordered. Explaining my confinement to the girls was a real problem. Maiah and Sarah weren't even three years old yet, but I had to put them in a full-time preschool just so I could stay in bed. We also had a university student move in to help with the girls in the mornings and evenings. I supervised meals, household chores, and bedtime baths from my bed, which I could only leave for very short periods of time. I found myself calling friends and reading novel after novel. I also spent many quiet hours with Maiah and Sarah, reading stories to them and playing quiet games on my bed. Sometimes Todd would bring home a favorite video of theirs and we would all sit on the bed watching the movie and eating popcorn."

After experiencing premature labor at thirty-two weeks, Debbie was put on strict bed rest, up only for meals and to go to the bathroom. "I was sent home after a week in the hospital. Fortunately, my parents had traveled two thousand miles to look after us. Bed rest was boring, but tolerable because I like sedentary activities like reading, watching TV, and listening to music. I particularly enjoyed writing in my journal, which was relaxing and helped me organize my thoughts. I also wanted to forestall labor as long as possible, so I followed my doctor's orders carefully."

*Sexual Abstinence:* The third precaution meant to prevent premature labor is abstinence from sexual intercourse, orgasm, and stimulation of the woman's breasts and nipples; breast stimulation and orgasm may increase uterine contractions, and prostaglandins in seminal fluid may initiate softening of the cervix. What effect sexual abstinence will have on a specific couple depends on what changes they have experienced (which may range from lack of interest to increased desire) during pregnancy.

Debra discussed this with her obstetrician at a prenatal checkup. "Of all the precautions my doctor outlined, the most difficult for me was the abstinence from intercourse and orgasm, prescribed when I was six and a half months pregnant. Since the double hormones produced by the two placentas increased my sexual appetite, I found compliance with this precaution especially hard. Abstinence also created an emotional distance between Rick and me."

Sheri and Steve were surprised when their doctor casually announced that sex was prohibited after the sixth month. "With three months to go, this news was hard to take. The look on poor Steve's face said it all!"

Debbie had a very different reaction. From the beginning of her pregnancy, her obstetrician had indicated that intercourse was not advisable during the final months. At twenty-eight weeks, Debbie had a false alarm of premature labor and her doctor reminded Dale and her to reduce their sexual activity. "I know Dale was disappointed, but I was actually relieved. I was having backaches and my abdomen was huge. When my doctor said 'No more sex,' Dale got tense, but I relaxed."

## Medical Tests and Procedures

Because twin pregnancy is seen as high risk, it can become high tech as well, as many medical tests and procedures are used to evaluate or treat the expectant mother. How much and how often these are used depends on the presence and degree of medical complications. The more problems, the more intervention is likely to occur. This is true of both diagnostic and therapeutic procedures.

*Prenatal Checkups:* Routine tests done at prenatal visits are vital to assess the mother's and babies' well-being. Most of the time, test results will have a positive outcome, but if any of these tests or procedures indicate significant physical stress other medical follow-up will take place. It is important to ask how the information from the tests will be used and how it might change your medical care. It is good to ask about the accuracy, risks, and potential benefits from each one.

Fundal (uterine) measurements, palpation of the abdomen, and weight gain give information about fetal growth. Blood pressure

measurements, blood tests, and urine analysis for sugar and protein indicate how well the mother's body is responding to the
demands of pregnancy. It has become routine in most practices
for a pregnant woman to undergo a glucose tolerance test in the
second or third trimester to determine if she has gestational diabetes. For women pregnant with twins, ultrasounds and non-
stress tests are often done as an adjunct to the regular obstetrical
care.

*Ultrasound:* A ultrasound scan, also called sonagram, is one
of the most effective ways to confirm a multiple pregnancy. It is
also an importrant method of monitoring the remainder of a
multiple pregnancy and determining the growth of the developing
babies. An ultrasound scan uses very high frequency sound waves,
beyond the range of the human ear. These sound waves are
beamed into your abdomen and echo off your bladder, uterus,
placenta, and fetus into a computer which converts them into
pictures on a monitor.

During the scans the technician takes measurements of the
fetuses to estimate the due date and to determine their growth
and normal development. She also checks the health and the
location of the placentas. Ultrasounds are also used to evaluate problems such as unexplained bleeding or decreased fetal
movement. For some parents, ultrasounds can be reassuring and
informative. For others, they build anxiety, feel invasive, and un-
dermine confidence.

The procedure is painless, although the pregnant woman will
most likely feel uncomfortable, as she is required to drink many
glasses of water so her bladder is full when the procedure takes
place. By pushing the woman's uterus up above the pelvic bone
the full bladder helps make it easier for the technician to get a
clear picture of internal organs. The full bladder also enhances
the sound transmission, adding to the clarity of the picture. During this procedure, the woman lies on a table and a lubricant is
rubbed on her belly. A small device, the ultrasonic transducer, is
moved around on top of her belly to pick up the sound waves
and transmit the picture onto the monitor. During a scan, the
woman can look at the monitor with the technician. When it is

difficult for the untrained eye to recognize what is on the screen, most technicians will help you identify parts of the baby or babies as she takes measurements of the fetuses to determine their growth. When the ultrasound is done, some technicians may give the woman a negative, a picture, or a video of the procedure.

Debra was reassured by the information she received during her ultrasounds. "My first scan showed that the babies were growing very well and that their placentas were separate from each other. I felt that this was supporting evidence that I was carrying fraternal twins. This comforted me, because it increased my chances of having at least one girl. Two subsequent ultrasound scans taken weeks apart verified my own confidence that the babies were continuing to grow well. Sure that they were fine, I declined further scans until the time of birth, at which time their positions would be checked. I wanted to avoid any unnecessary tests and costs unless some other problem showed up."

Linda requested that an ultrasound be done during her second pregnancy. "When I found out that I was pregnant for the second time, my family and friends mercilessly teased me about having a second set of twins; boys this time. I adamantly protested, although in the back of my mind I knew my body was responding to this pregnancy exactly as it had with my previous one. I wanted to *rule out* twins!

"On the day of the ultrasound, I had Todd come with me to hold my hand. The technician put the transducer on my belly and immediately two little heads appeared in the picture. I burst into tears and Todd let out a happy yell. All I could think about was the high-risk months ahead of me: unending tests, bed rest, doctor appointments, and the likelihood of having premature babies again."

In situations where there is concern for the development of the twins, ultrasound can confirm normality. When Debbie had her third ultrasound at twenty-four weeks, her earlier concern about the smaller fetus and amniotic sac was lessened. "Along with checking fetal size, the doctor examined the babies' spinal columns and internal organs. Everything looked fine! I was so relieved. At the end of the exam, when the doctor asked if I were interested in knowing the babies' sexes, I said that it really didn't matter, but I suspected it was two boys; he agreed. An added bonus came at the end of the exam when the doctor surprised me with a videotape of the entire ultrasound. Our first 'home movie'!"

Finding out the sexes of your babies may be a pleasant side effect of ultrasound monitoring. However, unless amniocentesis is done on both twins, there is no guarantee that the physician's or technician's observations are 100 percent reliable. During Debbie's third ultrasound, a doctor told her she was carrying two boys, which she discovered was inaccurate when she gave birth to a boy and a girl! Leave room for inaccuracy!

*Amniocentesis:* Amniocentesis involves placing a fine needle through the abdominal wall and into the amniotic sac to withdraw small amounts of amniotic fluid which surrounds the fetus. This fluid provides various information about the babies. Administering an amniocentesis on a woman carrying twins is technically more difficult than performing one during a singleton pregnancy. The amniocentesis needle must be carefully placed to avoid injury to the babies and placentas. Sometimes even the most skillful physicians will find it impossible to do an amniocentesis on both twins, especially in later pregnancy when there is less amniotic fluid and the uterus is crowded with the babies. We recommend that parents discuss with their practitioners their ethical and emotional feelings regarding this procedure before it is carried out and fully discuss any potential risks. Amniocentesis can carry a slight risk of miscarriage, infection, premature labor, or tissue damage to the baby, placenta, or cord.

In early pregnancy it is often done on women over the age of thirty-five to determine if the fetus has a genetic abnormality. If an abnormality is detected in one identical twin, both will be affected, but genetic problems in one fraternal twin may not affect the co-twin. In either case, the parents are then faced with the decision to have the pregnancy terminated and lose both of the babies, have one of the babies terminated, or to go ahead with the pregnancy knowing that one or both will have a disability.

In later pregnancy, amniocentesis is most often done to evaluate the lung maturity of the baby or babies if delivery is imminent or needs to be induced. Occasionally, amniocentesis can relieve the excessive buildup of amniotic fluid, which, again, occurs more frequently with twins.

During Linda's second twin pregnancy, her water broke at thirty-three weeks. "My obstetrician requested an amniocentesis because he wanted to assess the condition of the boys before delivery. However, after a very lengthy ultrasound and many conferences between doctors, it was determined that I didn't have enough fluid to perform the test. I didn't know whether to worry more or be relieved that I couldn't have an amniocentesis."

Debbie's doctor suggested an amniocentesis be done when she went into premature labor at thirty-two and a half weeks. Debbie agreed. She knew the test was necessary; nevertheless, the thought of having it done petrified her. "I vividly imagined the needle piercing either the babies or the placenta in a vital spot. Unfortunately, Dale was unable to be with me during the test. When it was over, I realized that my fears had been groundless. The procedure was handled skillfully, and in some ways was very interesting to watch."


*Chorionic Villi Sampling:* Chorionic Villi Sampling (C.V.S.) is a procedure that is performed between the sixth and twelfth week of pregnancy. The sampling is done by taking a sample of tissue from the chorionic villi (a part of the placenta). This tissue can then be tested to determine whether or not certain genetic abnormalities exist in the developing baby. Of course, with fraternal twins sampling must be done on the chorionic villi of both twins to obtain each twin's unique genetic makeup.

C.V.S. is a possible alternative to amniocentesis and has the advantage of being less invasive. It also reveals information about the fetus earlier in the pregnancy than amniocentesis does. However, chorionic villi sampling is a relatively new procedure and some studies associate the procedure with an increased risk of miscarriage and deformities in the baby. As with all medical procedures, it is wise to discuss the risks and benefits of C.V.S. with your doctor before undergoing this test.

*Non-Stress Tests:* A non-stress test is used to check for placental functioning and the condition of the babies. A fetal monitor compares the babies' heart rates in response to Braxton-Hicks contractions and fetal movement. This is an important tool for assessing whether the babies are stressed due to the mother's high blood pressure, breakdown of placental functioning, over-crowding in the uterus, or other problems that affect the babies' growth. If a non-stress test has a negative reading, it is often repeated a day or two later. If the woman is far enough along in her pregnancy, and the test is still negative, it may be followed with a stress test, where contractions are initiated by breast stimulation or uterine stimulants to see how the baby reacts to stronger contractions. Depending on the response, labor may or may not be induced, or a cesarean may be performed.

When Debra started having signs of mild pre-eclampsia near the end of her pregnancy, she began having weekly non-stress tests. "It would take up to two hours to get a good reading on both babies. The nurse-practitioner and I giggled a lot about the babies' responses to all the poking and prodding, and came to feel that we knew what their personalities were. We even went so far as to predict that the first baby was a boy and the other was a girl, which was later proven correct!"

Sheri's first non-stress test took place at thirty-one weeks. "Instead of going to the clinic, my mom, my daughter, and I went to the hospital. My doctor wanted to use their more sensitive machines for this first test. The nurses propped me on a bed in one of the labor and delivery rooms, strapped two wide bands with small monitors around my belly, positioned the monitors, one over each baby. The machines graphed the babies' heartbeats on paper. It was exciting to sit there for an hour, feeling the babies move, and watch the heart rates rise and fall in response to their movements. The graphs also allowed my mom and Kallie to see all the movements I was feeling inside. It was a wonderful experience for all three of us. After I was thirty-three weeks along in the pregnancy, I started having weekly non-stress tests in the doctor's clinic to help monitor the babies' heartbeats because my blood pressure was starting to rise."

## Medical Problems in Multiple Pregnancy
· · · · · · · · · · · · · · · · · · · · · · · · · · · · · · · · ·

As with any pregnancy, medical problems may develop during the nine months that a woman is carrying her twins. In addition, if a woman has a chronic health condition, it may further complicate the pregnancy. When assessments or tests indicate the presence of a medical problem, further tests or treatments are recommended. With a multiple birth pregnancy, there are a few unique complications that may arise, although these are rare and few in number.

*Warning Signs:*   Some warning signs of trouble in a pregnancy are: persistent vomiting beyond the first trimester or severe vomiting anytime; signs of infection such as fever, chills, or a flulike feeling; burning on urination or vaginal burning or itching; swelling of face or hands; visual disturbances; severe, frequent, or continuous headaches; muscular irritability; spasms or convulsions; severe or unusual digestive or abdominal pain; fluid or bloody discharge from the vagina; and the absence or lessening of fetal movement. These symptoms may indicate any number of medical concerns and should be brought to the attention of the physician or midwife.

*Gestational Diabetes:*   When blood sugar levels are abnormally high during pregnancy, the mother is said to have *gestational diabetes,* which is a temporary and inadequate response to the body's increased demands on the pancreas for the production of insulin. Some contemporary studies indicate that blood sugar levels from well-nourished pregnant women are normally higher than the currently "acceptable" values for women who are not pregnant. Whole-blood glucose tolerance tests can confirm abnormal blood sugar levels and are commonly given during the second or third trimester of pregnancy. Women with true gestational diabetes are at a greater risk of developing pre-eclampsia, producing excess amniotic fluid, or developing adult-onset diabetes later in life. Their infants may be too small or too large, have respiratory problems, or, more rarely, be stillborn. The three most common symptoms of gestational diabetes are excessive thirst, hunger, and increased frequency and amount of urination.

With Linda's second twin pregnancy she was told that she had borderline gestational diabetes. Her doctor recommended a special diet that was calorie-restricted, low in carbohydrates, and high in protein. Linda also did a glucose test on her blood three times a day. Linda did her own research on gestational diabetes and on the caloric intake needed during pregnancy and finally confronted her doctor with questions about her diet. "I wondered if I was getting enough calories. I asked him if his diet was based on a woman with a twin pregnancy or with a singleton pregnancy because my information indicated that I actually needed more calories than his diet allowed. He agreed, and my caloric allotment was increased. Unfortunately, by this time it was near the end of my pregnancy and I had no room left for more food!"

Debra was also advised to decrease her caloric intake to manage her borderline gestational diabetes. She followed a diet based on her current body weight with allowances for increased weight gain. "After checking several resources, I came to believe that an across-the-board calorie restriction was inadequate for my twin pregnancy, so I followed a guideline of 32 calories and 1.3 grams of protein for every two pounds of body weight instead. I believe this was a healthier choice for me. Still, I questioned whether that increased amount of protein was enough for the amount of stress I was under."

*Pre-Eclampsia and Eclampsia (Toxemia):* Pre-eclampsia generally appears in the third trimester of pregnancy. It occurs in 20 to 30 percent of all twin pregnancies compared to 6 to 7 percent in all pregnancies combined. The exact cause of this condition is not known for certain, but is believed to be related to reduced kidney or liver functioning in the mother. It ranges from mild to severe.

Pre-eclampsia, which used to be referred to as toxemia, is characterized by high blood pressure, protein in the urine, and fluid retention in the legs, hands, and face. Some women may develop only high blood pressure, called pregnancy-induced hypertension, and not show any other symptoms that characterize pre-eclampsia. During pregnancy many factors, including inade-

quate diet (especially protein), ingestion of alcohol or drugs, infections, chronic diseases such as diabetes or recurrent kidney
infections, and physical or emotional stress can increase the
chance of pre-eclampsia developing. A doctor may recommend
some or all of the following when pre-eclampsia occurs—bed
rest, elevation of the legs, resting on the left side to enhance fetal
blood circulation, reducing the use of salt, increasing protein in
the diet. Sometimes medications to control rising blood pressure
are prescribed. In addition, increased medical supervision to
monitor the health of the mother and babies is indicated.

The reason for careful monitoring and treatment is that severe
pre-eclampsia can lead to *eclampsia* if left untreated. Eclampsia
has a very low incidence rate; with good prenatal care, this more
serious complication is usually prevented. It is marked by severe
headaches, visual disturbances, extremely elevated blood pressure, and hyperactive reflexes. Eclampsia can become a life-threatening condition characterized by convulsions, possible coma, and,
rarely, death.

Sheri learned that she was pre-eclampsic when her fourth ultrasound was done at thirty-six and a half weeks. "My blood
pressure was high enough that, along with my blood vessels, the
babies' vessels in their (shared) placenta and umbilical cords were
constricting and they weren't receiving enough nutrition. We
needed to decide whether Emmy and Tessa would be better off
inside or out. The doctor ordered some blood tests and scheduled
a detailed ultrasound, called a *biophysical profile,* which would
provide a rating of the babies' muscle tone, body movements, and
breathing ability, as well as the amount of amniotic fluid, and the
blood flow resistance through the umbilical cord.

"An ultrasound was part of the profile exam, in which the
technician watched and scored both babies in several developmental areas. Both twins scored very well. They didn't appear to
be under stress, but they were measured as too small for their
gestational age. After a call to my doctor, a radiologist performed
an amniocentesis to determine the maturity of my twins' lungs.

"Later that evening, Steve and I sat in our doctor's office, going
over the results of the tests with him. Since my blood pressure
was dangerously high and the amniocentesis showed that the ba-

bies' lungs were mature, everything pointed toward delivering the babies as soon as possible. My doctor booked us into the next available cesarean room at the hospital. Our babies were scheduled to be born the next day at 4:00 P.M."

In the last few weeks of her pregnancy, Debra also began to show signs of mild pre-eclampsia. "This required more frequent prenatal visits to undergo non-stress tests. Since I was no longer able to drive, I had to find rides to the doctor, which is not so easy when one lives 25 miles away. All this proved to be quite stressful, which was counterproductive to the recommended treatment. To help my body cope, I increased the amount of protein in my meals and rested more, especially on my left side. I could sense when I overexerted myself, and it showed up in the blood tests that examined my liver and kidney function."

Fourteen days before her due date, Florien made her weekly visit to the midwife and discovered that her blood pressure had risen considerably. "I had some urine tests done and made an appointment to see the doctor four days later. Meanwhile, it was rest, relaxation, feet up, and no salt.

"In spite of this, at my follow-up visit a few days later, my blood pressure was still high, I was starting to retain water, and the urine tests showed protein was present. Since I was over thirty-eight weeks along, I checked into the hospital a few hours later so my doctor could induce labor."

*Placenta Previa: Placenta previa* occurs in about one in every 200 pregnancies and is twice as likely to happen in twin as in singleton pregnancies. This condition occurs when all or part of the placenta is lying near or directly over the cervix. It is most often recognized when it causes painless bleeding, which is the result of a minor tear in the placental attachment to the uterus or partial detachment of the placenta from the uterus. Bed rest is recommended when bleeding occurs; sometimes the expectant mother is hospitalized until the bleeding stops or, in severe cases, until delivery. Most of the time, if placenta previa occurs in the earlier months of pregnancy, the placenta will grow up and out of the way of the cervix. If it remains, cesarean delivery is required. However, with a partial placenta previa either a vaginal or a cesarean birth can occur depending upon the exact location of the placenta and the amount of blood loss.

Linda remembers one afternoon in the twenty-eighth week of her second pregnancy. "I woke up from a nap and thought I had urinated or, worse yet, ruptured my membranes. I was alarmed and scared when I realized the liquid running down my leg was blood. I felt nothing, no cramps or pain. Todd rushed me to the hospital, where my doctor ordered an ultrasound. The diagnosis was a partial placenta previa. I continued to have several bleeding episodes off and on until my thirty-third week of pregnancy. Each time I was hospitalized, sometimes only for a few hours, then discharged on complete bed rest. I was told that my delivery could be either vaginal or cesarean, but more than likely I would have to have a cesarean."

*Preterm Labor:*  One of the biggest medical concerns in a multiple pregnancy is premature labor and the subsequent early births of the twins. Statistically, 50 to 60 percent of multiples are born before the thirty-seventh week of gestation. Prematurity is not desirable, as the babies, with less mature bodily functions, are prone to have some problems adjusting to the outer world.

The actual definition of preterm labor is the onset of regular uterine contractions before the end of the thirty-seventh week of pregnancy. These contractions cause the cervix to dilate (open) to at least 2 centimeters and to efface (thin out) by 75 percent. Contractions that cause progressive changes in the cervix or contractions that come ten or less minutes apart are also warning signs that labor has begun.

In at least half of the cases of premature labor, the cause is unknown. The most widely held theories attribute preterm labor to placental insufficiency and low blood volume, most commonly due to inadequate nutrition or substance abuse; overdistention of the uterus from multiple pregnancy, excessive amniotic fluid, or a large baby; illness in the mother such as infection, diabetes, or pre-eclampsia; stress in the intrauterine environment, which is more likely in multiple pregnancy; and breaking of the amniotic sac.

*Chronic Health Conditions in Pregnancy:* Years ago many women with chronic health problems were discouraged from getting pregnant. Today with careful medical attention, such pregnancies often can be brought to a successful conclusion.

Debbie had problems when her asthma flared up. "As I began my second trimester I had the misfortune of catching a bad cold, which triggered a chronic problem with asthma. I had started my pregnancy with strict instructions to take no medications at all; now I was faithfully taking several prescriptions as well as breathing treatments. I wondered if this could harm my babies, but my obstetrician and allergist both assured me that the medications were safe; not taking the medication could cause me to have serious breathing problems which would decrease the oxygen to my babies. This put things in perspective, but still, I worried."

Linda also has a chronic condition that caused her problems during the early months of her pregnancies. "My severe morning sickness had already taken its toll on my body. Then to complicate matters, I have Addison's disease, a dysfunction of the body's adrenal glands. I take medication to control the disease and this required careful monitoring during the pregnancy.

"During the second month of my first pregnancy my doctor increased my medication to control the Addison's disease when I became severely dehydrated and weak. He was quick to assure me that it would not harm the baby, but I couldn't help being skeptical. I questioned the increase in the dosage, and read everything I could find on each one. At this time it was not known that I was carrying twins, and I was concerned about only one baby. I would have worried twice as much if I'd known there were two."

Linda developed another problem that required additional medical treatment. "Midway through both of my pregnancies, chills set in, followed by a high fever. I was told to take Tylenol which helped until the fever returned a week later. I went in to see my doctor, who suspected a kidney infection. A urinalysis confirmed the diagnosis, so I was off to the hospital again, this time in tears. I was put on IV fluids and antibiotics. I could not help being concerned about the babies. To reassure me, the nurse shared the results of the heart rate monitoring that had been done on the babies. Their hearts were strong and normal. Of all the tests and procedures I endured, this one I welcomed."

## Medical Problems in the Developing Babies

*Vanishing Twin Syndrome:* The *vanishing twin syndrome* occurs during the first trimester of pregnancy when one twin stops developing and is either miscarried or absorbed into the uterus, while the other twin continues to grow and develop normally. Sometimes the pregnant woman bleeds and thinks she has miscarried her baby, only to discover that she is still pregnant. She may never know that she was carrying twins. Other times, twins may have been diagnosed by ultrasound early in pregnancy, with the subsequent miscarriage of one baby, leaving the expectant parents to grieve this loss.

Debbie relates that, "My first ultrasound at nine weeks showed three amniotic sacs. The first sac was good-sized, with a thriving embryo inside of it. The second sac was smaller, but still showed a fetus and a heartbeat. The third sac appeared to be empty. When I read about the vanishing twin syndrome, I felt certain that this was happening to the third fetus. At the end of my twelfth week, I had a watery, bloody stained vaginal discharge as I slept one night. A second ultrasound done the following day showed two thriving fetuses, but the third sac was totally gone. Apparently, that was what I had miscarried. I was relieved and disappointed at the same time."

*Intrauterine Growth Retardation:* For various reasons, twins may have *intrauterine growth retardation.* In general, twins are smaller at birth than singletons of the same gestational age. Sometimes this is due to competition for nutrients and/or over-crowding in the uterus. Other times it is due to the mother's medical problems, such as eclampsia. At birth, the twins may have low blood sugar and may have large heads in relation to their body size. One or both twins may be affected. Most twins born with this type of growth problem have no other serious complications, and develop normally.

At thirty-six and a half weeks, Sheri was due for her fourth ultrasound, and going into it, things looked pretty good.

"After the measurements were done on Tessa, the technician told us that she weighed only four and a half pounds. She had gained only one pound in the last month, not the two she should have. The technician soon announced that Emmy was also too small for her age. After the ultrasound, my doctor told us that I was pre-eclampsic and that my babies might not be receiving adequate nutrition. We scheduled a biophysical profile to be done the next day.

*Twin-to-Twin Transfusion Syndrome:* When identical twins share a placenta, it is possible for the babies to get unequal amounts of nutrients. This occurs in 10 to 15 percent of identical twins and is known as the *twin-to-twin transfusion* syndrome. In this condition, tiny fissures in the blood vessels within the shared placenta allow the blood designated for one baby, the donor, to be passed into the system of the other baby, the recipient. The donor baby has a decrease in his blood supply, and is usually small and anemic. However, the larger fetus, the recipient, tends to suffer most, with possible jaundice, respiratory disorders, or even heart failure. It is sometimes necessary to do exchange transfusions on one or both of the twins after birth.

*Entangled Umbilical Cords:* Approximately 2 to 4 percent of identical twins share a single amniotic sac. With no membrane to separate them in the womb, their umbilical cords may become entangled with each other, threatening the babies' growth. If entanglement is severe, it can cause loss of life by cutting off either baby's lifeline to the placenta. As with intrauterine growth retardation and twin-to-twin transfusion, *entangled umbilical cords* are found in such a small portion of twin births that it is not generally a cause for concern.

Sheri was one of the few women who did have this condition, but was not aware of it until the time of her twins' births. "During our second ultrasound at twenty-six weeks, the technician couldn't

find an amniotic membrane separating the babies, but she assumed
it was there. She said the membranes were very thin and sometimes hard to see. At successive ultrasounds, the technicians all
mentioned the same thing, but none seemed concerned. We never
even considered that the membrane wasn't actually there. We
didn't find out the truth until Emmy and Tessa's birth and I am
glad. If I had known that Emmy and Tessa's cords were tangled,
it would have scared me for the remainder of the pregnancy. As
it was both of our babies were healthy at birth; we considered
ourselves fortunate."

## Getting Ready for Your Twins

While the health of the mother and babies are foremost in
many parents' minds during pregnancy, much time is also spent
in preparing to bring the babies home and care for them. Getting
a home prepared for two babies can be both a time-consuming
and expensive job. By having the goal of getting everything ready
before the seventh month of our pregnancies, we were able to
actively participate in purchasing needed items and rearranging
our households while we still felt fairly energetic. Some of us
started to think about getting help for after the babies were born
and how we would manage our finances. We started to think about
choices: breast-feeding or bottle-feeding, cloth versus disposable
diapers. Of course, some women do not find out that they are
carrying twins until very late in the pregnancy or during the
delivery. It is important to remember that, even in these situations, things can work out as friends, family and hospital staff
assist you in getting your needs met.

Some of the twin books available in bookstores and libraries
offer lists of suggested layette and equipment needs. While these
lists are very helpful, perhaps the best resource is other mothers
of twins who can tell you what they have tried and what worked
best for them. Contacting mothers-of-twins clubs and other community parenting groups is a good way to find these women.

Having twins can be very expensive, especially if these are your
first children and you try to purchase all new equipment and

clothing. Costs can be cut by buying good quality, secondhand items. Once the initial expenses are behind you, it becomes easier to plan ahead for the regular necessities in caring for your twins.

*Preparing to Care for Newborn Twins:* Part of the preparation of caring for newborn twins can be done long before the twins are born. Choosing a pediatrician and readying the nursery are two practical ways to start. Yet, it can also be useful to make other decisions about the twins' care. Discussions between partners about division of the workload and household responsibilities should be started during pregnancy; other day-to-day issues can also be considered.

Debbie made decisions about how she would feed and diaper her twins. "I gave a lot of thought to whether or not to breast-feed exclusively. I had breast-fed Chris with no supplements. It had been wonderful, but it involved a major commitment of time and energy because I was never able to express milk and had to be with him for every feeding. With twins, I knew that the demands would be doubled and that I would be overwhelmed unless Dale could help by giving them supplemental bottles. Since I was never successful at expressing milk, it was clear to me that I would need to supplement with formula. I felt some guilt about this, because I knew that breast-feeding would be best for the babies. But I had to do what was easiest, least stressful, and therefore best, for me, and try not to feel too guilty."

With the feeding issue settled, Debbie next made a decision about whether or not to use cloth diapers. "I chose a diaper service. I was surprised to find that with twins it was more economical and nearly as convenient as using disposables.

"The clear conscience I felt for not polluting the environment that the twins would inherit offset the lingering guilt I felt for deciding in favor of formula supplements!"

Debra made up her mind about breast-feeding her twins very early. "I had a lot of confidence that I could provide enough milk for twins and I felt this was best for them nutritionally and emotionally. It would also save money, both by not purchasing formula and by reducing the chances that my babies would get sick and need medical care.

"For financial and environmental reasons, I chose to wash my own cloth diapers, as we had just purchased a large-capacity washing machine and dryer. I made sure I had one week's worth of infant clothing for each baby, so I would only have to wash clothing once a week."

*Choosing a Doctor for the Babies:*   Many expectant parents of twins are concerned about who will provide the medical care for their babies after they are born, especially if the twins are born prematurely or have medical complications at birth. We all had such concerns and some of us began our selection of a doctor for our babies well in advance of their due date. We each chose a physician who was qualified and suited to our personalities and needs.

During Florien's sixth month of pregnancy, she sought opinions from her friends who had infants or young children. From their recommendations, she chose three pediatricians and scheduled appointments with them. "Devin and I only met two of the three pediatricians we had planned to see. After meeting the second one, we knew that he was the one we wanted to care for our newborn twins. The thing that impressed us most about him was that he spoke to us as though we were intelligent, caring parents. He took the time to explain new medical terminology and made us feel secure in asking any questions we had about the health care of our children. He told us he would attempt to be at their delivery and would work with the neonatologist in the NICU, if our newborns needed such care. He gained our trust and respect during that initial interview and to this day he hasn't let us down."

Beyond liking and respecting a doctor, it is important to have the answers to a few questions. Does his office run efficiently? How available is the physician? Can he see you in the evening or on weekends? When he is out, who covers for him? Are the physicians who cover for him also physicians you can trust? How does he feel about circumcisions, especially if the boy is premature? These are just a few of the types of questions parents should learn the answers to before choosing a physician to avoid disappointments and misunderstandings in the future.

## Getting Ready for the Birth
· · · · · · · · · · · · · · · · · · · · · · · · · · · ·

*Childbirth Classes:* As expectant mothers near the mid-point of their pregnancies, they will feel a need to get ready for the births of the twins. We found childbirth classes to be helpful in educating ourselves and our partners about the birth process in general, and about twin births in particular.

Childbirth classes can be a good resource in helping expectant mothers to manage their pregnancies and their deliveries, and for information on infant care after the twins are born. We all made a point of telling our instructor that we were carrying twins. Because of this, they were able to provide us with information about pregnancy and birth processes which was relevant to twins. Some educators even provided relaxation techniques and exercises appropriate for a woman carrying twins!

We suggest completing a childbirth class before the end of the sixth or seventh month of pregnancy, because the chance of going into premature labor is very real. Two of us who had high risk symptoms chose to take childbirth classes as early as the fifth month; they were more comfortable sitting through the classes than the rest of us because by the end of our twin pregnancies, most of us had a difficult time sitting comfortably for very long!

We encourage pregnant women to attend classes with a partner, even if he or she has been to childbirth classes before. The more our partners knew, the more supportive they were when the time to give birth arrived! If your partner is not able or willing to attend with you, ask a friend or relative to be your support person.

Linda's doctor suggested that she and Todd take childbirth classes early in their first pregnancy, because of the increased chance of premature delivery of twins. "We heeded his advice and enrolled in a Lamaze class in my fifth month. By the time I delivered Sarah and Maiah the class was still busy learning how to breathe!"

Even though Florien wasn't on "complete bed rest" orders from her doctor, she asked for a private session in her home in addition to the class she and Devin enrolled in at the local hospital.

Debra arranged to have a private lesson with her former childbirth educator to specifically discuss the birth of twins. "We spent three hours talking, especially about breech delivery and the pros and cons of possible medical procedures that might be proposed. I used this information to negotiate a detailed birth plan with my doctor."

*Designing a Birth Plan:*   Designing a birth plan may seem like going overboard to some people; to others it is a means of regaining some control over an unpredictable situation. It is an excellent way of letting your medical team know exactly what your preferences are and can also be a good tool for discussing what types of delivery options are possible, given an individual situation. A few of us took the time to write up a birth plan in an effort to relay our wants and needs to our care providers and support people during the delivery.

Debra negotiated a birth plan with her obstetrician, with an emphasis on avoiding a cesarean birth unless absolutely necessary. "I told him this was important to me for two reasons. The first was that I wanted to keep as many of the positive elements as possible of my previous home birth intact during the hospital delivery. The second was that I wished to avoid the recovery of surgical delivery while simultaneously caring for two more children. My doctor carefully answered all my questions, respected my concerns and feelings, and volunteered to attend my delivery even if he was not on call."

When Florien was pregnant with her twins, she wrote a request list for the birth. This was given to her obstetrician, midwives, and pediatrician, and she planned to bring a copy to the hospital when labor started. "My birth plan was two pages long and very thorough. It stated our desire for the use of only the necessary technological intervention or medications required for a safe delivery. It included a limited visitor list, and specified that we wanted the minimum number of hospital staff to be present at the delivery. Most of our requests were discussed and negotiated with our doctor before the delivery time arrived.

"I also shared my plan with the class instructor during a private session with her at our home, and got her opinions about the realities of multiple births in the hospital. I highly recommend one-on-one meetings with hospital staff to anyone carrying twins.

"When I finally went into labor, though, complications occurred that did not allow for most of what was written on my plan. However, my medical team's awareness of my concerns was enough for me to feel comfortable with the last-minute decisions that needed to be made."

Even pregnancies being managed for premature labor can be discussed to discover the doctor's recommendations and the woman's feelings about the premature labor. Debbie explains that when she was ready to leave the hospital after her first episode of premature labor was under control, she and her obstetrician sat down and discussed a plan to manage the remainder of her pregnancy, and the birth options. "He explained that I needed to continue on oral Terbutaline [a drug that suppresses uterine contractions], which I was to take faithfully around the clock. I was to be on strict bed rest, up only for meals and to go to the bathroom. If labor started more than four weeks before my due date, I would have a cesarean section. The cesarean would minimize birth trauma for Michael, who was in the breech position. If I went into labor close to term, when the babies were fully mature, we would attempt a vaginal delivery. Early in my pregnancy I had been against having a cesarean section; now I just wanted to have these babies safely, even if it meant an operation."

## Going into Labor

*Facing the Possibility of Having Premature Twins:* The premature birth of twins can happen, even when every reasonable precaution has been taken, so we recommend that every woman pregnant with twins consider it as a possibility. The more mentally and emotionally prepared a woman is for premature labor, the easier it will be to deal with the added stress of controlling premature labor medically or having babies in the neonatal intensive care unit. In addition to reading books about prematurity, we recommend that you visit the NICU in the hospital where you will give birth. If the hospital doesn't have an NICU, locate the NICU nearest you and make arrangements to tour it if possible.

Dale and Debbie toured a neonatal intensive care unit (NICU) when she was hospitalized at thirty-two weeks to treat the contractions of premature labor. "Dale walked; I rode in a wheelchair. We met the neonatal nurses and neonatologists. This turned out to be a valuable experience. We saw premature babies of all sizes and ages, and three- and four-pound babies that had once been one- and two-pound babies. Now they were doing well and were nearly ready to go home. We asked every question we could think of, and were reassured that although many preemies are initially quite ill, most of them do just fine. The doctors and nurses were all highly skilled and caring. We came away knowing that, although prematurity is never ideal, it can usually be dealt with successfully."

Florien recognized the potential chance that she could give birth to her twins prematurely and made an effort to help prepare herself in case this were to happen. "During our childbirth class, Devin and I walked down to the neonatal intensive care unit and gazed at the current twins in residence during the breaks. Observing the tiny babies and their families helped us to balance our fears with our hopes. The skill and confidence that the NICU staff showed with the fragile preemies brought the reassurance that if our babies were born prematurely, they would receive excellent care."

*Signs of Labor:*  It is important to know the signs of labor because some of the common aches and pains of pregnancy can be just that, or they could be preliminary signs of labor. This is especially important in a twin pregnancy because of the possibility of premature labor. Potential warnings of impending labor are a dull abdominal or menstrual-type cramping, an increase or change in vaginal discharge, and feeling sick or flulike.

Definite signs of labor are water leaking or gushing from the vagina, mucus plug coming from the vagina, and contractions or cramps that come 10 or less minutes apart and continue to occur longer than one hour. If any of these happen, call your physician or nurse midwife immediately, because they are best qualified to differentiate between a false alarm and labor.

*Managing Premature Labor:* When women go into labor prematurely, or before the thirty-seventh week of pregnancy, efforts will be made to stop it. Some women can be successfully treated at home with complete bed rest. Medications may also be used to control contractions. Sheri thought she was going into premature labor when she started having Braxton-Hicks contractions at thirty-three weeks. Although she knew that Braxton-Hicks contractions are not a sign of true labor, she made an appointment with her obstetrician to be sure.

"My doctor determined that these were Braxton-Hicks contractions, but because of their frequency and regularity he put me on Terbutaline to stop them and asked me to rest in bed as often as I could. The Terbutaline made me feel as though I had drunk three cups of coffee and had run around the block. After a week or so, the contractions stopped at night. I was then allowed to discontinue the medication before bedtime. After another week, the contractions stopped altogether and I gladly put those pills away."

Other women will need more aggressive treatment to manage their labor. In these cases, the pregnant woman is hospitalized and given a drug such as magnesium sulfate, which is given intravenously and stops labor by relaxing the muscles of the uterus. An ultrasound is often done on the babies and an amniocentesis performed to determine the babies' lung development. If the uterine contractions cannot be stopped and the woman is at thirty-four weeks of pregnancy or less, a steroid injection is given which speeds up the development of the babies' lungs, minimizing the risk of respiratory distress syndrome. If one or both of the babies' amniotic sacs breaks, labor cannot be stopped indefinitely because of the risk of infection, but it may be delayed for a day or so.

When Debbie was thirty-two and a half weeks pregnant, she went into premature labor. "The contractions I had were not particularly uncomfortable, but they persisted more than an hour even after I rested. I went to see my doctor to have him examine me; still, I was pretty sure it was nothing more than Braxton-Hicks contractions. To my surprise and disappointment, he told me that my cervix was almost completely effaced and was beginning to dilate. I was immediately admitted to the hospital. In an attempt to stop labor, they placed me on bed rest, started an IV, and strapped a monitor around my abdomen to record my contractions and the babies' heart rates. I was given magnesium sulfate in my IV to stop labor contractions and the steroid, Betamethasone, by injection to mature the babies' lungs.

"After a few days of hospital bed rest, my contractions decreased in frequency and strength. My obstetrician explained that I could not be maintained on magnesium sulfate, which I didn't mind because it made me feel drugged and uncoordinated. He put me on oral Terbutaline; that made me feel shaky and hyperactive, but at least I felt alert, a distinct improvement. I had an ultrasound and an amniocentesis performed and as more days passed, productive labor ceased and I was allowed to go home on oral medication and with complete bed rest."

Debbie was at home on bed rest for two weeks. Her obstetrician confided to her that he had never thought she would make it that far. "With renewed conviction, I believed I really might carry to term. But this was not to be. On the first day of spring, during my thirty-fifth week of pregnancy, my water broke. Our babies were ready to be born."

Linda began labor when she was thirty weeks along in her pregnancy. "At the end of my seventh month, we had a chance to go to Ashland, Oregon, three hours' travel from our home in Eugene. I had always wanted to go to the famous Shakespearean Festival held there every year, and the thought of spending a few days in a different setting was exhilarating. My doctor, however, was not as enthusiastic as I was about the trip. He reluctantly agreed to it only when I promised to take plenty of naps and to stay off my feet.

"The day before we left, my muscles ached and the babies seemed to be kicking more than usual. I felt tired, too, but couldn't put my finger on the problem. The next morning, I still didn't feel right, and considered calling off the trip. But I didn't want to spend the next few days at home, so I convinced myself everything was fine. We arrived in Ashland for a light lunch, and then had a nap in the hotel.

"That evening, Todd and I went out with friends for a quiet dinner, then went to bed. At 2:30 A.M. I woke up. I returned from the bathroom and was lying in bed when all of a sudden, I felt a warm gush of liquid between my legs. My water had broken.

"I tried to remain calm as I shook Todd awake and told him what had happened. He called the doctor.

"We were instructed to start immediately for Sacred Heart Hospital in Eugene, the closest facility with a neonatal intensive care unit. Todd propped me up in the back seat of our car and we sped to the hospital, 180 miles distant. An unspoken question lay between us: 'Would we make it in time?' "

*Going into Labor at Term (Or Close to It!):* No matter how prepared you think you are, even full-term labor and birth can hold surprises. Due dates are only estimates of arrival times and sometimes things conspire to foil your best-laid plans.

Sheri and Steve had a decision to make after the biophysical profile and her non-stress test results were available. "I was thirty-seven weeks along when I got the results, and everything pointed toward delivering the babies as soon as possible. My doctor booked us into the next available cesarean room at the hospital; our babies would be born the next day at 4:00 P.M. After our meeting with the doctor, I went to a Christmas party. When I got back home at 10:30, we called our parents about the next day's plan and went to bed just before midnight. I had just gotten all my pillows situated around me when my water broke. Off we went to the hospital."

Debra was able to go into term labor on her own. "After thirty-seven weeks of pregnancy, I left worries of prematurity behind me. My pre-eclampsia was worsening, however; so when my doctor threatened hospitalization, I called my parents to come up earlier than planned. Their caretaking brought about immediate improvement. On my next prenatal visit at thirty-eight weeks, I couldn't help asking my doctor a question that was foremost on my mind: Could I have sex now? I figured that if I had got that far, I deserved it. He grinned in reply. Rick and I took full advantage of this opportunity, but we only had one week to make up for lost time. I went into labor at 39 weeks."

## Our Thoughts and Reflections

SHERI:    Because I am an eternal optimist, I spent my pregnancy feeling confident that the twins' births would go fine. I had occasional worries, but I didn't allow myself to become consumed by them. This, and the fact that I took good care of myself physically, made my pregnancy a great experience. My pregnancy was the only period of time that I got more attention than the twins!

LINDA:    I thought if I followed my doctor's orders precisely, stayed off my feet, and ate well-balanced meals, I would carry both sets of my twins to term. Was I ever wrong! The bottom line is that every woman's body responds differently to a twin pregnancy, and there are still many factors beyond our control.

DEBBIE:    From the very start, my twin pregnancy was high stress, beginning with in vitro fertilization and continuing with nausea, acne, asthma, varicose veins, backaches, and finally premature labor. There was always one more discomfort or medical problem to deal with. I wish I had thought of my twin pregnancy as a potential challenge from the very start; then I could have tackled those eight months with a different attitude. Instead, I naively imagined it would be a problem-free and totally wonderful experience, so I was constantly disappointed by my unmet expectations. A more realistic outlook would have made my pregnancy much more enjoyable.

FLORIEN:    I feel very fortunate because I had a relatively easy twin pregnancy. Even though I had discomforts and Devin and I needed to make changes in our lives in preparation for starting a family, I viewed my pregnancy as a challenge and honestly, I really enjoyed being pregnant with twins!

DEBRA:    Though I was uncomfortable at times, I was fascinated by my body's ability to meet the challenge of growing two healthy babies. I always had enjoyed being pregnant, reveling in those primal feelings of creating life, being part of something so elemental, yet so magnificent. The challenge in my pregnancy was to adjust to twin motherhood. My advice to others who are having a hard time facing the reality of having twins is to seek and accept help—in any way you need. Also, don't let other people's naive comments about the blessings of twins invalidate your concerns.

# Chapter 3

# "Baby A ... Baby B"

## The Birth Experience

Whether the birth of twins occurs vaginally or by cesarean surgery (or both), it is truly an amazing experience. Nothing compares to it, and no two experiences are alike. There can be great drama and suspense. You can be frightened one minute and ecstatic the next. You can also just be relieved that it is all over. You will remember it forever, both the good and not-so-good parts. The following pages are filled with our special memories of how our sets of "Baby A and Baby B" entered the world. Because of the personal nature of our birth stories, the format of this chapter differs from that of other chapters. You may share some similarities with our experiences, but mostly, your labor and birth will be uniquely your own.

### How Will Your Babies Be Born?

The birth of multiples has some added variables that cause it to be treated by most practitioners as *high-risk*. While some complications happen with greater frequency in twin births than with singletons, many normal and uncomplicated births do occur. One of the key influences in how your birthing process will proceed is your doctor's or midwife's beliefs about the management of twin labor and birth. Their individual statistics will vary as to the number of twins they deliver vaginally, by cesarean, or in combination—when the first twin is born vaginally and the second by cesarean. It is useful to know what your practitioner's statistics are if you wish to increase your chances of a vaginal delivery.

Some practitioners consider all multiple pregnancies an indication for cesarean birth, while others may attempt a vaginal delivery of twins only if both babies are positioned head down at the time of delivery. Others may, if the first twin is delivered in a head-down position, attempt to deliver the second twin vaginally if he is in the breech position or if he can be repositioned from a transverse position. Other factors that influence the method of delivery are: whether a woman has had a previous cesarean, whether she will be having premature or low birth weight babies, or whether she is beyond the fortieth week of gestation. If you are expecting a vaginal delivery, you may also wish to discuss some of these issues with your practitioner: freedom to change positions or walk around during labor; the use of medications for pain relief or to stimulate contractions; when and if electronic fetal monitors (machines that keep track of your contractions and the babies' heart rates) should be used; and under what set of circumstances a cesarean would be elected. When you actively participate in planning your twins' birth, you can be sure that your preferences will be a factor in the method of delivery chosen as your pregnancy and labor proceed.

*Labor Begins:* The management of your labor and delivery will depend quite a lot on how far along you are in your pregnancy when your labor starts. Labor that begins prematurely (before thirty-seven weeks) will be handled differently than labor that begins at full term. Recognizing the early signs of labor is paramount to preventing premature birth as well as preparing for a term birth. One or more of the following symptoms may be preliminary signs of labor: a nagging or intermittent backache; soft or diarrhealike stools; feeling flulike or sick; increased vaginal discharge; three- to four-pound weight loss; a burst of energy or an urge to put your life/house/closets in order (the "nesting instinct"); pressure or cramping in the lower abdomen that comes and goes; or contractions that come consistently ten minutes apart for more than an hour, even after you have tried drinking fluids and lying down. More definite signs of impending labor are: loss of the mucus plug (a blood-tinged clear or creamy-colored discharge); contractions that are increasing in frequency, length, and intensity; and breaking of the bag of waters, which may result in a sudden gush of fluid or a trickling leak.

The development of any of the preliminary or definite signs of labor should be followed by a phone call to your practitioner to notify him or her of the situation. It is especially important to call immediately when the bag of waters breaks because prolapse of the umbilical cord (the cord coming out before the baby) needs to be ruled out. Be reassured that this is not a very common occurrence but there is a higher incidence of it when the first baby is in the breech position or not engaged into the pelvis, or when the membranes rupture prematurely. When the waters break well before the babies are due, it comes as a great shock, as it did for Linda.

*Linda's Early Arrival:* "As we raced to the hospital 180 miles away, I tried to understand why my membranes ruptured early. Though my pregnancy had been complicated, I had taken every precaution to prevent premature labor. Now I was going into labor, and I was scared to death.

"We reached the hospital and by the time I was settled in the labor room, I was experiencing mild contractions. My doctor was at my side almost immediately. He explained to Todd and me that the birth would be delayed as long as possible to make sure the babies' lungs were strong. I was given Terbutaline to stop my contractions and Betamethasone to help the babies' lungs mature and hopefully prevent respiratory complications. The babies and I were monitored closely to observe the effects of these medications. By the second day, the contractions were under control and the babies' heart rates looked strong and stable. Now we just had to sit tight as long as we could.

"This was easier said than done. I ached from lying on my back and my insides felt bruised from the babies' kicking inside without amniotic fluid to cushion them. My heart raced, my nerves were stretched to the breaking point, and I felt hot, all from the medications. I couldn't sleep, especially listening to the sounds of other women in labor. Their muffled groans reminded me of the stories I'd heard about birth and made me even more anxious. I practiced my breathing exercises during *their* labors!

"Worst of all was the endless waiting, in spite of knowing this was best for the babies. Todd, my parents, and our friends worked extra hard to keep my spirits up. Finally, on the fifth day, the contractions could no longer respond to the medication and I was allowed to go into labor. An ultrasound revealed that both babies were head down, so my doctor was comfortable with my attempting a vaginal delivery. I was officially in active labor."

*Vaginal Delivery of Twins:*   The first stage of labor during twin births is much the same as for a singleton. During this stage, the involuntary contractions of the uterine muscles work to open the cervix, the necklike structure of the uterus that opens into the vagina. The action of the muscles pushes the baby against the cervix, and also causes the cervix to shorten, thin out, and then expand and open around the baby's head (or, occasionally, the buttocks). The thinning and shortening is called effacement, and is measured in percent, from 0 to 100. The opening is termed dilation and is measured in centimeters, from 0 to approximately 10. The first stage of labor is opening the "first door" and usually takes the most time. With multiple birth, this stage usually happens only once, before the delivery of the first baby. When this point is reached, the second stage of labor begins. Now the mother assists the uterus in pushing the first baby through the vagina, as the baby works through the pelvic bone structure and out to the vaginal opening, or "second door." Then the other baby makes this same part of the trip through the birth canal and out into the world. The placentas from each baby are expelled in the third and last stage of birth, although occasionally one will come after each birth. How long the process takes, what it feels like, and the responses of the mother and babies to the physical and emotional demands of the experience vary enormously.

*The Births of Linda's First Twins:* "My early first stage labor pains were surprisingly easy; I was even able to carry on normal conversation. By afternoon, my contractions became fast and strong and I started to dilate rapidly. Every contraction pressed on my spine, and Todd coached me while my mother rubbed my back. They were doing a good job, but I wasn't. I found it difficult to do my breathing patterns during real labor; instead, I held my breath during the contractions and gasped for air between them. After several of these strong contractions, I was checked for dilation and told I was already at 8 centimeters.

"Just when I thought I couldn't take it anymore, I was wheeled into the delivery room. Everything happened so fast from that point that I remember very little about the actual delivery. With a few pushes and minutes later, our first child was born: a girl we named Sarah. I heard her weak cry and then she was rushed out of the room. I wondered if she was all right until the doctor's 'Stop pushing!' brought my mind back to the work I still had to do. The second baby had turned sideways in my uterus, and my doctor was working to reposition it.

"Meanwhile, the other doctors and nurses prepared for a possible cesarean. I wanted to scream. How unfair! Fortunately, the doctor was able to move the baby into a head-down position and 15 minutes later, our second daughter—Maiah—came into the world. She, too, was rushed away immediately. A short while later, the nurses brought both babies into the delivery room for a quick look. It was a relief to finally see them, but such a brief encounter was disappointing. My arms were aching to hold them, yet I wasn't allowed to. Sarah weighed 3 pounds 8 ounces, and Maiah weighed 3 pounds 5 ounces. My heart went out with them as they were carried out of the room. This was not how I had pictured the scene after the birth. I wanted to cry, both from relief and frustration. I was relieved that both babies were breathing on their own, and frustrated because we were separated. I felt cheated out of sharing their first precious moments of life."

*Just in Case:* Many parents of prematurely born infants experience a similar sadness about being left out of the first meeting with their babies. Though parents intellectually understand the reasons for the babies being taken immediately to the neonatal intensive care unit for evaluation and treatment, their hearts may feel deprived. The whole experience of premature labor and birth is emotionally charged. In addition to the usual concerns about delivery that all parents have, there are worries about how the babies will cope with immature body systems, especially breathing. We suggest that parents acquaint themselves with the feelings, potential problems, and procedures that may be encountered. Some of these are explored in the next chapter and in other excellent resources listed at the end of this book. We also recommend that parents talk with their health care providers and local hospital representatives about their specific practices and policies. Gather information, so you can participate in the decision-making process and learn to care for your babies in the NICU nursery, ahead of time if possible, rather than trying to absorb it during a stressful and emotionally turbulent time. Linda's second set of twins were also premature and brought home this fact—even though she had been through the experience before, the impact was no less powerful.

*The Births of Linda's Second Twins:* "I just couldn't believe it when at 33 weeks into my second pregnancy, my bag of waters ruptured again; unlike my previous pregnancy, though, the sac tore just slightly, causing a slow leak. Besides doing all the healthy things I did in my first pregnancy, I had been on weeks of bed rest, taken oral Terbutaline to prevent contractions, and used a home uterine monitoring service that kept me constantly in touch with nursing staff. I had never dealt with the possibility of another preterm labor, so I was emotionally unprepared for what lay ahead.

"We rushed to the hospital in the middle of the night. Everything was handled as it was in my first pregnancy: the medications to stop the labor and mature the babies' lungs, the monitoring, the discomfort, and the waiting. This time, however, we only had to wait twenty-four hours, for the monitor was showing one baby in distress. At 3:30 A.M., Todd was summoned to the hospital, and the decision was made to do an emergency cesarean. I was prepped and rushed into surgery before I had a chance to realize what was happening. Everyone hurried so fast and looked so serious, I felt a little neglected as a person. Within minutes, the spinal anesthesia took effect and shortly our first baby was born, a son whom we named Keegan; our second baby, Colin, was delivered a minute later with his umbilical cord wrapped around his leg. This is what had caused his heart rate to slow, but luckily had not caused any serious problems. Once again, after a brief glimpse of the boys, they were rushed to the NICU. My body was numb from the anesthesia but my mind was also numb from such an emotional upheaval.

"Later that day, through a haze of medications, I was wheeled into the NICU to see my babies. I couldn't get over how beautiful they looked. Although they were premature, they had lots of red hair and fine features. Even though the boys were doing well and I knew what to expect about the potential problems and NICU routine for premature infants, I had conflicting feelings. I had wanted a normal term pregnancy and delivery so badly and I was disappointed in myself. I just felt lousy."

*Surprise Beginnings:*   Linda's reactions to the birth experiences with her premature twins are not unusual, although she is certainly in the minority for having to go through it twice! Debbie's and Sheri's twins also came earlier than expected and their labors were also initiated by the breaking of the bag of waters. Debbie's initial premature labor had been controlled by drugs and bed rest, but once her waters broke at thirty-five and a half weeks, it was time to return to the hospital for delivery.

*Checking in:*   "Because I had been in the hospital three weeks earlier to stop premature labor, Dale and I were already familiar with the routine of checking in and getting hooked up to the monitor that tracked my contractions and the babies' heart rates. But that had been the dress rehearsal, this was the real thing. The nurse told me that my doctor was on vacation, so one of his associates would be delivering our babies. I was glad I had made a point of meeting all his partners prior to delivery, just in case this happened. Once the doctor arrived, he reviewed the monitor tracings and then did one last ultrasound. The first baby, the one we had named James, was still head down, deep in my pelvis, and so would be the firstborn. It was his amniotic sac that had broken. Michael was still in the breech position, with his sac intact. The doctor and I reviewed the birth plan I had worked out with my regular physician. Earlier in my pregnancy, natural childbirth had been a priority. Now all I wanted was my babies to be born safely. We felt a cesarean section was the best choice. Preparations for the surgery began immediately."

*Cesarean Birth Procedures:* Once a decision is made for cesarean birth, hospital staff begin prepping the mother for surgery. Most often, the following procedures take place: the mother's blood is drawn to be typed and cross-matched; an IV is inserted in her arm or hand for administering fluids, medication, or blood; one or both of her arms may be restrained; her lower abdomen and upper pubic hair is shaved and coated with an antiseptic solution; a catheter is inserted into her bladder; she is fitted with a blood pressure cuff; and a cardiac monitor is attached. Sometimes a preoperative medication is given to relax the mother, but this may be waived if she wishes to avoid feeling sleepy or groggy during the surgery; try and discuss this with your practitioner beforehand. Most hospitals today use spinal anesthesia so that the mother can be awake and alert for the birth and her support person can be with her. In hospitals that are dedicated to family-centered birth, fathers or support persons who wish to accompany the mother into surgery scrub up and change into sterile clothing while the mother is being prepped. Once this work is completed, the anesthesia is administered. This may be a spinal or epidural, both of which act to numb the body from the waist down. General anesthesia, given in an IV and/or through a mask, results in unconsciousness, and is primarily reserved for emergencies or failed spinals. Once the anesthesia takes effect and the mother is stabilized, the birth begins. Debbie tells about the exciting moments.

*The Births of Debbie's Twins:* "The preparation and anesthetization went like clockwork, and the fears that I had about having a spinal anesthetic quickly went away. When Dale waltzed into the operating room, all dressed in his green scrubs and smiling like a kid at Christmastime, I relaxed even more. He stood near my head and kept me company. One of the nurses draped a sterile cloth just above my abdomen, and even though I knew this was necessary to keep a sterile field, I was disappointed that my view of the babies' births would be obstructed. Our chosen pediatrician and a hospital neonatologist came into the room and chatted with us while they waited for their parts in the births. We talked excitedly about meeting our boys, James and Michael, for the first time.

"The incision was made and minutes later, our 'Baby A' greeted the world. Our pediatrician said, 'Isn't this the one you were going to call James?' As Dale and I nodded our heads in agreement, he continued, 'Well if that's the case, *he's* missing some very important equipment!' He smiled and brought the baby to us. Finally it sank in—we had a girl! She was a perfect, adorable, dark-haired beauty . . . and she looked like Dale. We stroked her fingers and toes as the pediatrician reassured us that she was good-sized and looked healthy. Then he took her away to do a thorough examination. Only sixty seconds later, Michael was born, handsome and round-faced, resembling my father. Dale cut Michael's umbilical cord and proudly carried him out to the NICU to join his sister. As I lay there, having my incision repaired, the reality of giving birth to my twins finally hit me. I had two healthy babies and they were *not* both boys. Having a boy and a girl had been my secret desire all along. Thank you, God!

"Once in the recovery room, I was overcome with fits of uncontrollable shaking and the feeling was made worse by the fact that I couldn't feel anything below the waist. The nurse said my shuddering was not uncommon, although it was more severe than usual. With a warm blanket and some oxygen, I felt better, but the tremors didn't stop entirely until the anesthesia wore off hours later. In the meantime, our pediatrician stopped in to give me an updated report on the babies' condition. Our daughter, 'James,' was 6 pounds 1 ounce and our son, Michael, was 5 pounds 13 ounces. They were doing well and breathing without difficulty but they would be treated in the NICU with the standard precautions for premature babies: heart rate and respiratory monitors, a warming isolette, and IVs. He advised me to get some sleep for I wouldn't be able to nurse this first night. In some ways, this was a relief because I was weak, in pain, and very tired.

"Alone in my room I closed my eyes and eventually drifted off to sleep, only to be awakened by cramping pains in my abdomen. It took me a minute or two to understand that this was not premature labor but the result of the cesarean birth. My last thought as I finally dozed off for the rest of the night was that my daughter needed a more appropriate name. What would we call her?"

*A Planned Cesarean Birth:* Debbie's decision to have a cesarean took place at the time she went into labor; however, there are times when a cesarean is preplanned because of medical problems with the mothers or babies. A cesarean delivery is the safest method when there is a prolapsed cord, when the first baby is in a transverse or sideways position in the uterus, when the placenta lies partially or completely over the cervix (placenta previa), or when the placenta begins to separate from the walls of the uterus before the babies are born (abruption of the placenta). Other problems with the mother, such as pre-eclampsia, high blood pressure, herpes, diabetes, or a serious infection precipitate a planned cesarean. Occasionally, a planned cesarean is chosen if infants are believed to be in distress or are not growing well in the intrauterine environment. For instance, after it was discovered that Sheri was pre-eclampsic and a biophysical profile revealed that her babies were small for their gestational age, her doctor scheduled her cesarean for the following day. However, nature had plans of its own—just after midnight her waters broke.

*The Births of Sheri's Twins:* "Steve was snoring soundly when I shook him awake and whispered that I thought my water had broken. Then, as I rolled over, the water started gushing and my voice quickly escalated to a frantic 'Get me a towel!' Still half asleep, he leaped out of bed and retrieved some towels. We were both secretly pleased to take the exciting midnight ride to the hospital rather than go through a boring 4:00 P.M. check-in.

"By the time we arrived, contractions were coming three minutes apart. After I was hooked up to the fetal monitors, we sat around waiting for my doctor, who arrived about three hours later. Though I was thankful to experience labor one last time, I'd had enough. The contractions had intensified, I had gotten the shakes, and I was feeling nauseated. The first words out of my doctor's mouth were, 'I see you've been in labor just long enough to reaffirm your decision to have the C-section.' I was definitely ready for the pain to stop and the babies to be born.

"When they started the surgery, I was still shaking so badly that I asked Steve to hold my head for me. I hated feeling so out of control. My doctor whistled and hummed through the incision and the birth of our first twin, Tessa. That came to a stop when he realized that the umbilical cords of both twins were twisted together. Steve said it looked like a huge, thick braid. No wonder we had never seen the amniotic membrane separating the twins. Emmy and Tessa were in the same sac, skin to skin. Luckily, the cords were long and the winding had never seriously tightened them. It turned out that the C-section was the best choice after all, for the intertwined cords could have been a problem during a vaginal delivery, when Tessa's passage through the birth canal might have crushed Emmy's cord.

"As if that weren't enough excitement, when the doctor tried to take Emmy out, he found that my uterus had contracted and pushed her up underneath my ribs. After failing to dislodge her, my doctor apologized for having to enlarge my incision vertically, for this meant I would not be able to have any future vaginal deliveries. This didn't matter to me, I just wanted Emmy out unharmed. Though it seemed much longer, Emmy was born just three minutes after Tessa. Steve let go of my head and hands to cut her umbilical cord. Honestly, once the babies were out safely, my next thoughts were, *Good, now I can have some Demerol to relax me so I can stop shaking and get some sleep!*

"At this point, Emmy and Tessa were placed in warming beds a few feet away. They had no difficulty breathing but they were a bit underweight for thirty-seven weeks. Tessa weighed 4 pounds 7 ounces, and Emmy was 4 pounds 6 ounces. They both had lots of dark hair, which made them look more like full-term babies. Because they were three weeks early, they were taken to the NICU for the first twenty-four hours for observation.

"Two hours later, as I was being taken to my postpartum room, the nurse took a detour through the NICU so I could see my babies. She parked my gurney in between them. Tessa looked just like Emmy, except for having little red blotches called 'stork bites' on her eyelids. I was told they would fade away in a few months, but until then, it was a great way to tell the babies apart.

*Emergency Situations:* Sheri's birthing experience illustrates one of those unforeseen events in multiple birth. Cord entanglement is unique to the 1 to 2 percent of twins that share both membranes of the placenta. Other challenges that may come up during delivery are related to the presentation and position of the babies, especially the second twin. This includes the breech, transverse, compound, or, most rarely, locked positions. A compound presentation involves an arm or hand that is coming through the pelvis at the same time as the head, decreasing the room available for birth. Locked positions occur when parts of both babies' bodies are in the way of each other, preventing the birth of either one of them. Difficult birth positions may sometimes be resolved through manipulation of the babies by the attending practitioners, but if this is not successful a cesarean may be necessary for delivery of one or both twins. Emergency situations that necessitate cesarean birth may arise during labor after preventive, alternative, or medical techniques have failed. These include fetal distress; prolonged or arrested labor, due to ineffective contractions or to a disproportionate fit of the head/buttocks to the pelvis; and an induced labor that fails to result in a vaginal birth.

*Inducing Labor:* Labor is induced for some of the same reasons that a cesarean may be considered. In addition, induction is often done in an overdue pregnancy when there is concern for the babies' well-being. One way labor can be induced artificially is by breaking the bag of waters. However, once this is done, it is usually best for the babies to be delivered within twenty-four to forty-eight hours to avoid infection. Because of this, the labor is often induced when the cervix is somewhat effaced or dilated. If it is not, the practitioner may try to soften the cervix by applying prostaglandin gel and/or by administering Pitocin, a synthetic version of oxytocin, the main hormone that stimulates the uterus to contract. Alternatively, Pitocin can be used to induce labor instead of breaking the amniotic sac, or to bring on contractions if the previous methods are ineffective. Pitocin was used to induce Florien's labor ten days before her due date because her sudden onset of pre-eclampsia had worsened, despite attempts to control it at home.

*The Births of Florien's Twins:* "Devin and I checked into the hospital in the afternoon, and a short while later I was attached to monitors and an IV that began releasing Pitocin into my bloodstream. It wasn't long before the monitor showed I was having contractions, but I couldn't feel them at all. Later that evening, the Pitocin was stopped so that everyone could get a good night's rest. Everyone but Devin. He went home to start packing for our move into a new house.

"At 6:00 the next morning, the IV was started again. My midwife and Devin joined us at 8:00 A.M., and by 9:00 A.M. I was finally starting to feel mild contractions. I had dilated to 6 centimeters by noon, but when I was checked later, I had regressed to 5. I questioned the possibility of this. My midwife explained that sometimes, when the uterus is so overstretched, it doesn't hold its muscle tone and may become ineffective for labor. It may also begin to swell, which might account for the decrease in dilation of my cervix. Meanwhile, I was beginning to feel terrible shooting pains down my legs during the stronger contractions, and this was so painful that I was focused more on this than on my labor. I was told that the babies' positions could be putting pressure on the nerves of my legs during contractions. There was nothing that could be done about it, although leg massages and heating pads helped a little.

"After three hours of experiencing severe pain in my legs and no progress in dilation, the option of having a cesarean was proposed. Although we were given the choice to see if anything would change during the next three hours, Devin and I doubted that it would, and so we opted for the cesarean. Once the decision was made, the hospital staff worked quickly as preparations were begun for surgery. The midwife was now our photographer, and Devin my hand-holder. I had heard stories of how painful the administration of the spinal anesthetic could be, yet for me it was a rather quick and easy process. The surgery, however, held a few surprises.

"My arms were strapped down during the delivery, which was something I didn't expect and was reluctant to endure. The staff explained that this was necessary because my arms might involuntarily spasm—and indeed, minutes later, my temporarily paralyzed arms did begin jolting around under the broad straps. It seemed like only moments passed before my sons were born. I could only glance at them since my arms were strapped down and I was trying hard to understand and endure what was happening to me.

"Immediately after the boys were out of my womb, the numbness of the anesthetic rose from below my chest clear up to my neck. It was very frightening to feel a sense of helplessness as I did not have any sense of control over my bodily functions, and was not aware of my own breathing. I kept asking for oxygen, hoping the sensation of breathing would return soon. It did return, but only after the anesthetic wore off, hours later. My experience was not the usual result of spinal anesthesia, but apparently this reaction happens to some people.

"While Devin and the midwife were admiring the babies, I only wanted my incision repaired so I could be returned to the privacy of my room. With my energy at such a low ebb, I was relieved when everyone journeyed down to the nursery to weigh and test the babies. I fell asleep immediately.

"Several hours later I awoke, feeling much better and ready to visit with Devin and my sons. Now I could really hold and admire them. I fell in love with them immediately. They looked amazingly similar; they weighed 6 pounds 10 ounces and 6 pounds 13 ounces. The only way I could tell them apart was that Baby A's hair stood straight up! I was enjoying my visit with them but was still feeling too unstable and weak to try breast-feeding them yet. I didn't mind this hiatus, for I felt confident that there would be plenty of time in the near future to breast-feed and bond with the boys. They looked rested and happy, so I knew I could try to get some sleep and that they would be fine."

*New Moms Need Loving, Too!* A new mother may have few emotional or physical reserves to draw on after a cesarean delivery or difficult vaginal birth. She should know that it is not only OK but also necessary to meet her own needs before she takes on the responsibility of caring for her babies. Even when vaginal twin births go smoothly, as Debra's did, there is still a need for some extra tender loving care. Though Debra's birth turned out to be relatively easy, postpartum held some difficulties for her.

*The Births of Debra's Twins:* "I felt my first contraction at 1:00 in the afternoon of the day I delivered. Somehow I think I knew this was the day, because all that morning I was very animated, finishing up last-minute tasks and giving instructions to my mom. Ten minutes after that first contraction, another came, along with a dark red blood clot. Since my checkup two days prior had indicated I was already 5 centimeters dilated, and because I lived a half hour away from the hospital, I knew I shouldn't waste any time getting there. I made the appropriate phone calls and hurried my parents and children to get ready to leave. While waiting for them, I noticed some heavier-than-normal bleeding, and once we were on our way, I urged my dad to drive faster. As the bleeding continued, I became increasingly alarmed.

"When we arrived at the hospital, I was taken immediately to the maternity unit and preparations for surgery were begun. My doctor and my midwife arrived a few minutes later and began investigating possible causes for the bleeding. They were able to rule out anything serious, and suggested the cause to be a small tear in my cervix. We all relaxed at this news and everything was calm when Rick, who had come straight from work, joined us.

"By 4:00 P.M., my dilation reached 9 centimeters but stayed there for another hour. Apparently my cervix was getting slack and starting to swell. My blood pressure was also rising and becoming a concern, so we decided to stimulate my contractions with Pitocin to hasten the delivery. A short while later, I came to the conclusion that a little pushing might help the situation, too. With my midwife pressing the rim of the cervix over the baby's head and some voluntary pushing, we succeeded in reaching full dilation. It only took a few more pushes for my son to be born.

"Amid the smiles and tears of joy, with my son clutched to my chest, I was oblivious to the doctor's actions. He broke the bag of waters of the second twin and was checking its position. Suddenly, my son was taken from my arms and the anesthesiologist placed a mask over my face. I thought I had missed some signal or decision and immediately panicked. My doctor said that the second baby, whom we had planned to deliver in the breech position, had turned head down, but had an arm over the head and the cord between. This was a compound presentation and meant we would have to deliver by cesarean if the situation could not be corrected. My fears and the suspense intensified as my doctor worked determinedly. Holding the baby's hand and cord back with one hand, the doctor attached a vacuum extractor to its head. He had me push while he applied some traction, and soon our cooperative effort succeeded in seating the baby's head safely into the cervix. With a few more pushes, the second baby made its debut.

"With the announcement of a baby girl, everyone in the room yelled, and my daughter screamed and went red all over. I think the fast birth and the noise upset her, for it took a long time before she calmed down in my arms. I was elated that the birth turned out so well, that the babies were gorgeous and healthy, and that everyone whom I had wanted to be present was there.

"We had quite a party once I returned to my room. The babies were introduced to their older brothers and passed all around. I did find it a little strange to relate to two infants instead of being totally engrossed in just one, but I also learned in those moments that one *can* fall in love with two babies at once. An hour or so later, Rick and Jason took the babies to the nursery, then shortly returned with their vital statistics: Richard weighed 6 pounds 14 ounces and Aislynn was 8 pounds 7 ounces! I was very proud of that.

"My high spirits in the first couple of hours had completely overridden some weak and shaky feelings I had begun to experience. I was bleeding fairly heavily and my high blood pressure had continued to climb, so I was given Phenobarbitol. Once everyone went home, I could feel the effects of the medication. The nurses said that they would have to watch the babies in the nursery until I was stabilized. I felt sad that I couldn't have them room in with me as I had planned, and I asked the nurses to promise me to bring them back when they cried."

*Expect the Unexpected:* We are amazed at the variety of birth experiences that occurred among the five of us, and we acknowledge that none of us had any of the major difficulties that some parents encounter. We can safely say that finding out that you are having multiples makes you very conscious of the unexpected and in many ways prepares you to be more flexible. A lowering of expectations was one of several things that contributed to an overall positive birth experience for us. In addition, practicing healthy behaviors, becoming informed of our choices, developing trusting relationships with our care providers, and actively participating in decision making helped us to feel in control. This was very empowering and helped us to cope with the unknown and those things that we couldn't control. When there were undesirable outcomes, we learned that there are many ways to cope with or make up for the aftermaths. These came to light in the hours and days following birth.

## Postpartum Recovery

Being pregnant with twins (or more!) one minute and becoming "unpregnant" in the next can be a smooth transition for some and wreak havoc on others. Once the babies are born, a period of rapid adjustment by the body and mind must take place. The physical changes the body undergoes in the postpartum hours and days are truly amazing. Add to this the emotional upheaval commonly associated with birth and you can appreciate the wondrous capacity that humans have to adapt. The level of vulnerability you experience at this time may feel very rewarding and exciting or very risky and scary. Perhaps such openness readies us for the work that lies ahead—loving and caring for our babies. It may be hard to think of this tumultuous period as having such a purpose, but pay attention to the messages you receive from your body, heart, and mind. They serve as a signal or as a protective mechanism. If you feel hungry, eat; if you feel tired, rest. If you don't want to see visitors right away, don't; there will be plenty of time to share your babies with the rest of the world. Linda had very contrasting postpartum experiences after the births of her two sets of twins, each a reflection of the circumstances that existed at the two points in time.

*I Wanna/Don't Wanna Go Home!* "When Todd and my parents joined me in the recovery room after the girls were born, the atmosphere was jubilant. Todd kept telling everyone how brave I was. I felt like a real hero. But when I held my daughters for the first time the following afternoon, I knew the hardest part was about to come. The girls would have to remain in the NICU until they weighed at least four pounds. Once I resigned myself to that fact, I was highly motivated to go home so I could pump my milk, get rested, and prepare for their homecoming. That was my way of maintaining the connection between us.

"On the other hand, going home after the boys were born was the very last thing I wanted to do. I just about begged my doctor to extend my stay in the hospital, but he said there was no medical reason for doing so. I was emotionally and physically drained. I was also apprehensive, for not only did I already know how much work it would be to pump milk, make daily trips to the hospital, and later to cope with babies on monitors, but now I also had two other children to care for on top of that. I was completely overwhelmed, and felt like a baby who needed to be taken care of myself."

*Listen to the Feelings:* Linda's postpartum feelings turned out to be a weather vane for her sense of well-being for weeks to come. After her first birth, she felt ready to take on the demands of caring for her daughters. All in all, she felt she coped very well. After her sons were born, her anxiety about dealing with the demands of her larger family while trying to heal from her disappointment was well-founded. It took her several weeks to work through her feelings. We think that emotional distress should be a recognized medical reason for a longer postpartum stay, for both the mother's and family's long-term well-being are at stake. It is the individual mother's, families', and practitioners' responsibility to pay close attention to the feelings that arise in the days, weeks, and months following birth. Only then can parents care for themselves better, ask for—and in some cases, demand—and receive social support from others. When our needs are met, we feel right and good. Both Sheri's and Florien's postpartum experiences highlight this point.

*It's OK to Let Others Care for You:*  Florien stayed in the hospital for five days following her cesarean birth. She remarks, "I was groggy a lot of the time from the pain medications and was having great difficulty in walking following the surgery, so I was content to be waited on. This way I could concentrate on my babies, whom I had with me constantly, day and night. During the day, Devin and my family and friends were busy doing the most helpful thing anyone could do for a new mother: packing our belongings, moving to our new home, unpacking, and setting up our household to be ready for my homecoming. That was a gift for which I will be forever grateful."

Sheri was pleased by how well everything went with the babies. "The nursing staff had concerns about Emmy's and Tessa's ability to nurse, but these were relieved the first time I nursed my twins, when they latched on and never looked back. Ouch! By that same afternoon, their IVs and heart monitors were removed, and they were moved into the regular nursery. We were glad to nurse and visit with them without cords dangling all around. Later that evening, I was able to walk down to the nursery. Looking through the windows, I stared at them sleeping peacefully. I was on such an emotional high I couldn't even sleep.

"The next two days went by in a blur of feedings. Because the babies had to gain weight, they had to be fed every three hours. I would nurse one baby, who had been weighed on an electronic scale, then that baby was returned to the nursery for weighing and some formula supplementation while I nursed the second baby. When Baby Number Two was finished, we'd go back to the nursery for weighing and supplementation. Between this and diaper changes, bottle fixing, and shuffling back and forth, the process took an hour and a half. It could be quite a juggling act, and sometimes I worried that the babies might get mixed up by the staff. I could tell my babies apart, and they each had bands and necklaces, but still I wondered if we should have painted a finger or toe with nail polish, just in case. I had read about doing this with identical twins.

"The day of discharge came too quickly for me. The babies were gaining weight and thriving, but I felt I was just running on empty, getting only four hours of broken sleep each night. This was tolerable while my only responsibility was to feed the twins, and the wonderful nurses were waiting on me hand and foot. Once we were home, getting no sleep made things crazy."

*You Deserve a Break Today:* Debbie admits she underestimated the amount of pain and discomfort she would have after surgery and pushed herself too hard, too soon. She had heard other women say that having a cesarean was no big deal, almost ignoring the fact that it was major surgery. Though everyone will have different physical and emotional responses to cesarean birth, there is a common misconception that it is "easier" than vaginal birth. While that may be true for women who have prolonged or difficult vaginal deliveries, the notion that cesarean birth is generally less painful than vaginal birth should be disregarded. Having had both, Debbie says she'd take vaginal birth any day, barring any issues of safety.

*I Wish, I Wish:* Debbie really didn't expect to feel like she did after the birth. "At first I thought I was being a baby, but then I acknowledged to myself that my body had been through a lot. I had been on bed rest for three weeks prior to delivery so I had no stamina or muscle tone and my back ached. In addition, my incision was sore and it was difficult to move about. Making trips down to the NICU and pumping breast milk was an ordeal.

I wish I had requested a postpartum room closer to the NICU and used a wheelchair when I was tired. Despite the physical pain, the worst part about it was feeling sad that I couldn't have my babies to hold and enjoy when I wanted to. I wish I had been more assertive about asking the nurses to take me to see my babies. I should have treated myself according to how I felt and what I needed, rather than waiting for the nurses to anticipate my needs and offer help. Believe me, I have learned to do both."

*Asking and Listening:* Debbie's story reflects a need for better communication between parents and health care providers. A number of things can be done to improve this. Health care practitioners can ask more questions, assessing a patient's emotional as well as physical well-being. This would help the quiet, compliant patient who may not feel comfortable speaking up. The new parents must express their desires forthrightly, rather than expecting others to read their minds. Staff members are only human, and are often under stress or overworked; you can say, "I don't feel listened to," when you feel your concerns have not been addressed. Everyone should keep in mind that it is *your* body and they are *your* babies. Debra's experience after her birth illustrates the importance of staff and parents communicating clearly.

*It's Important to Me:* "After such a wonderful birth, the rest of that night turned out to be fairly miserable. As hard as I tried, I couldn't get any sleep. The IV in my arm hurt; I was still getting Pitocin, which was causing heavy cramps; I was terribly thirsty and drank six pitchers of water, forcing me to get up to go to the bathroom frequently; my muscles ached; and just when I thought I could doze off, someone would come in to check my blood pressure, give me more medication, or *something.* I worried that my babies were crying and no one was responding. Every time I asked about them, I was told that they were sleeping. After several hours went by, I began to wonder if I was just being told that because I was having so many problems. It was hard to believe that both of them had not been awake but I also couldn't believe I was not being told the truth. The labor and delivery nurses had been so good to me during the birth. I didn't know what to think or do.

"Perhaps the nurses were just trying to protect me, but now I know that I could have asked to see the babies' charts and the nurses' notes. The next day, I also realized that my instructions about demand feeding should have been written on the babies' charts, rather than communicated over the intercom. I had sent my two sleeping babies back to the nursery at 8:00 on the second night of my stay so I could try to sleep, and requested that each be brought to me when they woke up. I awoke at midnight and called the nursery. Both babies were awake and brought to me, but they had been fed sugar water, something I had specifically asked the nurses *not* to do. I tried to nurse the twins, but their tummies were full, and Ricky just threw everything up. I was upset because I felt that I had been deprived of something important to me. I wanted to spend as much time with my babies as I could before I went home. From previous experience, I believed this would help me bond closer with my twins. I couldn't wait to go home so I could do what I wanted."

*There's No Place Like Home:* New parents can feel as fragile as they think their infants are and many new families go home to tackle the challenging task of recovering physically and emotionally from the birth while learning to meet the needs of their infants with little or no help. As good as home might look, it is *essential* that a new family have supportive care for the next few weeks. This means having help with household duties and meal preparation as well as emotional support. Don't be shy about enlisting family and/or friends. If they are not available, there are services that can provide housekeepers and/or baby nurses on a full- or part-time basis.

*A Few Words About Bonding:* There has been a lot of controversy about bonding, especially in regard to multiple births. Many parents are worried that they don't feel or experience what they expect they should. Be reassured that nature has built into the childbearing cycle many safeguards for insuring the attachment between parents and children, especially with humans, for we care for our offspring longer than any other mammals. Pregnancy and childbirth are an important part of this bonding, and should be respected and treated as such.

Because the birth of multiples is more likely to involve separation of mother and babies at birth due to prematurity, cesarean birth, or other difficulties, we suggest parents not put so much pressure on themselves at this time if things don't go as planned. It helps just as much to focus attention on prenatal bonding and on adequate help and support in the months that follow birth. Be aware of and sensitive to other influences on the bonding process, such as: the parents' own childhood experiences; cultural practices that inhibit or enhance parental instincts or inclinations; relationships with others, especially the spouse or partner and the grandparents; present life challenges or demands; previous or current pregnancy experiences; medical and social care of the pregnant family; and events occurring both at birth and in the postpartum period. Parents specifically wonder about the effects of involuntary separation on the parent-child relationship, when babies are premature or sick. Linda and Debbie, whose twins had to remain in NICU due to prematurity, speak to these concerns and many others in the next chapter.

## Our Thoughts and Reflections

SHERI: Except for a few minor inconveniences associated with the cesarean birth, I had an uneventful recovery in the hospital. People started pouring in by 7:00 the morning after the twins' births. The spotlight felt wonderful and terrible at the same time. It was my first chance to show off my babies and I didn't want to miss seeing anyone. I wish now I'd rested and allowed the three sets of grandparents to show off the twins.

LINDA: Like many mothers, I had some preconceived ideas about the birth of my twins. But even though the births didn't go the way I'd hoped, they were each special in their own way.

My advice is: Don't be hard on yourself or dwell on the fact that your twin delivery may not be ideal. Rather, enjoy what you can and cherish the results of your efforts.

DEBBIE: Giving birth to twins cannot be described as enjoyable or fun, but it is one of life's great experiences. My advice is twofold. First, attack labor as a challenge. Think of labor as climbing a great mountain peak, and birth as reaching the summit: It's a lot of very hard work, but the view is worth it!

Secondly, when the moment of each birth arrives, focus and concentrate to remember each sound and smell—and particularly, each beautiful baby's face. Have someone take photographs or videotapes if you want, but make a conscious effort to remember.

FLORIEN: Giving birth is always a special event for any woman but giving birth to twins is by far extra special and unique. You may prepare and plan for a smooth delivery, but often twin deliveries don't go as expected. The most important thing about Max and Otto's delivery was that they were born healthy. Whatever it took to reach this end was my primary concern throughout my pregnancy and their births.

DEBRA: I was so glad I made the effort to educate and prepare myself about all aspects of labor and delivery of my twins. When it came down to the actual delivery I had to put my trust in my doctor's skills and instincts. I think this was possible because we had worked as a team throughout the pregnancy and had developed good communication. I let him know what was important to me and he too shared his concerns and we both showed flexibility.

# "The babies will need to stay"

## Premature Twins

**D**espite fine medical care, good nutrition, and moderate exercise, two of us gave birth to our twins prematurely. This chapter is about our babies' medical treatment in the neonatal intensive care unit (NICU) as well as our gradual adjustment to being mothers of premature twins. We hope you find the information we have to share to be both useful and reassuring.

### Prematurity

Premature infants are defined as those babies born at or before the end of the thirty-sixth week of pregnancy, when the vital organs and regulatory systems of the baby are not fully developed. This physiological immaturity is the source of the many medical problems which can trouble the premature baby after birth. Nearly 50 percent of all twins, compared to only 7 to 10 percent of singletons, begin life facing the struggles of prematurity.

Both sets of Linda's twins were born two months premature: They weighed about three and a half pounds each and had medical problems which were treated for two weeks in an NICU. Debbie's twins, born at thirty-five and a half weeks, were both good-sized at about 6 pounds, and looked as strong and healthy as full-term babies. But, like Linda's twins, their regulatory systems and ability to feed were not fully developed, so they spent about a week in an NICU.

## Low Birth Weight

Any infant born at or near term weighing less than 5.5 pounds is defined as having low birthweight; however, low birthweight is distinct from prematurity and occurs in about 60 percent of all twin births. Sheri's twins, Emmy and Tessa, were born at thirty-seven weeks gestation, each weighing only 4 pounds. Yet they were well developed and healthy, and not considered premature. Occasionally, low birthweight babies develop medical problems related to their small size which may require care in an NICU.

## The Neonatal Intensive Care Unit (NICU)

The NICU is a nursery equipped with highly technical medical machinery and staffed by physicians and nurses skilled in the care of premature babies and other seriously ill infants. Because NICUs are highly specialized, they are not located in every hospital. Instead, they service a wide area of communities and sometimes care for ill babies who come from many miles away.

NICUs have an atmosphere and design all their own, quite unlike the lighthearted mood and colorful murals found in a regular newborn nursery. Strange noises, beeping alarms, flashing lights, and an array of complex medical equipment are the norm in the NICU.

Most babies in the NICU don't look big, cute, and cuddly like full-term infants. They look small, skinny, and wrinkled as they lay in either the protective, controlled environment of their isolettes (clear, covered, rectangular-shaped bassinets that have porthole-type openings on the sides large enough to allow adult hands to reach in and care for the babies), or baby-sized open-air tables that are warmed with infrared heating units and allow for easy acccess of medical equipment and personnel.

Most of the babies are connected to monitors which track their heart and respiratory rates. Many have intravenous (IV) tubes in their hands or feet to deliver fluids and medications. Some receive oxygen through nasal tubes or a ventilator. Some, too weak or immature to be bottled or breast-fed, have feeding tubes in their noses or mouths from which to take formula or breast milk. No two babies in the NICU are alike but they all have this in common: They all look very, very vulnerable.

In this environment, it is the doctors and nurses who are responsible for the babies' care, and it is all too easy for parents to underestimate their own importance and unique value to their babies. Linda remembers her first reactions: "Walking past all those fragile premature babies to get to our babies, lying alone in their isolettes, left me feeling overwhelmed. I felt afraid and uncertain."

Even Debbie, who is a pediatric nurse and comfortable in a hospital setting, felt uneasy the first few times she went to the NICU: "I hated going there. I hated the antiseptic smell that was present in the waiting room outside the NICU. I hated washing my hands for the required three minutes to remove germs. I hated taking off my jewelry and putting on the special hospital gown. I hated it all, not because it was so hard to do, but because it frightened me and reminded me that my babies were sick. The first time I actually entered the NICU and saw my twins with IVs in their tiny feet and monitor leads strapped to their doll-like chests, this feeling of fear only grew stronger. To this day, if I go past the NICU and pause to remember, I feel a pit in my stomach and get weak in my knees."

After the first few days, Linda and Debbie grew more at ease with their babies' temporary homes in the intensive care units. They asked lots of questions about their twins' care: Why did the twins have IVs? Why were the heart-respiratory monitors necessary? Was it all right to hold and touch their twins? Did the nurses have tips on how to feed preemies? The stream of questions seemed unending, but the nurses and physicians answered them all without complaint. With their questions answered, Debbie and

Linda were able to feel comfortable with the equipment and procedures and to become active participants in the care of their twins.

## Common Problems Associated with Prematurity

Premature infants are more likely than term infants to develop life-threatening medical problems in the first days and weeks of their lives. Among all premature infants, statistics show that: (a) the greater the prematurity, the greater the amount and severity of medical complications that might occur; (b) premature boys tend to have more medical complications than premature girls; and (c) in twins, the second born is more likely than the first born to develop medical problems after birth.

As important as these statistics are, it is important to remember that premature babies are unique, and statistics cannot predict how well any individual baby will do after birth. For example, both sets of Linda's twins had fewer complications than statistics indicated were likely. And Debbie's boy, Michael, was a stronger and healthier premature infant than his first-born twin sister! Some of the more common medical problems of prematurity are lowered resistance to infection, dehydration, jaundice, inability to regulate body temperature, underdeveloped heart and respiratory regulatory systems, respiratory distress, intracranial hemorrhage, and feeding problems. Both Linda's and Debbie's twins had some, but not all, of these difficulties.

*Lowered Resistance to Infection:*　All premature babies are considered to be more prone to infection than full-term infants because they have less sophisticated immune systems. For this reason, NICUs limit visitors. Those persons who are allowed to visit must carefully wash their hands and wear gowns, as Debbie described earlier. Even with these precautions, the babies in the NICU are carefully observed for signs of infection. When a baby develops a bacterial infection, he is treated intravenously with antibiotics and is often isolated from the other infants in the intensive care unit, to avoid the spread of infection. Viral infections do not respond to antibiotics, but they are also potentially serious. So a baby with a viral illness also may be isolated as he receives medical care to treat the symptoms of his illness.

*Dehydration:*  Another very common problem of prematurity is dehydration. Even full-term infants experience a certain amount of fluid loss in the first few days after birth as they adjust to life outside the womb, but healthy newborns soon compensate for this water loss with good intake at their feedings. However, premature babies are at risk of developing severe dehydration because their water loss is often accentuated by poor feeding, the warmth and dryness of their isolettes, or the bright lights used to treat jaundice.

In the NICU, the doctors and nurses evaluate a baby's level of hydration by watching his weight gain and occasionally testing his urine or blood. When dehydration occurs, intravenous fluids are given until the baby is taking adequate amounts of fluid and nutrients by mouth. Debbie's set of twins and both of Linda's were jaundiced and had IVs to prevent dehydration during treatment.

*Jaundice:*  Jaundice results from having an excess of bilirubin in the bloodstream, causing the skin and whites of the eyes to turn yellow. It is not uncommon in newborn infants, but can be dangerous, especially for premature infants, if high levels accumulate in the child's body. All of Debbie's and Linda's babies devloped jaundice and had to undergo phototherapy.

A form of therapy which helps the babies' bodies to break down and remove the excess bilirubin, phototherapy usually only lasts a day or two. Special fluorescent lights are placed to shine directly onto the infant. During phototherapy the baby is entirely naked so the body can absorb the light rays; only the eyes are covered with patches to protect them from the light. Debbie couldn't help thinking that both of her twins looked like teeny-tiny Lone Rangers.

A new development in the treatment of jaundice, which was not yet available to Debbie's or Linda's twins, is the "bili blanket," a form of phototherapy in which the infant wears a specially designed blanket sleeper that emits the light rays necessary to break down bilirubin. A nice feature of the bili blanket is that the child's head and eyes are free of contact with the lights, so he needn't wear eye patches and can continue to enjoy eye contact with people and things around him during the therapy.

*Regulation of Body Temperature:* When Debbie's twins were treated for jaundice and they lay naked under the phototherapy lamps, she became acutely aware of each of her babies' smallness and frailty. Having so little body fat and such underdeveloped muscles causes problems for all premature babies as they try, with little success, to regulate their body temperatures. The lack of insulating body fat makes it nearly impossible for premature babies to protect themselves from even minor temperature changes in their environment. And with poor muscle tone, they cannot shiver to produce body heat to ward off chills.

To counteract this inability to warm themselves, almost all babies in the NICU wear tiny stocking caps on their heads and lie in the climate-controlled environment of a warming bed, or isolette. As babies mature and are able to tolerate changes in air temperature, they are moved into open-air cribs. This is a day parents wait for, because it is a signal that their baby is one step closer to being discharged.

*The Development of Apnea and Bradycardia:* Just as the premature baby has difficulty regulating his body temperature, he also has trouble regulating his heart and respiratory rates. Apnea, a common respiratory problem, is a cessation of breathing that lasts more than fifteen seconds. More simply put, the baby just "forgets" to breathe. Bradycardia occurs when the heartbeat is slower than normal. Apnea and bradycardia may occur independently of each other, or they may occur nearly simultaneously. Debbie's little girl, Joanna, frequently had episodes of apnea which were almost always followed by a brief period of bradycardia. Other times, especially when she gagged or burped during feedings, her heart rate would drop, while her breathing continued normally.

Heart and respiratory rates are carefully followed in an NICU
through the use of heart and respiratory monitors, which are set
to sound alarms when breathing stops or heart rates rise too high
or fall too low. When Joanna's alarm sounded a nurse—or Debbie
or Dale, if they were present—would stroke Joanna's back or tap
the soles of her feet to stimulate her to restart breathing and
increase her heart rate.

Debbie remembers, "It would usually only take ten or fifteen
seconds to get Joanna back to normal, but these seconds were
agonizing. Each time it happened I would wonder: 'What if she
doesn't start breathing again?' Of course, I knew the nurses had
procedures to follow in such cases, but the thought haunted me."

While episodes of apnea and bradycardia are not unusual for
premature babies, many children have rare, scattered episodes
that are soon outgrown. Michael had only one occurrence of apnea
during his entire hospital stay, and all of Linda's babies had only
rare problems with either apnea or bradycardia. For Joanna, however, they were a frequent daily occurrence that were not outgrown. To treat these episodes, her pediatrician prescribed
Theophylline. After a few days on the drug, Joanna's episodes
greatly decreased and the medication was stopped.

Before Joanna was discharged from the hospital she had a
pneumocardiogram to study her heart and respiratory rates. This
test was done on all of Linda's twins as well, as is commonly the
case for babies preparing to leave the NICU. A pneumocardiogram is a long-term (usually 12 to 24 hours) study of heart and
respiratory rates. Any recorded episodes of apnea or bradycardia
are considered abnormal and will likely result in an infant being
sent home on a portable heart-respiratory monitor; the parents
are instructed in its use as well as infant cardiopulmonary resuscitation. Linda's twin boys, Keegan and Colin, her daughter Maiah,
and Debbie's daughter Joanna all needed monitors because of
abnormal pneumocardiograms; Linda's Sarah and Debbie's Michael, who both had normal test results, were sent home on them
as a precautionary measure.

*Respiratory Distress:*  Both Linda and Debbie's twins were
fortunate to avoid the most serious respiratory problem: respi-

ratory distress syndrome. Respiratory distress syndrome (also known as hyaline membrane disease) occurs when the underdeveloped lungs of the premature infant cannot expand and contract as they should with each inspiration. Instead the lungs collapse, leaving the infant struggling for air.

In a full-term pregnancy, surfactant lines the lungs of the fetus in the last weeks, allowing the lungs to function normally after birth. When a baby is born prematurely, there may be insufficient amounts of surfactant in the lungs, causing some degree of respiratory distress. Respiratory distress syndrome was once a deadly threat, but today it is most often treated successfully through the use of special volume- and pressure-controlled respirators, which assist the babies' breathing until they can breathe well on their own.

*Intracranial (Brain) Hemorrhage:* Intracranial hemorrhage is another grave complication of prematurity. It does not occur commonly, but does happen often enough to be briefly mentioned. An intracranial hemorrhage develops when the fragile blood vessels of the premature infant rupture and bleed into the brain. This may happen spontaneously or may occur as a result of another illness or medical problem.

The words *intracranial hemorrhage* are frightening. And the condition is a serious one—exactly how serious depends on the extent of the hemorrhage. Physicians often prescribe medications hoping to prevent a hemorrhage or reduce its effects if and when it occurs. Although an intracranial hemorrhage has the potential to be debilitating and even life-threatening, the long-term outlook for most infants is good.

*Problems Related to Feeding:* For Debbie and Linda, the most frustrating challenge of their twins' prematurity was dealing with feeding problems. Feeding problems are common in premature babies because they tire easily, their sucking reflexes are often underdeveloped, and they may have trouble swallowing and sucking at the same time. As a result, premature infants have difficulty gaining weight and sometimes become dehydrated. NICU personnel closely follow each baby's ability to feed and the pattern of weight gain or loss. Attaining a predetermined weight while showing a consistent weight gain and adequate feeding ability are important factors in determining a baby's readiness for discharge.

Both sets of Linda's twins faced an uphill battle with feeding; they were too immature at birth to nurse or feed from a bottle. They were fed through tubes for several days before advancing to small feedings from bottles especially equipped with preemie nipples, which are easy to suck from. It was several more days before they were strong enough to nurse.

When Linda's twins graduated from feeding tubes, they were placed on a three-hour feeding schedule. Most of these feedings were taken from a bottle containing specific amounts of previously expressed breast milk. Linda was only able to nurse her twins every second or third feeding, because the doctors felt that breast-feeding, which is more strenuous than bottle-feeding, was too tiring for her babies. A disadvantage of bottle- and breast-feeding a newborn is the possibility that the baby may become confused in trying to learn the different styles of sucking required in each type of feeding. As a result, the baby may not feed as well or may not take to nursing as easily as he or she otherwise might have. Fortunately, neither Linda nor Debbie's twins had this problem.

Another challenge presented itself. Debbie's twins never required tube feedings, but like Linda's twins they had limited opportunities to breast-feed. This limitation hampered both Debbie and Linda's production of breast milk. To compensate for this, they stimulated their milk production by using an electric breast pump on each breast every three to four hours for ten to fifteen minutes—around the clock!

While they were in the hospital electric breast pumps were supplied for them. Once they went home they arranged to rent the pumps from La Leche League and bought dual breast attachments which emptied both breasts simultaneously and made this time-consuming job a little bit easier.

While producing an adequate supply of breast milk was hard work, actually trying to feed their premature twins was even more difficult. Clumsiness and disinterest in feeding are common problems for premature babies, although, as with everything, some babies do better than others! Debbie's Michael had the reputation in the NICU as being an "easy-feeder." Whether it was bottle- or breast-feeding, he sucked eagerly and finished quickly. Joanna was another story!

Debbie remembers clearly: "Joanna was only a month early and I really did not expect her to have any feeding problems, but boy, did she! For the first several weeks it seemed like she was always either uninterested or too sleepy to eat. To get her to swallow even the minimum amounts of formula or expressed breast milk, we had to use every feeding technique known to the NICU staff. First, I lifted her out of her warm blankets, removed her booties, and stroked the soles of her feet as I spoke to her. This usually aroused her to a semidrowsy, semialert state. Before she could fall back to sleep, I quickly placed the nipple of the bottle in her mouth. Often she resisted sucking. Sometimes she nodded off after a few swallows of formula despite my best efforts. In either case, I reacted by massaging the roof of her mouth with the nipple. This dripped formula into the back of her throat which she was obliged (nearly forced, actually) to swallow."

Teaching a premature baby to suckle from the breast can be just as frustrating. Linda found herself in tears during her initial nursing sessions with her girls, when neither one wanted to suckle, and each immediately fell asleep. And Debbie's Joanna didn't take to nursing any better than she did to bottle feeding. Time after time, she refused to suck and repeatedly pushed Debbie's nipple out of her mouth with her tongue.

Lack of success in feeding your infant can take an emotional toll on you. Debbie remembers: "At first my moods rose and fell with Joanna's weight gain. Then it clicked in my head that her poor feeding wasn't a rejection of me, but a reflection of her prematurity. Then I felt better, and with time my persistence in feeding her paid off." Linda felt less discouraged when a nurse shared an important insight, explaining the value of skin-to-skin contact between Linda and her twins. She pointed out that even when no milk is taken, both mother and baby benefit from close contact. Awareness of this reassured Linda that she had much to offer her twins.

As time passed, with plenty of perseverance and emotional support, the feeding of our twins grew easier and more rewarding. Even some of the early setbacks became a source of fond memories. Linda remembers her first experience pumping breast milk. "My first day home from the hospital, I spent all morning pumping and came out of the bedroom with less than an ounce of milk. Todd was wonderfully supportive. I was embarrassed to have him take such a small amount of milk to the hospital, but I had been instructed to send every drop. I worried about how that meager quantity would be divided between two babies but my milk never reached Sarah and Maiah. When Todd arrived at the hospital, he put the bottle of milk in his pants pocket. Hurrying to get through the electric entrance doors of the NICU, he smashed his pocket along with the plastic bottle, and my breast milk ran down his leg. Todd knew how much I had gone through to get those few drops of milk, so he was unable to tell me what happened. I heard the story later, from a nurse, and laughed until I cried."

## The Emotional Adjustment

Even though Linda had tried to prepare herself for the possibility of a premature birth by reading a book about prematurity and Debbie had toured the NICU and met NICU personnel during her first episode of premature labor, neither of them was emotionally prepared for the reality of premature birth. Debbie says, "I must have been in denial or something, but even after my premature labor, and the order for complete bed rest and special medications, I still thought I would carry my twins to term. Leaving my twins behind in the NICU when I was discharged was a scary, depressing thing. I felt cheated; I'd lost my beautiful dream of leaving the hospital with my twins, one cradled in each of my arms."

Linda had a similar grieving process: "With my first set of twins, I quickly accepted the babies' prematurity. But during my second pregnancy, I had unrealistically convinced myself that I would carry my babies to term. I was devastated when I went into labor at 33 weeks, and grieved my lost pregnancy like the loss of a family member. I mourned for weeks, even after the boys came home."

Add to this the constant worry that a parent feels about the medical condition of her child and you begin to understand the full spectrum of feelings brought on by the birth of premature twins. Linda remembers, "At first, when the babies were born and most fragile, I thought: 'Will one or both of my babies die?' As they grew stronger, these ideas were replaced with: 'Will they be normal?' "

Debbie, who tends to be a worrier, always had one more nagging question, one more doubt. The quality of many of her days was measured by the nurses' reports that greeted her as she entered the NICU. Pronouncements, such as: "The babies each gained an ounce again today!" or "Your baby only had two apnea spells all shift" were known to make Debbie's day on more than one occasion!

During this period of emotional upheaval, Linda and Debbie found that sharing their feelings with their spouses, nurses, doctors, hospital social workers, and other parents of premature babies was very helpful.

Extended family and friends can also be an important source of emotional support. Debbie and Linda both came home to the welcoming arms of their parents. Debbie remembers, "Having my parents there to greet us when Dale and I arrived from the hospital helped me to refocus my attention and put things in perspective. I was relieved that my parents were able to extend their visit until both babies were home, too."

Finally, another source of comfort which should not be overlooked is spiritual support. Linda remembers, "My visits to the hospital chapel to think and pray were important to my emotional well-being. Amid the chaos, here was a place for meditation where I could quietly make sense of all that was happening."

## Bonding

Much has been said and written about the bonding process that occurs between mother and baby in the first hours of a baby's life. Unlike the delivery of a healthy term baby, there are no private moments for parents to cuddle and caress their premature infants at birth. When parents and premature baby finally do meet up again in the NICU, a barrier of medical technology and their baby's physical frailty stands between them.

Parents of premature infants often feel badly when they lose these first precious moments with their children. "In the delivery room our pediatrician let me briefly touch and stroke Michael and Joanna as he held them, but I never actually got to hold them close. I had to lie on the table as they finished my C-section and watch as my babies were carried away from me. I really, really felt awful about that."

Another very common reaction to having ill premature infants is to feel isolated from your children. Linda recalls, "I tried to bond with the babies while they were in the hospital, but some days I came away from the NICU feeling that the girls belonged to the nurses more than they did to Todd and me. Taking every opportunity to touch and help with their care helped us to develop an attachment to our babies. Most of our genuine bonding didn't occur until later, though, when we were able to cuddle our babies in the privacy of our home. Although our bonding was delayed, it was no less wonderful."

Sometimes bonding occurs at the oddest moment and in the seemingly least significant way. "I still remember clearly," says Debbie, "the first time I saw Joanna in the NICU. Sixteen hours had passed since I had seen her briefly at her birth. As I held her sleeping in my arms, I tried to remember how she looked at her birth; but I couldn't. I said to her, 'Are you really mine? Hmmm, little girl? Do you know who I am?' Immediately she opened her eyes and looked at me intently as if she were saying to me, 'Of course, I know who you are. Now please, Mom, may I get some sleep?' I knew our bonding could not have been better or deeper or stronger had it happened seconds after her birth."

Although Linda and Debbie had no problems bonding with their twins, it can pose a problem for some parents of premature infants. The medical problems, the frail, almost birdlike appearance of many premature infants, the parent's worry that he or she might somehow unwittingly hurt their tiny baby or unplug some vital piece of medical equipment—all are obstacles to parent-child bonding. In extreme cases, it is not unusual for parents to emotionally withdraw from their baby in anticipation of his death, while at the same time loving their child and hoping he survives. These seemingly conflicting feelings of hope, fear, detachment, and love are normal and are known as anticipatory grief.

Difficulties in bonding with premature infants are not unusual, but they must not be ignored or denied. Speak to a hospital social worker, counselor, or chaplain about your feelings. Ask hospital nursing staff how to handle medical equipment and how to care for and feed your babies. You will feel more comfortable with your twins and begin to form an emotional bond that will last a lifetime.

## Going Home

Discharge from the NICU will occur when the baby's doctor is satisfied that the baby is medically stable, breathing well, feeding well, gaining weight consistently, and able to tolerate being in an open-air crib without heat lamps. For each premature infant this will come at a different time. Twins, even identical twins, will not progress at the same rate in the NICU, and it is not unusual for the discharge of twins to occur on different days.

Conflicting feelings will abound: sadness about leaving one twin, joy at having the other in your arms, relief that the baby is well enough to come home, fear that the baby is now your full responsibility. Debbie experienced all these emotions. "Leaving the NICU with just one twin, I was torn between the happiness of taking Michael home and the sadness of leaving Joanna behind."

The mixed feelings persisted at home. There were advantages to taking Michael home before Joanna. With Joanna in the NICU, it gave Debbie the opportunity to adjust to Michael's demanding schedule before having to deal with Joanna's schedule, too. And with daily trips to the NICU to see Joanna, Debbie had the chance to speak with the nurses about Michael's progress at home as well as Joanna's progress in the hospital. There were disadvantages as well. Debbie remembers, "I felt guilty about needing to spend so much time at home with Michael that it made it impossible for me to get to the hospital for more than one brief period each day. I was always tired, and it was hard to enjoy Michael or Joanna. When I was with one, I always felt I should be with the other. It was a no-win situation that left me physically and emotionally exhausted."

Linda and Todd had similar reactions when Maiah and Sarah left the NICU on separate days, so they decided on a different course of action for the boys. "We were given the choice of taking Keegan home or waiting until a follow-up pneumocardiogram could be done which was scheduled for the same day as Colin's proposed discharge. We chose to leave Keegan in the hospital, and it turned out they were both discharged on the same day."

When Linda's and Debbie's twins were discharged, both they and their husbands received thorough instructions on how to use and care for the portable heart and respiratory monitors. Instruction in infant cardiopulmonary resuscitation (CPR) and anti-choking techniques were taught. The babies' feeding schedules were reviewed and last-minute questions were answered. Then, it was time to leave the NICU.

## Adjusting to Having Both Babies Out of the Hospital

The euphoria of having your twins all to yourself is brief, as soon as the awesome responsibility of caring for two premature infants becomes evident. Linda and Todd didn't even make it home before their troubles began. "You've never felt true frustration if you haven't tried to put a five-pound premature infant who is attached by several wires to a cardiopulmonary monitor into a car seat! Believe me, it isn't easy. I stuffed towels underneath the twins and used rolled-up receiving blankets to support their heads and shoulders. I tried to support their heads as best I could, but I was still afraid their chins would fall against their chests and cut off their airways."

No matter how prepared parents may be, the first few days at home with premature twins is a period of adjustment. Debbie says, "A few days after both twins came home, my parents had to return to Wisconsin. That's when the real work began. There was housework and all our older son's needs. Michael and Joanna both had three-hour feeding schedules; but they still weren't nursing at every feeding so I had to use an electric breast pump every three to four hours, 10 to 15 minutes at a time. Add to that the diaper changes, bathing, cuddling, and soothing that all babies need, and you can see why two hours of sleep at a time seemed like a luxury!"

Linda agrees. "How can I describe how hectic it was? Our girls were our first children and they came home one at a time. It was difficult, but compared to how it was with the boys, it almost seems easy. To say life was chaotic would be an understatement!"

It's true that adjusting to life at home with premature twins is stressful, but it is what Debbie, Linda, and their husbands had been waiting for, hoping for, and praying for since their babies' births. It was the difficult beginning of what would become a very rewarding journey.

## A Special Note

It would be less than honest to give the impression that the NICU stories of all premature twins end as happily as Linda and Debbie's did. While most complications of prematurity can be treated successfully these days, the fact remains that a small number of infants survive prematurity with developmental delays, chronic medical problems, or lifelong disabling conditions.

An even smaller number of infants do not survive prematurity at all. Having never encountered circumstances such as these, we cannot offer any personal advice or hard-earned wisdom. However, there are some good books that deal with these sensitive issues. There are also support networks for parents who have one or more disabled twins and for parents who have lost one or both of their twins. These resources are listed in the suggested reading and resource section of our book.

## Our Thoughts and Reflections

LINDA:    Because so many twins are born prematurely, I think it is a good idea to acquaint yourself with the NICU before your babies are born.

Another thing that helped me through this period was to have a positive attitude. I daily reminded myself that my babies were in good hands and would be home soon. I focused on their weight gains and increased feedings, without dwelling on their minor setbacks. I wasn't always able to smile away the tears, but I made an effort to be optimistic.

DEBBIE:    Each day my twins were in the NICU was a challenge as I struggled to face my fears, deal with the demands of caring for my older boy, Chris, keep up with housework, recover from my C-section, and make visits to the hospital.

As the days passed my twins grew stronger. Life got easier and a tiny bit more predictable. When Dale and I were finally able to take Michael and Joanna home, we were overjoyed. There was a lot of hard work ahead of us, but we were only aware of how thrilled we were to have passed this milestone successfully!

Chapter 5

# "You really have your hands full!"

## *The First Six Months*

**C**ongratulations! After many long months and a great deal of worry, you finally have your babies at home all to yourself. So now what? Does the word *"Help!"* come to mind? Stay calm. Despite the fact that these next few months will be very demanding, we are living proof that they can be survived.

As you read about our experiences with our newborn twins, you will appreciate that, as a mother of young twins, "You really do have your hands full."

### *Coming Home*

*Getting Adjusted:* One thing that made our homecomings easier was the fact that all of us had at least one willing and able grandparent waiting there to help. Some had traveled great distances and some had only come across town, but they all immediately pitched in to help. All five of us agree that extra help and support is paramount in those first few weeks at home, whether someone comes to live in or just comes by with a dinner.

None of us fully realized what caring for infant twins would involve, so bringing our babies home evoked many different feelings in each of us. Florien and Linda, both first-time parents, had reactions that ranged from overconfidence to overwhelmed.

Five days after Florien's cesarean, she was ready to go home with Max and Otto. "Devin and I were very excited about officially starting our lives together as a family. Neither of us was nervous. I had been around many babies in my work, and we had a number of friends with young infants. Devin was a natural at being a dad. Our confidence in our ability to care for, handle, and love our children was high. We were full of anticipation about the changes in store for us, as a family and as individuals."

Linda had read in child care books that the first months would be the most difficult, and felt unprepared for the overwhelming task of caring for twins. "I had no practical knowledge of mothering. Fortunately, Sarah and Maiah were unaware of my lack of experience."

Debbie, Sheri, and Debra all had other children, but they knew that having twins meant they'd experience a whole new realm of parenthood. All the normal boundaries would be stretched. Their past experience would help them, but they, too, were in uncharted territory.

Sheri's daughter was four and a half years old and Debbie's son was seven when their twins were born. Both families had lots of help and support in the first few weeks, so they had similar experiences when they got home. Sheri and Steve's family members all lived in town, though, and were a great help to her whenever she needed it. Debbie's, on the other hand, were from out of state, and had to leave after a few weeks. That's when the real work started for her.

"Dale and I tried to develop a daily routine and make some sense out of double three-hour feedings, double diapers, double bathings, double crying—not to mention continuing to be the parents of another child who very much needed to discover where he fit into all of these. It was a very difficult adjustment."

In addition to bringing her twins home, Debra had other issues to deal with. Her husband, Rick, was in the middle of remodeling their house, and though she had one son in high school, she had another who was just short of three years old. "As soon as I was in the door, Muggy excitedly showed me his new big-boy bed that Rick had just finished building, as we needed Muggy's crib for the babies. I made a big deal about his being a big boy now and needing a larger bed.

"I was disappointed that the expansion of our master bedroom, where the babies would be, was not yet usable. It was frustrating to come home to an unfinished nest. I was forced to spend the first few days at home organizing the babies' space, instead of resting and recuperating."

*Heart/Respiratory Monitors:* The experience of having their babies on heart/respiratory monitors was extremely stressful for both Linda's and Debbie's families. The monitors were the size of portable radios; each had a terminal and three lead wires that attached to the babies' chests. Adhesive patches secured the leads to the skin. Linda recalls, "We had to be careful to keep the wires separated, since both babies were in the same crib. To cut down on the confusion, we labeled each monitor with the baby's name.

"The portable monitors, which were very sensitive and often sent off false alarms, required constant adjustment. Crying, abrupt movement, or poor skin contact with the patches often activated an alarm. As if those first sleepless weeks with two babies weren't hard enough, we also had the disrupted sleep and anxiety of false alarms ringing several times nightly.

"I remember the worst night very well. At 2:30 A.M. I awoke to the sound of Maiah's alarm. I was out of bed in a second. Maiah was fine, but the alarm was still buzzing. I checked all the leads to make sure no wires were disconnected. Nothing seemed wrong, but each time I reset the monitor, the alarm went off. In desperation, I replaced all the patches, which required working all of the old adhesive off with baby oil. By this time, Maiah was screaming; removing the patches hurts the babies' fragile skin. I was so frustrated, I started crying too, and soon Sarah joined in.

"When Todd woke up and found all of us in tears, he immediately called the hospital's twenty-four-hour service number. A technician came to the house, and the problem turned out to be faulty wiring. After that night, we convinced our pediatrician to allow us to discontinue the heart monitors.

"I was not apprehensive about doing without the monitors; in fact, we all slept better after they were gone. The babies seemed much more comfortable without wires attached to them, and I was finally able to give them a tub bath without worrying about getting water on the connective patches."

For Debbie, the monitors were a reassuring necessity, but they also grew to be a frustrating reality. "I couldn't pick up a baby and move any useful distance without also picking up the monitor. As a result, we tended to spend most of our waking hours in the same room, which did very little for my morale. At least once a day, a monitor sounded a false alarm."

"We lived with these machines for four and a half months, at which time both babies had a twelve-hour sleep study done on them. This involved having a special machine attached to each monitor to record their heart and respiratory rates for a twelve-hour period during the night. The results were normal and the monitors were discontinued. Without the security that the monitors provided, Dale and I were a bit nervous, but after a few nights we adjusted."

## Feeding Our Babies

During our twins' first few months of life, we spent more time feeding them than anything else, so we had many questions. Our initial concerns centered around whether to feed with breast milk or formula, how to hold twins during feedings, and whether or not to feed on demand.

*Breast-feeding, Bottles, and Formula:* Breast milk or formula is the only food babies need for their first four to six months. The issue of whether to breast- or formula-feed twins is a complicated one, as many factors go into the decision. Returning to work, and providing the opportunity for others to feed the twins, may indicate choosing formula for some. Excellent nutrition for baby and closer bonding are the most common reasons women choose to breast-feed. Be it bottles or breasts, the reality is that having twins means there is double the amount of work and concern attached.

Overall, we found that our personal feelings and needs were the most important influences when we made decisions in this area. During our pregnancies, all five of us gave thought to and made choices about feeding methods. After the twins were born, we had to learn from our mistakes, sift through a variety of advice, and compromise a bit. The first thing that can throw a monkey wrench into feeding plans is the premature birth of the twins.

*Feeding Schedules:* Some premature newborns are too small, too weak, or too sick to suck from the bottle or breast. For these infants tube feedings are often used until the infant matures. Then bottle-feeding or breast-feeding is introduced, and offered at regular intervals. A feeding timetable is fairly standard for small or premature infants, even after they leave the hospital. As babies demonstrate a good, consistent weight gain, they are advanced to an on-demand schedule.

Sheri's twins had a three-hour feeding schedule. "Emmy and Tessa were born only three weeks early; they were strong, had no complications, and had a developed sucking reflex. But we were still sent home on a three-hour feeding schedule because of their low birthweight (due to my high blood pressure). Fortunately, Emmy and Tessa gained weight rapidly, and were feeding on demand by four weeks."

Debbie had both twins home by the time they were nine days old, and they were both on three-hour feeding schedules. "Our doctor only wanted them to nurse every third feeding so they wouldn't become fatigued. This made life very complicated as I had to make formula, breast-feed, and pump my breasts to keep my milk supply up."

"Despite our best efforts, the three-hour feeding schedule was grueling. When Dale was available, he and I took turns making the formula and bottle-feeding the babies. We found it easiest to make an entire day's supply of formula in the evening after the children were asleep. In order to maximize our sleep at night, we shared the nighttime feedings. Dale had the 11:00 P.M. and 5:00

A.M. shifts while I had the 8:00 P.M. and 2:00 A.M. shifts. This worked better in theory than in practice, but once in a while we'd each get a four- or five-hour block of sleep, which seemed like heaven.

"Thankfully, the three-hour schedule didn't last long. By the time the twins were three weeks old, each had gained nearly two pounds and they were advanced to a four-hour schedule. Two weeks after that, they were allowed to eat whenver they seemed hungry. I nursed the babies at most of their feedings; however, we made it a point to use formula occasionally to give me a break. By the time the twins were two months old, Michael was taking one bottle of formula in the evening when my milk was low and he got frustrated, while Joanna adamantly refused to take any more bottles and patiently waited for my milk to let down."

Linda's twins were also sent home on a three-hour feeding schedule. "Nursing my twins every three hours helped to increase my milk supply, but it was exhausting. Some days, it seemed I barely had enough milk to satisfy both babies, but then a day or two later, my supply of milk would adjust to their demands. I soon decided that I needed to sleep through the 6:00 A.M. feeding, so Todd gave the babies bottles of breast milk which I had pumped the day before. He really enjoyed bonding with Sarah and Maiah during those early morning feedings and the few extra hours of sleep were important to my health and well-being."

Debra's full-term twins came home with no strict feeding schedules; she breast-fed them on demand. But she had a rocky start. "My milk didn't come in until the fourth day. And by then I had two ravenous babies on my hands because my milk supply wasn't keeping up with their demands.

"I think several things contributed to this problem: a lack of rest, the babies' full-term weight, and some long delays between feedings at the hospital that hindered the natural production process. The problem was compounded when the babies started napping for three hours or more per day, both at the same time. I let them sleep because I needed the break, but it turned out to be a poor tradeoff because the lack of stimulation to my breasts hampered milk production at this critical time.

"It was hard to remain adamant about strictly breast-feeding when confronted with hungry babies, so after the first week I began to supplement my breast milk with an ounce or more of formula after each nursing. When I realized that this was counterproductive and saw how long it took to wash and prepare bottles in the short amount of time that was left to me, I regained my resolve to breast-feed only.

"I called my midwife. She explained the importance of frequent breast-feeding and gave me a breast pump to use while the babies were sleeping; this would stimulate production and I could feed them with the extra milk if they were still hungry after nursing. She also advised that I nurse them every two hours over the next twenty-four, to build up my supply. Her advice worked, and within a week I was able to completely eliminate the supplemental formula. Nursing turned out to be more satisfying and enjoyable than bottle-feeding. I'm glad I kept trying until I got it right."

*Nutrition and Breast-feeding:* Building up a good milk supply for breast-feeding is dependent on frequent nursing, as much as eight to twelve times in twenty-four hours. The stimulation to the nipples and emptying of the breast increases milk production. To further aid supply, and to keep the mother's stamina and energy level up, a nutritious diet and adequate fluids are also important.

Linda's appetite while breast-feeding was tremendous. "To help my milk production meet the babies' demands, I ate as many nutritious meals as I could and drank a minimum of eight glasses of milk or other fluids every day. As recommended, I had a glass of water beside me whenever I sat down to nurse."

Eating well yourself and feeding your babies are equally important, interrelated tasks. Maintaining a healthy diet is difficult because it is often hard to find the time to sit down and eat. Many mothers of newborn twins find it easier to snack on nutritious foods throughout the day than to try to fit meals in between baby feedings.

*Coordinating Feedings:* Twin siblings sometimes have extremely different temperaments. Keeping them on the same feeding and sleeping schedules can be a challenge, but it makes life with two babies much more manageable.

For Debbie, this was easiest after her babies started feeding on demand. "It allowed the twins to start lengthening the time between their feedings. At night when one baby would wake, I'd feed him or her and just before that baby finished eating, I'd have Dale wake and change the diapers of the second baby. Then we'd trade babies. I would feed Baby Number Two while Dale changed the first one." This system of feeding one baby right after the other is highly recommended by parents of twins and is what we term as *on demand*. Actually, on demand of the baby who wakes first, the schedule is fairly simple and obvious. Nevertheless, it can sometimes be hard to stick to. For instance, if the first baby feeds sluggishly, the other baby has to wait. This forces Baby Number Two more fully awake, so he or she doesn't want to go back to sleep for several hours.

Florien and David used a similar system when they were both available. When Florien had to feed them by herself it went a bit differently. "I would nurse, burp, and change one baby and then the other one, giving the waiting baby a pacifier to temporarily satisfy his sucking need. I had been told by a nurse at the hospital that this was the best way to get the babies on the same feeding schedule, so it was what I did from the day they were born. I used this method during the day at home, when we were away from the house, and even at night."

Sheri solved her scheduling problem by inventing a "Who ate what, and when?" chart for the babies. "One full day of alternating breasts and babies left my head spinning. I drew blanks trying to recall the last time they'd eaten. Reasoning that this was unnecessary mental strain, I opted for a chart. I drew a line down the center of a pad of paper, and used half of the page for Emmy and half for Tessa. For each feeding, on the same horizontal line, I wrote down the time and which breast for which baby. The chart and pen I kept tucked inside a large box of nursing pads which always was within arm's reach."

Coodinating feedings was also Debra's next hurdle. "At first, things were so haphazard that I never felt sure about which twin got how much and when. I called another mother of twins, who suggested several alternatives. I decided to try feeding one baby on only one breast at each session and I made a point of changing the sides they nursed on at each feeding. I chose to feed them every two to two-and-a-half hours during the day and let them feed on demand at night: when one twin woke up, I nursed that one back to sleep, and then woke and fed the other twin. In spite of all the challenges, one month after delivery, nursing was going smoothly and the twins were healthy and growing rapidly."

*Positions for Feeding Two Babies:* There are many different positions in which to hold and feed infants. The most common maneuver, whether breast-feeding or bottle-feeding, requires that a baby be cradled in the crook of your arm. When there are two babies, and only two arms, this can be tricky. Our best advice is to experiment with hands, arms, legs, pillows, chairs, and footrests, until you find a few positions that allow you and your babies to be comfortable during feedings. One method to avoid, though it may be tempting, is to prop a bottle in a baby's mouth. The baby could easily choke on too much milk, besides babies need and enjoy the physical closeness that occurs during feedings. We found that many nursing positions work well for bottle-feeding, too. For best success, make sure the babies' heads are facing toward the nipple. Regardless of the feeding method, it takes time for both baby and feeder to feel competent at it.

For Sheri, nursing the babies together was intensely overstimulating at first. "I just didn't like the feeling. It made my whole body tingle and ache. So for the first couple of weeks, I fed Emmy and Tessa one at a time. This involved a tremendous amount of baby shuffling, but when I had help taking babies back and forth, it was a pleasurable experience. When I was alone, there was a lot of crying. (The babies usually cried, too!)

"A few times I tried pumping my breasts, but I could never get enough milk to make the effort of working my hand-held breast pump worthwhile. I really wanted to breast-feed exclusively, and fortunately by the third week, nursing Emmy and Tessa together was losing its sting. I was actually starting to enjoy it and I devised a position to fit my tall frame. The babies sat on my thighs, facing each other, feet touching, while I held their outside legs and reclined a little. In this position, the babies latched right on to nurse. Their downside arms hung into my armpits and their other hands always held tightly to the centerpiece of my bra. Sometimes they even held hands. This upright position worked beautifully. It greatly reduced the twins' coughing and choking on too much milk. If one did cough, I would extend my elbow a little and let her sit up. She'd catch her breath and easily latch back on.

"Steve nicknamed this method the 'speed feed' because it was considerably faster than nursing them separately. I could relax back into our big recliner chair with all three of my girls. (Kallie often snuggled up next to one elbow.)"

With a little practice, Linda found that the easiet nursing position for her was to sit on the couch and hold the babies like footballs, both heads down and facing each breast, with their bodies and legs under her arms and draped alongside her chest. "Their heads and bodies were supported by pillows, and eventually they developed enough head control that I no longer needed help to position them. I alternated breasts and babies during feeding to give each child equal left and right visual stimulation. Even though the girls nursed at the same time, it took them 45 minutes to an hour to finish. Later, when the girls got bigger, it became difficult to hold two wriggly, squirming babies at the same time, so I began feeding them separately."

When Debbie was home alone, she would either nurse them both at the same time, cradling each in one arm, face-to-face, or nurse one in a regular hold while bottle-feeding the other. "As I sat on the couch, the bottle-fed baby lay close to my thigh, head by my knee, looking up at me. I was careful to touch and smile at both babies as they ate.

"With my arms full of babies, I found some products of modern technology that were extremely helpful at feeding time. My cordless telephone, answering machine, and portable intercom saved me from even more baby juggling."

For Florien, nursing the twins at home was tiring, but not too physically stressful. "I preferred to hold one baby in a football hold and the other in a regular hold if I was feeding them simultaneously. If I felt like feeding them separately, I gave the second baby a pacifier to suck on while waiting to be fed.

"One thing I never got used to was the fact that when you have twins, you and they are considered public property, whether or not you are breast-feeding. I learned to find quiet corners and to be subtle in my feeding techniques when we were in public."

*Burping:* A good portion of the time dedicated to feeding is spent burping babies. Debra's babies became very uncomfortable and woke up after falling asleep if they were not burped adequately. "Aislynn and Ricky were quick to latch on and nurse, but getting a good burp out of them was time-consuming. During the night it was really hard to stay awake while trying to pat stubborn air bubbles out of the babies. If I gave up too soon and put them down, twenty minutes later they woke up from stomach discomfort.

"When this happened, they often acted as if they were still hungry. At first, I was easily misled into feeding them some more, compounding the problem. After I learned to wait the situation out, it sometimes took time, but a large burp always came up and the baby would settle right down."

Out of necessity, Sheri learned to entertain and/or burp one baby while simultaneously feeding the other. "I nursed one baby in a regular nursing hold, her head in the crook of my left arm. With my left hand, I held the other baby's head and chest up while she 'sat' on my knee, and patted her back with my right hand. I constantly reminded myself that I was truly amazing for performing this daring feat of twin motherhood!"

Linda used the most common position for burping her babies. She would gently ease the baby upright, and with his head lying over her shoulder, pat his back. This method works well, but the simple truth from Linda was that "Burping the babies one at a time only worked when I had help, or had the babies' feedings perfectly orchestrated."

*Growth:* When babies are premature, low birthweight, or have any significant health problems, their milk intake will be carefully monitored in the hospital. Their ability to thrive is directly related to their ability to gain weight.

One by one, our babies got on track and we were sent home with the advice that six to eight wet diapers per day (from each baby) is a good sign that feeding is going well. For some of us, this information was enough. Others had doubts. Sheri found a solution to ease her mind.

At her babies' one week birthday, she had her doctor's orders to bring Emmy and Tessa in for a weight and progress check. "The girls were thriving, and the doctor was reassured. But I continued to have worries. Aware of my concern, my mother found a baby scale at a secondhand shop. The scale allowed us to weigh the babies daily and reinforce the fact that they were doing well. It was just the encouragement I needed!"

Florien's boys had good birthweights, but gained slowly after that. Her pediatrician assured her that the gain was steady—and that was the most important point. "He explained that almost 90 percent of the nourishment comes within the first five minutes of breast-feeding, so we needn't be alarmed when our babies finished nursing within a few minutes. As a precaution he recommended that they be followed by the federal WIC (Women, Infant, and Children) program which we were eligible for. There, the boys could receive regular and frequent checkups.

"After a year of tracking Max and Otto they saw a steady positive trend in the boys' growth patterns and we were told that the twins would always be on the small side. Devin and I had guessed this all along because neither one of us are very big people to begin with!"

If your health care provider is concerned about weight gain in your breast-fed twins, you may wish to contact a lactation consultant before considering formula supplementation. Feeding your babies formula may hinder your production of milk and spoil plans to breast-feed exclusively. The lactation consultant may be able to help your babies gain weight through a few changes in your breast-feeding practices, but this should always be done in agreement with your practitioner.

*Weaning:* The definition of the word *wean* is to withhold mother's milk from the young of a mammal and substitute other nourishment. It sounds quite simple, but the actual logistics can be complicated depending upon when and why weaning is taking place. A woman must take into account her babies' age and nutritional requirements, then factor in each of her babies' personal preferences as well as her own. Last, but not least, she'll have to deal with the emotions that she and her babies have about the whole process. There are, however, some basic ground rules for weaning.

Weaning from breast-feeding is best when done slowly, dropping one feeding at a time, over a period of several weeks or months. In this way the mother's breasts don't become engorged and the baby can make the adjustment gradually.

Some of us breast-fed our twins beyond the first six months, but the overwhelming job of mothering four small children took a physical and emotional toll on Linda after her second set of twins was born. "I decided that one way to gain back some personal space was to wean Colin and Keegan at five and a half months. I couldn't keep up with the demands of breast-feeding twin infants and chasing twin three-year-olds. Most times when I fed the boys, the girls wanted to be on or next to me. It was just too much trying to balance all four of them."

For Sheri, too, breast-feeding was becoming tedious and she started weaning her twins at five months. "I knew that I'd done my babies a great service by feeding them breast milk that long, and I was frustrated at having to stop what I was doing in order to nurse them during the day. The alluring alternative was to lay them on the carpet near me, and as they held and drank their own bottles, I could fold laundry, do paperwork, or clean. I would smile and talk to them while I worked, and when they were full they simply stopped drinking and rolled over to play with a toy. This newfound freedom was too hard to resist so I gradually gave up all but one feeding to bottles of formula. Both babies became constipated, and I had to try several different formulas before discovering one that they could comfortably process.

"In a covered pitcher, I mixed enough formula for the whole day and stored it in the refrigerator. At feeding time, I simply poured the formula into two bottles. For the first few months, I warmed their bottles in the microwave for fifteen seconds each. I was always careful to shake the formula after heating, to mix up any hot spots created by the microwave. I always tasted the formula myself before I gave it to them."

"One month later, just before Emmy and Tessa turned six months old, I was still nursing them in the morning. Four bottles of formula spanned the day and evening feedings. I really enjoyed this schedule; it granted me freedom, yet I could still feel good about breast-feeding. Regrettably, at that point my milk started drying up. It hit me one morning when the babies seemed listless after nursing—they were still hungry! I could have tried to get my milk supply back up by increasing my breast-feeding periods, but it seemed like the right time to quit nursing altogether."

Both Linda and Sheri felt some sadness at the end of their breast-feeding experience, but they also felt relieved and satisfied that they'd done their best for their babies. They both gained a new sense of freedom, too, which they agree made them happier women and better mothers. Later Sheri said, "I still get occasional pangs of guilt at not nursing Emmy and Tessa longer, but I made the right decision for myself, at that time, and I'm not doing anyone any good by feeling guilty."

*Solid Food:*  Starting twins on solid foods is a big step. Most full-term babies become ready between four and six months of age, although premature infants may lag behind. According to the American Association of Pediatrics (AAP), babies are ready for the introduction of solid foods when all of the following are present: The babies weigh more than 12 pounds, have good control of their head and neck muscles, make chewing movements with their mouths, act hungry even though they are being breastfed several times a day or taking more than 35 to 40 ounces of formula in a twenty-four-hour period, and are very interested in "adult" food.

The twins' new interest in food can be an exciting development for the whole family. A person can't take a bite in their presence without them staring straight at the fork.

By five months of age, Florien's boys became very interested in what she and Devin were eating. "Max and Otto were eagerly looking at and grabbing for food off of our plates. Our pediatrician suggested that we try offering them baby cereal, and he assured us that it was fine to start solid food at this age if the babies truly appeared interested.

"We started with two teaspoons of rice cereal because it was the least likely food to cause allergies and it settles most easily in the babies' tummies. As directed, we thinned it with breast milk, juice, or applesauce. We were careful not to make it taste too sweet, though, or the boys would have balked at other, less sweet foods.

"I wanted to continue to feed the boys at the same time so I arranged them comfortably in their baby carriers on the floor in front of me. I fed them bites, alternating between one baby and the other. In this way I didn't have either one crying to be fed and I got the job done all at once. As they became more competent at sitting, we used infant chairs that attached to our kitchen table. Once the babies were fed and content, Devin and I would eat. It was just too much mess and confusion feeding them and ourselves at the same time."

Debbie's experience with her first son, Chris, was much different than what transpired with the twins. "I started Chris on rice cereal when he was four months old and he gobbled down his two daily feedings, but when I tried to do the same with Michael and Joanna, they spit out the cereal. My pediatrician told me that babies have no real nutritional need for solid food at four months of age, so I happily waited. I did, however, introduce them to apple juice and prune juice. Joanna seemed to enjoy an ounce or two of apple juice, diluted to half strength with water. And Michael, who was having problems with constipation, needed an ounce of diluted prune juice every two days."

## Caring for Our Babies

Caring for two babies will consume nearly every waking (and sleeping!) moment of your life for the next few months. Clearly, there are many issues that new parents of twins must face. Learning all that you can about baby care will make life much easier.

*Crying and Comforting:*   Coping with infant crying is one of the hardest parts of parenting newborns. But crying is the only way that babies can communicate that they need something. Parents are programmed to be disturbed by crying so that they respond, and relieve or comfort the infant. A baby will usually be able to modify crying so that it sounds different for each basic need, and parents can learn how to differentiate the tones. Some cries are more obvious: hunger, fatigue, wet or dirty diapers. But babies have more subtle needs, too. Wanting to be held, to have more or less stimulation, or to have something to suck on are equally vital to an infant's well-being.

There were many times when we couldn't figure out why our babies were crying, so trial and error was our only recourse. *All* of us became distressed by prolonged crying, especially when *both* babies cried at once, so we asked for help and took a break.

Coping with fussy babies can be much easier when you have a wide variety of soothing techniques at your disposal. No one method works forever. The bigger the bag of tricks you have to choose from, the more successful you will be in calming your babies.

It took Debra a couple of weeks to feel that she could handle both fussy babies at the same time. "It's funny how you have to use your entire body to do things while holding two babies. I'd hold a baby in my arms and rock or bounce the other one on my legs. Or I'd use a foot to bounce one in a springy infant seat or to roll a stroller back and forth. Having been a waitress for ten years proved an advantage; I could juggle and balance easily, and my arms were strong.

"I was also dependent on what I call 'extended family substitutes' like rocking chairs, baby swings, infant seats. While these can't give you moral support or a needed hug, when it comes to coping, anything that works is fair game."

Dale and Debbie spent many hours comforting and cuddling babies, too. "We all took turns at this, and learned to be creative. Chris, after a bit of a rough start, blossomed as a loving big brother. Dale and I carried the babies, rocked them, wore them in front packs, and put them in swings, and placed them atop a running dryer. I also sang a lot. Sometimes the singing was loud (a shade below screaming) and the lyrics went: 'I can't take it anymore. I can't take it anymore. I'm gonna go *crazy!*' It helped."

Early on, Florien purchased swings for her twins, and found them to be real lifesavers. "They not only allowed the boys to observe me as I cooked or cleaned, but were also wonderful for calming Max and Otto when they were fussy. Best of all, they were run by batteries; all I had to do was turn them on.

"Most importantly, we found that limiting the amount of activity around the babies was very useful in calming them. Turning off the TV or radio, dimming the lights, unplugging the phone. . . . Car rides in the evening and walks in the stroller also provided a relaxing change of environment for the babies and for Devin and me."

Sheri's twins went beyond mere fussiness and posed a big challenge to her and Steve. She remembers, "When Emmy and Tessa were two weeks old, we took a four-hour car trip to Seattle. The babies slept all the way there, but late that night they started screaming. They cried every night after that for nearly four months. The diagnosis was infant colic."

*Colic* is a syndrome described as uncontrollable crying in a healthy baby, lasting more than a total of ninety minutes a day and tending to recur day after day. Some infants are most upset in the evening, some cry during the day. Some are colicky for only two or three weeks, while others continue having colicky episodes until they are three or four months old. We emphasize "healthy" because a baby who cries uncontrollably must be examined by a physician who could rule out an organic or physical cause for the crying. There are several theories and myths surrounding colic and these can be found with potential solutions in books on the subject. The simple reality for parents of twins is that one or two colicky babies creates additional stress in an already demanding situation. Sheri and Steve tried anything and everything to cope with Emmy and Tessa's colic.

"Our lives became ruled by their nighttime colic and daytime fussiness. Hoping to alleviate their discomfort, our pediatrician gave me a list of foods to avoid, suggesting that any of them could be an irritant which passed to the babies through my breast milk.

"The avoidance list was comprised of chocolate, dairy products containing cows' milk (although yogurt was allowed), onions, garlic, tomatoes and tomato sauce, broccoli, cabbage, mushrooms, peanuts and peanut butter, mustard, peas, and any pork product. Any other foods known to be fatty, spicy, or gas-producing were also eliminated. There were times when I reasoned that my careful diet of fish, chicken, rice, and fruit couldn't possibly be affecting their colic that much. These thoughts usually came as I rationalized eating chocolate cookies or candy. Hours later, as the colic worsened, I lectured myself severely for my lapse.

"Constant, droning monotones that flooded out other stimuli soothed our savage babies. Running water helped to calm them. The washer, dryer, and vacuum were also very useful. Best of all were stove and bathroom fans. Emmy and Tessa always napped with their bassinets crammed into our back bathroom, the fan running. Later, when they outgrew the bassinets, I set up my nursery monitor as an intercom. With the transmitter in the bathroom and the receiver by their beds, we piped in the fan's noise.

"I'd learned that slight pressure on their tummies helped sometimes. Perching the babies up high, one on each collarbone, I held onto their inside armpits while their bottoms rested on my forearms. I walked in circles and watched soap operas. Eventually, my arms would get tired, but this position calmed them for quite a while. An even better position was standing, feet apart, with one baby straddling each hip, facing out. I held their tummies in my hands and gently jiggled up and down on my toes. Simultaneously, I swayed from side to side, and Emmy and Tessa bobbed there, relieved.

"After all else failed, I made a repeat visit to our pediatrician and got a prescription for Levsin, an oral medication that is primarily used for peptic ulcers.

"We didn't like the idea of giving the babies medication, but the Levsin drops definitely helped. Emmy and Tessa had a few drops at every feeding. When evening came, they were awake and uncomfortable, but not screaming. While we walked them around they stayed calm."

Most babies grow out of colic by three or four months of age. Parents who are dealing with colicky twins need to get frequent breaks throughout the day and to ask for help from others. Keeping the home environment as calm and peaceful as possible helps parents and babies alike. Remember also that colic is not the result of bad parenting. Additional suggestions for relieving colic include warm baths, infant massage, and holding or carrying the babies in a baby pack.

*Getting Babies to Sleep:*   Often the end result of calming a fussy baby is that he or she falls asleep. This can be a great relief for everyone involved—but if it becomes a regular pattern, the baby may never learn to fall asleep by himself.

To teach babies to fall asleep on their own, there are several proven strategies. The most obvious is putting them to bed anytime they are sleepy or drowsy, giving them the opportunity fall asleep without being held or fed. It may also help to wrap them in a blanket and place them next to something soft, but firm, like crib bumper pads. Most twins especially like sleeping together when they are newborns.

Florien let her boys share a crib for the first five months. "We put the crib in our room to start with, so night feedings would be easier and the second bedroom would be available for out-of-town company. There was plenty of room for both babies in one crib, and it took up less space in our bedroom. Max and Otto never seemed to bother one another when they slept; rather, they seemed comforted by having each other so near after spending nine months in the womb together."

Another suggestion that may help sleepy babies drift off to sleep on their own is soothing music, which may be a tape recording, musical mobile, or the voice of a loved one. There's also the age-old method of patting or rubbing babies on their backs at a slow rhythm. And some babies will drop off to sleep in rocking cradles or beds. As a last resort, some parents try a car ride to lull resistant infants to sleep.

On her long trips to and from her country home, Debra discovered that riding in the car nearly always put her babies to sleep. "On really rough days, I took them for a ride on purpose, just to get a break. It was so nice, surrounded by silence, but the quiet only lasted until we got back home. Invariably, when I turned the motor off, Aislynn and Ricky woke up."

As we all know too well, frustrated parents will sometimes do almost anything to get a baby to sleep, even if it means having to break bad habits later. Sheri nursed her babies to sleep from the start. "I soon realized that this was a mistake. I taught Emmy and Tessa to associate falling asleep with nursing, so they resisted sleep unless I was holding and feeding them.

"By the time they were four months old, the twins were sleeping for a six-hour stretch through the night. Sometimes they would stir, but rarely did they need my comforting to get back to sleep. This was a signal to me that they knew how to comfort themselves, and weren't in real need of my nursing them to sleep.

"So, one night after their 11:00 P.M. feeding, we put Emmy and Tessa into their bassinets while they were still awake. We left the door open and a night-light on. They cried for nearly twenty minutes. Listening to them cry was heart-wrenching, but we reassured each other that it was the right thing to do. After we made that initial commitment and stuck by it, we felt fine. After only three days, the babies had learned to go to sleep by themselves.

"Leaving their room was never easy, but we went through the same routine every night and the pattern became our family ritual for bedtime. The babies didn't like it sometimes, but they knew what to expect and it helped them to settle down. They'd fuss a bit and then listen to each other as they drifted off to sleep. It was wonderful for all five of us."

Regardless of whether you try to make changes in your infants' method of falling asleep, beginning to establish bedtime rituals can lay the foundation for future bedtime successes. Bathing, listening to music, and including a special item, such as a soft blanket or stuffed animal, will signal that it is time for bed. During the night, when the babies wake for feedings, stick to the business of feeding and changing them; do not encourage social interactions. If babies get the impression that nighttime is play time, they will stay awake for it.

*Sleeping through the Night:* Night waking is another area of concern for new parents. Almost everyone hopes babies will establish adult sleep patterns as early as possible. The reality is that infants are designed to wake up for feeding in their early months. Each baby has an individual time line that dictates when he or she is ready to sleep for longer stretches of time. Some parents are lucky to have children who sleep for long periods from birth, but this is not commonly the case. Some babies sleep relatively little; others, especially those who are premature or low birthweight, need to be awakened for feedings.

When full-term babies are three to four months old most can sleep for four- to six-hour stretches at night. Some babies fall into this pattern naturally, while others continue to wake up every two to four hours. Both situations can be entirely normal at this age. But if babies are still night-waking by the time they grow to be five or six months old, they may need some coaching to change their habits.

There are many different theories about, and methods of, teaching babies to sleep through the night. Most parents of newborn twins are especially interested in all of them. Each has advantages and disadvantages that parents have to weigh, recognizing that these techniques should not be used until a baby is four to six months old. Until then parents should follow their babies' instincts and needs, as it is fruitless to attempt to force a young infant to sleep through the night—they are simply not capable of it.

The five of us read books, talked to our pediatricians, had discussions with friends, and then tried everything!

Linda didn't have sleeping problems with her babies, because she always encouraged them to get themselves back to sleep whenever they awoke during the night. "When I heard any of them cry, I would listen for a few minutes before getting up, and often they went back to sleep. I decided that fifteen minutes was a reasonable length of time to let them cry, but I never had to wait that long. They usually went back to sleep within five minutes. If they continued to cry, I knew they needed me and I went to them without hesitation."

By the fifth month of sharing a bedroom with Max and Otto, Florien and Devin were ready to make some changes. "We decided to let them sleep in their own room because the little sounds that they made during the night were waking us up. We hoped that if I fed them at 11:00 they would only wake up once in the night for a feeding, before waking up to start their day. It seemed like a great idea.

"Unfortunately, the move ended up being hard on me. Devin was able to sleep better than before, but the babies continued to wake for their 2:30 A.M. feeding. I had to wake up fully and take the babies, one at a time, to feed them in the living room. The lack of sleep took its toll on me, so we spoke to our pediatrician for some advice.

"He told us that the boys were old enough to sleep for six hours. So we decided to try a system in which I would let the boys cry for a minute when they woke up. Then I would go in and tell them that I was near, but I wouldn't pick them up. Each night we increased the length of time that we let the boys cry, up to ten minutes, before entering the room. I was careful not to pick them up, although there were times that I would rub their backs for a moment to calm them down.

"This system worked beautifully, and after several days the boys fell asleep quietly, and stayed asleep for six whole hours! It was hard on us to let them cry the first few nights, but it had a very positive outcome for all of us. We and the babies woke up better rested and happier."

Debra found a totally different way of getting more sleep when she became exhausted from frequent night-waking. "Both babies slept in one crib, just a few feet away from our bed. Usually around 11:00 P.M., the twins would finally be asleep. Anywhere from thirty minutes to two hours later, at least one of them would be awake again. Their sleep schedules were so sporadic and unpredictable, I could only hope for two hours of uninterrupted sleep per night.

"Because I was apprehensive about the twins waking each other, as soon as I heard one of them fussing, I'd pick that baby up. I later learned that babies will often wake slightly and make noises, or fuss in the transitions between their sleep cycles. If you delay your response long enough to determine whether it's one of the transitional noises or an 'I need you' cry, you'll learn the difference and the baby will learn how to go to sleep by him- or herself. Because I didn't do this, my babies slept lightly and woke up often.

"What helped at that point was my decision to allow the babies to sleep with us when they were four months old. Our "family bed" might have been controversial, but it worked for us. The babies slept longer, and when they did wake up, I didn't have to rouse myself fully. They would nurse and fall right back to sleep. And I, in turn, got more sleep. Of course, we were somewhat crowded, but it was worth it because it was comforting to be together in a state of peace, unlike during the more stressful daytime."

As demonstrated by the variety of solutions we tried, each family has to find the right situation regarding where, how, and when their babies fall asleep.

*Illness:* Many babies develop their first colds and other minor illnesses during their first six months. This is especially likely if a baby has older siblings or is frequently around other children in day-care or social settings. Even experienced parents find these first illnesses stressful, for who can watch a small infant, ill and feverish, without feeling helpless and concerned? The worry goes double with twins because what one baby catches, the other usually gets, too.

Although most of the illnesses that children contract are mild and resolve with time and tender loving care, it's important to consult with your twins' physician to determine how he or she wants you to handle your specific situation. Always take time to chat with the doctor or nurse about your concerns and start asking questions at the twins' first well-checkups. You can't be expected to memorize everything your doctor tells you, so don't hesitate to write things down. If your doctor doesn't have time or interest in answering your questions, consider finding a new physician who better meets your needs.

Debbie always felt better knowing what the red flags were. "My pediatrician gave me one good rule of thumb. He said that for the first three months, if either of the babies developed even a low-grade fever, he wanted to see them. He and his nurse also gave me more specific information as I needed it when the kids had their first bouts with colds and intestinal viruses. His best advice was that if I didn't feel comfortable with how my kids were feeling during any illness, I should call and talk to his nurse. I used this advice often and many times this averted a visit to the office."

A discussion of childhood illnesses isn't complete without mentioning immunizations. During the first six months of a child's life, physicians recommend that the baby begin his initial series of immunizations for diphtheria, pertussis (whooping cough) and tetanus (the DPT injection), haemophilus influenzae (injection), hepatitis B (injection), and polio (oral). Others, such as the injection for measles, mumps and rubella (MMR) will be given at a later age.

Florien did lots of planning before taking her babies in for their immunizations. "First the nurse gave the oral polio while the boys were still happy and quiet. Then I sat down and held the baby to be immunized in a bear hug, facing my chest, with his arms folded up in front, and his legs hanging down on either side of my legs. I held him tightly so he couldn't wriggle or use his hands during the injection. The nurse squatted down, held his leg tightly, and gave one injection into his thigh. Then she'd go to his other thigh to give the other shot.

"Just before the shots I calmly told each baby of his impending pain and showed him the source, but I assured him that the pain only lasts a second and that the vaccine would make him strong. I then quickly comforted him. When the first baby calmed down, which usually only took a few minutes, that baby was held by a nurse or helper; and the process started all over with baby number two. It was really hard to be part of all this pain for them, but I knew I had to be strong for Max and Otto."

Some immunizations, particularly the pertussis part of the DPT shot, may have side effects such as fever and crankiness. The vast majority of side effects are minor and temporary, but it is wise to discuss your concerns with your doctor before the immunizations are due. He or she can then compare the risks of immunization with the risk and potential outcome of having one of these serious illnesses. In most cases, the risk of contracting one of these illnesses is far greater than the risk of a serious reaction to an immunization. For this reason most states have immunization requirements for children.

Most often, parents choose to immunize their children on the schedule recommended at their doctor's office. But the vaccines can be expensive if you have them given there. If limited finances are an issue, the most inexpensive place to get immunizations is the local health department. Some health departments only give immunizations on certain days of the week during specific hours; this can be an inconvenience, but the savings can make the effort worthwhile.

Parents eventually find their own ways to handle the children's health care, as did we. Our best advice is to find a health care provider that you trust, use him or her wisely, and make informed choices based on the best interests of your children.

*Diapers:* Trivial as the subject seems, diapers are a major concern for new parents, especially those faced with diapering two babies. Our individual decisions to use cloth diapers, disposable diapers, or a combination of both were shaped by many different factors.

Most parents of twins find that they need sixty to seventy diapers per week for each baby. This fact lured Sheri to the convenience of disposables, but the price tag was over twenty dollars per week. Economic and environmental concerns led Linda, Florien, and Debbie to use cloth diapers. They all used a diaper service that had weekly home pickup and delivery of clean, well-sanitized cotton diapers. Soiled diapers required no rinsing and were bagged inside deodorized containers, so there was no odor problem. The cost of diaper service was about thirteen dollars per week. Debra also used cloth diapers but lived outside the service's delivery area, so she bought and washed her own diapers. This took considerable time and energy but cost only eight dollars per week, plus her investment in eight dozen diapers.

*Pacifiers:*   We all used pacifiers to some degree and for different reasons. Sheri used them for a few months when her babies were small. "When my daughter Kallie was born, she didn't want to take a pacifier. Emmy happily sucked on a pacifier, and Tessa spit it out every time I gave her one. Then one day both babies were acting as though they were hungry, but would spit out my breast as soon as they got milk. I gave them the pacifiers and Emmy was immediately soothed. Tessa fought it at first, but I knew it was what she needed, too. I held and rocked her with the pacifier in her mouth. Initially she wailed, but eventually she caught on and was greatly comforted.

"I read that a baby's urge to suck reaches its peak around the fourth month. More and more, the babies were calmed and interested in playing with rattles and other toys. I also realized that the twins weren't emotionally attached to the pacifiers at this age, so weaning them away gradually wasn't necessary. After four months I just threw the pacifiers in the trash one day and they were gone!"

Debbie's twins had different ideas. "Michael didn't use a pacifier to fall asleep, but was immediately soothed by them. On the other hand, Joanna refused a pacifier because she preferred her thumb. Joanna continued to suck her thumb for several years, but at six months, Michael became more interested in toys and never missed his pacifier when it disappeared."

Debra used pacifiers for Aislynn and Ricky until they were almost a year old. Ricky seemed more willing to give it up than Aislynn, though. "My daughter had always been a little harder to comfort, and sucking seemed to be the one thing that calmed her down, so I weaned her from it more gradually."

*Bathing and Dressing:*   Dressing and bathing two babies is most efficient when done in assembly line fashion. It doesn't matter if you bathe and dress the babies one at a time, or bathe them together followed by dressing them together; just get a system in your head and stick to it. The more help you have, the more spots you can fill on the line. Be careful to keep your helpers on task; sometimes it's easier to do it yourself, if too many hands end up duplicating work. Bathing and dressing your babies can be a very special playtime if they go smoothly. If they don't, be prepared for utter chaos.

Debra tried to simplify the physical work involved in caring for Aislynn and Ricky in every way possible. "I only bathed them every few days, but washed their bottoms off under the bathroom sink or tub faucet after messy diapers; it took less time to wash and rinse the babies than it took to wash and rinse out wash cloths. It was also great for diaper rash prevention.

"At night, I dressed the twins in cotton gowns or kimonos, which made it much easier to change them. I also used lap cover pads underneath the babies to keep the crib sheets cleaner longer. This saved on laundry and changing time."

Like Debra and other new parents, Debbie's focus was also on economizing her time and energy. "My twins never really enjoyed their baths, so to reduce the stress for all of us, we gave them weekly baths in a plastic baby tub, though we washed their faces and bottoms daily. I rarely tried to bathe the babies on my own; I arranged a 'date' with Dale to help do the honors.

"After bathing, if the babies were headed for bed we dressed them in long, sleeping bag–type sleepers with pull-strings at the bottoms. That way the babies stayed warm and changing diapers was a snap. During the day, I dressed Michael and Joanna in stretchy, one-piece sleepers if we were staying at home. When we went out, I steered clear of cutesy or frilly outfits and chose practical, comfortable, wash-and-wear outfits for the babies *and* for myself."

*Enjoying Our Twins:* Before we knew it our babies moved from occasionally needing comfort to constantly wanting entertainment and social interaction. As our twins grew older, they smiled, cooed, rolled over, and reached for toys.

Florien learned that it's never too early to enjoy and play with your twins. "I sang silly, made-up songs and gently wiggled their arms and feet. As they grew, I continued to play with them and their toys, modeling how to use them."

By the time Debra's twins were four months old they had outgrown their infant seats, so she put them in walkers. "They quickly learned to scoot around. We got a kick out of watching them flit from side to side across a room, like little crabs. We also suspended a Johnny-jump-up in a doorway. They bounced like frogs, giggling the whole time."

Todd and Linda made a concerted effort to fit enjoyable family activities into their hectic schedule. "In the evenings we took walks, with the girls snuggled in their packs. Todd strapped both baby packs to his chest and walked through the neighborhood while my mother and I tried to keep up.

"A more relaxing recreation for us was gardening. I parked the babies' stroller in the shade while I pulled weeds and harvested vegetables. Sarah and Maiah were usually content to nap or to watch the trees blowing in the breeze."

Debbie and Dale took countless photographs and made many videotapes of Michael and Joanna. "Both photos and videotapes were anxiously awaited by our extended families, who were far away."

How you choose to interact with your twins will naturally depend on your particular circumstances, but try not to get so bogged down with baby care that you overlook opportunities to have fun with them. The latter happened to Debra and it's her biggest regret.

She related, "It's funny, when I look back at their baby pictures, my memories are so vague. They are smiling and laughing, but it is hard to remember. If I could do one thing differently, it would be to store away at least one happy memory every day."

*Caring for Ourselves:*   All five of us look back and have our own regrets about things we might have done differently when our twins were infants, but we all agree that we did the best that we could do at the time. The one thing we now realize is that taking good care of ourselves should have been a priority. Often we put our personal needs at the bottom of our to-do lists, and everyone around us suffered nearly as much as we did.

*Sleep Deprivation in Parents:*   Sleep deprivation is of major concern to the parents of newborn twins, because a serious lack of sleep can turn happy, optimistic parents into grouchy, depressed individuals. The most common advice is to sleep whenever the babies sleep, no matter what. This seems obvious, but sometimes babies won't sleep at the same time, and it's often hard to overcome the idea that by sleeping you're wasting the only free time you've got!

Florien often napped with her boys during the day, which left her house less than immaculate during those early months. "Instead of cleaning, Devin and I decided to focus our attention on caring for our sons. I found that if I didn't get at least five hours of sleep out of every twenty-four, my life was a blur and my tolerance level diminished markedly. Whenever I had a choice between napping and vacuuming, I napped. As the boys slept longer and required fewer feedings, I needed fewer naps and housework became more manageable. Then, to revitalize ourselves, Devin and I coped by getting out of the house individually for periods as short as half an hour."

In Debbie's case, "The early weeks with the babies' three-hour, round-the-clock feeding schedule were grueling. I didn't sleep more than one and a half to two hours at a time. To make matters worse, it was probably a month before I stopped having backaches and pain from the cesarean. Most of the time I felt like a wreck. My mind was mush and my body was weak. I couldn't finish sentences coherently and I had no energy.

"I was so tired that I even had difficulty keeping track of the babies' whereabouts. One time when Michael was particularly fussy, I put him in a large baby basket and placed him safely on the running dryer to calm him. I left him there for just a minute or two and came right back to fold some laundry. As I entered the utility room and saw the basket on the dryer, I remembered that Michael was in it. But for a moment I was confused as to who that baby was and how he got on my dryer! I began to wonder if I would ever feel normal or be clear-headed again."

Existing in a state of endless exhaustion is a reality for families with newborn multiples, and it can literally be overwhelming. Without realizing it, Debra was becoming seriously sleep deprived. "The good thing about nighttime was that it was quieter than daytime, and I didn't have to deal with anyone else's needs. But the constant fatigue took its toll. Sometimes I resented the babies for being the cause of my broken sleep. When I had those feelings at night, I didn't exactly pick them up with loving care, which made me feel even worse.

"As the days and nights blurred into each other, it seemed as if I were spending most of my time on the couch or in the rocking chair, trying to get both babies to nap at once so I could get some sleep. When I did have some spare time, I couldn't decide what to do with it: eat? pick up the clutter? take a shower? play with Muggy? do laundry? brush my hair? pay bills? I began feeling like a battery that was continuously draining, lacking the energy even to respond to the babies' smiles or to play with them."

Unknowingly, Debra was struggling with more than sleep deprivation. The feelings that she describes reveal several symptoms of postpartum depression.

*Postpartum Depression:*   After a woman has a baby, she usually experiences a variety of emotional mood swings. The ups and downs aren't fun, but they are quite normal. This period of roller-coaster emotions can last for up to three weeks, and is commonly referred to as "the baby blues." Soon, though, sleeping schedules and surging hormones settle down, at least for most of us. Unfortunately, for some it doesn't. Then you're dealing with postpartum depression.

Debra says: "It was much like drowning might be, trying to keep on top of everything and succeeding just long enough to take a few gulps of air before sinking again. Negative feelings began to pile up—helplessness, inadequacy, guilt, and resentment. My spirit felt withered, like the vegetables that withered in our garden because I couldn't find the time to gather them. All those wonderful experiences of snuggling, kissing, and laughing with my babies did occur, but sometimes it felt as though I were laughing on the outside, while crying on the inside.

"Many weeks passed in a blur, and they were full of awful feelings I had never experienced before. The anger, resentment, and subsequent guilt made me hate myself. I wondered what was wrong with me. The urge to "fly the coop" surged through me and it took all my self-control to keep from running away. As time went on, I had fewer and fewer enjoyable times with my babies. I knew it would be hard to raise twins, but to only occasionally enjoy them, to feel guilt over that, and to act like such a monster was like nothing I could have imagined.

"I knew this was unhealthy for my children; and I felt so ashamed. I isolated myself, not wanting others to know what was happening to me. When I had to go out in public, I was such a good actress that one of my friends said she would nominate me for mother of the year! How ironic!"

One in five mothers of multiples develops some degree of postpartum depression compared to only one in ten mothers of singletons. This discrepancy is likely due to the increased stress that mothers of multiples experience. Emotional and physical stress impairs the rebalancing of hormones that needs to occur after childbirth. Certain hormones provide a sense of well-being; when the levels are too low or absent, a woman can develop postpartum depression, ranging from mild to severe.

Unfortunately, many women like Debra do not recognize the depression and do not receive treatment for it. The self-blame, shame, and isolation further impair a woman's ability to seek out help. It also overrides the attachment and nurturing feelings a mother has toward her children, causing her to feel unworthy and to question her capacity to love and care for them. Not having the positive feelings for her babies that she expected may trigger a grief reaction. There may also be physical signs of stress such as chest pain and hyperventilation. If you think you have postpartum depression, talk to your physician or others who are educated on the subject. Although postpartum depression is painfully real, it is also quite treatable.

Postpartum depression affects every member of the family, so treatment that includes the mother and her close family members is the most effective. Without treatment, it took Debra a few years to work through her depression. It is an individual matter, so its severity and length will vary greatly.

Debra wishes she had identified and learned how to deal with the problem much sooner. "The most important thing to know is that postpartum depression is not your fault and that it is a treatable condition. Family members must be supportive and they may even have to assist the woman in getting treatment, if she cannot help herself. The worst thing that can happen is for a woman to feel totally alone in the struggle. Somehow, I managed to work through it, but it was a long painful journey."

## Our Thoughts and Reflections

SHERI:   Emmy and Tessa's six-month birthday was a huge milestone in their lives and ours. Looking back, I realized that the physical work involved in caring for our babies did not turn out to be the most stressful part of raising our twins. The challenge came in coping with the many changes in our lifestyle and the effect these changes had on our family.

LINDA:   By the end of the first six months with the girls, Todd and I felt like seasoned parents. We had learned the skills of parenting by applying common sense, with a lot of love and patience. Teamwork eased most of the fuss and hassles, and enabled us to bond as a family.

DEBBIE:   My attitude greatly strengthened my ability to cope in the first months after the twins were born. I had my spiritual beliefs, which were a great consolation; it also helped to keep life in perspective and remember that other ordinary women just like myself have raised, are raising, and will raise twins. Thankfully, the best days often followed the worst ones. I stored memories of those days in my mind and reflected on them with the certainty that there would be more. Lastly, I understood that those most demanding first months were just that, the first few months. There would be an end to sleepless nights, colicky babies, and frequent feeding schedules. I only had to endure.

FLORIEN:   There were two things that really helped us get through the first six months of Max and Otto's lives. The first was that Devin and I really made an effort to get as much rest as we could and to give each other short breaks, if and when it was possible. Secondly, we took the time and effort to learn our sons' signals. Parenting is not intrinsic, it is learned. As parents, we felt that it was our responsibility to take the time to learn how to parent our children if we wanted rewards from the job.

DEBRA:  Extracting the significant events from the blur of those first few months has been difficult for me, but it has enabled me to share the perspective of a survivor. Having twins has changed my life for the better and has fostered personal growth more than any other single event in my life to date, but I could not possibly have known it at the time. I've learned since that I had more choices than I allowed myself at that time; I could have asked for, even demanded, the help and support I needed to meet the needs of my family.

# Chapter 6

# "I just don't know how you do it"

## *Establishing*
## *Support*
## *Systems*

**W**e found that to do the best job we could of mothering our twins, we needed to develop effective and ongoing support systems. Our reactions to the casual remark, "I just don't know how you do it!" depended greatly on whether we tried to "do it" with or without support. There are many differences in the kind of support we each needed and eventually found. Take advantage of our hindsight, then begin to plan for and develop your own network of support, so you can "do it" too.

### *Why Support Is Vital*

Having adequate support was a major determining factor in how much we enjoyed the experience of mothering our twins. When they were infants, we first believed it was possible to handle everything by ourselves, but then reality set in and stress began to take its toll. The frequency and degree of stress each of us felt turned out to be directly related to the demands on our time and energy versus the amount of support available to us.

The demands came in many forms. Going through so many

changes, from pregnancy to twin parenthood, demanded a lot of our energy, especially emotionally. Other demands came from within and were characterized by the "I shoulds" that we heaped upon ourselves. These were the pressures to accomplish tasks, to act or feel certain ways, or to be successful in our efforts. Most of the time, however, our demands were external, and involved those things we felt we must do to care for our families, manage our households, or work outside the home. Over time we learned to minimize these demands as much as possible, which reduced our stress considerably.

Balancing out these demands with support, in the form of those people, things, activities, or beliefs that sustained, assisted, or strengthened us, helped. Some of our support systems were internal, based on our self-esteem, self-confidence, or spiritual beliefs; they were the "I cans," providing us with the inner strength we needed to keep going and, most importantly, to reach out for and accept help from others. External support came from relying on other people or taking time out for ourselves. We had to be able to say "I need" in order to build up good support systems to counterbalance the inevitable demands of parenthood.

Those of us who experienced very high or long-term stress will share firsthand the effect it had on us and our families. We eventually reduced it to manageable levels. To do this we had to change certain areas of our lives, develop an effective support network, or acquire professional help. If, during the pregnancy, we had built solid support networks to rely on after the twins were born, we might have prevented or minimized much of the stress we experienced.

## Support During Pregnancy

During a multiple pregnancy, many parents feel a great deal of stress and anxiety from all the changes, the medical implications, and the work needed to get ready for two (or more) babies. For the mother, growing the babies pushes her body to its physical limits, so taking good care of herself is just as important for her as it is for the babies. A healthy diet, mild exercise, and rest will help both parents cope better with the stress. Another way parents can support themselves is to find someone who they can talk to about their concerns and feelings and who will listen without making judgments or giving advice. Family members or friends, health or parent educators, medical care providers, spiritual advisors, support groups, counselors, and other parents of twins are possible sources of emotional support.

Sheri felt lucky to have found a special source of support during her pregnancy. "One of the best parts of my pregnancy came when I started attending biweekly support group meetings for mothers of twins. Seeing all those babies with their moms really helped me to visualize mothering twins. It also calmed many of my fears about the babies coming too early and not making it. I could see that the group members had a real bond and that they helped solve problems for each other that only other mothers of twins can solve."

Getting information and support during pregnancy like Sheri did can build inner courage if you have worries about how you will care for your twins. Most parents work through these and other worries without great difficulty. But feeling constantly overwhelmed, depressed, withdrawn, or highly anxious may signal stress that has grown beyond your ability to cope, and professional help may be warranted. Debra experienced this during her pregnancy, but was unaware that she needed help.

"I tried to deal with all my worries by myself because that was the way I had always functioned. I didn't talk to anyone about my thoughts and feelings because I felt no one would understand, and I was ashamed of the negative ones. Now I know that I was not the only woman pregnant with twins to be so upset about it or to be afraid for my future. I definitely should have had some help coping with the emotional issues."

## Planning Ahead During Pregnancy

Addressing emotional needs is just as important as the tangible preparations a family makes for multiple parenthood. Debra put thought and effort into things that could be taken care of before the twins arrived, to make certain areas of life easier. "In my house, meal preparation could be a big ordeal. So, once I was on bed rest, I took full advantage of the time and made lists, lists, and more lists. First I planned meals for six months, then made up a master grocery list. We stocked up on staples, paper goods, and frozen and canned foods. I got our financial records in order and revised our budget system."

Sheri found other ways to get organized before her twins were born. "In the early fall, I carpooled Kallie and several of her friends to preschool for extra days so that during the winter, when I was on bed rest during late pregnancy and caring for my newly born babies, I would have no carpool duties. Piles of mending, touch-ups of paint on the walls, oven cleaning, unruly closets, and haircuts for Kallie and me were all taken care of. By seven months along, we had the babies' room furnished and stocked with already washed and sorted baby clothes."

Preparations like these go hand in hand with planning for the outside help you will also need. There are many services you may wish to become familiar with should you need them later. Early in her pregnancy, Florien searched the community for resources that she felt would be of value to her family in the future.

"I called a Mothers of Twins club and a local parent education and support organization for information about having and raising twins. We also spoke to a hospital social worker about getting financial help if we incurred extraordinary medical bills from the birth or afterward. Knowing that we would eventually have a need for babysitters, I checked the phone directory for potential child care options or referral services. I really did my research and it paid off by reducing my worries after the babies were born."

The first few months of twin parenthood can be more rewarding if as many things as possible were taken care of before your babies arrive. Most importantly, think about who can provide ongoing help after the twins are born. Start with those who are closest to you—they are a crucial part of your support network.

## Getting Help from Others
· · · · · · · · · · · · · · · · · · · · · · · · · ·

*Husbands/Partners:*   Usually the first person that a mother of twins looks to for help is her partner or husband. For many couples, parenthood is a joint venture in which the responsibilities of caring for the household and children are mutually shared. Some families share all the necessary tasks and others designate certain ones to each partner. It doesn't matter how the details are worked out, just that they are talked about and agreed on. Being specific about what kind of help each person needs and wants increases cooperation. Making assumptions about each other's role can lead to unrealistic expectations and the building up of resentments, making good teamwork difficult. With two sets of twins, Linda and Todd had to develop a workable approach to caring for their children. Linda claims that Todd was, and still is, her best support person.

"Todd was a wonderful parent from the very beginning, and I feel lucky to have such a supportive partner. When I was having a particularly difficult time coping, I found Todd to be level headed. It was such a relief to have someone who understood what I was going through and who was always willing to listen. Todd assured me that I was doing a good job of mothering the twins, and his terrific sense of humor helped to ease my fears. On extremely stressful days, I would sometimes find cheerful, encouraging notes taped to the babies' cribs."

Debbie's husband, Dale, took a week's vacation from work after the twins were born, allowing him to be involved twenty-four hours a day. "Dale loved being with the babies; he looked forward to having his turn feeding or comforting them. He was an enthusiastic and understanding partner, equally sharing the other work in running the house or helping Chris with school-work. Even after he went back to work, he consistently returned home eager to meet the demands of our family. I don't know what I would have done without him. Sometimes I wondered if the wrong parent was staying home to raise the children!"

Many working fathers plan to take some time off after their

babies are born, although it is usually for a short period of time. Most likely this is due to financial considerations, but sometimes it is because men are expected to put their work first at all times. Although parental leave acts have been passed recently, most parents cannot take advantage of them. They provide little or no financial compensation, which is especially hard on families of multiples. The early months after childbirth are a formative period for the family, and if possible, an investment in time together will have long-term benefits for the children and parents.

Florien and Devin were fortunate to have a more flexible situation which allowed them nearly equal opportunity to parent their newborn twins. Devin worked part-time for the first six months after the boys were born. "Having Devin home to help as I recovered from my cesarean surgery and during those exhausting first months is probably the main reason I kept my sanity. Having two extra hands to help with diaper changes and feeding meant that I could have personal time for errands or breaks. It also gave each of us a chance to play with the babies individually. I think this was particularly important to Devin, for Otto and Max were able to establish a positive, reciprocal relationship with their father at an early age.

"I can't imagine how my life would be without Devin's emotional and physical support. Mutual love, respect, and concern do not come easily at all times, especially when you are exhausted, but require the dedication of both marriage partners. We had to develop new patterns of communication, learn to work as a team, and offer each other help when needed."

Sheri and Steve's relationship was also based on a solid partnership. "Steve is my partner in the truest sense of the word. As we drifted off to sleep he frequently whispered what a great job I was doing. Continually interested and involved in even the smallest decisions, his finest quality was that he was always right beside me caring for one of the babies. I didn't have to ask him for help, no matter what the chore. He gave my job his highest respect."

Working cooperatively and in a supportive manner may require some purposeful communication for many couples. Debra and Rick did not really talk about the kind of support they needed from each other, so there were many unspoken assumptions once the twins came. Debra has realized that this lack of communication contributed greatly to conflict in their relationship.

"We had already established a system of providing certain areas of family support. Rick held a time-consuming and stressful job that was our primary source of financial support; he was doing construction on our house, and took care of outdoor chores. That left the household tasks and care of the children to me. When the twins came along, I became overwhelmed and expected Rick to come to the rescue. He couldn't recognize that I was having problems and needed more support from him. He told me later that he thought I was handling things very well, as I always had, although he noticed I was more tired and grouchy. When he didn't read my signs of stress and jump in to help me, I strongly resented it.

"Eventually, we simply threw in the towel and gave up trying to work it out. There were far too many responsibilities for just two people, and neither one of us could get a break. We really needed help from other people."

*Relatives and Friends:* Relatives who live nearby and are able and willing to help can make a tremendous difference in how a family adjusts to twin parenthood in the early weeks. We were all fortunate in that our extended families were able to stay with us during at least part of this critical time. Some of us also had ongoing help from relatives far beyond the postpartum weeks, and a few benefitted from the continuous help of older children. Parents of twins who count on relatives for consistent help find that the contribution is immense. This is especially true for single parents.

You can also turn to friends for occasional aid. Although support from friends may be limited to specific types of help or shorter intervals, their roles in our lives were invaluable. Sheri admits she was incredibly lucky to have lots of family and friends around from the very beginning.

"Steve's and my parents all lived here in town, and because Steve's parents had long ago divorced and both remarried, we had three (count 'em, three) sets of willing and able grandparents nearby. There were also aunts and uncles, so we were never at a loss for help or babysitting. The first few weeks after the girls were born, Steve's and my mom took turns staying with me while Steve was out of town. Having all these relatives to offer help and to call upon throughout this period (and ever since) has given us the relief and freedom we need.

"Once life got a little more predictable with the babies on a four-hour feeding schedule, I would have my friends come by 'for a feeding.' That way, when Emmy and Tessa slept, I could have time to be alone. I loved having all these people around almost anytime I needed someone, but I also needed time to be by myself."

Because Sheri let her friends and family know specifically how she wanted help from them, everyone felt good about their participation. Many people who offer help are not always sure what they can do. It worked best for us when we suggested specific ways our assistants could help with the housework, meals, shopping, and caring for an older sibling or for the twins. Our most effective helpers were those people who were able to be supportive of our parenting choices and style, especially regarding issues of breast-feeding, responding to crying, and the need for holding babies. Sometimes we had to set limits with certain people, as unwelcome advice and undermining comments could undo otherwise well-meant kinds of support. On the other hand, support from our experienced, supportive parents made life much easier, especially for first-time parents like Linda and Florien. Linda's mother was able to stay with her for eight weeks after her first set of premature twins came home. Linda and Todd were grateful for the extra hands and emotional support she provided.

"My mom had the experience and we had the new-parent motivation. What a team we made! She advised us occasionally, but mostly did a lot of listening. I think between the three of us we experimented with all sorts of solutions to crying, feeding, and sleeping problems.

"After my mom left, my neighbors and friends occasionally filled in with household help, babysitting, and bringing in meals. Some of them, especially the ones with no children, came over just to hold one or both of the twins. That gave me a chance to take a break or get something done. Most importantly, my friends called often and asked how I was doing. They were sympathetic listeners and gave me tons of encouragement.

"In contrast, after the boys came home, my parenting experience was much more difficult. My mom needed to stay with my dad, who had recently experienced a stroke. My sister came a few weeks later and visited for two weeks. She and I talked out many of my feelings but there wasn't enough time to work it all out.

"The friends who had encouraged me after the girls were born seemed to vanish for one reason or another. I think some of them thought I was a pro at handling twins and did not need the help, while others might have been intimidated by the sheer magnitude of it all. A few were busy with expanding families of their own. I found myself feeling abandoned after the boys were born; I had not consciously realized the difference having emotional support could make when you come home to care for your new babies."

For Florien and Devin, coming home meant more than simply bringing Max and Otto to their new home. Since friends and relatives had just helped them move to a new duplex while Florien was in the hospital, it meant that there were still boxes to unpack and a house to be made comfortable to live in.

"When the boys and I arrived, most of the furniture was already in place, the cupboards and refrigerator were stocked, and vases of flowers were scattered throughout the house as a warm welcome. On our second day home, Devin's mother arrived. She stayed four days and assisted us in making the transition from hospital to home.

"After she left, my oldest sister Toni came for a week to help out. It was like having a best friend there, for she was a great listener and complimented me frequently on my mothering skills. Toward the end of her visit, my mom and dad arrived for an eight-day stay. They were thrilled to spend time with their newborn twin grandsons, especially my mom, who is a twin herself. I was sad when my parents had to leave; it didn't seem fair that they and all my brothers and sisters back home in Connecticut could not share the experience of having newborn twins in the family.

It also meant that I would have to find other sources of continued support.

"The friendships I developed and maintained during my six years in Eugene were a significant part of my support system after the babies were born. I could visit these friends at any time or ask them to come relieve me for an hour, so I could take a short walk or do a quick errand. They also checked in with me once in a while to see how I was doing."

Debbie and Dale also depended on a combination of family and friends for continuous support. After Michael and Joanna came home, Debbie's parents, who had arrived weeks earlier while Debbie was on bed rest, extended their visit to help her and Dale settle into their new responsibilities. "I thank God they decided to stay one more week while we adjusted to life at home with twins. Dale and I pretty much tended to the twins while my mother kept house, cooked meals, and watched over Chris, and my father brightened our spirits with his stories of the Wild West and music from the Big Band era. When the week ended, I didn't want them to go.

"However, we were not alone. Dale's sister, Pam, who lives in the same town as we do, called and visited often. Friends and neighbors came forward with offers to run errands, make meals, entertain Chris, babysit for us, and help me take the twins to doctor's appointments. During the early weeks, one particularly courageous friend watched the twins for eight hours on two separate occasions just so I could get some sleep. Dale's parents, who live in Hawaii, were unable to come visit, so they offered us financial support instead. We used the money to hire a housekeeper for several weeks."

All of Debra's relatives lived out of state, but her mom was able to stay with her for two weeks after the twins were born. "She was so helpful and nurturing. She took much of the burden of housework from me, often completing a task just as I was thinking about doing it. She anticipated my needs as well, and helped with the babies both day and night. I was just getting the hang of handling both babies at once when it came time for her to return home and back to her job.

"My mom offered to stay longer, hoping her employer would understand the necessity of her absence. I was worried that she was risking her job, so I convinced her I could manage, especially with my sister-in-law coming the following week. Letting her go was better for her than it was for me; it was the most painful parting I've ever experienced. I thought at the time that another few days wouldn't matter that much. It turned out to be like the difference between learning to swim in shallow versus deep water; I was just not ready to plunge into twenty-four-hour care of my twins. I still felt like I needed to be taken care of myself.

"The adult side of me also took over during the visit of my sister-in-law, Jeanne, and her two adult daughters. Because I knew that when they left, I'd really be on my own, I didn't allow them to help with the babies as much as they wanted to. However, they were great at cuddling and comforting Aislynn and Ricky as much as I let them. I really missed those extra arms once they went back home. It would be weeks before I would get a temporary household helper that I located after putting in a desperate call to a family social service agency."

*Volunteer and/or Hired Help:*    When help from family and friends is lacking or needs to be supplemented, expand your search to other resources. Start with your own neighborhood, looking for a preteen, teenager, older adult, or senior citizen who might enjoy an invitation to simply play with the babies while you rest or get something else done. Just by chance, when Sheri's girls were six months old, she happened across a ten-year-old girl who lived in their neighborhood and turned out to be a tremendous help to her.

"While I was weeding the lawn one summer day, a neighbor and her daughter came down the street to see the babies. The young girl knelt shyly next to the stroller, while her mother explained, 'Sara just loves babies.' Trying not to fall all over myself, I suggested that Sara was more than welcome to take the twins for a walk. She gladly accepted, and has been like another mother to them ever since. She runs errands with us and is my best babysitter."

Not everyone is so fortunate as to have a person like Sara walk right up and volunteer to help, but don't be afraid to ask through local churches, schools, senior centers, or social clubs. Look in your phone book under social service organizations. Check with community agencies or your local hospital for a list of organizations that may provide services or respite care to families for free or for a minimal charge. Debra found out about the home care service she used through a county agency.

"Having twins qualified us to use the service, but our income level required that we pay a portion of the cost. I decided we could afford it for a few weeks. As it turned out, the person they sent happened to live just five miles away from me. She came once a week for two hours, and it was nice to see the house clean all at once for a change. While she worked, we chatted; she had raised six children of her own and was very understanding and supportive. The last time she came, I let her hold the babies while I cleaned the house! I loved that arrangement, for what I really needed was a break from mothering. Regretfully, I had to discontinue her service after one month, but she said she would be willing to babysit on occasion. I took her up on that offer a few times but mostly, from that point, it was solo flying.

"Later I realized that resources do exist in rural areas, but they may be different from those in urban locales. Trust that some friends and neighbors will respond positively to requests for help. If I had posted a sign at the local store, gas station, or post office, perhaps just saying, 'Would you like to hold a baby or two?' it might have attracted favorable attention. Even phone contact with a crisis hotline could have broken through the isolation I felt so badly. I have learned that being truly self-reliant doesn't mean doing everything by yourself, it means doing whatever it takes to increase one's own well-being."

For some people, hiring someone may be the best solution to having help. While it may be difficult to rationalize the expense, understand that an investment in good support will be justified in the long run. It can minimize health care costs, and may even prevent the need for family counseling or therapy! In addition to contacting the sources already mentioned, you can look for hired help through ads for housekeepers, nannies, child care persons, or college students. Some large urban areas may have *doula* services, a postpartum care program. A *doula* (a Greek word meaning "to serve") comes into the home to care for a new family. Doulas do general housework, run errands, provide older child care, prepare meals, and assist with infant care. Longer term day or live-in help is also a possibility. Nannies care primarily for the children but some will also perform various household duties. An older adult or college student may be interested in doing household duties and child care in exchange for room and board. If none of these options is available to you, don't overlook resources in your community that may be able to fill the very important need for parents.

*Community Support:*    Emotional support for parents is harder to come by these days, as people move far away from their extended families, but it can be found in the form of parent support groups. These groups provide an opportunity to be with others who are dealing with similar issues and concerns. Directories, information and crisis phone lines, or community services often have listings of these kinds of services for parents. Types of parent support groups range from general groups for all parents to the specific groups for teen parents, single parents, parents of disabled children, parents of premature infants, and parents of multiples. We met through participation in support groups offered by a local organization, called Birth to Three. The program brings together parents who live near each other and who have babies close to the same age. Meetings include time for educational topics to promote good parenting skills and positive attitudes toward child rearing, as well as time for information sharing. Many groups work out additional social activities and child care exchanges. Florien joined a group two months after her boys were born.

"I found that most parents deal with similar basic issues as we all expressed our concerns and shared the techniques we each used to soothe and feed our babies, or to get them to sleep. Even with such practical support, I found that something was missing. I knew that the help I needed regarding how to manage and parent two infants at the same time would only come from other mothers of twins, so I approached Birth to Three about starting a group for parents of multiples.

"The first step we took was to contact the State Department of Vital Statistics for names of parents who had delivered twins during the previous year. We sent a letter announcing a first organizational meeting, and made follow-up phone calls. Six families attended that first meeting. Once the word got out, we had a large and dedicated group. Though I initiated the program, Debra and I cofacilitated the group for a while so all the responsibilities for getting the project off the ground would not fall on one person. We met every other week, with child care provided by the University of Oregon psychology department. (A professor there was doing a study on twin temperament and observed our children while we had our meetings in relative peace.) For me, to finally have contact with parents of multiples was (and still is) nothing less than a lifesaver.

"I have used the group not only for sharing practical parenting information, but for heartfelt emotional support, exchanging child care, handling emergencies, finding solutions to problems that other friends could not relate to, or that parenting books failed to address . . . the list goes on and on. Perhaps best of all, I have made friends through these groups that will last a lifetime!"

The rest of us were able to benefit from Florien's effort in forming the support group for parents of multiples. Debra's twins were one and a half years old when she started with the original group. "The group came along at a time when I was desperately needing support. The group sponsored workshops on stress management, self-esteem, and communication skills that really made a difference in my life. I could see that my family had some serious problems, which led me to get further help. These were the first steps down the road to major changes and recovery that continues to this day. The support group gave me the knowledge and courage to seek out professional help and to surround myself with additional supportive people."

Sheri had started coming to the support group during her pregnancy, so once her girls were born she made a point of continuing to come for the twice-monthly meetings. "They were my garrison through that first difficult winter when Emmy and Tessa's colic hung on for sixteen weeks. I learned to talk, eat, nurse, and change diapers simultaneously among others who were doing the same thing! Caring advice was just the fortification that I needed to keep going. An added bonus was that getting myself, Kallie, and the babies to the meetings taught me how to plan for other outings without fear of disaster. I could venture to the group, and if I forgot something or needed help I was among skillful allies. Best of all, though, was the group's commitment to Mom's Night Out. Once a month we met for dessert, or drinks, or hot tubbing—without the kids!"

Our groups are similar to other support groups for parents of multiples that can be found everywhere. Most communities have clubs for families with multiples that provide support, social activities, or clothing and equipment exchanges. If there is not one where you live, check the resources listed in the appendix for information on forming a group in your community. When attendance at a parent support group is not possible, seek out interaction with other parents in different places. The YMCA, La Leche League groups, library story times, or parks are a few possibilities. Some parents actually develop informal meetings from such contacts. Linda met two mothers of twins just this way while out walking with her girls in the stroller.

In this day and age it is wise to use caution when making friends this way, although our experience has been that parents of twins have a common bond, and will enjoy exchanging a funny story or a few words of encouragement when they meet. It never hurts to exchange a phone number; who knows, a long friendship may come of it. Even strangers can provide a boost to self-esteem. On occasion, when Todd was out of town for days on end, Linda sought out what she called "stranger support" when she felt the need for adult recognition of her hard work.

"To activate stranger support, I dressed the girls up in identical clothes, packed up the twin stroller, and headed for the mall. There I proudly walked the twins up and down in front of the windows, all in the pretext of shopping. Strangers would stop and talk to me about my beautiful babies and make comments about how proud I must be and how lucky I was. They marveled at my ability to handle the two of them at once. By the time I reached the end of the mall, my head was so full of compliments that I forgot my earlier despair. With all these pats on the back, I was ready to go home and face my situation alone again."

Sheri had a similar experience after spending a long day shopping with her children. "Already feeling overwhelmed, we were trying to leave the mall when chaos erupted. I was holding both babies, who were crying, of course, while Kallie pushed the stroller full of shopping bags. A couple of them spilled onto the floor, so I tried to tell Kallie how to reload them. A woman who had no packages and was heading out the same door offered to carry the bags for us. I smiled feebly and said, 'Thank you, that would be wonderful.' When we reached the car, a few twins questions later, she helped me load up."

"That day I learned to accept help when it was offered. Many times people had volunteered to open doors and carry bags, and my immediate response had always been, 'No thanks, I can get it.' I realized now that some assistance could make things much easier and that people sincerely like to help. It felt great to acknowledge that allowing others to help was another way of supporting myself."

*Supporting Yourself:* Just as important as getting support from those around you is finding ways to nurture yourself. Although most of the time the needs of the children must be put first, time should also be set aside for meeting yours. Florien had a good explanation of why this is so essential.

"Despite the support my husband, friends, and community offered me, I realized that I also needed to provide support for myself. When I had a bad day and nothing was going right, I pictured my body, mind, and soul as a tall glass full of water. Whenever I changed a diaper, dropped an egg on the floor, disagreed with Devin, or was late for an appointment, a sip of water was taken from my glass. Soon, unless more water was added to the glass as nourishment, it would be completely empty. I tried hard not to reach an 'empty' state, as that meant that I would have no more energy to give my children, my husband, or myself. Instead, I allowed myself a small amount of time each day to enjoy a cup of tea and relax, or perhaps call a long-neglected friend or one of my sisters to chat. It was very important to be good to myself in order to become revitalized. 'Refilling my glass' on a regular basis gave me the will to change yet another diaper, the energy to meet my children's needs, and the spontaneity to share in their play."

Linda had some favorite things she did for herself. "A daily two- to three-mile jog around a nearby trail relieved my tension and gave me time to think. It helped me to maintain my weight and get back into shape while being a refreshing break from motherhood. The exercise also served to balance out my alternate reward system—desserts! A truly stressful day earned a chocolate mousse brownie from a nearby bakery. I could walk there with both girls in their stroller. They usually fell asleep on the way so I could get through the checkout line and be home again in twenty minutes. Though I had to exercise even harder to work off the extra calories, it was worth it. Other ways I rewarded myself were arranging for child care so I could take myself out to lunch, go shopping or to the library, take piano lessons, or write in peace and quiet. Getting in the habit of making time for myself became even more critical after I had the boys. It has been harder to achieve, but I make it happen."

Sheri's insurance plan, to have friends come over only during the twins' waking hours, repeated dividends at other times of the day. "I didn't feel guilty about taking time for myself while the girls napped. Instead, I spent this time doing whatever I wanted to do, from crying over my favorite soap opera to pulling weeds in a remote corner of the yard. I could decide on the spur of a moment what I needed to do with my time, and didn't let other things nag at me to be done. Sometimes I even let housework become a refreshing break. I felt so scatterbrained and tired most of the time that concentrating on something not related to child care actually gave me energy."

It is important to find time for activities that are satisfying and nurturing. Women may especially have difficulty defining these kinds of personal needs and justifying the time and energy it takes to meet them because cultural messages have long emphasized putting the needs of the family first. This is one of those "I shoulds," that cause many women to neglect themselves, and some of us were guilty of that, too. Under the stress of caring for our families, we learned that not taking care of ourselves had a cost, both for us and for those we were caring for.

## When Stress Hits Overload

Even when you have supportive family and friends, the daily reality of caring for twins can be dotted with truly overwhelming moments. Despite feeling deep love and caring for their children, all parents will have times that they feel resentful, angry, or unable to cope. However, when these moments become a string of hours or days, or harmful thoughts become harmful actions, help is needed immediately and adjustments have to be made. Under stress, Debbie sometimes wondered if she might get out of control.

"When I was home alone with Michael and Joanna, things fell apart. Perhaps if my twins had not been premature and colicky, I might have handled everything better, but in those first few weeks they cried inconsolably for hours at a time, and I never had a free moment. I got so tired and frustrated trying to soothe them that I thought I would explode. I tried to cry, but I couldn't. Instead, the fatigue and frustration made me so distraught that I felt like I just wanted to grab one of them by the ankles and throw him or her against the wall. These were frightening impulses and I managed to control them. Still, when I felt this way, I too often picked them up roughly or held them tightly. I was entirely mortified that I, whom I considered to be mature and well-adjusted, could be capable of having these thoughts and feeling this way.

"After a few of these scary episodes, I realized that it was necessary to share my feelings with someone I trusted before I lost complete control of myself. For me, that person was my husband, Dale. Thankfully, he was the perfect listener, supportive, loving, and nonjudgmental. I'm not sure how I would have handled my shame and guilt if he had been accusatory and unforgiving.

"The first thing he did was reassure me that the alarming

thoughts and feelings I had were responses to the stress and exhaustion, not the result of being a bad mother. Once I understood this, I was able to remedy my situation. Dale and I agreed that at those times when Michael and Joanna continued to cry after I'd done all I could to comfort them, and I was growing anxious listening to their screams, I should leave the room and take a short break. We also decided that I should make a conscious effort to get out of the house with the babies once a day. Even a walk around the neighborhood would probably ease the feelings of isolation brought on by being housebound day after day. We also made a pact to hire a babysitter and go out together once or twice a month after the twins were taken off their heart and respiratory monitors. In addition, I discovered that an effective way of releasing my pent-up anger and anxiety was to get out of the view of the babies and pound my fists into pillows or couch cushions as I screamed and groaned in frustration.

"These measures did wonders for me. This is not to say that I didn't have any further episodes of feeling nearly out of control. These feelings did return from time to time on particularly rough days, but I knew I could restrain them and that was half the battle.

"The other half was to reduce the degree of tension I experienced on even the best days and decrease the frequency of the rough days. To do this, I realized that I needed to change some areas of my personality.

"The first change that I had to make was to ask for help when I needed it. I began to see that it benefitted no one, last of all me, to be a martyr-mother! In fact, saying 'please help me' when feeling overburdened, and saying 'yes, thank you' when sincere offers of assistance were presented to me, made me feel good and instilled in me the desire to help others in the future, just as I was being helped now.

"Next, I realized that I needed to set limits on how I used my rare and valuable free time; I had to learn to say no when it was in my best interest to do so. This included declining inconvenient phone calls and social visitors, as well as refusing to do volunteer activities that I had gladly done before the twins were born.

"I also gave myself personal rewards for a job well done. Sometimes it was a hot bath, or a candy bar, or a quiet moment at the end of the day. Other times it was meeting with other mothers of twins to talk about shared problems or to relax and just have fun. What I chose was not as important as being sure I did something for myself on a regular basis, something that rewarded me for being me."

The months following the birth of Keegan and Colin were very difficult for Linda, but not for obvious reasons. Understandably, she felt physically drained from her cesarean and the lack of sleep at first, but she was surprised to feel like, as she describes it, an "emotional wreck" for weeks beyond that.

"There was such a contrast between my feelings after the two births. After giving birth to Sarah and Maiah, I sailed smoothly through the postpartum period, but after the boys, I found myself wondering if I were going crazy. As I feverishly moved from one child to another, I felt disconnected from all of them. My temper was short with the girls and I was constantly yelling. I cried almost every day. At some point it dawned on me that I might have postpartum depression.

"As soon as I could, I went to the library and read everything I found on the subject. Once I had an explanation for what was happening to me, I started to feel better. I shared the information with Todd and voiced my feelings of not being ready to mother the boys. He was very understanding and also quite relieved to know what was bothering me. It took a few more weeks and some more crying before I came out completely from under my dark cloud of depression, but as the days passed, I could feel myself becoming whole again and the bond growing stronger between the boys and me.

"I also learned a valuable lesson. Ever since that time, I can immediately tell when I'm getting stressed out, which usually happens on the days that I can't get out of the house to jog or simply carve out a peaceful moment in the day for myself. I can no longer take it for granted that time will make things better. I have to make it happen."

Debbie and Linda were able to overcome their difficult times through personal and family support. When these same resources are lacking or unavailable, a much different scenario may ensue. This was the case for Debra. The intense fears and threatening feelings she had were actually warning signs that she had taken on too much without adequate support. At the time, she blamed herself.

"I got so down that it affected my ability to function. I would go without a shower or getting dressed for two or three days at a time. I remember one Saturday that I just sat in the rocking chair all day, holding my sweet babies, rocking and crying. I told Rick I didn't think I could handle it anymore. He asked me if I was going off the deep end on him. I said no, I just needed some help. No more was said but he must have thought I meant physical help, because he started to assist with more household tasks after our talk. I thought it was obvious that I meant more than that.

"Assuming that I couldn't count on help from him, I tried to call a crisis line. They gave me a few numbers for parents under stress. After dredging up the energy to dial the phone, my frustration was compounded when I was told that there was a waiting list and that priority also went to parents who had physically abused their children. I was referred to a counselor but we could not afford the hourly fee, and we had no insurance to cover the cost. I finally gave up. A sense of hopelessness and shame mixed with a new resolve to survive. This brought acceptance and resignation, which actually made me feel more in control. I knew then that it was up to me to make the situation better.

"The first thing I did was find more time for myself. This required a change in my decision to breast-feed exclusively. When the twins were nine months old, I started giving them a supplemental bottle so I could get away for longer breaks. I felt much better after doing this a few times and realized I should have done it much sooner.

"I think a large part of my anger was fear of losing my identity in motherhood. Once I had some free time, I had a strong desire to get in touch with other parts of myself again, to do things not related to mothering. With these positive experiences, I felt less guilt and we enjoyed each other more. These good feelings also motivated me to seek out more social support in the community.

About the time Aislynn and Ricky were fifteen months old, the parents of twins support group was formed. Now we had a place to go that was good for all of us.

"Another real turning point came through a stress management workshop that I attended. I discovered that what I still needed most was time for myself, for I had not made that a priority. This gave me the knowledge and strength to seek out professional help I could afford and to surround myself with other supportive people."

*Inner Support:* Whether overwhelming moments of twin parenthood are few and far between or a crushing constraint, the ability to survive them comes from inner support. You have to look inside yourself and draw upon as many sources as you can to face each challenge, one minute, one hour, one day at a time. In the most awful moments, look into your heart, for there you will find strength and wisdom you never knew you had.

Debbie relied heavily on spiritual strength. "I have always been an introspective and spiritual person, and thankfully, I was wise enough to see that I couldn't do my best if I neglected these spiritual needs. This is not to say that I attended church regularly; on the contrary, my church attendance dropped to an all-time low during the first year or two after Michael and Joanna were born. I did, however, keep my personal communication with God open and active. During the most challenging times, I prayed for and received inner strength. In quieter moments, I prayed for wisdom and perspective. I believe I received it as I considered people who might have much greater troubles than I did. Soon I realized that raising twins was not the most difficult challenge that I or any other parent could face in a lifetime. Because I knew that my connection to God would never fail me, I was capable of handling the responsibilities that were given to me. That is not to say that prayer and reflection made me the perfect mother. Rather, continuing to explore my spiritual side made me stronger and more capable of meeting the challenge of caring for twins."

Like everyone, Sheri had up and down moments while caring for her family, but a special attitude got her through them. "My natural optimism permitted me to look at the bright side of the picture. Sometimes things were so ridiculous it was actually funny. If I looked at my life like a situation comedy, I could always find something positive about it. I made having an attitude about having a good attitude a top priority, and it worked very well for me."

Through the toughest times, Debra kept telling herself that she was strong and capable, too. "On really trying days, I thought of my mother raising her nine children and my aunt who had two sets of twins, back to back. Both sides of my family came from strong and long-lived ancestry, and I constantly reminded myself that life would get easier as the twins got older. The best outcome of this experience is that by working through it, I have added to my inner support. I now know that when I struggle with a problem or challenge, it is trying to teach me something about myself. I know I can count on myself to reach out for what I need; I can get myself back into balance if I get overloaded; I can entertain a certain degree of stress, for it makes me feel creative and productive; and I can give compassion and understanding toward people, especially parents, as they struggle with their own troubles."

## Our Thoughts and Reflections

SHERI:   I have seen so many women feel guilty about taking a break or have heard other people call them selfish if they were not devoting every moment of their lives to their children or to their partner. It is so unfair to expect women to give so much and not take time for their own needs. I highly recommend getting in touch with yourself and your belief systems, then exposing yourself to books or seminars that can help you cultivate healthier attitudes. Since I have become aware of how good self-esteem and high motivation helped me have a happy experience of mothering my twins, it has empowered me to go even further with my other life goals.

LINDA:   At first I tried to get by on my own inner strength but that wore thin very quickly. Once I got over my resistance to asking other people for help, my life became a lot easier and more rewarding. At the time in my life when I'm doing the most for others, I have learned the importance of taking care of myself. Although my family will always be very important to me, I will also always strive to be true to *myself*.

DEBBIE:  Dale and I prepared well for the challenge of parenting our twins, and we worked very hard at trying to meet the needs of our children, perhaps too hard. We shouldered most of the burden ourselves. If I had it all to do over again, I would have hired a babysitter once a week so I could have had a few hours to spend any way I wanted. I would budget it in as a necessary expense, like medical care. It would have been better, I think, if I had not leaned so heavily on Dale for support. I think he would agree that we both should have rewarded ourselves more often for the tremendous effort we both put forth. After all, we were worth it.

FLORIEN:  Devin and I have encouraged each other to pursue personal interests and friendships, while maintaining a loving partnership. I think this is particularly beneficial to Max and Otto because, being identical, they have amazingly similar personalities. It provides an opportunity to observe their parents as individuals as well as a couple, thus fostering their own personal growth and uniqueness and their relationship as identical twins. In addition, they witness how we access various support networks, and don't rely solely on each other. It provides a model of how to "make it" successfully in a society that makes many demands and to utilize many forms of support.

DEBRA:  The hardest part for me in this whole experience has been to let go of the notion that I, and we, alone were solely responsible for everything that went sour in our family and our relationships after our twins were born. I attribute these feelings to the pioneer spirit that says 'Thou shalt strike out on your own and stand alone in the wilderness.' Well, I have done that, and I don't think it is a healthy way to raise a family. With respect for individual autonomy in today's culture, we must find a way to reestablish the benefits of living in extended family cultures, where children are raised in the context of parental and community support, and individuals are responsible both to themselves and to the group as a whole. In a society that is daily making more and more demands of parents and holding them accountable for the outcome of their child-rearing, there is an obligation to provide parents with the support they need to nurture the next generation.

Chapter 7

# "Oh, look, twins!"

## Out and
## About
## with
## Twins

Whether you travel across town or across the country with young twins, the experience can be exhausting. However, if you plan carefully and pack well, your outings can be not only bearable but enjoyable. We have discovered that, no matter who you are and how you live, there are some common *do*s and *don't*s when it comes to traveling with young twins.

Taking twins on outings of any kind requires a certain amount of ingenuity, planning, flexibility, and courage. It also requires a few trials and errors and emotional and physical adjustments as parents learn to handle and care for their twins under the watchful eyes of the public. Nonetheless, the five of us agree that the rewards are definitely worth all the effort.

Within this chapter lies our hard-earned wisdom; what we learned and what we wished we'd known before going out and about with twins. Apply our tips to your own situation, and you needn't repeat our misadventures. Instead, you and your twins can travel as seasoned veterans, basking in the attention of total strangers who will undoubtedly notice you and exclaim, "Oh, look, twins!"

## Taking That First Step Out the Door

A new mother of twins may be so overwhelmed by the idea of being alone with two babies in unfamiliar surroundings that she is hesitant to venture out of the safety and comfort of her home. Debbie remembers all too well: "During the first few months after Michael and Joanna were born, I focused on the effort it required to get out of the house and all the things that could go wrong. It may take a while to build up enough confidence to confront the outside world but once the first trip is taken, both you and the babies will enjoy and appreciate each new experience."

In order to become accustomed to going out, start slow; a walk around the block or a short walk to a friend or relative's house is fine. If you need an extra pair of hands the first few times out (until you gain confidence) take them. Your goal is to move at your own and the babies' pace. Nobody else can judge your comfort zone so if you're not ready to go somewhere or do something, then wait!

## Gearing Up

Practically speaking, the race starter's phrase, "Get ready, get set . . . go," is a good motto to remember when preparing for any outing with twins. The first step is to consider the gear you'll need for a particular activity. But before you rush out to buy every item you think you'll need for traveling comfort, there are several things to take into account. Will you be the only parent/caretaker with the babies or will you usually have another adult along? Backpacks are great for older babies, but they only carry one child per adult. A prime consideration may be cost. Buying all new equipment can be expensive, so, to save money, you may need to think about utilizing secondhand stores, garage sales, swap meets, and friends who can lend you equipment.

Bear in mind the physical surroundings you are likely to encounter while on outings and vacations. Do you like to camp, hike, bike, walk the beach, spend time in the city or at suburban malls? On walks, will you come upon gravel roads, narrow passageways, or elevators?

It is impossible to examine every factor involved in your life-style, but planning ahead will be well worth your effort. To help you search for the right supplies there are books dedicated to the single topic of equipment for infants and consumer guides that discuss the advantages and disadvantages of various models and functions of equipment. In addition, other mothers of twins are a valuable source of information about the kinds of baby gear that they found most useful.

*Twin Strollers*: A twin stroller is undoubtedly the most useful piece of equipment you can own for taking twins out and about. A stroller is not only a handy way to get to and enjoy your destination, but it is also a nice way to experience the great outdoors and reap the benefits of a good long walk. Once the babies experience the pleasure of strolling, they will look forward to their outings as much as you do.

These days, strollers come in a variety of styles and are designed to meet the many needs of both parents and babies. In the tandem one baby rides behind the other; in the umbrella-style the babies ride side by side; and in the limousine the babies sit facing each other.

In looking for a stroller that is quick and easy to set up and down, be sure it is also sturdy and comfortable enough to hold two *growing* children. A well-built, reliable twin stroller is not inexpensive, but it will save you the inevitable extra cost of having to replace a flimsy, poorly built one.

All five of us chose the limousine stroller because it was easy to collapse and maneuver through narrow doorways and crowded areas.

Debra mentions that, "It is important to look at the wheels. My stroller was great for city use, but the wheels got bent when I tried to use it at home in the country. That prevented me from getting outdoors for a walk."

When Florien traveled by plane, she used a borrowed side-by-side umbrella stroller. "I found that my limousine stroller was too large to fit in the plane's overhead compartment; while the side-by-side fit easily. This was especially important when we arrived in the airports and I needed to get around with two children between flights."

Having a single-seat umbrella stroller can also come in handy. Linda says, "Some days, I placed one baby in the single stroller and carried the other baby in a chest pack. On the return walk, I switched babies so the other one could enjoy the close body contact. This way, we got in some cuddling with our exercise."

*Baby Packs*:   The baby pack, although widely used in other countries only became popular in America in the sixties. The physical closeness between the baby and the adult provides a warm secure body position for the baby and encourages bonding. Not all people are comfortable wearing a pack and usually two people are necessary, each carrying one baby. When twins are very small, it is possible to wear one baby in front and one in back or use a double pack.

However, packs aren't for everyone. Florien attempted to use baby packs when she went on short outings but did not find them useful. "Devin would have one front pack and I'd have the other. It never worked for me because the baby I was carrying would try to nurse through my clothes and I'd start to leak milk all over myself. I was a mess!"

*Harnesses*:   Some parents use baby harnesses when their babies are older. Within our group only Florien tried them, and the result was less than favorable.

"A friend of mine suggested using harnesses. She had used them with her toddler-aged twins and found that it gave them the freedom to explore in close proximity to her.

"Unfortunately, they were not the answer to our problem. I had two active toddlers, trying to go off in two different directions while attached to me. My legs and arms couldn't be pulled that far! Eventually, one twin would drop to the ground in tears because he couldn't go where he wanted to go and I ended up carrying two kicking and crying boys to the car to go home. Our next method of dealing with the situation worked much better—

for a few months, I didn't take them out alone. I waited until they understood my directions for safety better first."

*Portable Cribs*: On a large scale, the benefits of portable cribs are fairly evident. No matter where you travel you will always have a "safe space" for the babies to play and sleep. However, they are fairly expensive if bought new. This might be a good item to borrow, buy secondhand, or rent as you need it.

An adaptation of the portable crib is the portable corral play yard, which has the advantage of being designed for outdoor use; it has no floor and can be set up into a variety of configurations. Linda used hers often, with both sets of twins. "Some days, we went no further than our own backyard, where I set up the play yard under the apple trees. The babies loved the grass and playing with our dog through the fence, while I relaxed knowing they were happy and safe."

*Hanging High Chairs*: The hanging high chairs are useful for meals at restaurants, outdoors (picnic tables), and at other people's homes when high chairs are not available. They are even nice to have at home as an alternative or low-cost, space-saving substitute for high chairs. Florien used them exclusively. "We had a fairly small home and decided that two high chairs would take up a lot of room so we used portable hanging chairs that hooked on to our table as soon as the boys were able to sit up well. This also allowed us to eat together as a family once they started eating finger foods and self-feeding."

*Infant Seats*: Infant seats are great for use at home as well as when you are out and about because they provide a convenient seat that easily sets on counters or on other surfaces. These curved seats offer gentle support for young babies; they can sit and watch the world, or catch a nap. Nowadays, some grocery stores have shopping carts already equipped with infant seats across the top; another type can be brought from home to place in the main basket. Most of us used our infant seats often; however, as an attempt to economize, Debbie never bought any. She simply bought sturdy lightweight car seats and used them as both car seats and infant seats.

*Car Seats*:   Car seats are required by law in most states, and it is important for parents to thoroughly research the available selections. There are a number of car seat models and designs available at a variety of costs. Car seats are handy for other modes of transportation besides automobiles, such as airplanes. Parents who cannot afford new car seats can rent them from many state and local service agencies. We do not recommend purchasing used car seats, unless you can determine that a particular seat meets current federal safety standards. All car seats are only effective if you use them and use them properly.

*Diaper Bags*:   Although the diaper bag may not be considered a piece of equipment, the five of us agree it was vital to our survival on outings. A few of us carried fully equipped diaper bags to keep in the stroller, while some chose to equip a bag to keep in their car. Debbie even had one diaper bag that she used for outings and another in the car just in case she forgot her regular diaper bag. Sheri had a similar strategy. "I made certain that the car was equipped with extra food, diapers, and clothing. Kept in the trunk, my small bag contained some Cheerios, extra baby sweatsuits, socks, diapers, and most importantly, a travel pack of baby wipes."

Florien's diaper bag had to have clothes and toys to last the entire time away, and still be able to fit onto the stroller. "Besides all the necessary things for Max and Otto, I made a snack for myself to keep my energy level up. I also brought two pacifiers in case they became hungry at the same time and needed something to suck on while waiting their turn to nurse. And, during the early months, when I had problems with my breasts leaking, I brought extra clothes for myself."

Debra, too, says, "I set up a changing station in the back of our station wagon and kept it stocked so I didn't have to pack a diaper bag for each trip." Linda added a book to her diaper bag supplies to read during quiet moments in the park while the babies napped.

## *Planning Short Outings*
· · · · · · · · · · · · · · · · · · · · · · ·

After a parent has purchased, borrowed, or rented the necessary equipment, the next step is to get organized. Both careful preparation and scheduling are important for a smooth outing. Debra remembers, "Since going to town entailed at least a four-hour trip, I supplied our car with that in mind. For us, the three things that enabled a smoothly running operation were our roomy station wagon, the twin stroller, and a feeding and changing area in the car. Other things that helped were not planning to arrive anywhere before 11:00 A.M. and frequenting places with drive-up windows."

Florien planned her trips around feeding schedules. "It took me approximately an hour to prepare to leave the house. Besides nursing each child just before we left, I had to change diapers and load a diaper bag."

All five of us found that short morning outings work best because everyone was well rested. Sheri agrees that the foundation for a happy trip was laid by having her twins on a fairly dependable sleeping and eating schedule. "When the babies were small, it sometimes seemed foolish to wake one just because the other had awakened, but it was the only way to keep their schedules in synch. Planning around Emmy and Tessa's routine was essential to successfully getting out of the house. After they woke up and were fed and happy, we'd head for the door."

In addition, understanding your twins and your own limitations are also important. Debbie says, "Despite my careful planning, not all our outings went well, especially in the early months. Many was the time that I dragged a crying and whining Michael or Joanna from shop to shop, finally being forced to cut the trip short. Even on the best days, I returned home emotionally and physically drained. I soon realized that I didn't have the energy to take my infant twins on long outings every day; instead, I alternated our days out with days at home, which kept us all happy."

Florien learned that sticking *too* rigidly to a schedule can also prove to be stressful. "There was one time that I really regretted taking the boys out. When they were five months old, I joined a water aerobics class and scheduled the boys for the child care provided by the facility. One morning, we arrived at the YMCA a few minutes before class only to find the parking lot full. I drove around the lot and neighborhood streets looking for a nearby place to park.

"Class started as I continued to search for a parking space, and I considered forgetting about the class for the day. Finally, I parked in a ten-minute parking zone in front of the building and ran inside, leaving the twins in my locked car. I was angry with myself for leaving them alone and angry at the YMCA for not having enough parking spaces for everyone. The staff members patiently listened as I ranted and raved; when I wound down, they calmly said there was nothing they could do about my problem. I ended up back home.

"It was obvious on reflection that I had put unrealistic expectations on myself that day. I learned that being a parent of young babies means that one does not always end up doing what one sets out to do. Risking the safety of my children and causing myself additional stress was not healthy or wise. 'Be flexible' became my motto."

One final way to make outings easier is to have another person go with you to help out. Sheri did this often when her twins were infants. "My mother gladly went anywhere with me and the girls. She came along on doctor visits, where the wait and the shots were uncomfortable for everyone, and on the most mundane grocery store junkets. She was an extra set of loving arms and hands that were indispensable to me."

*The Grocery Store*:   Short trips to the grocery store are one of the most frequent outings we make with our twins; food is the one item which will push a reluctant mother out the door, and out of necessity the babies are packed up to go along. The five of us have tried: pushing a grocery cart and pulling the twin stroller, using two grocery carts, putting both babies in carriers in one grocery cart, placing one baby in a chest pack and the other in the cart, or simply loading the groceries around the babies in the stroller. Each of these methods has a tendency to attract undue attention and requires a bit of effort to accomplish. Count

on spending twice the normal amount of time needed to shop—
people will stop to talk to you as you and your twins parade by.

Linda found a local grocery store that has free child-care for
children two to six years of age. "I'm sure I'm one of the few
mothers in town that has four children within this age range. Now
I leave all the kids and take a full unhurried ninety minutes to
shop."

Drive-up windows at quick markets are convenient for buying
bread and milk without the hassle of getting everyone out of the
car. Debra often frequented places with drive-up windows, both
for errands (banking, groceries) and for fast food. Sheri has another suggestion. "I used 'one-stop' stores that met all my needs
at one location. I discovered a little open-air mall a few blocks
from our home. Along with a large grocery store, it has a dry
cleaner, a shoe repair, a drug store, and a McDonald's. Even in
the winter, we could stop at a couple of stores per trip. The babies
loved to be outdoors for the few minutes between buildings, yet
we were sheltered from the weather."

*Dining Out*:   Although all of us have used the convenience
of drive-up restaurants, there are occasions where sit down dining
is preferred (or unavoidable). Our restaurant experiences have
been as varied as the restaurants themselves.

The best restaurant for children is one that has a playground
where parents can sit at a table close to the play area and eat while
watching their children happily playing. A pleasant formal dining
experience is harder to achieve, especially when the twins are
between one and two years old. Linda remembers, "When our
girls were infants, some of our first excursions were to restaurants.
We always arrived right after feeding the babies. Full and content,
they were usually happy to sit in their carriers and watch us eat
until they fell asleep. Sometimes this plan didn't work, and both
babies would fuss while we held them on our laps and tried to
eat. As the twins grew out of infancy our visits to more formal
restaurants ceased because it's nearly impossible to keep two 18-
month-olds happy and patient in a restaurant. When our twins
turned three and their table manners improved, restaurant dining
became a special treat for us all once again."

*Recreational Day Trips:* Recreational outings are a high priority to the five of us and the ones we enjoy most. Trips to playgrounds and parks, picnics, visiting wading pools or lakes, bicycle rides, and hikes are just a few of the adventures we have shared with our twins.

Debra found the nearby countryside a perfect place for her day trips. "When the walls closed in on me at home, I could take a break by going for a ride through the peaceful countryside. This always lifted my spirits and put things in perspective. Sometimes I'd pick Muggy up from preschool and we'd take the long way home so we could have an uninterrupted talk. During the summer, we all drove to a nearby lake that had a clean, grassy area to relax. I took along a small plastic swimming pool and filled it with lake water so I didn't have to worry about watching three little ones in deep water."

Even more adventurous outings, like sailing, moderately difficult hiking trips, and cross-country skiing are possible. Linda's fondest memory is a mountain hike involving the whole family: "Todd and I carried the boys in backpacks, and we held hands with four-year-old Sarah and Maiah. Together, we climbed a narrow trail to the top of a mountain lookout. Even our dog helped out by carrying his backpack full of diapers, snacks, and juice."

Visiting the playground is also a bit of a challenge; one person watching two active young children in a park situation can be overwhelming. However, small parks located on quiet streets or enclosed playgrounds with only one entrance and equipment scaled for toddlers and preschoolers are much less stressful for a mother. In larger parks, we found it more difficult to monitor our twins' activities as they ran to teeter-totters, high slides, and merry-go-rounds. A safety consideration for a parent looking for a suitable playground for children of any age is the ground surface. Sand, bark-o-mulch, or tiny round pebbles make a much softer and safer landing than concrete.

A nice alternative to the outdoor playground is a toddler gym or indoor playground. Sheri says, "In our area, a small group of women got together and opened a co-op indoor playground for children under five years of age. Yearly dues were used to purchase toddler riding toys and climbing equipment and to rent a

gymnasium. Each member signed up to open or close the playground twice a month; this involved getting the toys out of, or
putting them back into, their storage area at the appropriate times.
The inside playground was an ideal place for Emmy and Tessa to
run and play safely with kids their own age. In addition, there
was an area for all the parents to sit and talk, so a delightful
atmosphere of support and friendship developed."

*Other Possibilities*:    Finding places to go with twins does
require imagination. Indoor shopping malls where a mother and
her babies can stroll before shopping hours begin are wonderful
for exercise and diversion during adverse weather. Libraries are
also good places to go. Often they have toddler storytimes and
child-centered events scheduled as well as information about
other community activities. Local park and recreation departments sometimes offer "Mom and Toddler" classes along with a
variety of other preschool programs. If all else fails, do as Sheri
did: Ask other mothers. "I decided to muster my courage and
ask strangers with toddlers or preschoolers for tips; they were
always kind, helpful, and informative. A world of opportunities
opened when I swallowed my shyness and talked to other parents."
All five of us agree that isolation can lead to depression. Don't
sit home: Find out what's available in your area and go exploring,
twins and all.

*How To Get There*:    Although many parents will find the
easiest and fastest way to get to their destination is by car, other
means of transportation should not be overlooked. Of course, the
most obvious is walking, and we all did this often. For trips close
to home, walking with the twins in the stroller often saves wear
and tear on both the car and mom's nerves. In addition, the benefit
of fresh air and exercise often relieves a mother's stress when the
babies are fussy.

Public transportation—bus, train, or subway—is another alternative which can be exciting for the twins, especially when they
are older. During Oregon's rainy weather, Florien sometimes rode
around with her twins on the bus just to entertain them. Still
another way to travel is by bicycle. Linda used a two-child cart

that she pulled behind her bicycle for trips to the park. "The girls always became excited whenever I got our helmets out; they knew we were going on a bike ride. Some afternoons, I would pack a lunch and take them for a ride along the river." Otherwise, two attachable child bicycle seats can be used for older twins, if two adults make a trip.

*A Few More Tips:*    Linda found dressing her two sets of twins in brightly colored matching sweatshirts made keeping track of them at the park easier. Another tip is to carry a fanny pack when walking preschool-aged twins; your hands will be free to handle each twin's hand. Or better yet, buy little backpacks for each child and let them carry their own gear. They'll love it! Sheri found it important to always know where her house keys were. "Arriving at home with babies and shopping bags to juggle at the front door made me establish a rule: I always put my keys in the outside pocket of the diaper bag." Some of us found willing helpers when we asked neighbor girls to come along on short trips to watch the babies while we ran our errands.

By being prepared and giving some time to planning, you will discover what works best for you and your twins. Use our advice, if helpful, but it's most important to gain insight from your own trials and errors. Thank goodness, we all learn as we go.

*Going to the Doctor's Office:*    Most outings with twins will be fun and not too stressful; however, in the first few months and on a yearly basis afterwards, there will be the not-so-fun visits to the doctor's office. We've found it helpful to take reinforcements along. The twins' father, grandparent, a friend, or even a trusted babysitter can be of great assistance. Another possibility is to take one baby to the doctor at a time, thus allowing you to give undivided attention to each child. When scheduling your twins' doctor appointments, make them first thing in the morning or just after lunch, before the doctor has a chance to get behind schedule. Debbie found this method a sure way to avoid long waits at the office.

No matter how harried you feel, it is important to remain calm and relaxed so the babies feel reassured. In this way, doctor appointments will be treated as a normal part of life, not a dreaded experience.

## The L-o-n-g-e-r Overnight Trip

Having mastered shorter outings makes parents feel more at ease on longer ones. Debra talks about their first overnight trip: "Once I became confident and efficient taking routine trips, I planned our first extended recreational excursion. When the twins were a year old, we decided to take a family trip together to the Oregon coast. We stayed in a nice motel, the weather was fairly dry and warm, and we were able to explore the beach, pulling the twins behind in a large red wagon. It was easy and relaxing and we had a great time."

*Camping*: The five of us are fortunate to live in an area where there are many wonderful places to camp. Although camping with children brings a whole new meaning to the great outdoors, it can still be fun with a little versatility. Debbie, Linda, Florien, and Sheri all found ways to take their young twins on overnight camping trips.

When Debbie and Dale decided to take their family on a week-long trip, they found a creative solution to their camping plans. "Since I wasn't thrilled to camp with four-month-old twins, Dale proposed that we abandon tent camping for the convenience of camping in a recreational vehicle (RV). Not too surprisingly, I jumped at the chance to rent an RV with all the conveniences of home."

Both Sheri and Linda went on shorter weekend camping trips and chose to use tents. Their experience with "roughing it" with twins was varied; some trips were more enjoyable than others. A few helpful tips for tent camping: take a lot of extra clothes, snack food, and sunscreen for the babies; use portable cribs and corral play yards for sleeping and napping; and use hook-on high chairs for picnic table meals. Another point to remember is that the convenience of camping in a park where there is running water, bathrooms, and showers might make the difference between having an enjoyable time or a terrible experience.

Florien and Devin had a wonderful time in a rustic cabin when their boys were toddlers. "It was a nice balance of enjoying the outdoors by canoeing, hiking, and fishing while having a sheltered warm place to sleep in at night. Later, when the boys were three years old, we took them tent camping in a remote area. On that trip, our most useful item was a portable child's toilet seat. Devin dug a pit toilet and they could sit comfortably to go to the bathroom."

We readily admit that it takes lots of energy to be outdoors overnight with young infants. However, with a little extra planning, it can be a truly rewarding and wonderful experience.

*Car Trips*:   Car traveling with young twins will also take an extra amount of planning and scheduling. Debra remembers: "The first car trip I took with the twins was without my husband, Rick, when Aislynn and Ricky were one and a half years old. I made sure the car was in good working order and planned for emergencies by packing a tool set, flares, and a first-aid kit. I left at 6:00 P.M.; the kids fell asleep as I drove until 3:00 A.M. I stopped at a rest area to sleep, folding down the seats and covering them with a foam pad to make a comfortable bed for all of us. At dawn, I got up to drive until the kids awoke and were ready for breakfast. That left only two more hours of driving until our destination in California. For the next couple of weeks, we traveled around visiting friends and family, using this same type of traveling schedule. I brought the kids' own comforters and pillows for familiarity and some relaxation tapes to wind them down in the evenings from the excitement of the trip."

This driving-at-night-while-the-kids-sleep schedule is a common strategy. However, the major drawback to this schedule is that once the destination is reached, the kids are rested and ready to go while their parents are exhausted from driving. Debbie used a variation of this when their entire family drove cross-country when the twins were three years old. Every morning they got up at sunrise, stopping every few hours for meals and sightseeing. By suppertime, they were finished driving for the day. A nice leisurely evening and early bedtime for everyone kept fatigue at a minimum. Whatever plan you use, it is nice if there is support and help waiting when you arrive at your destination, so that everyone can rest and unwind.

*Air Travel*:  Because several of us have families far away, long distance airplane travel has been necessary to visit family and friends. Getting young children in and out of planes and airport terminals and entertaining them during flights presents a different set of challenges. Florien, Debbie, and Debra all made airplane trips while their twins were young.

Planning an airplane trip starts with the plane reservations. Getting inappropriate seating assignments or booking connections from one flight to another too closely at a busy airport are guaranteed to start a vacation on a bad note. Florien says, "When the boys were eighteen months old, we decided to take advantage of the federal airline regulation that allowed no-cost travel for children less than two years of age when they sat on their parents' laps. We wanted to visit my family on the East Coast for ten days over the Christmas holidays; in order to reserve seats, I began to make plans three months in advance. I planned to reserve the bulkhead seats located at the front of the economy section of the airplane. Since there are no seats directly in front of the bulkhead, there is extra room for young children to stand and play." This sort of seating arrangement is often best for parents with young children, but not always readily available. Airlines like to keep these seats open for persons who have disabilities and who need extra leg room. These bulkhead seats are often unbooked until the day of the flight, especially during the busy holiday season. Some travel agents will book these seats for parents with young children; however, it is stipulated that other seating arrangements will have to be made if a person with a disability is on that flight.

Another problem Debbie and Florien ran into while making their reservations was that parents holding twins on their laps cannot sit in adjoining seats because federal law requires that each passenger (including nonpaying infants) have at his or her immediate disposal an oxygen mask, in case of an emergency. Airplanes are designed with only one extra mask for each section of seats; more than one baby in a sectioned row of seats would necessitate another mask. The best possible seating arrangement is for the parents to sit across the aisle from each other while each holds a child.

Being aware of federal regulations and making the proper seating reservations can start an airplane trip off right. Debbie remembers wryly, "We weren't informed by the ticket agent of any rules. It wasn't until we boarded the plane and sat down that a flight attendant approached us and politely but firmly explained that Dale and I would have to move apart. Unfortunately, the plane was crowded and the seats adjacent to us were already taken. It took a bit of 'musical chairs' before we were seated across the aisle from each other. We were fortunate that the flight attendants and the other passengers were so accommodating."

Florien's troubles were even worse when Devin and she were separated by several rows during their airplane trip. "With one toy bag and one diaper bag between us, we were constantly up and down, switching seats and trying to hold sleeping babies on our laps while other passengers climbed over us on their way to the bathroom or just to stretch their legs."

When making airline reservations, remember to allow ample time (at least an hour) between connections. Extra time allows for unhurried plane transfers and also makes up for delays and guards against the possibility of missed flight connections. Debbie found that when she couldn't find direct nonstop flights it was best to avoid making connections at the hub airports, which are the busiest. At these airports, she often spent a long time sitting on the plane with her bored twins as they waited for clearance to land or take off. And, of course, these sorts of delays also increased anxiety and the chance of missing the next flight connection!

Once the reservations are made, the next step is deciding what to take on the flight. Debbie says: "I learned to carry onto the airplane those items which we couldn't or wouldn't live without, in case our luggage went east when we went west. Things that fell into this category were toiletries, medications, the twins' favorite stuffed animals, our camera, the contents of my purse (my empty purse was packed in a suitcase for convenience), and a change of clothing for everyone. A small backpack for our eldest son, Chris, was filled with his special books, toys, and treats, and Michael and Joanna's diaper bag was stocked with diapers, bibs, small unbreakable toys, books, and snacks that weren't messy and didn't require refrigeration.

"When Michael and Joanna were less than 25 pounds and still light enough for Dale or me to carry on our backs, we traveled with an infant backpack carrier and two umbrella strollers. We checked in one stroller, keeping the other with us. Having one twin in a stroller and the other in a backpack ensured that at least one of us would have both hands free to carry luggage. As Michael and Joanna grew heavier, we kept both umbrella strollers with us for use when we deplaned."

Although at times the other passengers seem like a captive audience to everything that goes on between the parents and twins, try to stay calm and relaxed. Many young children will be entertained for a short period by being in a new and exciting environment while others will simply fall asleep. Don't forget to give babies a pacifier or allow them to nurse or feed from a bottle on takeoff and landing to decompress their ears. The sucking motion will relieve ear pressure and will keep the babies from experiencing pain. Young children can be instructed to swallow several times or be given gum or food to chew.

The planning does not stop with the plane trip; considering which items are needed at the final destination is also very important. At the top of the list are secure places to sleep, high chairs, car seats, and toys to play with. Most of these can be borrowed from family and friends or rented on arrival. Debbie found that packing a lot of toys isn't always necessary. "It seemed that the kids rarely needed real toys to play with at Grandma and Grandpa's house. A deck of cards, a set of dominos to stack and build on, and a pile of poker chips to slip through a slit in the top of an empty coffee can, combined with Grandma and Grandpa's company, were good for hours of fun. This sort of spontaneous entertainment requires little planning and lots of ingenuity, and provides plenty of fun."

Parents are concerned about the safety of young children in a home which has not been babyproofed. Debbie found she needed to do a quick babyproofing of her parents' and her in-laws' homes whenever she visited them. "Soon after arriving, we politely explained our predicament to our parents; then, with their approval, we proceeded to put away breakable or dangerous objects and to cover the low electrical outlets. Of course, no amount of babyproofing can replace watching your children closely."

Even though a parent may spend considerable time preparing and planning, the experience can still be overwhelming. Florien remembers her Christmas trip: "Everyone was always busy, busy, busy. My parents' home was bustling with visitors and was filled with excitement, which made it difficult to relax completely and enjoy ourselves. And although the boys proved to be adaptable travelers, they were a bit overcome at times. All the new faces, the many Christmas treats, and the time changes made it impossible for us to establish a workable routine which Max and Otto, being only eighteen months of age, needed."

We all agree on the need to establish a routine when making extended trips to vacation or to visit family and friends. Parents who continue regular eating, napping, and sleeping schedules for their children along with consistent discipline rules from home will find traveling much easier. This isn't always easy to do, but it pays great dividends in the form of good behavior and good attitudes on the part of the children and appreciation on the part of other family members and friends.

## The Twins as Public Property

After taking your twins out in public just a few times you will realize that other people see your babies as public property. There are no strangers; everyone stops to talk, tell their own twin stories, ask questions, or just offer advice. People tend to whisper and stare whenever they see twins, especially little babies. Sometimes this kind of attention brings encouragement.

Other times the unsolicited stares and conversation may make you uncomfortable. Florien remembers, "Many times I must have looked foolish handling both babies, diaper bag, and all the equipment with just two hands. When people looked at us, I never knew if they were staring at the twins or my struggles. I finally decided that it did not matter what others thought; the boys and I needed and enjoyed our daily outings."

Linda also found it difficult to be around curious strangers. "At first, their curiosity was a novelty; we were proud to show off our babies and politely listen to personal stories about other twins. Before long, however, the many questions and comments became more annoying than gratifying. Now when I go out with our two set of twins I feel like a freak. Everyone wants to know my whole fertility history and all the statistics on having two sets of twins."

Our differing reactions to the attentions of well-meaning strangers probably reflected our own differences in personality, because by and large we found most people to be very understanding and more than willing to lend a hand to open doors, carry packages, and briefly calm crying babies.

Always remember that no matter how prepared you are there will always be occasional stressful situations when you are out with your twins. However, nothing will benefit you and your babies more than being flexible and remaining relaxed even during the worst of situations.

## Our Thoughts and Reflections

SHERI: Journeying out into the world was sometimes difficult, but for me it was definitely worthwhile. It kept me from feeling trapped inside our house and let me interact with people. I always came home tired, but with a clearer perspective on my life.

LINDA: All the insight and experience I gained by taking Maiah and Sarah out as infants has inspired me on many occasions to take both sets of my twins out. There have been many more happy outings than there have been not-so-pleasant ones. Nowadays, I'm often seen with all four in tow.

DEBBIE: A less compulsive woman would have left much of the trip planning and scheduling to chance. But I really believe that my meticulous preparations made our vacations more relaxing and much more enjoyable. As I reflect on the trips and the memories my family has shared, I am convinced that traveling with young twins is worth the effort it takes.

FLORIEN:   Because I took my sons everywhere I could since they were infants, they were accustomed to being out and about. They proved to be terrific travelers who were readily adaptable and open to adventures. They also had a good sense of acceptable public manners, so I didn't need to watch their every move. Because of their response to traveling, I never hesitate to introduce them to new experiences and places near or far.

DEBRA:   My system of scheduling long-distance car trips and shortening driving distance has worked well for me. I enjoy my trips with the kids to see friends and family and I can't wait for these visits to come about. I find myself scheming for the next trip as soon as the last one is over. Have determination, will travel!

# Chapter 8

# "You look like you need a break"

## *Locating Child Care*

We all struggled to find child care that best suited our twins. We found that locating quality child care for twins was more complicated than searching on behalf of one infant or child. "Double" children seemed to double the problems. First, we had to locate sitters and facilities that were able and willing to accommodate twins, then compare them and decide which fit *our* requirements.

There are so many questions to be considered that the search can be mind-boggling and stressful. We hope to provide you with some perspective, and perhaps a few answers, so when your best friend says, "You look as if you need a break," you will know where to get one.

### *Realizing You Need a Twin-Sitter*

At some point following the birth of our twins, we realized that we needed to find that special someone to "twin-sit" while we were absent for short periods from home. Although we knew we needed a breather, actually finding that person to relieve us wasn't always accomplished quickly.

Florien remembers: "Only I can be my children's mother. Yet, by the time the boys were six months old, I realized that in order for me to be at my personal best, I not only deserved, but needed, a break from parenting once in a while. Trying to find both the time and someone who has all the qualities Devin and I required in a child care provider proved to be challenging and frustrating."

Debra also knew she needed a break; however, building an addition to their house to accommodate the twins limited their budget, meaning she couldn't afford the luxury of the relief a baby-tender would bring. "In the first year after having twins, breaks from mothering were very few and far between, which contributed greatly to my high stress level. Within my family, work and school schedules and the frustration that ensued when the babies were hard to comfort made relief from others sporadic."

Linda and Debbie weren't comfortable leaving their premature infants on heart-respiratory monitors in the care of a baby-sitter. Debbie was able to take a needed respite in the early months. "I did not hire any baby-sitters until Michael and Joanna were four months old and off their heart monitors. These machines were too technical and intimidating for the average person to feel comfortable with. Until the twins outgrew their need for the monitors, I was fortunate to have two friends who were registered nurses; they watched the babies when I had an appointment or needed a brief break to maintain my sanity."

After her first set of twins was born, Linda waited to hire a sitter until they were six months old. When she finally did get her much-needed break, she made it a full-day affair. "Todd said, 'I found a baby-sitter for Saturday, dear.' Sarah and Maiah had recently gotten rid of their monitors, and Todd had been asking me to spend a day cross-country skiing. I had been putting him off. Of course, I wanted to go skiing, but until now, I had only left them for brief periods with my husband.

"He wouldn't listen to my protests, so I planned for our trip. I prepared what was needed for the babies, but never gave my own gear a second thought. Thank goodness, Todd remembered my skis! I quizzed the new baby-sitter mercilessly, and left explicit instructions for her to follow.

"I set out grimly. The beautiful Oregon wilderness eased some of my worry, so Todd and I had a good time skiing and enjoyed our picnic lunch. However, I was relieved when we headed home. Poor weather conditions made the trip down the mountains agonizingly slow. I clenched my teeth and silently watched my watch. We were late. An hour from home, we stopped at the first available phone and learned that the twins were fine, but due for their next feeding. I didn't need to be told; my breasts were full and leaking. Todd tried to cheer me up, but I wasn't in a good mood. Finally, we pulled into the driveway. I raced into the house before Todd had a chance to turn off the motor and was relieved to see our baby-sitter on the couch with a book on her lap and both babies sleeping peacefully beside her. That first babysitting experience convinced me the girls could manage without my constant mothering."

## The Occasional Babysitting Arrangement

Occasional baby-sitters can be family members, teenagers, or senior citizens. The easiest way to find this type of baby-sitter is to ask for recommendations from friends and neighbors with children. They themselves might offer to help occasionally, or perhaps they can suggest someone from their own list of helpers. We found that the very best sources are often parents whose children have outgrown the need for sitters, as they can pass their sitters on to you. However, some mothers do not have to look any further than their own family for child care.

*Asking Family Members to Babysit:*  Family members can be some of the most loving baby-sitters available; after all, they have a lot invested in the welfare of your children. Sheri had numerous relatives available to watch Kallie and the twins. "Steve's mother was our savior. She was always willing to stay at our house with the kids, and the other five grandparents were nearby for backup support. With all these grandparents and countless aunts and uncles, Kallie, Emmy, and Tessa were well taken care of."

Although family members are a wonderful baby-sitter resource, and they often volunteer their services, we must remember not to take them for granted and rely on them exclusively. Debra worried about this problem with her teenage son, Jason, so they compensated him in different ways. "When Rick and I asked Jason to babysit for occasional evenings out, we gave him support for his social activities and pocket money when he needed it. This helped Jason feel appreciated; at the same time, it gave Rick and me the comfort of knowing that the best person for the job was tending the kids."

*Hiring Teenagers:*    For many mothers, the very word *baby-sitter* means hiring a teenager. We found many willing and able persons in this adolescent group. While most of us hired teenage girls, an increasing number of young men are capable of and interested in babysitting jobs. High school counselors, church pastors, and community youth directors are helpful resources for getting responsible teenage help.

However, Sheri opted for a more direct approach. "I began a baby-sitter list by talking to the kids who walked by our house after school. After stopping the teenagers, I asked if they were interested in babysitting; if they weren't, I asked for the names of some of their friends who might be interested. Even the younger kids were helpful. Familiar with the baby-sitters in our area, they offered me tips on who they liked best and why. My method worked splendidly and the list of baby-sitters grew."

Florien found teenage sitters through an acquaintance at work. "One of the directors at work had two daughters who were already actively providing respite care for children with disabilities. They proved to be wonderful sitters. They were responsible, creative, and full of endless energy; they knew emergency first aid and managed our two active little boys without difficulty. Best of all, they loved Max and Otto dearly."

Although teenagers make wonderful baby-sitters, there are a few drawbacks to hiring them. Teenagers are more apt to be inexperienced and/or unavailable, and enjoy socializing on the phone with friends and watching television while babysitting. While we had no control over our sitters' availability, issues such as phone and television usage and social visitors could be eliminated by discussing them and setting clear and firm rules before we left the house.

Still, our overall impression is that teenagers can be excellent sitters for twins. Linda sums up her experience: "I suppose all parents are apprehensive about leaving their babies with a teenager. My concerns proved to be unfounded. Thankfully, my positive experiences with Sarah and Maiah's young sitters has made me more open-minded about hiring baby-sitters from all age groups."

*Hiring Senior Citizens:* Retired persons are often an underutilized source as baby-sitters. Debbie hired a retired lady who had raised four children of her own. "I found her through a local church that had a women's group. I liked the idea of having an older woman sit with our children; I appreciated that she had capably raised four children and also liked the idea that she had a grandmotherly interest in the twins. That seemed especially nice since my parents and in-laws live so far away. The only potential drawback to hiring an older person is that some do not have the stamina to keep up with active twins for hours at a time. So it is important that the prospective sitter is clear about the physical demands, especially if the babysitting job turns into more than an occasional hour."

## A Few Suggestions Regarding Twin-Sitters

Selecting a baby-sitter recommended by someone whose opinion you value may be a good choice. However, keep in mind that not all baby-sitters make good twin-sitters. Putting twins to sleep, feeding them, and comforting them requires extra work and special care. A brief interview before hiring is a good idea: Always ask questions that reflect your concerns about handling twins (e.g., both babies crying at once, dual feeding schedule), as well as your particular babysitting situation.

Once a tentative selection of a baby-sitter is made it is wise to introduce her to your twins before the babysitting date. The sitter's interaction with the twins is a good indicator of how well the sitter and the twins will relate to each other in your absence.

Once the final selection is made, it's time to orient your new sitter to your home and your twins' routines. On the first visit, it is a good idea to have her show up 15 to 30 minutes ahead of your scheduled departure time. You can spend this extra time familiarizing her with the house and your twins. If your twins are identical, make sure she can tell them apart. Dress them in different colors, and leave a note with their names matched to the colors they are wearing. Tell your sitter about any behavior characteristics unique to only one twin (Keegan always grabs toys away from Colin, for example), and discuss how you want her to handle any difficulties, disagreements, or misbehaviors that might arise while you're gone.

Leave the baby-sitter with the phone number(s) where you can be reached as well as emergency phone numbers. Be clear as to your rules about allowing other people in the house while you are gone. If someone you know will be stopping by in your absence, tell your sitter his or her name and give her a description. This pertains to phone calls as well. A few of us found it easiest to leave our answering machines on, thus freeing the baby-sitter of the responsibility of handling phone calls while tending the twins. If you are still concerned about leaving your twins in the care of one person, you may want to consider hiring two baby-sitters at the same time.

*Hiring Two Sitters:*  A common question parents ask themselves when arranging babysitting for twins is, "Should I hire two sitters at a time?" While most of us used only one sitter at a time, some parents do decide to use two. Sheri found that two sitters worked well for her when Emmy and Tessa were infants.

"If one of their grandmas was babysitting, I'd have our neighbor, Sara, come to help during mealtimes. Or, if Sara was coming for the day, I'd have her bring a friend. This was a great way to meet Sara's friends who also liked to babysit. Then if Sarah couldn't make it, I had alternatives. Another positive aspect of leaving two sitters was that one could also give Kallie some much-needed attention. Most nights, Steve and I mustered just enough strength to read her a bedtime story before dozing off ourselves. When we had two sitters, Kallie could always depend on one of them to make popcorn and play 'Candyland' with her in the evening after the twins were asleep."

## Permanent Child Care Arrangements

Long-term, reliable child care is needed when a mother returns to work, continues her education, or has other regular commitments that require extended periods of time away from home. Child care may be provided in or outside of the home and is often paid on a monthly basis. Child care options can be narrowed down by asking yourself a few questions about the type of care you want for your children. Do you want group or individual child care? Do you prefer the environment of a home or facility? What is your budget? If you chose to employ someone in your home, do you want a person who is willing to do housekeeping as well as childcare?

Like many mothers, some of us returned to our jobs during our twins' first year. Once we returned to work, all of us faced the important question of who would be our twins' child care provider. In some families this responsibility is given to a relative, usually a grandparent, who volunteers to babysit while the parents are working. Although this may be true for some mothers, all of us found ourselves looking for other sources of help.

*Taking Your Twins to Work with You:* For a brief time, Florien did without child care by taking her infant twins to work. This is not usually an option for most mothers; even when it is, many twin moms wouldn't find it feasible, but it worked for Florien for a short time.

"When the boys were three months old, I took them to my recreation job, where I worked ten hours a week. I was pleasantly surprised to discover that the boys were welcome at my office. How lucky I was to have an understanding supervisor!

"I took the twins with me for two months. At first there were no problems. The boys needed feeding and an occasional diaper change, but they slept most of the time. Everything went well for a few weeks. My supervisors were pleased with my work and the office staff wasn't bothered by the babies' presence.

"However, as Otto and Max got older, I often had to put in extra hours to accomplish what should have taken me half the time. Their feedings became more frequent and longer as they began eating solid foods. They became squirmy, wriggling eels when I tried to change them, and required more and more time for interactive play. Since I wanted to play, too, I got even less work done. I soon realized I needed to find other help."

*Selecting a Person for Permanent Care:* One good source for finding regular child care is the newspaper classified ads; you may choose to answer an ad or place one of your own so you can lay out your specific needs and requirements. Another is community agencies, which may also provide referral services of certified child care providers in your area.

Interviewing a permanent sitter usually requires a longer process than the brief discussion used when choosing an occasional baby-sitter. In Debbie's household, she had the job of interviewing potential sitters; then she discussed her opinions and reactions with Dale. Their decision was mutual and had the benefit of being based on both subjective and objective views.

During the interview, it is always a good idea to ask for several references. Be sure and check out all former employers, and ask the other people they have worked for if they have been satisfied with the baby-sitter's job.

Once a baby-sitter is chosen, it is wise to agree on a brief trial period of employment. Debbie explains, "I always had a few trial visits for a new sitter. During this time, either the sitter or I was free to discontinue the relationship for any reason if we felt it wasn't working. If your selection process has been a thorough one, this probably won't be necessary, but it's a nice fallback situation for everyone involved."

*Familiarizing Your Permanent Sitter with Your Home:* Acquainting a new regular sitter with your home should be thorough and complete. Debbie describes her procedure. "At the initial visit, I oriented our new sitter to our home and discussed each of the children's likes and dislikes. I showed her where the first aid supplies were and pointed out the locations of our phones, labeled with our address and posted with emergency phone numbers. I had them learn which areas of the house were entirely childproof and which areas were absolutely off-limits to the children. I also explained to them our discipline procedures. When the time finally came for the sitter to watch the children, I felt confident that things would go well."

Although each of us followed similar routines with our new sitters, Debbie took her routine a step further when she requested that as a condition to employment the sitter take a course in infant/child cardiopulmonary resuscitation and antichoking techniques, which Debbie paid for. When her twins were infants Debbie also asked her sitter to keep an informal diary each day of what her children ate, when they slept, and when they had their diaper change.

"When I came home in the evening, all I had to do was look at the daily diary to know immediately what sort of day the children had. This made it much easier to plan and prepare for a good evening together. This confirmed my belief that in-home child care was best for our family."

*Child Care in Your Home:* The one advantage to having a person come into your home is that it provides a stable routine and familiar environment for your twins. Sometimes this type of child care is hard to arrange, but with a little persistence a suitable person can be found.

Florien found her in-home child care by a common method, word of mouth. "When the boys were eight months, I put an advertisement in the paper for child care help for ten to fifteen hours a week. To my dismay, only four women called, and I could tell very quickly over the phone that none of them would be capable of providing the care Devin and I desired for Otto and Max.

"In the middle of trying to locate a permanent sitter, a unique job opportunity arose; I was asked to be a group leader for a four-week educational exchange to England. Finally, another mother who I met in our twins group mentioned a local baby-sitting service. The sitter service was bonded and insured, and their employees were experienced child care providers. However, there were a few drawbacks: The service was more expensive than the usual baby-sitter and we would also have to pay for mileage.

"I requested the two sitters from the babysitting service that my friend had recommended, a mother and her daughter. It was important to us that the boys have consistency while I was gone, and we were unwilling to trust their care to several different and unknown people. We also decided that hiring two sitters would provide a backup when one couldn't make it, and would allow each of them necessary time off. The sitter service was reluctant to provide these women exclusively, but I was adamant. They finally agreed and we hired the women one month prior to my departure. Hiring the sitters early allowed everyone involved the opportunity to get to know one another and to become comfortable with the arrangement. This also allowed me to have some unrushed time to prepare for the trip and gave me the chance to demonstrate the parenting style we desired during my absence. All this preparation enabled me to leave home with a light heart, and things worked out splendidly."

Initially, Debbie also had trouble finding a person to come into her home when she returned to work part-time following her six-month maternity leave. "When the babies were two months old, I began my search. I told everyone I knew and trusted that I needed a sitter to come to our home while I worked Friday and every other Saturday.

"My older son Chris had gone to day-care facilities and had done well there; however, I still had memories of the early morning hustle and bustle as I tried to get him and all his toddler paraphernalia to the day-care center on time. I inevitably arrived at work feeling rushed and out of sorts. I didn't want to go that route again.

"After two months of searching, the only suitable person I had found was a college student who was studying to become a registered nanny. She was perfect, but she was only available on Saturdays. Fortunately, I had a flexible job-share partner who also is a good friend; I was able to work out a schedule where I worked every Saturday. I immediately hired the nanny-student to work for me on those Saturday mornings when Dale and I worked. This worked well for six months. Then I found a mother who agreed to babysit my kids provided she could bring her own young children with her to our house."

## When a Baby-sitter Brings Her Own Children

Sometimes the person most capable of watching twins is a woman with young children of her own, who needs to bring them with her when she babysits. The outcome of this type of baby-sitting situation depends on the mother involved and whether she is comfortable having other children in her home. This type of child care has two possible drawbacks. One is that the mother will devote all her attention and care to her own child, neglecting her responsibility to you and your twins. This is especially true when your twins are infants and will need one person's undivided attention. Another is the matter of discipline—if her methods differ from yours, clearly problems may develop. Be sure she knows your house rules and how you want your children disciplined, so she can be consistent if the children are involved in a ruckus.

Debbie shares her experience: "At first, it concerned me that the baby-sitter would need to bring her children (daughters aged five and two) with her when she came to our house to watch the twins and Chris. But I decided to give her a few trial visits. To my surprise, everything went well. This situation worked because her girls were quiet and well-behaved, and the twins, at twelve months, were just old enough to truly enjoy their company. Chris, who was nine by then, felt he was too grown up to play with 'babies and little girls.' He had many friends his age in the neighborhood and just wanted a sitter who would be kind and fair to him after he got home from school. She was wonderful, and treated all the children equally."

## *In-Home Child Care in the Caregiver's Home*
. . . . . . . . . . . . . . . . . . . . . . .

Child care provided in the caregiver's home is often one of the most affordable babysitting alternatives. Some in-home providers are licensed by the state and meet certain standards of care, but others are not, so you must carefully scrutinize each home and caregiver.

When Linda returned to work part-time she found a woman to take care of thirteen-month-old Sarah and Maiah. "Finding a good permanent day-care situation was an immediate priority. Finally, through our church bulletin, I found a woman who was tending three children in her home. She was able to give Sarah and Maiah the individual attention they needed to help them adjust to my returning to work."

A benefit of having child care away from your home is that you can schedule some time to be home alone while your twins are gone. Linda enjoyed taking her lunch break in the quiet of her own home. "I loved to come home for a peaceful leisurely lunch before I went to pick up Sarah and Maiah. It gave me a chance to wind down before seeing them. I also appreciated that when I got home from work the house was the same as I left it, not in a huge mess from the twins being at home all morning."

Although in-home child care has many advantages, not everyone will wish to or be able to use this type of care. As the need for child care has grown, day-care centers have sprung up all around the country.

## *Day-Care Centers*
. . . . . . . . . . . . . . . . . .

Day-care facilities are a first choice of many working parents as they offer predictable hours and reliable staff, but they do vary greatly in cost, availability, child-adult ratio, and quality of care. Some do not take infants, while others specialize in caring for babies. Some allow flexible drop-in or part-time hours, while others have fixed full-time attendance requirements. They also differ in the source of their funding, either private or public, which affects the cost. When evaluating day-care centers, be sure to determine that they are licensed and inspected: Inspections and audits of a licensed center cover areas such as health, safety, and financial responsibility. A facility will be more likely to maintain high standards when subject to such scrutiny.

Because many factors need to be taken into consideration, it is a good idea to have a clear picture of the sort of day-care situation you are looking for. Then when you are ready to begin your search ask for personal recommendations from family, friends, and neighbors.

If you don't get any firsthand referrals then you'll have to use other sources. The telephone book has a listing for centers, and some grocery store or community message boards list neighborhood availabilities. Before you visit a center, call and ask questions to find out everything you can about the facility, director, and the staff. Then do an on-site evaluation and a thorough check of references.

When you visit a day-care center consider dropping in unannounced, instead of making an appointment. Linda explains: "When I first started looking for a center, I decided to just drop in to visit instead of calling for an appointment. I realized if I called ahead the directors would want me to visit during nap time, when all was quiet. This wouldn't give me a fair idea of how things were actually run. I wanted to observe the facility when they weren't prepared to greet me, so I chose to stop by during more hectic times. In this way, I was able to get a feel of the overall atmosphere and how the staff handled the stress of commotion."

After you arrive at the day-care facility, be alert to your initial impression of the atmosphere, as it will give you a good indication of whether or not the staff enjoy their work and care about the children. Are the children happily playing or isolated and quiet? Is the general mood cheerful and relaxed? Is the staff patient when dealing with the children? And if, like Linda, you dropped in, was the staff comfortable with an unannounced visitor? If you yourself aren't comfortable, you can be sure your twins won't thrive in that atmosphere.

The environment should be clean and safe and have adequate space for children to play safely inside and outdoors. Are there toys, equipment, and activities geared toward the different stages of child development? Is the equipment in good repair and sturdy enough for active children?

Ask the day-care director about their health precautions. What do they do to limit the spread of infectious diseases? Can children come to the center with a minor illness? Do the staff and children wash their hands after using the bathroom (or diaper changes) and before handling foods? Are there routine sanitization procedures? Is the staff trained in first aid?

Staff-parent interaction is also an important element in every day-care facility. The initial interview is a good place to address your concerns and it serves as a good barometer of the center's receptiveness to parent input. In good day-care centers, there is an open line of communication between parents and staff. As a mother of twins you may have additional questions to ask. Is the staff receptive to the idea that twins are individuals, but also aware that they have a unique relationship with their twin siblings?

Florien tells how she located a day-care center for Max and Otto. "When I returned to graduate school part-time, I needed a facility with flexible hours to accommodate my changing class schedule. I discovered the university had its own facility, staffed with experienced teachers and early childhood education students. After visiting the facility, I decided to enroll the boys for several reasons. Not only did the staff and environment meet all my expectations, but I liked the idea of having the boys close by. I could drop them off before class, but I was also near if one of them became ill or even if I just wanted to drop in and check on them. Besides, they gave a second child discount, thus making the cost fall within our budget."

Debbie, on the other hand, did a thorough investigation and finally decided that the disadvantages outweighed the advantages of using a day-care center. "I learned that it would be expensive to have both Michael and Joanna in day-care at the same time and I would still have to find and pay a sitter for their older brother, Chris, after school. After I figured out the actual costs and considered the inconvenience of transporting infant twins to day-care, I decided I could hire someone to come to my home for about the same cost, maybe even less. In addition, I would have the benefits of keeping Michael and Joanna at home."

## Live-In Help/Nannies

Live-in help is another option when you have extra living space and need long-term child care. Certified nannies generally provide a high standard of care, but are the most expensive type of live-in help. Some parents of twins choose to hire older adults or college students who are interested in exchanging live-in help for room and board. Nannies can be located through a nanny service or other employment agencies, while students can be found through university newspaper ads or a campus job information office. When choosing who will provide your live-in assistance, the process will go more quickly and easily if you know exactly what type of person you want and are clear as to your babysitting needs. If you hire students, keep in mind that schedules will change from term to term and that they will want to move on once their education is complete. If you need help at set hours during the day or want someone who is more likely to make a longer-term commitment, then perhaps a student isn't right for your situation.

Although locating a person who is willing to give live-in child-care can be time-consuming, *do not rush the process!* Finding a quality person who is congenial to your home life is an absolute necessity.

Linda and Todd chose to hire a college student to live in when they had their second set of twins. "Right before I found out I was pregnant with twins for the second time, Todd received a promotion to a higher management position. His new job required that he fly out of town on Monday mornings and return home on Thursday evenings. With the discovery of my twin pregnancy, I panicked, thinking about all those evenings alone with infant and three-year-old twins. We agreed to find someone who could provide constant care. At first, we considered a nanny but found that to be too expensive. Next, we searched for a college student, for we were fortunate to have a spare room over our garage and to live only two miles from a university. A female student moved in during the last part of my pregnancy and exchanged some child care hours for room and board. This met all our needs and I especially liked knowing she was there for me during the night, if an emergency arose."

## Other Child Care Possibilities

*Hiring Mother's Helpers:*  Preteenagers can be a great help watching the twins when you remain at home busy with other duties. These children may be too young to be left alone with twin babies, but their presence can provide much-needed relief. Their enthusiasm and energy often make up for what they lack in experience.

Sheri frequently hired young sitters. "The nine-to-eleven-year-old kids really enjoyed getting down on the floor to play with my twins and their toys. At first, I had them babysit while I was at home cleaning house or cooking dinner. I could hear them with the twins and they could help me at changing and feeding times. After they and the twins were older, I left them at home alone with the twins, feeling confident in their babysitting abilities because I trained them myself."

*Co-Op Babysitting and Exchanging Care with Friends:* In some instances, exchanging child care with friends on an individual basis or in a group situation can work well when child care needs are occasional. Linda exchanged care with another mother of two children. "This always worked out nicely when everyone was gone and I enjoyed the peace and quiet of my home. But I always had to keep in mind that when it was my time to reciprocate I ended up watching six kids. After spending the day with six children, I really appreciated just having four of my own!"

Yet Florien found that exchanging child care worked well for her family and regularly exchanged care with another family with twins for almost four years. "I had originally asked my friends with singletons if they wanted to trade child care. Not one of them took me up on the offer. They found the prospect of caring for three babies or toddlers overwhelming. They could 'maybe' manage two children of similar ages, but they weren't interested in trying to coordinate three children who needed diaper changes and feedings.

"Through my twins support group, I discovered another family with twins one month younger than Max and Otto that was interested in such an arrangement. They also had a son who was two years older than our twins, but it still worked out fine for both families. The other mom and I were able to relax and run errands while the children were being cared for by a competent friend, and the boys made wonderful playmates.

"I think the reason it worked so well is that we treated it like a job during the hours we had the other children in our home. We devoted all the time to playing and caring for the children, knowing that we could accomplish nothing else. We kept to our feeding, diapering, and nap routines in order to keep everything manageable and even found time to paint murals on the garage, go to parks, and dress up as superheroes. I also felt it went well because we knew how to manage small groups of children, just by the fact the we had twins to begin with."

Debra exchanged child care with a group of neighbors. "Right before Aislynn and Ricky turned three years old, I linked up with a network of people willing to do part-time child care." Although Debra didn't have to start her own group, this is always something that can be accomplished through mothers of twins groups.


*Sitters Who Stay Overnight:* Finding someone to watch your twins when you are gone overnight can be an intimidating task. However, it can be accomplished by following the same guidelines used in selecting any other type of child care, with a few added precautions. The sitter will need to be comfortable dealing with the discipline, feeding, and sleeping problems likely to crop up in a twenty-four-hour or longer period of time. Go over your procedures in detail with your baby-sitter until you are satisfied she understands them clearly. It is also wise to let neighbors, family, or friends know you will be gone, so they can look in on your children or phone your baby-sitter to see how things are going.

When Todd and Linda left town on vacation, Linda made an extra effort to make sure everything ran smoothly in their absence. "When our twins were young, Todd and I were able to schedule a few trips away from town. We were fortunate that my parents or Todd's parents stayed with the twins. The familiar faces and surroundings made it easier for the children. We always left a signed, notarized letter giving our parents full authority to act in case of a medical emergency and gave a similar letter to our pediatrician giving him the right to treat the children. Before we left, I made sure the laundry was done, meals were prepared ahead, and instructions were taped on the fridge specifying feeding, napping, and nighttime schedules. It seemed that the preparations for our trips took as long as the trip lasted."

## A Last Word for the Children

Throughout this chapter, we have given our advice and shared our perspective on what was important to us as we found child care for our twins. However, when making child care decisions the feelings of two very important people must be considered: the twins! We cannot neglect their feelings. As the twins get older and are able to express their desires, needs, and fears about baby-sitters, it will be easier to elicit their reactions to a particular babysitting situation, but even as infants it is important to determine that they are happy with their child care provider.

When Sheri's twins were infants and couldn't voice their feelings, she listened to their older sister. "Kallie was old enough to give me a complete report about each sitter when I got home. I'd casually ask her what she and the baby-sitter had done while I was gone and if she thought Emmy and Tessa had been happy. And whenever possible, I'd let her choose a sitter."

Even if you don't have an older child to give a complete report, you can tell a lot by the twins' facial expressions when they see their baby-sitter. Look carefully for signals of trouble and don't hesitate to follow your gut feelings if you think the child care situation you've chosen is a poor one.

# "And you must be Mommy's little helper!"

## *The Adjustment of Older Siblings to Twins*

Being the older sibling of twins is not easy. When the twins are oohed and aahed over in public, older siblings are often ignored. At best, they are given a pat on the head and the standard line, "And you must be Mommy's little helper!"

At home, life isn't much better. Once the twins are born, the siblings' needs are delayed while the infant twins are cared for. School-age or teenage siblings may even find themselves in the position (whether they want it or not), of being baby-sitters and assistants to their moms or dads.

Although the addition of twins to a family is often hard on the older children, a positive adjustment is possible. Parents can help by anticipating the pitfalls and preparing for them thoughtfully. When problems develop after the twins' arrival, take heart: Solutions can be found and worked through.

### *Sharing the News*

When we told our children that they would soon be the big brothers and sisters of twins, we got a variety of responses. Each of us listened carefully as our children expressed themselves. We knew this was the first step toward their acceptance of the twins.

Linda's girls, Sarah and Maiah, took the news calmly. "The girls didn't think anything of it when I told them I was pregnant with two babies. Being only three years old and twins themselves, they thought two babies at a time were par for the course! All they could think about was how exciting it would be for each of them to have a baby to care for."

Sheri wondered if her only child, four-year-old Kallie, would be jealous. "I worried that Kallie would be upset because she and I were so close. When my home pregnancy test showed a positive result, I waited anxiously for her reaction. Thankfully, Kallie was overjoyed. From that point on, it was *our* pregnancy. After we learned I was having twins, Kallie became even more protective of me. She covered me with blankets when I rested and frequently made peanut butter and jelly sandwiches for both of us."

Initially Debbie's son, Chris, who was then seven, felt ready to be a big brother. Debbie remembers: "Chris was tired of being an only child and was nearly as ecstatic as Dale and I were. He bragged to anyone who would listen that 'he' was going to have twins. But after mulling it over with his friends for a few weeks his excitement about having twins was rapidly replaced with anxiety. Out of the blue, he expressed concern that once the babies were born there wouldn't be enough money for birthday and Christmas presents, and asked how we were going to keep the babies out of his room and away from his toys once they could crawl."

Debra vividly recalls the day she told her older son, Jason, then thirteen, that she was expecting twins. "Jason echoed the same concerns I had about the shortage of living space and the stress on finances, and I could tell by his face that he was wondering how much babysitting he'd be in for. But he also enjoyed a close relationship with his younger brother, Muggy, and he said that it would be 'neat' to have two babies." Muggy was only two and a half years old at the time. She recalls: "In very simple terms I told Muggy I was pregnant, and as my tummy grew larger I encouraged him to touch it and talk to the babies. He was delighted with the idea, but I don't think he really understood what it would mean. I realized then that I would have to find more creative ways to help him get ready for the twins."

## Preparing Children for Twins

There are many ways to prepare children for twin siblings, all of which must be tailored to meet the individual needs, age, and personality of the child involved. For all children it is important to include information about what twins are, to allow them an opportunity to express their feelings and concerns, and to reassure them that although family life will be altered, they will continue to be loved and cared for.

An older child will benefit from open, honest conversations addressing all the feelings and worries he or she might have. Debra used this approach with Jason. "I validated his concerns that shortages of living space and money were issues that Rick and I also worried about. I told him that I didn't know how it would all work out, but that it was Rick's and my responsibility and we would handle things. I also reminded him that once the addition to the house was ready we would have more living space.

"Jason was also concerned that he would have to do more around the house once the twins were born. I had to admit he was right. I explained that I felt badly about this, and I shared with him my belief that good things can and do come out of hard times. At the time, there wasn't much more to say. Some of his worries resolved with time; others became ongoing issues."

A younger child will need more than a sharing of feelings and verbal reassurance to understand the concept of twin infants and the impact they will have on the family. Additional ways to prepare younger children are: acting out play with dolls or stuffed animals representing the twins; reminiscing with them about their own infancies; looking through baby books and old baby clothes; including them on a tour of the nursery at the hospital where the twins will be born; and arranging for them to observe and interact with small babies.

In preparing your child, it is a good idea to include another significant adult in the process. Involving the father, grandparents, favorite aunt, or baby-sitter will be fun for the child and strengthen his bond with them. These strengthened relationships may prove valuable after the twins are born and his mother is less available.

Debbie borrowed a little bit from all these approaches in preparing Chris, but she focused on two primary areas—informational conversation about twins and practical experience with babies. She explains: "Chris is the kind of child who likes to know everything about everything, so Dale and I did a lot of talking to him about twins. We picked times when we wouldn't be interrupted or distracted. We explained what twins were and told him that we expected ours would be fraternal. I let him touch my abdomen and feel the babies move. He even looked at my medical books about pregnancy.

"We reassured him that we would have enough money to take care of him and the twins and that we would make every effort to keep his things safe from curious, crawling babies. And we reminded him that he would always be our one and only, special Chris.

"Chris vacillated between thinking of them as smiling, sweet dolls who would be his constant companions or as miniature monsters who would continually cry and be bent on destroying all his toys.

"To fight these misconceptions, Dale and I arranged for Chris to spend low-keyed supervised time with a few of our friends' babies. It gave him a realistic view of life with infants, and he found he enjoyed it. We also encouraged constructive play by buying him two toy stuffed baby animals (he was too self-conscious to get dolls), complete with pacifiers and blankets. He named them, cuddled them, disciplined them, and displayed them proudly in his bedroom. After a few months, he became comfortable with the idea of twins. Once again he looked forward to and bragged about the birth of his twins."

Kallie was younger than Chris, and more eager to have twin siblings. Sheri and Steve's style of preparation reflected these differences. "It wasn't difficult getting Kallie ready for the twins. In fact, it was kind of fun because she was eager to be a big sister.

As my abdomen grew larger, I took advantage of opportunities to show Kallie my naked belly and talk with her about how the babies were growing. She loved to feel my tight skin and was fascinated by my stretching belly button.

"Kallie and I reminisced about her infancy and sorted through her old baby clothes. She and I talked to the twins inside of me and told them stories of Kallie's babyhood, which tickled Kallie and reminded her how special she was to Steve and me. We also had fun poring through baby name books together.

"Kallie was thoroughly thrilled with the idea of having twins, but she only wanted sisters! Fortunately, my second ultrasound showed two baby girls. Kallie was jubilant and Steve and I were spared the struggle of convincing our headstrong little girl that baby boys were as lovable as baby girls!"

Linda had a rough time because she was on bed rest for a good portion of her second pregnancy. "Overall, it was easier explaining the babies to Sarah and Maiah than explaining my confinement to bed. They couldn't understand why I couldn't play with them; as a result, they gave their caregiver a hard time. Often they ran into my bedroom, crying over minor problems, and flung themselves on my bed. The one good thing that came from this was that during the time I was on bed rest, the girls had the opportunity to get used to being cared for during the day by someone besides me. When Keegan and Colin were born and I still needed live-in help, they were accustomed to it. In fact, they actually did better after the boys were born!"

Debra also had difficulties to contend with as she prepared Muggy for his twin siblings. However, her concerns did not result from Muggy's reactions or behavior, but from her own feelings of loss and sorrow as she anticipated a change in their relationship. She explains: "I thought that preparing Muggy for the twins would be simple, but it wasn't. As I looked through photo albums with him, recalling how special he was and telling him how proud I was of his growth and accomplishments, I became aware that he was no longer my little baby boy. A necessary and natural separation was growing between us, and I grieved about it.

"The irony of this was that Muggy had no way of understanding or processing the fact that he would have to let go, too. Although

I used two dolls to show him the amount of care that two babies would need, I never found a way to talk to him about the feelings he might have after the twins were born and my attention turned toward them. Another pressing concern was how Muggy would react to the rearrangement of our household to make space for the twins."

As in Debra's case, many families with older children will find it necessary to alter their living space, especially the children's sleeping arrangements, to accommodate the expected twins. These changes, especially a child's transition from crib to bed, should be done as early as possible during the pregnancy, so the older child doesn't feel displaced by the twins. Including children in the alterations by allowing them to participate, even on the simplest level, will remind them that they are valued members of the family. A young child may enjoy shopping for a few baby items, and an older child will appreciate having input on how space is used and where furniture is located in his room. These approaches won't guarantee smooth sailing but they go a long way toward defusing anger and encouraging cooperation.

## When the Twins Come Home

No amount of talk, creative play, or wishful thinking can eliminate the very real struggles that occur when the twins come home. Just as each child responds in his own ways to the news that his mother is pregnant with twins, so will he or she respond uniquely to the reality of the demands and chaos of life with infant twins. A child's age and personality, the amount of emotional and financial support available to the family in the first months, the parents' abilities to cope with the changes, to assist each other, and to be sensitive to their older child's needs will all effect how the older sibling responds and relates to the twins.

The sibling should be given the opportunity to visit the new twins in the hospital, and encouraged to touch and handle the babies as is appropriate for his age and ability. Even if the twins are in an NICU, a sibling can wash and gown up and visit briefly if he or she is well supervised and has been told what to expect.

When the babies are discharged, if it isn't possible to bring the older child along, it will be important for him to spend a few special moments with his mother when she gets home.

In the following days, when friends and relatives visit to bring gifts and fuss over the twins, sibling jealousy will be less intense if you remind your visitors to show interest in your other children. It would also be wise to have gifts on hand to give your children at strategic moments.

Debbie remembers, "I hadn't really thought too much about getting Chris little gifts when the twins were born. In fact, I thought the idea was ridiculous, but then I noticed Chris sitting forlornly during one of my baby showers as Dale and I opened up one baby gift after another. I realized he felt left out. At my last baby shower a thoughtful friend bought a little gift for Chris, too. When he saw it, his face lit up like a Christmas tree! I decided to do the same for him when the twins were born."

When Linda was pregnant with Keegan and Colin, a friend suggested that she bring a "Hello" gift to the girls from the boys when Linda came home from the hospital. Linda recommends it: "The girls were thrilled. There was an added bonus; the new toys also distracted Sarah and Maiah during those first few hectic hours after we arrived home."

Gifts and thoughtfulness can lessen the negative impact on the older siblings for a little while; however, as the weeks pass, frustration, jealousy, sadness, anger, and resentment will grow to one degree or another in all children. Ours were no exception.

Debra remembers her troubles with Muggy: "Muggy just fell apart after Ricky and Aislynn came home. He tried to get attention by misbehaving and challenging the limits we had established. He would do things he knew he wasn't supposed to. It seemed that every time I asked him something, he would scream, 'No!' and run away. Thankfully, most of his anger was directed at me, not the twins. It was uncanny the way he seemed to know when I was most vulnerable, which was usually when I was breastfeeding both infants, and I invariably ended up yelling at him. These continual battles caused me to feel resentful toward him after a while. Eventually, we got into a vicious cycle: The more he acted up, the less positive interaction we had and the harder it was to give him what he needed."

Jason made an easier adjustment even though his life changed quite radically. Debra recalls, "Jason celebrated his fourteenth birthday one week after the twins were born. He started his freshman year in high school and played on the football team. When he came home he had chores to do, including kitchen cleanup after dinner. He helped with the babies often and played with Muggy, too. When I had time to think about it, I guiltily observed that he had become a caretaker and that my involvement with him was only peripheral. Rick and I had raised him to be self-sufficient, but I think he must have felt somewhat abandoned.

"Sometimes he did resort to negative tactics to get attention from Rick and me, and he occasionally used passive resistance to rebel against the responsibility. As the twins got older, he started to tease them to let off some of his resentment. Most of the time, however, he acted in a mature and nurturing way toward Ricky and Aislynn. Through his teen years, he gave us little trouble and a lot of help."

Debbie's son, Chris, had difficulties adjusting to his role as big brother of twins. "Because Chris had been an only child for almost eight years, Dale and I anticipated that he'd be jealous, angry, and resentful. His actual reaction fell somewhere between the worst we had imagined and the best we had hoped for.

"When Michael and Joanna first came home from the hospital, Chris did very well, mostly because my parents were still staying with us and were able to give him lots of special attention. After they returned to the Midwest and Chris was faced with the stark reality of being the big brother to twin infants, life became less than ideal for him. It seemed that every time he made a request of Dale or me, he heard, 'Just a minute, I'm with the babies,' or 'Chris, can't you do that yourself?' The more Dale and I put him off, the more demanding he became.

"Soon our once capable and independent eight-year-old was so stressed out that he was crying because he couldn't tie his shoes fast enough, or was whining that no one loved him because he had to make his own after-school snacks. Instead of trying to understand why he was behaving this way, I just grew impatient with him because his antics were inconvenient and frustrating. My attitude did nothing but worsen the situation.

"I might have continued to deny the depth of Chris's emotional pain for some time to come if I hadn't been slapped in the face with its results. Chris had completed a spelling assignment at school and brought it home with the rest of his papers for Dale and me to review. In this assignment, he had to use the words *hate, always,* and *sleeping* in sentences. Just one month after Michael and Joanna were born, Chris had written: 'I hate my brother and sister. The babies are always crying. My mother is usually sleeping when I get home.'

"As I read these sentences, I was filled with sadness and shame for letting myself grow so out of touch with my son. I knew that Dale and I had been less sensitive to his demands, but I had rationalized that his needs temporarily must come second to those of Michael and Joanna. Now, as I looked at his school work, I realized that this was not only untrue, but unfair, too. I didn't know exactly how to handle this, but I knew it was time for another one of our long talks."

Linda's daughters, Maiah and Sarah, did well for the first few weeks after their twin brothers came home. Linda says, "After months of bed rest, I was up and about at last. Although I couldn't give them lots of attention, they had each other and two new brothers to help care for. They enjoyed running to get diapers and helping with feedings. I relied on them a lot and they really came through, but eventually the stress and lack of attention took its toll. After a few months of being my enthusiastic helpers, they revolted in a big way: They literally acted like babies. They crawled on the floor, sought attention by crying and whining, and demanded to sleep in their old cribs."

Sheri's daughter, Kallie, who had been looking forward to the births of her twin sisters, continued to do well after they came home. Sheri remembers, "Kallie carried babies and supplies to me with endless care and energy. She understood how fragile the twins were, so she handled them with kid gloves. Often one baby would wake and cry while I was nursing the other, and if Kallie was home, she would lift the crying baby from the cradle and carefully bring her to me. After feedings, Kallie reminded me to fill in the 'Who ate what and when?' chart, and later, when the twins were taking bottles, she always held and fed one baby.

"Best of all, Kallie was always willing to run for a diaper or a rag in an emergency. Though I tried not to take advantage of her, I'm sure I did, because she was always right there wanting to help."

The only difficulties Kallie had early on were a result of the increased responsibility she took in her own life. Sheri continues: "Kallie had always been independent, but for the first time in her life I wasn't a very enthusiastic mommy, I was a very tired mommy. Choosing her clothes, getting herself dressed, and brushing her hair all became tasks that she now did with little help from me. Her preschool teacher observed that while Kallie was doing well socially at school, she didn't want to practice reading or writing anymore and played mostly with dolls. Her teacher felt Kallie's disinterest in academics stemmed from the changes and stress she felt at home after the twins were born. This wasn't a big problem, but one we had to recognize and deal with."

*Helping Your Children Adjust to the Changes:*    Most of the anger, resentment, and misbehavior that our older children experienced after the twins came home were directly related to a decrease in attention from their parents. At first, this realization was accompanied by a certain amount of guilt, but reason prevailed as we understood that we were not superhuman. Our lives had become unavoidably complicated as former routine was often replaced by utter pandemonium. Still, we knew circumstances for our older children could be improved, so we sought to make the necessary changes to improve them.

Since Kallie had made the smoothest adjustment, with her only problem being disinterest in preacademic work at preschool, Sheri needed only patience and the wisdom not to pressure Kallie academically. Kallie's preschool teacher and she agreed to hold back on these activities until Kallie showed a renewed interest on her own, which she did a few weeks later.

Linda's problems with Sarah and Maiah were a little trickier, but Todd and she came up with creative ways to deal with them.

"Todd, friends, and family made concerted efforts to give them undivided attention by taking them on special outings or spending time with them here at home. In addition, we told the girls that they could play-act being babies for a few hours every day. During those hours, we put them in diapers, gave them bottles, and let them crawl in and out of the empty crib. I realize that this sounds a little flaky, but it worked. They got what they wanted—they were treated like babies—and I got what I wanted—control of the situation. Within several days, their interest in the baby game waned and I had my three-year-old girls back."

Muggy's angry, rebellious behavior presented Debra with a bigger dilemma. During a phone conversation, Debra shared her concerns with her mother and came to agree with her mother's impression. "My mother felt that Muggy's behavior stemmed from his feelings of insecurity and the decrease in my attention. Her advice was to ignore as much of the negative behavior as I could, and to pour on the hugs and kisses to help heal his pain. She also suggested I tell him that I missed our closeness, too.

"I gave her advice a try. Slowly, but surely, my new responses reduced his negative behavior. There were still times when I was so depressed that I found it difficult to be compassionate with him or consistent in how I treated him, and at these times the distance between us grew and his behavior worsened. If I had been able to give Muggy more frequent affection with consistent attention instead of occasional doses of TLC, we may have been able to keep his insecurity at bay. I have beaten myself up a lot about this, but now I understand that I didn't have enough personal resources to give Muggy all he needed."

Feeling so overwhelmed, Debra was also unable to give Jason the amount of attention she would have liked. To give him a much-needed break from his household responsibilities, she sent him on a three-week vacation to California to visit his grandparents. Still, she feels that none of this was adequate compensation for all he did.

In retrospect, Debra says, "I should have given Jason more emotional support. I couldn't have survived without him; but I rarely told him this at the time, and I wish I had. (Although I have told him countless times since then!) I also wish I had spent more time with him back then, just to be together and talk about what was going on in his life. I was so busy living day to day that I forgot that he needed my love and attention, just as much as Muggy and the twins did."

Chris is another example of the seemingly self-sufficient older child who was in great need of his mother's care. Debbie shares their situation: "When Dale and I read the spelling assignment that revealed Chris's true feelings about the twins, we were shocked into reality. Dale and I discussed this, trying to come up with a plan.

"First, and the most importantly, we finally acknowledged that the twins were getting our best energy. Chris wasn't being neglected, but he wasn't exactly being showered with attention either. I was the main source of his problem. Dale spent special time with Chris in the evenings or on weekends playing with him or taking him on excursions. On the other hand, my time with him was spent supervising his homework, insisting that he be more independent around the house, driving him to and from his various social engagements and sport commitments, or complaining that his chores weren't done. Most of our contact was far from being the fun or quality time we had previously shared.

"It became obvious that I needed to spend some time every day with Chris, doing something he (and hopefully I) enjoyed. At the time, cutting my free time even half an hour to be with Chris felt like the ultimate sacrifice.

"Of course, it wasn't a sacrifice. It was really an investment of love, a chance for Chris and me to rebuild friendship into our relationship. It was an opportunity for me to reacquaint myself with my older son during that all too brief time in his life when his mother was more important to him than his peers. The things we did together in the evenings were simple—we played board games; we played cards; we talked.

"Our activities together were far from exciting, but the time we spent together was meaningful and brought us closer. The benefits were many. When we spent time together, we were more considerate, helpful, and understanding of each other at other times of the day. When evenings went by without our shared recreation, our relationship suffered.

"Perhaps the most positive result of our time together was that it allowed Chris to feel loved and secure. As a result, he was able to give love freely to Michael and Joanna, which they returned many times over, and he helped more cheerfully with the twins and household chores."

*The Development of Bonds between Twins and Older Siblings:* After years of shared experience, be it good or bad, siblings will develop relationships with each other. Like all parents, we wanted our children to interact in warm and loving ways that would mature and strengthen with the passing years. Unfortunately, accomplishing this is easier said than done.

Sheri had concerns about the relationships between Kallie and each of the twins. She remembers: "Emmy's and Tessa's distinct personalities clearly surfaced when they were about nine months old, and while Tessa tended to go exploring and be less affectionate, Emmy still preferred to be held. When Kallie fed Emmy her bottle they smiled and cuddled, while Tessa gulped hers down and crawled away. It was only natural for Kallie to feel more drawn to Emmy. At first I didn't think much about it. But after a few weeks, some little things that Kallie was doing started to bother me. She always wanted Emmy to have the same color vitamin that she did, and she wanted Emmy to wear the prettier outfits. It wasn't as if she were mean to Tessa; Emmy just got her special attention and affection. Sometimes when she asked for something special for Emmy, I reminded her to be fair.

"The problem took care of itself when the twins were about eighteen months old and started to play together, excluding Kallie. Then it became two against one, with Emmy and Tessa dragging out Kallie's Barbie dolls and messing up her coloring books. Of course, being toddlers, the twins were into everyone's belongings, but Kallie felt as if it were a direct assault upon her. She began to treat the babies as a unit and stopped favoring Emmy. I was glad to see her preferential attitude come to an end."

Debbie's son Chris also showed a preference for one twin over the other. Debbie recalls: "Until the twins were two or three Chris consistently preferred Michael's to Joanna's company. At first, it started because Joanna was a fussier baby and he was uncomfortable around her crying. After a few months, Joanna outgrew her fussiness, but then Chris preferred Michael just because, 'He's a boy, Mom!' By the time Michael was a year and a half, and thoroughly in love with rough play and wrestling, his role as Chris's favorite was established.

"I am willing to accept that each of my kids will have different relationships with each of their siblings, but it really bothered me that Chris's perception of Joanna's worth as a buddy was based on the idea that she couldn't be fun because she was a girl. Dale and I suggested to Chris that he begin inviting her to play with him on occasion. He did, and she almost always said yes, which surprised and pleased Chris. To foster their relationship, occasionally Dale would run an errand or go on a short outing with just Chris and Joanna while I stayed home with Michael. Our plans were (mostly) successful. At this date, Chris still has a special bond with Mike, but he also has a growing relationship with Joanna. It will need nurturing and guidance, as he still likes to tease her to near hysteria, which doesn't exactly encourage warmth on her part. Still, I smile when she lovingly calls him her 'Crissy' and he calls her his 'Anna-Jo,' something I never thought possible two years ago."

Sarah and Maiah also showed occasional preferences for one twin brother or the other when the boys were about a year old. It wasn't a fixed fondness for one, but a fondness that was determined by which brother happened to be most cooperative and interested in being part of their various games of pretend. Linda dealt with this in a matter-of-fact way, simply letting the three children who were enjoying each other's company go off and play, while she spent special quiet time with the child who was left alone. "I never worried about one of the boys being left out or feeling rejected by the girls because both of them enjoyed their special time with me. Besides I knew that whoever was their favorite one week was bound to be the one left out of the fun the next week!"

Jason and Muggy rarely played favorites with Ricky or Aislynn, but they did develop bonds with the twins in their own ways. Jason easily cultivated a warm and protective relationship with his twin siblings while Muggy held back from the twins because they were clear rivals for Mom's and Dad's attention. By the time the twins were sociable one-year-olds and he was a self-confident three-year-old, he began to see the advantages of the situation and his relationship with each of them blossomed. Muggy reveled in his role as boss, which the twins conceded until they were about two years old. Then the quarrels began.

*Fighting, Fighting, and More Fighting:* Does the word *sibling* have to be synonymous with the word *fight*? While they do seem inescapably intertwined, we take solace in the knowledge that a certain amount of anger and tension between siblings is normal. As parents, it is our job to help our children deal with their feelings, not by stifling them or denying they exist, but by helping our children to express them in healthy and constructive ways.

Generally, when an argument arose between our twins and their siblings, we found that having them settle it between themselves worked best. Of course, when fights resulted in physical contact or mean-spirited name-calling, adult intervention was necessary. However, even in these situations our response was aimed at identifying the unacceptable behavior in a way the children could understand and briefly explaining our solution and/or the resulting consequences.

We share with you examples of what worked and didn't work with our children. Understand that some degree of sibling rivalry is bound to occur no matter what you do. Learning a variety of healthy ways to handle sibling conflict, and applying these approaches consistently and lovingly, is the best any parent can do.

Debra's twins had just turned two when sibling discord reared its ugly head at her house. "Muggy enjoyed bossing Ricky and Aislynn for about a year, but then the twins revolted by resisting his implied authority. At first, I played the mediator but soon they were coming to me to complain about every little thing one or the others had done. The fighting intensified and I finally realized that the kids felt that getting attention from me, even negative attention, was worth it. I eventually learned that keeping a watchful but quiet distance, while insisting they work it out, reduced the frequency of quarrels.

Of course, sometimes the verbal fighting escalated into physical aggression and then I intervened by separating them with an explanation that being angry is okay, but hitting is not acceptable. Within ten minutes of being separated they would be scheming to get back together."

Debra had an interesting revelation as she considered how and when her children fought. "I found that when the kids played outdoors they fought less often. Outdoors Muggy could take a watchful, leadership role which was appropriate. We had a two-acre section of our property tagged with red logger's tree tape designating where the kids were allowed to play. By the time Muggy was four or five, he was quite responsible in seeing that the twins stayed within this boundary. Before long, the power struggles decreased as Muggy, Ricky, and Aislynn redistributed their pecking order, with Muggy giving up some of his bossiness, and the twins becoming more assertive. Not that there weren't any more skirmishes, mind you, it just felt a little less like a war zone!"

Linda's house was filled with commotion for some time after the boys learned to crawl. Sarah and Maiah, who had been sharing and playing cooperatively for many months, were greatly distressed to discover that their baby brothers, Keegan and Colin, didn't understand or care to learn about sharing. As Keegan and Colin repeatedly grabbed toys from Sarah and Maiah, the girls grew increasingly upset. Some days they handled this well, other days they were driven to a tearful frenzy.

Initially, Linda and Todd dealt with this by putting gates up in the entry of Maiah and Sarah's bedroom so Keegan and Colin couldn't get to the girls' toys. Unfortunately, the girls also couldn't get through and Linda or Todd had to help the girls over the gate every time they went into or out of their room.

Their next solution was to purchase a babyproof doorknob cover. This snapped onto the doorknob and prevented the boys from opening the door, but the girls were strong enough to squeeze the doorknob and open it on their own. "Of course, the boys reacted to this barrier by pounding and crying at their door, but the toys were safe and the girls were happy."

Sheri had similar troubles between Kallie and her sisters.

"When Emmy and Tessa were 18 months old, they began playing cooperatively together. They ganged up on Kallie by rearranging the furniture in her Barbie house or taking apart Lego creations she had painstakingly built. For the first time, Kallie felt animosity toward her sisters. A day didn't go by that wasn't punctuated several times with Kallie's yelling, '*Mom*, get them out of my room!'

Acknowledging Kallie's feelings helped calm her, but we had to treat her fairly, too. All too often, Steve and I passed off Emmy and Tessa's naughty acts as 'baby behavior,' and didn't discipline them, because it was easier to tell Kallie to let the twins have what they wanted. This was, of course, the worst thing to do, because nothing made Kallie more jealous or furious than a double standard. Steve and I eventually moved Kallie's special toys out of the playroom and into her own bedroom, and we also let Emmy and Tessa know what was and was not acceptable behavior."

Debbie wishes she could say that with nearly eight years between Chris and the twins, there were fewer fights and arguments. "After I started giving Chris special time in the evening, life went smoothly until Mike and Joanna got to be about two years old and were very headstrong and very verbal.

"I was amazed to watch my ten-year-old son argue at a two-year-old level over some small toy or angry remark one of the twins made. It reminded me that Chris was in some ways still a young child, too.

"Unfortunately, this sort of bickering has persisted over this past year. Some days it isn't too bad; other days it occurs off and on for hours. Their fights usually seem to be over some small thing, but the issues behind the fights run deeper. For example, if Chris feels ignored by Dale and me, or if he is bored or stressed or angry about something else, then Mike and Joanna are convenient scapegoats. Other times, the twins provoke fights with Chris, because they resent his bossing them around, or they have hurt feelings because of something he said or did to them earlier in the day."

"When the twins were just two, Dale and I often had to referee the fights. By the time the twins were three, we encouraged our three children to verbally settle their disagreements between themselves. Certain rules are understood: If the source of the fight is a mutually desirable toy (yes, Chris sometimes fights for the same toy as Mike or Joanna!) they know the toy will be confiscated if the fight is not settled quickly.

"When hurt feelings are at issue, we ask them to talk about how it feels to have your feelings hurt, and suggest (we never demand) that an apology is in order when the time feels right. When the conflict is resolved we talk in simple ways to those involved to help them understand how they added to the fight by provoking someone or choosing not to peacefully resolve the conflict. When the argument is a ploy to get attention or an indirect way of expressing anger about something else, we remind them that asking for what you want or expressing your feelings directly are better solutions. Most importantly, Dale and I try to be healthy role models as we resolve our own disagreements."

Does all this really work? Debbie responds, "Well, my kids are great at identifying their feelings right before they punch their sibling in the arm or steal a toy!! But I don't think that this is such a bad place to start, because accepting and understanding emotions is an important part of learning safe and healthy ways to express feelings."

No matter which disciplinary approach is used, it must be used *consistently* if it is to be effective. Debra shares her experience: "If I were tired or stressed myself, I didn't have the energy to respond to the kids' arguments in the 'right' ways. I yelled right back at them to let off steam; it was almost like a reflex. Getting counseling for my personal problems helped me reduce my stress and anger. When I felt better, I was more effective as a parent and able to discipline more calmly and consistently: my kids knew what my expectations were and followed my limits. Before long, things turned around. I still have bad days, but at least now I know what I can do to make things better."

*When Anger Gets Out of Control:* Most children will respond to their new siblings much as ours did. They will alternate between anger and tenderness, frustration and happiness, resentment and pride. They will lash out at their parents by yelling, testing limits, and saying unkind things. As the twins grow into toddlerhood, the older siblings will occasionally direct their negative feelings toward them by starting their share of fights. Although these behaviors are difficult and tiresome to handle, they are normal and can be dealt with successfully, using common sense and good parenting techniques acquired by reading books on the subject, talking to other parents, and attending parenting classes.

Rarely an older sibling has such intense and overwhelming feelings of anger, resentment, or jealousy that he expresses them in more destructive ways. In a moment of rage, a toddler may topple over the bassinet when the baby is sleeping in it; a preschool-aged child may handle the twins roughly. A teenager may be morose and relate to the world and the people around him in an angry way. These behaviors can also be handled with good parenting and patience. However, if a child develops a persistently hostile or destructive pattern of relating, it is time to seek professional counseling for him or her.

*When Twins Are the Older Siblings:*  When considering the relationships between twins and their other siblings, attention is most often directed toward the difficulties that older children experience as they adjust to infant twins. This adjustment is quite striking; however, it can also be difficult for a singleton child entering the family where older twin siblings already exist, especially if the twins have a particularly close or exclusive relationship. Without thoughtful guidance by loving parents, the singleton child may contend with feelings of isolation, resentment, and low self-esteem.

Efforts aimed at reassuring the singleton child of his special uniqueness and enhancing the relationships between him and each of the twins should be encouraged. Other issues, such as sibling rivalry and fighting, undoubtedly will occur, and can be dealt with as one would deal with any set of twins and their singleton siblings.

## Our Thoughts and Reflections

SHERI:  Kallie occasionally sighs and tells me that she wishes her sisters were babies again because she could hold and love them with none of the hassles. Yet, she has also admitted that they have grown to be wonderful playmates, and appreciative and enthusiastic audiences for her plays and puppet shows!

LINDA: My girls are 6 now and my boys are three. Being just three years apart, their sibling relationships fluctuate on a daily basis. Some days, they all get along and play for hours. Other days, the boys throw the girls' things down the laundry chute and stand in front of the TV so the girls can't watch. Both sets of my twins are just beginning to sort through their feelings for each other, but I know that affection for each other will grow stronger as they get older.

DEBBIE: Having the twins has enriched Chris's life in many ways. Sure, he has experienced the responsibility and frustration that go along with being an older brother, but he also knows, and continues to know, the joy of unconditional admiration given only by younger to older siblings.

DEBRA: Jason benefited in many ways from having the twins to love and care for. He was able to express his nurturing qualities and relish their loving responses. He developed a very realistic view of the responsibilities and rewards of raising children. He will make a great father someday!

He told me once that although he sometimes felt overwhelmed by the twins, he also felt that the experience made him realize how strong and capable he was, which built his self-confidence.

Muggy, who initially had such a rough time adjusting to the twins, was very attached to them before long. He could see there were real advantages to having playmates. Having siblings has taught him about mutual caring, sharing power, and being considerate of others. My children enrich each other's lives as only brothers and sisters can.

Chapter 10

# "Start twinproofing"

## The Twins at Six to Twelve Months

**B**reathe a big sigh of relief: By the time they are six months old, you and your twins have probably left behind frequent feedings and some of the sleepless nights. Life will run more smoothly as routines emerge in your twins' lives. For some of us, this was also the time to deal with issues such as weaning, introducing solid foods, and developing good nighttime sleeping patterns. Still, much work lies ahead, because two crawling, standing, and teetering infants can keep one mother very busy! If you haven't already done it, now is the time to start *twinproofing*.

### Changes in Our Babies

As your twins develop during these next six months, they will change right before your eyes. Suddenly, they are older babies who are no longer content to remain where you leave them. Instead, they want to explore everything and to go everywhere as they taste, feel, and touch the world around them.

Sheri fondly recalls, "They yearned for wind in their faces and carpet fuzz in their fingers. At six months, Emmy and Tessa abandoned their favorite toys and headed for anything interesting at their eye level."

You will find that each child will progress at his or her own rate in all areas of growth and development. Fraternal twins are likely to show the greatest variation, but identical twins will also have their differences. However, if one twin falls significantly behind the other or you are concerned that something is wrong with a twin's development, do not hesitate to call or visit your doctor to discuss your concerns.

*Growth:* By the time your twins reach twelve months of age, they will be roughly two to three times their birthweight, and will have added three to four inches to their height. However, their growth during the second six months will not follow the steady increase of the first six; instead it is marked by plateaus, slight decreases, and occasional growth spurts. There are a few reasons for this: temporary decrease in food intake as solid foods are introduced, development of minor illnesses that curtail the appetite, increased activity that quickly uses up calories, and teething discomfort that causes occasional disinterest in feeding.

*Teething:* The eruption of teeth is just one more sign that your twins are growing out of infancy. Although a few babies may not have any teeth by their first birthday, many will have eight teeth, all incisors, which have made their appearance steadily over the previous six months.

Linda remembers how quickly Sarah and Maiah's mouths began to fill up. "Sarah and Maiah cut their first tooth within several days of each other. After that there were continual eruptions for months. The girls drooled more but otherwise this didn't seem to bother them."

Teething is not always pain-free. It can cause mild discomfort, fussiness, and drooling, but it is not believed to be responsible for fevers above 100.5F (rectally). When fevers higher than this occur, an illness is usually the cause.

Babies can get some relief from teething pain by chewing on bagels, zweiback toast, teething toys, or even a damp washcloth cooled in the freezer for an hour or so. For severe discomfort, some physicians recommend small doses of acetaminophen to decrease the pain on the toughest days.

As soon as your twins' teeth pop through the gum, it is time to think about dental care. A drink of water can be used to rinse out your twins' mouths after eating and drinking. Later, when they have more than one tooth, look for tiny particles of food lodged between their teeth and gently remove the pieces with a baby toothbrush or soft cloth. Also, find out if the water in your area is flouridated. If it is not, consult your dentist or pediatrician about giving your twins daily flouride drops.

*Developing Motor Skills:*   During these six months, babies develop many new motor skills. By the time your twins are one year old, they will amaze you with what they can do with their hands. They will be able to bring food and toys to their mouths, pick up different-sized objects with their thumb and index fingers, and bang two objects together and release them voluntarily. They will also be interested in reaching out for things in all directions. At this stage, twins begin to grab and touch each other, so watch out for innocent scratching and hair-pulling. Keep your camera handy to capture those special moments when they touch each other tenderly.

By seven to nine months of age, most babies can sit up alone and crawl with confidence. At a year, many are standing and some are taking their first steps. However there are wide variations in the acquisition of these skills. Some babies develop more slowly due to frequent illness, prematurity, or lack of interest, while others are precocious and progress ahead of schedule. Debra's twins Ricky and Aislynn acquired their motor skills early.

"When Aislynn and Ricky were six months old, I opened two sleeping bags and placed them on our linoleum floor for them to play on. I was amazed that, within a week, they were scooting and crawling around on the sleeping bags, and by the end of three weeks, they were pulling themselves up to furniture and attempting to walk without support. Ricky was overeager and fell over quite often so he became wary of letting go, but Aislynn took her first steps at eight and a half months and by nine months was walking all over the place. About a month later, Ricky finally let go and started toddling after her."

While Debra's fraternal twins showed equal ability in motor skills and passed many of their developmental milestones close to the same age, this does not always happen.

Debbie shares her experience. "By the time the twins were six months old, Joanna had been rolling around the house for some time, while Michael hated lying on his back or tummy and had rolled over only once or twice. He was satisfied to sit and play as Joanna practiced her attempts to crawl. Michael watched her with complete detachment until they were eight months old and Joanna crawled across the room. Suddenly, I could see on Michael's face the awe, the desire, and the intense frustration he was feeling as he studied Joanna's every move. A few days after Joanna's first official crawl, Michael began to practice his version, with impressive single-mindedness. About a month later, he was crawling around the house like an old pro!"

On the other hand, Florien feels that Max and Otto have followed a similar developmental timetable. "It's hard to explain, but Max's and Otto's bodies have always worked in synchronization. They learned to grasp objects, sit, crawl, stand up, and walk within hours or days of each other. Whenever they went exploring in the house they were always together. Even when they played, they usually remained within a few feet of each other."

*Play:* Many of your babies' waking hours are spent learning about their environment through play. As soon as they can roll over, they intentionally move toward interesting objects to examine them more closely. When infants are able to reach and hold things in their hands, they will pick up toys or everyday items to feel, touch, taste, and look at them. Before long, babies are seeking out preferred toys and activities.

We found that the most suitable toys for our twins at this age were things that were colorful and easy to hold, with smooth edges and no removable parts. If the toys rattled, rolled, or played music, they were guaranteed to be a hit. Having duplicates of favorite toys and extra playthings also made playtime more enjoyable.

Florien's boys enjoyed rolling balls, pushing cars, banging objects, and pulling small toys around by strings. They also loved the active play that their walkers provided them. "I placed toys or finger foods on the walkers' trays, and hooked small items onto the frame with plastic links. These brightly colored links saved me from having to follow Max and Otto about the house picking up dropped objects."

Like Florien, many parents find walkers to be fun for their children. However, they do present potential dangers. Certain models, especially older ones, tend to tip over if they meet resistance on the floor or if the baby is trying to reach for the ground and leans over too far. Walkers should never be used if there is any likelihood that a child will be near a stairway and accidentally tumble down. In addition, if walkers are used, children should not be in them for long periods of time. Babies between 6 and 12 months of age also need to spend time on the floor learning other important skills like sitting, crawling, and pulling themselves to a standing position.

Less active toys and everyday activities can also be entertaining. Our twins loved it when we listened to music and looked at picture books with them. They also liked banging on pots and pans, jingling measuring spoons, putting things in plastic bowls, and climbing into large cardboard boxes. Linda's twins made it a habit to follow her around the house and "help" her as she did housework. "At nine months of age, Keegan and Colin entertained themselves by playing in the empty laundry basket as their older sisters and I folded the wash. The boys had fun throwing toys into the basket and crawling in to retrieve them. When I made the beds, they loved getting lost in the bed covers and delighted in finding each other."

*Language Development:*   At this age, the babies' babbling sounds start to transform into more understandable spoken communication. Before this time, your twins have listened to your words and tried to copy them. Now they begin to formulate their own "first words" by making word approximations like *ba* for ball or *da* for dog.

To enhance the development of language, babies need a variety of auditory stimulation so they can understand how words are used. When babies babble and finally try to speak, it is not as important for parents to identify these first utterances as it is to encourage the attempts at verbal communication by smiling, listening, and talking back to their babies.

Florien made a point of reinforcing Max's and Otto's attempts to talk. "The boys were very curious about language. They babbled endlessly and I responded enthusiastically. At around six and a half months, they started using more expressive intonations. Devin and I had fun trying to guess what they were telling us, and at times thought we understood exactly what they were trying to say. A few months later the twins used 'Mama' and 'Dada' correctly. As the boys learned the joy and power of expressive language, they spoke constantly."

Some children may be saying several words by their first birthday, while others may not have yet produced a recognizable word. For example, Linda's girls were saying several words by twelve months of age; in contrast, her twin boys were babbling and appeared to understand some language, but did not yet say any distinct words. Linda shared these differences with her pediatrician, who explained that boys sometimes develop language skills more slowly than girls. He also told her that it is fairly common for the third and fourth child born close to older siblings to have expressive language delays because they do not get much opportunity for one-on-one conversation with adults. Finally, he added that some infants are just temperamentally inclined to be more verbal than their peers.

*Temperamental Differences:* Differences in temperament exist between every set of twins from the moment they are born. Usually, these differences become more and more apparent in the six-to-twelve-month stage. Commonly, fraternal twins show the most dissimilar temperaments.

Sometimes it is difficult to see the distinct dispositions of identical twins, as Florien discovered with some differences between Max and Otto.

"As infants and young children, the boys were very similar, but often made switches in their temperaments. Between six months and one year of age, they seemed to rotate every few days: One of them would want a little more attention or one would tire more easily than the other. These differences were subtle and not easily noticed."

Sheri's identical twins had more obvious differences: "Steve and I often shook our heads in disbelief at how different Emmy and Tessa could be. One would spend all her time crawling around exploring alone while the other wanted to be constantly held and entertained on our laps. Then after a few weeks they switched roles!"

Debra found the contrast in personalities that existed between her twins to be quite noticeable. "From their births, Aislynn was a people-lover and craved interaction with others. She smiled and babbled at anyone who came near. She was affectionate, yet had a volatile nature with constantly changing moods. One moment she would be laughing, and the next she would be screaming. In contrast, Ricky did not cry unless he was really hurt. Generally he was even-tempered, but he was shy around strangers and treated them as if they did not exist. He was more interested in objects than people, but he had a strong affection for his sister and they got along pretty well."

Debra's twins complemented each other at this point in their relationship so things went smoothly; however, this is not always the case. Differences developed between Debbie's Michael and Joanna which provided Debbie a bit of a challenge.

She remembers, "The big problems occurred when the twins were eleven and a half months old. Michael was walking well, while Joanna was just starting to take her first steps, but still preferred to crawl. As Michael swaggered around the house, Joanna crawled happily behind him. Unfortunately for Joanna, every few minutes Michael turned around, noticed her behind him, and became so excited to see her that he couldn't contain his enthusiasm. He attempted to hug and kiss her with such fervor that inevitably he tumbled on top of her, pushing her to the floor. Since she was a pound and a half lighter, one inch shorter, and not nearly as feisty as Michael, Joanna was no match for him. She screamed and lay passively beneath him until I rescued her. As I separated them, Michael was always happy and laughing, totally bewildered by Joanna's tearful reaction.

"This sort of interaction occurred frequently during their waking hours and became so distressing to Joanna that the mere sight of Michael moving toward her made her cry and crawl in the opposite direction as fast as she could. The best I could do in managing the situation was to give them separate nap times, to ignore the attacks as much as safety would allow, to encourage Joanna to assert herself, and to attempt to teach Michael to be gentle with his sister.

"A few weeks later, Michael playfully, authoritatively, and confidently pushed Joanna aside. Her reaction was to look him squarely in the eye and begin yelling at him unintelligibly. She flailed her arms around like a windmill, with such force that she knocked him down. Michael sat on the floor, wide-eyed, looking at her in disbelief. Michael tried to get up, but Joanna's wildly swinging arms knocked him down again. He looked stunned and suddenly dissolved into tears.

"The entire interaction was over in two minutes. Michael stopped his 'love assaults' on Joanna almost completely for several months. This is not to say that he never again attempted to wrestle with her. He continued to be the aggressor, and Dale and I continued to deal with this issue on one level or another for some time. There was, however, a noticeable adjustment in their relationship. Michael had accepted her limits and learned a valuable lesson about the consequences of aggressive behavior, while Joanna learned the positive benefits of asserting herself. And I learned the value of allowing them, within safety and reason, to work out their problems."

*Separation Anxiety:* Most of the developmental changes that occur in six-to-twelve-month-old babies are very rewarding. Learning to crawl or speak is a struggle, but once crawling is accomplished or the first word is spoken, everyone in the family is pleased and proud.

Unfortunately, the stages of emotional growth that babies pass through as they grow toward confidence and independence can be frustrating for both babies and parents. During this six-month period, infants are learning to express feelings of anger, jealousy, and love. One moment they are happy and smiling at everyone, and the next they are crying as if their hearts are broken.

Their capacity to love grows in leaps and bounds and their loyalty and attachment to their primary caregiver deepens so much that the fear of losing this person, even for brief moments, overwhelms them. This fear, known as *separation anxiety,* influences their behavior until it is resolved.

During this period of separation anxiety the mother is the center of her child's universe, and he wants her constant and undivided attention. While twins may have some consolation in each other's company, they still want their mother nearby at all times. This can be an overwhelming burden for the mother as her adoring babies crawl after her everywhere she goes. Even quick trips to the bathroom can be met with anger and frustration as her twins pound on the closed door, demanding entrance.

You can ease your twins' anxiety by remaining within their sight and hearing whenever possible. Give them lots of love and assurance, but remember that you are only one person and cannot possibly meet their every demand.

Florien's most difficult time came when she prepared dinner. "During the day I spent a lot of time with Max and Otto and things went well; but when I turned my full attention to meal preparation, they often cried for me and sought my attention by crawling around my feet and pulling on my legs. One day, I put them in their wind-up swings and set them where they could watch me. When they outgrew the swings, I moved them into walkers where they could play happily while I cooked."

Debra agrees that it was a tough juggling act trying to be "everything" for her twins. "Ricky and Aislynn followed me throughout the house, sometimes whining to be held or played with. I gave them as much attention as I could, but sometimes it wasn't enough, because they wanted me, and only me, nearly every waking moment. When I had to go out and leave them, I tried to have Rick or Jason watch them instead of a baby-sitter. When it came time to walk out the door, I'd kiss them good-bye, tell them matter-of-factly that I had to go but would be coming back. Despite their protest I calmly left, knowing they were in good hands and realizing they would stop crying shortly after I left."

This is a difficult time for parents and twins; fortunately, it only lasts a few months. As babies grow secure in their parents' love, and realize that a separation from their mother is only temporary, they will become more independent and leave this phase behind. Meanwhile, anyone who appears to threaten the connection with their mother is met with protest.

*Fear of Strangers:*  Babies of this age often have a fear of strangers, which is in part an extension of their separation anxiety. However, child psychologists also say that sometimes it isn't the stranger himself who is so threatening, but rather what he or she *does* that frightens babies. Imagine it from an infant's point of view. An unfamiliar adult, smiling broadly and babbling in baby talk, comes close and abruptly reaches for the baby to tickle, pinch, or kiss him, or worse yet threatens to remove him from his mother's arms. This invasion of the infant's personal space is simply too intense for a young child.

Sheri found this fear to be frustrating. "There I would be with both babies happily perched on my lap. The twins would be delighted to laugh, smile, or play peek-a-boo with complete strangers from across the room. But if one of those people walked close, my twins would shriek in terror. Even though I understood the reasons for their fear, it was embarrassing. Until Emmy and Tessa outgrew this stage, I warned all but close friends to please keep their distance."

This intense fear of strangers usually passes within a month or two. When it is gone, the twins move fearlessly ahead to explore everyone and everything around them.

## Everyday Issues
· · · · · · · · · · · · · · · ·

*Feeding and Weaning:*  During babies' first year of life, breast milk or formula is their primary source of nutrients. However, weaning from breast or bottle is sometimes attempted during this stage and solid foods are often introduced. The mother is faced with the practical dilemma of how to accomplish this.

At six months of age, all our twins were on at least four to eight feedings a day, drinking from six to eight ounces of formula or breast milk at each feeding. By the time they were seven or eight months old, their milk intake had decreased, and most were taking their first solid foods. During this period, some of us found that the milk feeding methods developed earlier continued to work well, while others made changes by weaning their babies from breast-feeding or by supplementing breast-feeding with occasional bottles of formula.

Florien started weaning her boys from the breast when she learned that in five months she would be leaving on a four-week trip to England. "I began weaning Max and Otto when they were five months old, but I worked at it gradually. First I stopped their least favorite feeding, and substituted a bottle of formula. Then every few weeks I eliminated another feeding and added more formula, until I had only one feeding left. In this way, my breasts never got engorged, the boys had several months to make the adjustment and I was able to time it perfectly. One week prior to my departure, I had them completely weaned and on formula."

Linda weaned her girls from breast-feedings at eight and a half months. "By then, Sarah was more interested in the bottle than the breast-feeding, and she had also started biting me. Maiah wasn't yet ready to stop, so I continued breast-feeding her. The bottles plus breast-feeding schedule became inconvenient, so I encouraged Maiah to make the transition to bottle alone, which she did within several days.

"Even though I was intellectually ready for the girls to wean, I found that when the time came I wasn't ready emotionally. After exclusively bottle-feeding for a few days, I missed the feeling of special closeness that breast-feeding gave me; I tried to get the girls to nurse again, but they cried for their bottles and I cried along with them. I realized we couldn't go back to breast-feeding, so we settled down to a regular bottle schedule, my breast milk dried up, and I accepted the inevitable—my babies were growing up."

Debra wasn't ready to wean her twins, but she did want to add supplemental formula feedings so she could get some breaks from nursing. "When Aislynn and Ricky were nine months old, I decided to replace one nursing a day with a bottle. The next month, I substituted another bottle of formula for a second daytime nursing. My breasts adapted to these changes by continuing to produce enough milk for the remainder of the feedings, and I had the best of both worlds—the convenience of nursing and the freedom to take a well-deserved break from it when I needed to."

Sheri, who had changed from breast-feeding to formula feeding when Emmy and Tessa were five months old, weaned them from bottles to cups when they were a year old. "The evening bottle was the first to go. As I had never put the babies to bed with their bottles anyway, we played right through their usual 6:00 P.M. feeding and they didn't bat an eyelash. I had a hard time convincing myself and Steve that they would sleep until morning on the cup of formula that they drank at their five o'clock dinnertime, but they slept all night.

"Two days later the morning bottle disappeared and we simply ate breakfast when the girls woke up. This replaced our previous morning schedule of my shower coinciding with the twins feeding themselves bottles; I had to get up and get going before Emmy and Tessa did. That morning, I replaced their mealtime bottles with covered cups. Though the girls balked and fussed for a couple of days I held firm, and the bottles were gone forever."

*Solid Foods:* Some mothers choose to introduce their infants to baby cereals as early as four months of age, but this should only be done after consulting with a health care provider, who can determine a baby's readiness. More often solid foods are introduced when the babies are about six months of age, although babies born prematurely may start later.

It is useful to follow certain guidelines when introducing solid foods. Easily digestible cereals make the best first foods; rice cereal is the most easily tolerated. Then you can advance your twins to strained fruits, then strained vegetables, introducing only one new food a week by offering a few teaspoons of it once or twice a day. It is important to start one new food at a time because this gives you the opportunity to note whether your babies have an allergic reaction or digestive intolerance to a particular food. When babies tolerate strained foods well, food of a thicker consistency can be given. Mashed fruits and vegetables, or easily gummed foods like Cheerios and zweiback toast work well. As more and more solid foods are introduced, babies will need less formula or breast milk, but this is still an important part of their diet. By the time babies are one year old, about half of their daily caloric intake should be provided by milk and half by solid foods.

Avoid foods such as apple chunks or slices, grapes, hot dogs, peanut butter, nuts, and other hard uncooked vegetables until your babies have a full set of teeth. Even then, these foods will need to be cut into small enough pieces for your twins to chew, so they do not present a choking hazard.

Whether to use commercially prepared or homemade baby food is something else to consider. All of us introduced solids using the ready-made cereal. Some continued to use store-bought products, while other chose to make the transition to home-cooked baby foods. Debra made economical, yet convenient, homemade baby foods by cooking small portions of food, blending them in a food processor, pouring them into ice trays and freezing them. She kept the food cubes in freezer bags and heated portions as needed.

Even those of us who used home-cooked foods found it useful to have a few jars of commercial baby food tucked away in the cupboard for the sake of convenience. Whether we made or bought our baby food, we all tried to avoid added salt, excess sugar, strong spices, caffeine, and artificial colors and flavors in our babies' food.

When it came time to start Max and Otto on solid foods, Florien was not sure what to expect, but she was pleasantly surprised. "Max and Otto learned to take solid foods quite easily. They were introduced to packaged rice cereal at five months of age, and by seven months were enjoying a variety of baby foods. My twins were eager eaters, so while it was messy, feedings were not stressful. Until they were able to sit independently for 15 minutes without tiring, I fed them in their infant seats on the floor with a large towel under them to catch the mess. We used big bibs and

I always had a couple of wet washcloths nearby. I spoon-fed one of the boys and then the other.

"When they were able to sit well unsupported, I put each of them in a portable hanging chair that I hung on our kitchen table. I sat in a chair between them and kept the bowl of food on my lap out of their reach. As they wanted to try and spoon-feed themselves, I let them, but was cautious to be sure they got enough to eat."

Linda was excited by the prospect of starting the girls on solids at six months, but soon met with a few frustrations. "I had read several excellent books on infant nutrition and had all my home-made baby food recipes on hand. Unless you have twins you can't begin to understand the frustration of trying to feed two un-cooperative mouths. I was still in the midst of weaning them, so they were nursing *and* taking bottles *and* starting solids, which made mealtimes complicated. First I gave them a little formula at mealtimes before giving them solid food. Then I fed one baby with a spoon while I breast-fed the other. When I was done, I switched and repeated the process. This was done at the table; one baby sat on an infant seat in front of me so I faced that baby at eye level, while I held the other baby to my breast, trying to keep one baby from sliding off my lap as the other spit cereal in my face. Eventually, I tried sitting both babies in their carriers, spoon-feeding them in tandem, then ending their meals with bottles. This worked better, but the twins still took a while to get used to the idea of solid foods."

Debbie's twins had very different reactions to solid foods. "I started solid foods when Michael and Joanna were about nine months old, because I was in no hurry to deal with the mess or added expense of baby food. Joanna quickly advanced to finger foods and happily fed herself Cheerios, toast, teething biscuits, and anything else she could get her hands on. But Michael would only eat strained baby foods, and if the tiniest grain of textured food found its way into his mouth, he acted as if he were being poisoned. I just went along with his preferences, trying not to worry about it while I gave Joanna chunky junior foods. To my dismay, Michael's negative attitude toward textured foods continued until he got his first set of molars at 15 months—then he made up for lost time and soon was eating nearly everything."

Sheri had no problem getting her twins to eat solids; instead she struggled to find the least messy and most comfortable way to do it. At first she fed her twins as they sat in their walkers while she sat on the linoleum floor, facing the twins, with one foot on the floor under each baby. In this position she could brace them while she spooned in their meals! By the time her girls were seven months old, they started making a huge mess at mealtimes, which prompted her to switch from walkers to high chairs.

By nine months of age, your twins may also want to use their grasping skills to self-feed finger foods. They may even want to try to use spoons, although they will not be able to do this well until they are about two years old. Encouraging your babies to participate in and enjoy their mealtime is ideal, but letting twins feed themselves results in a huge mess. Not only do they manage to cover themselves with food, but the floor and nearby surroundings suffer as well.

Whether or not you allow your twins to feed themselves will depend on your tolerance of messes and your general level of patience. Using oversized plastic bibs, spreading out vinyl tablecloths or linoleum remnants under the high chairs, or even moving the high chairs outside to a patio during the summer months (so you can hose down the mess afterwards) are a few suggestions.

While it may be work for you, feeding should be a pleasant experience for your twins. Otherwise feeding problems may develop. If mealtime is a source of anxiety because disapproving parents complain of messes, or overly doting parents attempt to force-feed, a baby may become disinterested. Our advice is not to let meals become a battleground between you and your twins. Instead, save some energy for another challenge of this age: sleeping problems.

*Helping Twins Fall Asleep:* One of the most frustrating sleeping problems of older infancy is a baby's inability to fall asleep on his own at naptime or bedtime. Some babies delay sleep when they are excited, tense, or overtired from the activities of a busy day. Other babies are hesitant to be separated from their parents because they do not clearly understand that their parents will return when they awaken. Still other infants have trouble sleeping because they have never learned to fall asleep on their own.

Fatigue, tension, and overexcitement tend to be self-limiting problems that occur at hectic times in a baby's life. A warm bath, extra cuddling and holding, and quiet time with the baby's mother or father are usually enough to bring on sleep. Avoid days too full of activity and follow a schedule of regular naptimes and bedtimes. Florien says, "Whenever I overextended Max and Otto by taking them on too many errands before naptime or keeping them up late because of my schedule, they would be so tired that they had difficulty getting to sleep. If I kept their sleeping times fairly routine, they got tired and fell asleep right on schedule."

Infants who cannot fall asleep because they are fearful of separating from their parents present a different situation. This nighttime separation anxiety often, but not always, coincides with similar problems during the daytime, and it appears to occur more often in infants who are separated from their primary caregiver during the day.

There are a variety of ways to deal with nighttime separation anxiety, all of which are aimed at making infants feel loved and secure. For the mother who is unable to be with her twins during the day, because of work or other commitments, it is important that she spend quality time with them in the early evening. It is also important for all parents to develop relaxing bedtime routines for their infants.

Florien tells of her experience: "Whenever possible, Devin and I were both involved in getting Max and Otto to bed. After their baths, we either looked at books with them or cuddled and rocked them as we sat and listened to music. Then when it was time for bed, we turned on their night-light, gave them hugs and kisses, lay them down, and quietly left the room, leaving their door ajar. With their room lightly lit and the sound of our conversation drifting in through their doorway, they fell asleep without difficulty."

Some twins will need more than a good bedtime routine to separate comfortably from their parents. These babies often find the security they seek through an attachment to a comfort object. A sucked thumb or pacifier can serve this purpose for many infants. However, if parents want to discontinue them before their children are ready to do so, these habits can prove bothersome. A better alternative is to offer babies the opportunity to attach to a cuddly object of comfort, such as a stuffed animal or soft blanket.

This sort of comfort object has a special place in a child's heart, and comes to represent the love he feels for his parents. When choosing special "lovies" for twins, we suggest that parents pick something different for each one, so the items can be easily distinguished. We also recommend buying one or two extra comfort objects that are identical to the original. That way, if you lose the first one, need to wash it, or it wears out, you have a ready and acceptable substitute. Remember to limit bedtime objects to only one or two or there will be no end to your twins' requests for more!

Comfort objects can be very important to some babies, while others could care less. By the time Debbie's twins were a year old, they were attached to two teddy bears that went to bed with them every night. Sheri's girls had a pile of lightweight receiving blankets from which one was chosen to sleep with at night. On the other hand, Linda looked and looked for something that would lull Keegan and Colin into a peaceful slumber. "When Keegan and Colin were going through separation anxiety, they had trouble going to sleep at night. Unfortunately, Sarah and Maiah were still young enough to require a great deal of bedtime interaction themselves. In order to direct some of my attention to the girls, I tried to force the boys to attach themselves to a comfort habit. I bought them teddy bears, my mom made them little blankets, and I encouraged them to use pacifiers. They rejected them all! Finally, I played them classical music tapes in a portable cassette player when they went to bed. They loved it! As long as they had their music, they could get to sleep anywhere."

Twins who have not learned how to fall asleep on their own because their parents have rocked them to sleep or fed them until they fell asleep will be resistant as they get older. You can help them make this adjustment by introducing a pleasant bedtime routine and offering them a comfort object, but sometimes this will not be enough when the twins strongly associate their parents' presence with sleep.

In these situations, some pediatricians recommend that when bedtime routines are completed, parents say good-night and leave the room matter-of-factly, even if their babies cry for them. If the crying persists, they suggest that parents come in and check on their infants every 5 to 10 minutes, offering brief verbal reassurances and quick caresses, but they advise against picking up the babies as this reinforces the cycle of their calling for comfort to put them to sleep. With this sort of controlled attention, infants usually fall asleep within 15 minutes or less on the first night and within a few days they will be falling asleep on their own with few complaints.

A variation of this technique is for a parent to stay in the room with the child, verbally comforting him, but not picking him up unless he becomes hysterical. The hysterical baby should be comforted, but as soon as the baby is calmed down, he should be put back to bed. Eventually the baby learns that he must put himself to sleep, but still feels supported by his parent's presence.

The inability of twins to fall asleep on their own is not just a nighttime issue, it can also be a problem during naptime. The solutions to nighttime sleeping problems can be applied to naptime problems, with slight variations. Debbie explains, "I never had trouble getting the twins to fall asleep at night, but I sure had problems at naptime. After a few whimpers, Joanna would be asleep. Michael was another story. Within 15 minutes, he'd have them both awake with his crying. I couldn't figure out how to calm him, and I was desperate to have them nap, so I started putting him in his electric swing. He was out like a light in minutes and stayed asleep for an hour or two. From the first time I did this, I knew I was setting a bad precedent; but at the time, I just didn't have the energy to deal with it in any other way.

"A couple of weeks later when I was in a better frame of mind, I started letting Michael fall asleep in the swing; then when I knew he was in a deep sleep I put him in his crib. That way he got used to waking up in his room with Joanna in the crib next to him. After a few days of this, I started to spend fifteen to twenty minutes of quiet time with Michael and Joanna in their room before putting them down for naps. To my surprise and relief, within a week Michael was napping without difficulty."

*Dealing with Nighttime Waking:* Once you have put your twins to sleep, the struggle may not be over, as 10 to 15 percent of children this age do not sleep through the night. Although there is no physiological need for this nighttime waking, there are some common causes. Some infants awaken because they hear a noise, or feel too cool or too warm. Once awake, they may not be able to return to sleep if they are too uncomfortable or fear being separated from their parents.

Other infants awaken because they experience nightmares or nightfrights. It is not known what form these dreams take, but the infant wakes up suddenly, screaming in terror. This can be distinguished from all other types of nightwaking in that the crying occurs simultaneously with awakening. This is not the fussing and fuming of an angry or fretful baby building to a crescendo over minutes; it happens with dramatic suddenness.

Lastly, infants of this age who are still being nursed, bottle-fed, diapered, cuddled, or comforted whenever they fuss during the night learn to awaken seeking food and attention. How you decide to handle your twins' nighttime waking depends not only on the cause of the waking but also on your value system and your ability to tolerate interrupted sleep.

If your twins are waking because they are too cold or too warm, or they sleep in a noisy part of the house, your solutions are best aimed at the root of the problem. Perhaps warmer or cooler pajamas will do the trick. Maybe the crib can be located further from the source of the noise. While these actions will keep the initial problem from recurring, once your twins awaken and are frightened you must then deal with that problem. If both babies awaken and cry, it is ideal to have both mother and father get up, so that each twin can be calmed promptly. Words of reassurance and a tender pat on the back are often all that is necessary. If one or both of your twins continues to fuss, you may want to leave the room and return to check on them at regular intervals until they fall asleep.

The baby who awakens because of a bad dream is surprisingly easy to comfort. It is often possible to reassure him or her so quickly that the other twin never awakens. When a baby has recurrent nightmare episodes, it is wise to look for a source of stress in his or her life. If the baby who is having nightfrights is in the midst of weaning, consider postponing or slowing the process down for a week or two. If you have been preoccupied lately, refocus attention on the baby who is having the sleeping troubles. Looking for daytime frustrations and dealing with those issues often eases the anxiety that is expressing itself at night.

Of all the sleeping problems that exist in infancy, we suspect that twins awaken to seek food or attention more often than singletons. Young twins often share a room, if not a crib. Their parents, ever desirous of peace and quiet, are quick to feed and comfort the first twin to avoid awakening the other one.

This is exactly what happened to Debbie. "As soon as one of the twins fussed, I went to that one and nursed him or her so that the other didn't wake up. One night it would be Michael; another night it would be Joanna. By the time they were five months old, they both were waking up every morning at 4:00 A.M. to nurse. I lived with this routine until I was nearly crazy from resentment and lack of uninterrupted sleep. I knew that their sleeping problems were all my doing; when they were eight months old, I was finally upset enough to do something about it.

"Dale and I did some reading on the subject, talked to our pediatrician, and decided that I was going to stop nursing the twins at 4:00 A.M. We picked a Friday night, when Dale and I were both prepared to lose sleep. We put Michael and Joanna to bed knowing that there would be no breast-feeding in the middle of the night, but probably lots of screaming. They didn't disappoint us! They screamed for almost an hour. We checked on them every five to ten minutes and offered verbal reassurance, but we didn't pick them up, change their diapers, or feed them.

"It was a very tough night for the entire family, but we were certain that this was the best way for us to handle the situation. Finally they did fall asleep, and slept until 7:00 A.M. The next night they awakened again at 4:00 A.M., and screamed for about twenty minutes before falling asleep. The following night they only grumbled in their sleep for a few minutes in the wee hours. The fourth night they slept solidly until 6:00 A.M., which became their new pattern.

"Admittedly, six is not my preferred time to arise, but it was a heck of a lot better than four!"

Although this type of approach to nighttime waking is recommended by some experts, it is not for everyone. Debra used a completely different method to handle her twins' nighttime waking. She explains, "Rick and I had allowed Ricky and Aislynn to sleep in our bed from the time they were four months old. They woke up three to four times each night and I nursed them right back to sleep, but the trade-off was the development of a nurse-to-sleep pattern. Still, I never thought of letting them cry it out, as it seemed too harsh to me. However, as the twins got older and more restless during sleep, we did make some changes.

"When they were 10 months old, Rick and I decided to move one large bed next to ours. I was able to nurse the twins to sleep in their bed, then crawl into ours, which I was happy to share again with just Rick. If I got too tired by early morning to get back into our bed, I just slept with the babies until it was time to get up. This alternative allowed us to gradually accustom the twins to sleeping in a bed of their own. It didn't stop them from waking up at night to nurse, but I didn't mind the feeding and I felt good about the choice I'd made."

The differing ways that Debbie and Debra handled their twins' sleeping problems underscores the fact that no two parents are alike and no one way is right. Identifying your needs and the twins' needs, learning what others suggest, and applying it all with a dose of common sense is a good place to start.

*Coping with the Twins' Minor Illnesses:*  When one twin gets sick, often he or she passes the infection on to his twin sibling. With two sick babies, even a minor illness has a major impact on family life. The management of any particular illness is something that should be discussed with your twins' doctor; however, we can offer you some insight into the practical reality of dealing with sick twins.

One of our great frustrations was trying to give our twins

medication. As newborns, they did not fight it, but by six months of age they became experts at spitting and splattering every bit of medicine we tried to give them. Soon we gathered some information and learned a few techniques that made giving oral medication easier.

First we made the important discovery that all medications are not created equal. Some brands taste terrible, while others taste quite good. When your doctor writes a prescription or recommends an over-the-counter medication, ask him if he can prescribe or suggest something with a pleasing flavor. When you go to the drugstore to get the medicine, ask the pharmacist if there is a difference in taste between the generic and the brand-name forms. Brand-name medications will always cost a bit more, but sometimes the quality of flavoring is superior and makes the added expense worth it.

Despite these suggestions, there may still be instances when one or both twins rejects a medication by spitting it all over you, themselves, and the floor. When this happens, you'll need other strategies.

It may be possible to mix the medicine with a small amount of juice or food that you are sure your twins will eat at one feeding. In this case, you will need to check with your pharmacist to learn if your particular medication is inactivated by or incompatible with any foods.

Some babies taste the medicine and refuse the food; some parents are uncomfortable disguising medicine in food. In these cases, the straightforward approach is best. For this, you will want to give the medication using an oral dosage syringe, which can be purchased at most drugstores.

Always draw up the medication and have it ready to administer before approaching one of your twins. If you do not have another adult available to help hold the baby as you give the medication, rest assured you can do it yourself. Simply wrap the baby's body in a blanket, being sure to securely trap the arms against his/her sides. Then, set the baby in an infant seat or in your lap in a sitting position.

Give the medicine by placing the oral syringe into your baby's mouth, next to his cheek. Slowly squeeze a small amount of it into this mouth, and wait for him to swallow before giving him more. Repeat this until it is done.

Never squirt the entire contents of the syringe into your baby's mouth, as this causes choking. At the very least, failure is assured as he sputters and spits it back at you. If your child repeatedly spits out doses of a prescribed medication, you should call your doctor. He can then decide if missed doses should be repeated, or if a switch in medication is necessary. It is never a good idea to stop a prescribed medication just because your child does not like the taste or because you are tired of trying to administer it.

Caring for sick infant twins takes its toll. Debbie shares her experience. "By the time Michael and Joanna were six months old, no matter how careful I was, they were both ill at least once a month. Thankfully, the illnesses were not serious. Regardless of the symptoms or the treatments, one thing remained constant: their need for generous doses of parental tender loving care.

"By the time the twins were nearing a year old, I had grown accustomed to a good night's sleep and to having free moments during the day as they played on the floor. Having my nine- or ten-month-old twins sick was just like having newborns again. After a few days of one of their illnesses, I was as irritable and as needy as my sick children and the last thing I felt like being was tender and loving."

Linda felt it was hardest on her when only one child was sick. She explains: "The healthy twin was in a constant state of frustration, having no way of understanding that I was giving most of my attention to the other twin because he or she was ill. At first, I dealt with this by holding both twins and feeling totally consumed by their needs. It was a no-win situation. After a few bouts of illnesses, I started getting babysitters on the worst days, so the well twin could be entertained as I tended to the sick one. Doing this eased the pressure on all of us."

Debbie also found ways to ease her stress. "I cut back on my other responsibilities. I let the housekeeping go and streamlined meal preparation. I also used the phone as a lifeline, calling friends with children to compare notes on illnesses, but the best part was simply hearing a friendly voice. We laughed as we agreed that motherhood was an impossible task and I hung up feeling restored, ready to give to my kids again."

## Our Evolving Family
· · · · · · · · · · · · · · · · · · · ·

*Enjoying Our Twins:* When a mother is immersed in the day-to-day work of caring for twins, it is all too easy to forget to have fun with them. Believe it or not, it is possible to enjoy them, especially during the second half of their first year when they are increasingly social, not too mobile (hopefully), and incredibly adorable!

Even mundane interactions with your twins can spontaneously meet your and their needs in deeply satisfying ways. Sheri found that "There were times on the best days when I felt completely in synch with Emmy and Tessa. I was adept at reading their signals and met their needs promptly and effectively. The unspoken communication, appreciation, and love that existed between us was complete. When I had days like this, I felt such complete fulfillment that I cannot describe it."

These special moments that Sheri describes are an essential part of the rewards of mothering, but they alone are not enough to sustain a happy and healthy parent-child relationship. There must also be time for fun.

Florien says, "Otto and Max were so much fun by the time they reached eight months. They loved playing pat-a-cake and peekaboo. The more attention Devin and I gave them the more excited they got. It was apparent that they enjoyed interacting with Devin and me."

Aislynn and Ricky were very silly at this age, and Debra often found herself laughing at them both. "We called Aislynn *Happy Girl* because her china blue eyes lit up when she laughed. She also earned the title of *Miss Wacko* because she shook her head from side to side for no apparent reason. We would ask her, 'Are you wacko?' when we saw her doing this, and she quickly learned to do it more in response to the question. When she began walking, her head-shaking caused her to lose her balance, however, so her antics became more demure. Getting around was itself the major form of play at this age, but Aislynn did show an affinity for cloth and paper or banging on things. Unfortunately, Ricky's head was a handy drum.

"Ricky was very tolerant of his sister's mistreatment because he usually had his attention on small things that fit in his hands—or better yet, his mouth. I had to watch him closely and constantly inspect the area for possible booty for our *Mister Vacuum*. Both the children were happy-go-lucky most of the time in spite of the fact that their mother was a mess!"

Pursuing activities outside the home is another source of fun when twins reach this age. Linda and Todd, who both enjoy swimming, decided to introduce their girls to the water when they were seven months old. Linda remembers, "Todd and I took swimming classes with Sarah and Maiah, so we each had a baby to play with during class. Todd and I had such fun, and the twins adapted to the water like little fish. Maiah was the class clown; she floated in our arms with her toes in her mouth. Other times she got so relaxed that she actually fell asleep while floating on her back. Sarah splashed and kicked as we supported her tiny body. The girls were delighted with this new environment and Todd and I felt good expanding their world."

Swimming classes are not the ideal recreational activity for every family. Children who hate their baths are bound to think of swimming lessons as torture, even if their parents are in the water with them.

Popular activities for older infants are walks in the stroller and playing outdoors. Sheri remembers, "Emmy and Tessa turned six months old at the beginning of summer. We spent lots of wonderful afternoons strolling through our neighborhood and returning home to explore our backyard. The girls loved being outdoors so much that they didn't mind when I finally corralled them in the playpen with toys so I could get some yardwork done or Steve could get the barbecue going."

As our twins grew closer to us and to each other and more capable of relating to the world around them, everything became more fun, especially holidays. Debbie brings this to life: "Halloween was a kick! I found two inexpensive pram suits made of heavy pile. One was made to resemble a lion, and the other a dalmation. We dressed the twins in these, put black eyeliner whiskers on their faces, and took them out with their older brother, Chris, for trick or treating. Michael and Joanna didn't quite understand what was happening, but they were entranced and it was great fun for the rest of us, too.

"Our Thanksgiving and Christmas celebrations were equally festive, although we had to make adjustments. At Christmas, our tree was inside a baby play-yard fence, and there were no decorations within reach of curious babies. At dinner, Michael and Joanna ate strained turkey and cranberry sauce and made a complete mess of our formal holiday meal, contributing to our memories and evolving holiday traditions. It started us all happily imagining what the holidays would be like when we were all a year older."

*Twinproofing:* A major undertaking for all of us during this six-month period was twinproofing our homes. This required careful thought and planning as we hurried to stay one step ahead of our babies' curiosity and physical development. The more mobile our inquisitive twins became, the more things we had to move away, lock up, and corral off!

Common potential dangers are stairs, windows, medications, hanging curtain strings, movable and breakable objects, wobbly furniture, plants, radiators, fireplaces, electrical outlets, poisonous substances, and any item small enough to cause choking. Another possible danger can be pets. Family pets like dogs and cats may resent small children who pull and push at them and get all their masters' love and attention. Linda says, "We had our standard poodle for five years before we had any children, so I knew he would be jealous and compete for our attention. Although he was a good-natured animal, I didn't want to risk having him snap at the girls, so Todd and I had him stay outdoors."

It is also wise to take precautions to prepare for an accidental poisoning, as Debbie did. "I didn't like to think that this could happen to my children, because I had all our medicines in safety-lock containers up high in our closet, but I had to face the possibility that an accident could happen. So I posted the 1-800 number of Poison Control and our pediatrician's phone number near the telephone. I also purchased a bottle of dated Syrup of Ipecac for each twin in case I needed it to induce vomiting."

Florien and Devin did a very thorough job of twinproofing for their curious little boys. "I found that we did more complete babyproofing than we would have if we'd only had one baby, simply because it was easier than it was to follow our active twins and constantly say no. Gates went up and drawers were securely latched. Devin and I kept all the twins' toys low, moved our possessions up, and left the kitchen cupboard containing plastic containers unlatched, so they were accessible to the boys. This was the only kitchen area they were allowed to play in and then only when meals were not being prepared. All other areas in the kitchen and bathroom were off limits."

In addition to regular babyproofing, Sheri and Steve had the challenge of finding methods that protected their twins, but still allowed Kallie, at age five, access to the things she needed. One of these things was the toilet. "After trying some inexpensive and impossible-to-open toilet latches, we discovered one called Lid-Lok. It was neat-looking, snapped on with no tools, and was easy for Kallie to open and close. It was more expensive than the other brands and I'll admit that I hesitated before buying it, but it turned out to be the wisest money I ever spent."

Linda had extra difficulties when she tried to babyproof for her second set of twins. "Sarah and Maiah, at age three, were constantly thwarting my efforts to babyproof. What I moved up out of the babies' way, the girls reached and moved back to the floor for their convenience. Unwittingly, the girls would move chairs that I had just pushed safely out of their way. Before I knew it, Keegan and Colin were pulling these chairs over on themselves. The girls usually forgot to close the bathroom door after they used it, and they often left their little toys all over the floor. It was a constant nightmare for me to keep objects out of the boys' mouths."

The best preparations for babyproofing in the world are no substitute for good, careful supervision of the twins. Sheri learned this important lesson in a frightening way. "One morning I was hosting an authors' meeting at my house and we were gathered in the kitchen. Suddenly the doorbell rang. The twins were playing at our feet, so I scooped up Emmy to go answer the door, leaving Tessa behind. I assumed that the others would watch her, but I never actually asked one of them to do so. I dashed to get Kallie ready to leave with her friend, and passed my friends who were on their way to the living room. I held Emmy as Kallie and I stood in the open doorway and wrestled with her coat. Then Kallie ran to her friend's car and I stepped out on the porch to wave good-bye. My thought flew to Tessa, but I remembered that I had left her with my friends. When I came back into the living room, I set Emmy down and noticed that Tessa was not there.

"Without asking my friends, I assumed that she had been left in the kitchen, but it was empty! I headed back to the living room, but I still did not see her, so I questioned my co-authors as to her whereabouts. They looked at me blankly; no one had been watching her. My heart dropped to my stomach as I did a quick survey of the bedroom and found nothing. I began to call her name as I ran through the house, searching behind chairs and under beds. I was really frightened by the time I had combed our master bedroom, still without success. Then, as I started out of the bedroom, I glanced out the window to see Tessa sitting in the middle of the driveway.

"Tessa did not appear to be afraid or upset, and when I retrieved her she was annoyed by my tearful hugs and kisses. After it was all over and Tessa was safe in the house, I concluded she had crawled onto the porch and behind the screen door when I was helping Kallie with her coat. She was probably right behind me as I waved good-bye to Kallie. If she had been outside a few minutes longer, she could have crawled into the street. Since that incident, the children are secured before I tend to another thing; I never assume that other adults are watching my children unless I ask them to do so."

## *Our Thoughts and Reflections*

SHERI:   Although Emmy and Tessa were harder to keep track of, their attention span had increased markedly by the time they were a year old. I was truly enjoying the time I spent with the twins.

FLORIEN: Taking time to play with Max and Otto was the greatest investment Devin and I made during this time of their lives. Through play we were able to help instill a sense of curiosity and a sense of security in each boy at the same time.

The thing that helped keep me sane enough to enjoy my babies and to view their play as fun, not work, was having them on the same routine for feeding, naps, diapering . . . most everything. It gave me the structure in my day to do all the "have-to's" and still have time for fun.

LINDA: By the second stage of infancy the double diapering, stereo crying, and endless feedings weren't as overwhelming. I could finally see past the work and actually enjoy our two happy babies. For the time being, I had life under control. I tried to establish good habits that we could build on and that would make our life easier in the toddler months ahead.

DEBBIE: Although the second six months of Michael's and Joanna's lives were easier than the first six months, I wouldn't want to give the impression that they were a *lot* easier. Because my twins were often ill with ear and sinus infections, I still felt overwhelmed on many days. I looked forward to the time when life would feel truly manageable.

DEBRA: There was just as much work involved in parenting older infants as there was in parenting newborns, but it was a more playful and gratifying time. During the summer months, I found the twins' mobility to be a definite advantage. They were thrilled to be outdoors, and I shared their exhilaration. We were all on the move now, but in different ways.

*Chapter 11*

# "We need to talk"

## *Couple Relationships*

The most important relationship within the family is the one between the parents. Yet in all our families, it was this relationship that suffered most after the birth of our twins, simply because there was so little time or energy left to devote to each other. Whether our twins were newborn, young toddlers, or preschoolers, it was easy to neglect our relationships with our spouses. Inevitably this caused problems. Eventually we all came to grips with the results of this unintentional (and nearly unavoidable) lack of attention.

When the problems were small, the most effective way we found to get back on track with our spouses was a well-chosen moment when we would lovingly approach them and say, "We need to talk." The larger problems could not be solved this easily. Our solutions, and the wisdom we gained in the process, are the stories we share now.

### *Having Twins Brings Changes to the Couple Relationship*

The birth of twins is a stressful event in even the best of marriages. Each of our marital relationships underwent many changes after the twins were born. Some were the direct result of the added responsibilities of twin parenthood coinciding with little time spent with our partners. Others were caused by unhealthy patterns of relating that had been part of our marriages for some time. Resentment, unfulfilled expectations, limited energy, and emotional and physical changes also taxed relationships. For the first-time parents there was the additional transition from "couple" to "family."

The birth of our twins precipitated for all of us a growth process that ultimately brought each couple (and family) closer together. The driving force behind our willingness to work through these difficulties was the desire to keep our marital relationship strong and healthy for the security of our children, as well as ourselves. Of course, this took a lot of hard work and commitment. Without it, our marriages might have come apart at the seams or broken apart altogether.

Linda remembers the effect that first-time parenthood had on her relationship with Todd. "We had a solid marriage built of love, trust, and good communication skills to fall back on when our first twins were born. But nothing could completely prepare us for the jump from being a couple to becoming a family of six with two sets of twins in just four years. Overall, I think we have done remarkably well. Of course, we've had some problems and I can remember times when we lost sight of each other as lovers, friends, and confidants. We were just too busy. In those first weeks after the births of each set of twins, the only time we had to share together was the brief minutes before sleep. But instead of words of passion we snuggled together and whispered sweet nothings like, 'Did you take out the dirty diapers?' 'Did you remember to cover the babies?' and 'Is the clean laundry in the dryer?' "

Devin and Florien, who were also first-time parents, adapted well to parenthood initially. However, they started noticing some strain in their relationship as the boys neared one year of age. "Before Otto and Max were born, my relationship with Devin was loving, comfortable, and carefree. Our personal values seemed to mesh well, and we looked forward to a life together which would one day include children. We did not have trouble communicating; there was always time to talk, go for walks, go on bike rides, or spend intimate time together.

"Our close relationship continued without much disruption for the first year after our sons were born. Devin and I were comfortable with our new role as parents. I worked two evenings a week and for a few hours on the weekends, and Devin worked part-time during the day. This gave each of us time to spend with our children as well as each other. We were very happy and felt blessed to have two healthy, active children. Our lives seemed to be full and complete.

"Yet somewhere along the way our individual values, expectations, and approaches with the boys started to differ. I believe these changes started during my trip to England when the boys were eleven months old. During the four weeks I was gone, two things happened that altered Devin's and my relationship.

"First, Devin did a wonderful job of caring for the boys and managing the house while I was gone. Prior to this, I had assumed most of the household chores, done most of the errands that made life go smoothly, taken primary care of the children, and made sure that everyone's emotional and physical needs got met. I had been Super Mom, Super Woman, and Super Wife without a second thought. Now that he had shown how well he handled some of the work I had previously done, I expected him to continue to do so.

"Secondly, during my trip I got a taste of life as it had been prior to my marriage. Before our marriage I had traveled extensively, visiting my parents' home countries and experiencing different cultures. After my trip to England, I was determined to have my sons enjoy the many wonders of travel and get to know my family and relatives better, so I set two long-range goals. One was to find work that would allow my family to travel and explore other parts of the world. The other was to find ways to visit my family more often, even though we lived three thousand miles apart.

"From this point, Devin's and my goals for work, life-style, and place of residence began a transformation. We did take time to discuss these changes and concerns as they arose, but we were finding more and more core differences in our preferences for where we wanted to live in relation to our extended families and our work, and how we spent our leisure time. This made our conversations more strained and subsequently less frequent. For the first time in our relationship, there was some distance between us."

Because Sheri and Steve had learned how to work out the marital tensions of parenthood when their first daughter was born, they simply applied the same rules when their twins were born and fared well. "After Emmy and Tessa came home we realized how lucky we were. We had lots of help, and our support network was strong. Plus, the insight and knowledge that Steve and I gained during Kallie's first few years held us together as friends and lovers during the tough first months with the twins."

Debbie and Dale were also experienced parents, but the births of Michael and Joanna still had a big impact on their relationship. "Before the twins were born, Dale and I enjoyed an easy, warm, and loving relationship. We never had to work at staying close and in touch with each other. It just happened naturally. Being the parents of one child did put some demands on our relationship, but as each year passed, Chris grew more self-sufficient and fit in easily with our life-style. Life for the three of us was pleasant and predictable. We functioned like three cogs in a machine, clicking away smoothly, each anticipating and responding to the needs of the other two.

"However, when Michael and Joanna were born prematurely, everything was thrown out of sync. During the first several months the babies had countless needs and Chris changed from our sweet, independent child into a whining, whimpering mess. Dale and I became exhausted and glassy-eyed automatons, moving from one child's needs or one household chore to another. There was little time to rest. Life was an unending list of duties to accomplish.

"Initially, the easiest way for me to deal with the ongoing stress was to withdraw from everyone, including Dale. I just wanted to sleep during every free moment. My thinking was simple; if I could only get enough rest, I might finally feel able to handle my responsibilities without going crazy! When evening came and all three children were asleep, I raced to my bed with a favorite book in hand. After a few minutes of reading, I was ready for some serious snoozing.

"I could feel emotional distance growing between Dale and me, but I was too tired to care. I reasoned that putting our relationship on hold for a while wouldn't really harm it. After all, I knew that we loved each other and I counted on him to understand and accommodate my temporary disinterest in intimacy of any kind.

"He did understand for about six weeks, then he insisted that I stay awake one evening and talk about 'us.' Even before he spoke, I knew what he was going to say and I knew he was right. We were drifting apart. Most of the time we were either abrupt and short-tempered or making accusations that the other wasn't doing his or her share around the house. Even our most pleasant conversations were brusque and to the point, more like hourly status reports than loving communication. At night, when we were finally alone, it was all we could do just to give each other an exhausted kiss and then fall asleep. For Dale and me, this was a new and disconcerting way of relating.

"We recognized that part of our problem was that the new demands on our time and energy exceeded our personal resources. We simply hadn't the chance to stay in touch with each other. In order to remain best friends and lovers, we knew we had to consciously set aside some time away from the children to enjoy each other's company."

For Debra and Rick, having twins altered their relationship radically. "Our marriage had been on shaky ground for a few years prior to the arrival of Aislynn and Ricky, but the good parts of our relationship had enabled us to gloss over the fact. Now, under the pressure of so many additional stresses, the cracks in the foundation began to widen until it felt as if the whole structure might collapse. We could no longer ignore our problems. During these years we were forced to take a look at our relationship, to get help, and to begin building an even stronger partnership than before.

"For the first eight or nine years after Rick and I married, 90 percent of our relationship was fantastic, which helped us to overlook or forgive the 10 percent that wasn't. Overall, we communicated well about most areas of our lives, but I had difficulty sharing my desires and needs. I was more focused on 'him,' or 'us,' or 'our plans.' Both Rick and I felt uncomfortable expressing negative feelings, so there were often misunderstandings. When we were tested by stresses that required the ability to communicate in these areas, our shortcomings became evident.

"Then I found out I was pregnant again. Rick managed to land a job that provided some of the security we sought, and we began to build a house for our growing family. These three factors lifted our spirits immensely and contributed to a renewed sense of commitment as well. We were getting along much better at this point, but parts of our marriage were still fragmented when we received the news that I was carrying twins. With all our new concerns, we had no time for the unfinished business between us.

"Of course, this unfinished business remained once the babies were born. Had I been able to tell Rick of my feelings and to ask directly for his help, he could have responded and we might have avoided the consequences of misjudging each other. The other side of communication is recognizing that someone is suffering stress or hurt, something especially hard to do when one is coping with one's own strong feelings.

"On his part, Rick did not expect much from me while the babies were infants, but he also didn't expect to be the target of my hostility or to feel unappreciated for his contributions. I have to give him credit for sticking around through all the chaos. He retreated into his own preoccupations, feeling alone with his burden of responsibility. We were two overwhelmed, estranged people, still committed to our marriage and family but feeling powerless to keep destructive forces at bay. Every facet of our relationship was affected. If only we had recognized the need to have time together to sort out the feelings and the misunderstandings, we might not have become so deeply entrenched in them."

## *Finding Time to Spend Together*
. . . . . . . . . . . . . . . . . . . . . . . . . . . . . . .

There is no doubt that after the twins are born there will be
less time for you and your partner to be alone together. This is
especially true during the first year of their lives. For most couples,
this decrease in time together is the major source of the negative
feelings that arise between them. Less time for small talk, intimate
exchanges, and discussion of problems leads to insecurities and
frustrations which can build up and grow out of proportion. It
became necessary to plan brief periods of time with our husbands
so this tension could be diffused and we could enjoy each other's
company. As each of us became more secure in our parenting
skills and our twins grew older and needed less of our attention,
time together was much easier to come by.

For the first year after Aislynn and Ricky were born, Debra
and Rick spent very little time together as a couple. The lack of
shared relaxation and recreation took its toll. "Rick and I seemed
to occupy separate worlds based on our notions of what each of
us should provide for our family. Rick felt a heavy financial responsibility and pressure to provide a better living environment.
At the time, he didn't realize that I and our children had more
immediate needs for his involvement with us. Meanwhile I concentrated solely on caring for the children, which left me little
time or energy to devote to other shared interests."

Linda and Todd were very conscious of the need for making
time for each other and tried different strategies to make it happen. "When the twins were babies and our schedule was so hectic,
once the day was over there wasn't any time left for the two of
us. Finally I came up with the idea of devoting a half hour or so
each evening to sitting down together, drinking a cup of tea, and
just talking. We tried to stick to this commitment, but some nights
we found ourselves in bed trying to talk through our yawns. When
we had to make do with only brief moments of conversation
during one day, I found that the next day was always more difficult.

"I soon realized that Todd and I needed time together. I needed
it to cope with the unending diapers, crying, and nursing. Todd
needed it so he could walk out the door in the morning, confident
that I was in a good frame of mind to handle my long day alone

with the babies. Understanding this made us both strive to keep our 'dates' in the evening."

Debbie and Dale also scheduled time to be together to enhance their relationship, but there was only one way to find that time in the first few months, before they had baby-sitters and evenings out. "I knew that it had to be carved out of our precious few hours of sleep; I absolutely *hated* the idea!! After all, I recently had started spending thirty minutes with Chris every evening, time I had already borrowed from my rapidly dwindling sleep time.

"I had an obvious conflict. My relationship with Dale was being jeopardized due to lack of attention. It was time to set priorities and I knew what choices we had to make.

"First of all, we committed ourselves to spending some time together each evening before falling asleep. We agreed that any conversations we had during this time were to focus on us, not the children. If this emotional intimacy led to sexual intimacy, so much the better.

"We also decided that during our waking hours we needed to treat each other with sensitivity and understanding. This included making conscious efforts to be loving and affectionate toward each other. A kiss as we passed in the hallway or a hug as we prepared dinner went a long way toward improving our morale. Finally, we planned to schedule an evening out together once or twice a month as soon as Michael and Joanna were off their heart monitors and we felt comfortable with baby-sitters.

"As much as possible, we tried to keep to this new routine. I don't mean to imply that our plan was always easy to follow. On occasion, our allotted time together felt like just one more duty on our list of endless responsibilities. Sometimes our prearranged attempts at intimacy left no room for spontaneity and ruined any possibility of romance. There were times when we were both so tired that neither one of us could carry our part of a coherent conversation, much less make love. When this happened, we simply agreed to take a night off from each other.

"After a week or two of close conversations and renewed intimacy, Dale and I began to feel like friends and lovers again."

## *The Renewal of Sexual Intimacy*

After the birth of a baby, not to mention two babies, it is common for a couple to experience a decrease in sexual intimacy. Sleep deprivation, the stress of caring for infant twins, the reduced time for emotional connections between partners, and the lack of opportunity for spontaneity are the biggest factors in decreasing sexual desire and activity. When anger or resentment runs deeply through a relationship, or one or both partners feel their contribution to the family is not validated, sexual intimacy will be threatened even more. In addition, if each partner's view of the other is changed so that they see each other more as parents and less as lovers, difficulties may arise.

Changes in a woman's body may also contribute to a decreased interest in sex. Sometimes a woman feels apprehensive about the prospect of milk leaking from her breasts during intercourse, or she does not feel sexy because her body is "not what it used to be." If she has had a C-section or an episiotomy that required stitches, her body will need time to heal before intercourse is comfortable. Hormonal changes also occur, and nurturing hormones may override the reproductive hormones, curbing her desire. Though this picture looks a little dim, in time a satisfying sexual relationship will return.

Finding a way to experience physical closeness with our partners when sexual intimacy was nearly nonexistent was a big challenge for all of us. We knew that physical contact was important to nurture our marital relationships and our self-esteem. For the first few months, we depended on alternate ways of expressing our love—hugs, a back rub, a kiss in the hallway, or cuddling while watching a TV show. When our bodies recovered from the demands of giving birth, our sexual desires returned if the relationship with our spouses was affectionate but unpressured. Then, as we experienced sex that was nurturing, stress-reducing, and just plain fun, it became self-perpetuating.

Unfortunately, the renewal of sexual intimacy is not always so simply accomplished. Todd and Linda's return to sexual activity took a while, mainly because of the extra physical demands being placed on Linda by her babies. "During my postnatal exam, I was told by my obstetrician that Todd and I could resume normal sexual activity in six weeks, but I told Todd that the doctor had said ten weeks. I needed those extra weeks to allow my over-worked body to adjust. I couldn't get used to satisfying two suck-ling babies and at the same time be intimate with Todd. When Todd found out the truth, he was very understanding, and slowly my body became accustomed to the extra maternal demands."

Though Sheri and Steve had established a close relationship, she denied their sexual needs for several months after the twins' birth. Trying to be supportive, Steve did not pressure Sheri, but eventually tension surfaced. "At first I discounted Steve's growing unhappiness, figuring it was just the demands of having twins that caused the tension. Yet deep down I knew that our intermittent sex life was the real reason for his frustration. Admittedly, I had become very disinterested in sex. My body was overstimulated from nursing two babies, and I was fulfilled emotionally by my closeness with them. Initially, I brushed aside the idea that there was a problem.

"After a few months, however, I began to feel the loss of intimacy between Steve and me. I knew I loved him, but wondered if I'd ever regain my desire and passion. Fortunately, Steve's un-easy feelings surfaced at the same time as mine, so we were able to talk: We reaffirmed our love for each other and rededicated ourselves to working harder at the sexual part of our relationship.

"To provide motivation, I went out and bought a frilly night-gown. When I bought it, my intention was to wear it *for Steve,* but I quickly realized that the lingerie made me feel more beau-tiful and sexy than I had in a long time. After I bought it I didn't make any immediate romantic plans, preferring the occasion to be spontaneous. And sure enough, a few nights later, the children all went to bed early. Voila!

"As Steve and I reestablished our sexual intimacy, I learned that my ability to mother my children was enhanced by a good partnership with him. Instead of looking at Steve as just another person who wanted something from me, I saw the strength that his friendship and love could give to me. I felt renewed and alive!"

The renewal of sexual intimacy will be more difficult when

there is a breakdown in the partner relationship. The distance that had grown between Debra and Rick naturally had a negative impact on their sex life. "For me, the fatigue, the negative feelings, and the physical closeness I had with the babies all day combined to reduce my desire to a minimum. Many times sex seemed like just another need to be met, though once I was aroused, the actual lovemaking was enjoyable and relaxing. But my overall disinterest contributed to Rick's growing feelings of frustration and rejection. Our once great sex life became another point of contention. Our sexual relationship didn't return to normal until many of the other issues in our marriage were worked through."

## Dividing the Work Load

Sharing household duties and child care is a challenge for all parents of twins, for it seems each parent needs to give 100 percent just to get through the day. If one partner can't or won't do his or her share, a conflict may result as the other partner takes on more than he or she can handle and resents it more and more with each passing day. Problems like this are best resolved promptly, so that simmering wounds don't damage the relationship. With an honest effort at cooperation, the work load can be divided fairly and each partner can feel mutually supported.

Linda and Todd were fortunate that the division of child care and household responsibilities never became an issue for them. "After the girls were born, Todd and I instinctively took over separate chores. We never discussed it, but we managed to get everything done with reasonable efficiency. Todd did all the cooking and helped out with many of the babies' demands while I did the housecleaning and nursed the girls. We both were exhausted by evening, but at least the day's work was completed when we fell into bed and we could start over again in the morning."

Linda and Todd's experience is unusual. In most relationships, a certain amount of juggling and rearranging of child care and household responsibilities must be discussed in order to reach a fair compromise. Sheri and Steve had straightforward talks about household duties during a time when each was well rested and ready to discuss them. Their decisions were always open to re-negotiation as individual and family needs changed with time.

"Yard work and gardening chores had always been pleasurable for me. When Emmy and Tessa were born, though, Steve took over the care of these areas. When he mowed the lawn, I found myself carrying babies from window to window, fretting and stewing because he wasn't helping me. One day, during an escalating role discussion, he challenged, 'Fine, you go mow the lawn!' So I did; and I loved every minute of it! As I mowed, I realized that many things he considered mundane chores would give me respite from mothering.

"We had another discussion about our household responsibilities and I shared my preference for watching all three children while he cooked dinner. I gave him time to unwind after work with a glass of wine and the evening news. Then I kept the children completely out of the kitchen while he prepared dinner. After we ate, he kept the kids at bay while I cleaned the kitchen.

"Later, Steve traded some of his cooking and cleaning chores for some of my duties feeding and dressing the twins. This was a nice change for the girls, who were able to have Daddy for more than just a playmate. With Steve's active help, the children became *our* children instead of *my* children. Emmy and Tessa seemed to notice this too, as they now could be calmed and comforted by either of us equally."

Debra made the mistake of assuming that Rick would see her need for assistance and voluntarily help with the house and children without being asked. "I thought he could realize how hard it was for me to handle everything. When he didn't respond in a positive manner, I felt abandoned and uncared for. When I brought the subject up, we ended up fighting about who was working harder or whose work was more important or valuable. Instead of problem solving like partners, we argued unproductively and never resolved anything."

## Resolving Day-to-Day Arguments

Successfully resolving the day-to-day conflicts of couples is of utmost importance to the well-being of the entire family. As problems arose within our marriages, we became aware of how and why they occurred, learned from our mistakes, and found key ways to right a bad situation.

First, and most importantly, we learned that it was best to solve problems when we were not under stress or, as is the case with twins, under *less* stress! During disagreements, it helped to avoid the trap of criticizing each other, to make stress the enemy. This kept the issues well focused and less emotionally charged. Additionally, when we handled our problems as they occurred, rather than letting them pile up, we defused a lot of potential anger. A good preventive step was to devise a plan of action for dealing with difficult situations before they actually arrived. Working together with our partners as a team was so much better than each of us trying to manage on our own.

Linda and Todd strongly believed that resolving arguments quickly was important to the health of their marriage and prevented a buildup of resentment and miscommunication. "With time so precious, it was critical to discuss issues and vent frustrations immediately. If a conflict wasn't dealt with at once, it sometimes took days before enough time was available to discuss it or work it through. We made a pact to never go to bed angry at each other. Sometimes we had to agree to put an issue on hold and discuss it later, but we kissed and made up in the meantime.

"Some of our disagreements seemed so silly, but were happening because of the pressure we both felt during those first few weeks and months. One disagreement started when Todd tried to fix our clothes washer. After a hard day at work, the last thing he wanted to do was spend an evening wringing out dirty diapers and taking apart greasy machinery. I had had a hard day, too, and became angry with his less than supportive comments. We were up to our elbows in wet diapers, yelling at each other. Finally unable to take any more, I threw down a diaper and stormed out of the room. Slamming out the back door, I convinced myself that I wasn't coming back, but once outside I realized that I didn't have my car keys or a coat. It was raining lightly, but I wasn't about to go back inside. I plopped down on the rock wall, feeling sorry for myself as the rain mixed with my tears. My visions of freedom slowly faded and my anger had dissipated by the time I crept silently in the house. I wanted to avoid Todd, but he was waiting for me. Instead of the confrontation I fully expected, he apologized for his bad temper and handed me a steaming mug of hot chocolate! We talked out our frustrations with the repaired washer humming in the background.

"When we had our second set of twins, some of the earlier problems resurfaced. I thought we had learned how to handle the stress, but we quickly fell back into our old pattern of ignoring each other as we tried to parent four children. Some of our days were so hectic, we didn't even have a spare moment to kiss.

"At least the second time around Todd and I were aware of what was happening. If nothing else, we had learned how to fight fair by sticking to the issue at hand and not dredging up old fights or flinging accusations at each other. Thus, we were able to resolve our conflicts quickly. I'm not saying it was (or is) easy. I still have to force myself to take that first step toward a compromise, but I know it is important to our relationship."

Florien and Devin made a point of fostering honest and frequent communication. Yet she realistically admits that there were hours, days, and sometimes weeks that went by when it was difficult to be open-minded and supportive of each other. "There were times that we didn't know where to start. Sometimes we didn't have the energy, and other times a confrontation was easier to ignore. Yet, we both consistently felt better when we took even a few minutes to talk about how our days were going, gave each other hugs, or cuddled in bed before going to sleep. When we didn't do these things, tension gradually increased and disagreements and misunderstandings were bound to happen.

"Minor disagreements that could be handled in a fair and respectful manner were discussed in front of the boys. A benefit of coming to terms over our smaller differences in this way was that Max and Otto were able to watch us present our differing views and feelings, discuss them, and reach agreeable decisions.

"Although Devin and I thought it was important to resolve

conflicts in front of the boys so they could learn constructive ways to handle disagreements, this wasn't always possible. When Devin and I had disagreements of a deeper nature, where close personal feelings and issues were at stake, we handled them in private. These discussions usually started out as arguments, but we would really try to calm down and respectfully listen to each other; then we'd come to an acceptable agreement or compromise. We can't always resolve our differences perfectly, but it is our goal, one we hope our sons will value and attempt to attain."

Debra and Rick had a more difficult time communicating, but their persistence and commitment got them through. "We talked about our communication problems during a trip to the coast, after Aislynn and Ricky's first birthday. Our conversation resulted in an agreement to start going out together, to spend quality time as a couple. This proved to be very helpful; we enjoyed each other's company during our 'dates' and began to feel connected again. During these unpressured moments we talked about many things, but avoided serious matters that could lead to arguments. Our communication skills were unequal to the heavier issues and we didn't want to spoil our special time. Consequently, the harder issues came up at home, usually when we were already stressed to the limit."

## Resolving the Bigger Problems

When the day-to-day conflicts between couples are not resolved to mutual satisfaction, deeper marital troubles may develop; these require more work than a reassuring hug or a short conversation. We found that good communication skills learned from attending parenting groups, talking with friends, and reading books, or from counselors were an important part of working out bigger marital troubles.

As the differences in Florien's and Devin's expectations of parenting and life-styles surfaced, they realized that these weren't little differences that would go away on their own. During several long conversations they each shared their feelings extensively, and came to some agreements.

"With a household to manage and two toddlers to care for, it was hard for me to find the energy in the evenings and on weekends to consistently meet Devin's emotional needs, too. In order for me to function at my best, I needed to replenish my energy by relaxing. Sometimes after the boys went to bed, I wanted to read the paper instead of talking. Gradually, I began to expect Devin to take care of his own needs, as I did mine. This wasn't necessarily an unreasonable expectation, but it *was* unreasonable of me to expect him to do this regularly without initially discussing it with him. Meanwhile, Devin was sensing but not knowing exactly what types of transformations I was making in my life. He was confused and defensive. Eventually we sat down and set new family and individual goals that reflected our needs, strengths, and desires. We recognize that these goals will probably change as time goes on.

"Now I try to spend at least a few minutes every evening with Devin to find out how he's doing and how things are going at work. I still expect him to carry his load in terms of housework and meeting daily family needs, but instead of telling him what to do (or as he would say, 'nagging him to do'), I try to *ask* him to do things. He, on the other hand, is taking more initiative and accepting more active responsibility for seeing that chores get done and our children's needs are met. We are learning to collaborate with each other instead of working against one another."

When the rift in the marital relationship is more severe, the best solution may be to seek professional help. Debra recounts the struggles she and Rick shared. "Our attempts to discuss serious problems almost always resulted in bitter arguments. Resentment and anger marshalled the punishing tactics of attacking with verbal abuse and withdrawal. We argued about everything from finances to housework. Seeking to rectify a deteriorating situation, we each demanded that the other change: 'If you would only . . . , things would be better!' We both secretly wondered if we really belonged together. We felt hatred for each other, then love, then hatred. One day I'd be content that our dreams were still intact, and the next I'd fantasize about moving out and starting a new life.

"At some point I began to ask myself what part I was playing in perpetuating this sickening merry-go-round ride. When I started asking these questions, I got answers. Self-help books on couple relationships shed light on what appeared to be an ongoing and intricately constructed real-life drama. Acknowledging the scripts within our marriage was much easier than changing them, though, and I soon realized that professional help and the support of others was needed.

"These resources helped me understand that I was not responsible for, nor capable of, changing anyone but myself. Once I stopped blaming and focusing on Rick so much, I made personal progress and found myself getting stronger as an individual and happier in all areas. However, the changes in me upset the dynamics of interaction between the two of us, which was a little scary and very threatening.

"I banked on the fact that Rick cared about us and was committed to our marriage. He had observed some positive changes in me, and I hoped that my sharing of the knowledge I had gained might induce him to seek out similar help. He was receptive to this only when it was expressed in an honest and sincere manner; I first made the mistake of blurting out my 'analyses' when we argued, which backfired completely. In spite of understandable reluctance in the beginning, Rick was open to the possibility of regaining happiness, and when the twins turned three he agreed to see a marriage counselor.

"We went to several counselors before we happened on the right one, who helped us to see our real strengths as individuals and as a couple, and to face the issues that put distance between us. Though we have a great deal of work ahead of us, we now know we will survive any other tests that life can devise. Only recently have we called an honest truce, put down all our weapons of retaliation, and embraced each other as friends and lovers once again."

## Revitalizing Our Relationships

At some point after your twins are born, a time will come when you have the luxury of focusing on the romantic aspects of your partner relationship. Planning to do this by the end of the twins' first year can give a very deserving couple an opportunity to deepen their bonds and renew their commitment to each other. For many couples with infant twins, stealing a few moments of time during the busy day to be with their partner has to suffice until the babies are old enough to be left for a more satisfactory overnight getaway. Needless to say, most parents worry about leaving their babies even for a few hours, but a well-trusted person can care for your babies very well and give you and your partner some much-needed time together.

Florien and Devin consider themselves lucky that Devin's parents live only forty-five minutes away and have always been comfortable caring for the twins. "Max and Otto were just ten months old when my in-laws first offered to take them for the weekend. The boys had just gotten over a virus that left them with sores in their mouths, so they preferred bottle-feeding over breast-feeding. I gave my in-laws some frozen packages of breast milk to feed them while the twins were at their house. While Devin and I were gone, I kept pumping my breasts to keep my milk supply up. Even though it may appear odd that Devin and I chose to go away for a weekend right after the boys were sick, we really felt a need to take this chance to be alone and strengthen our relationship. We felt strongly that they would be well cared for by their grandparents. We made a number of phone calls just to check in, but it went very well and was well worth it.

"Since then, my in-laws have occasionally taken the boys for a weekend, so Devin and I can be alone. The first day we are often so tired that we find ourselves enjoying our home with just one another to talk to and relax with. On the second day we usually feel revitalized and do something special together."

Debbie and Dale didn't arrange their first getaway until the twins were nearly a year and a half old. "The twins were nursing three times a day until they were past their first birthday. We also didn't have anyone to leave three children with and we didn't want to hire someone unfamiliar to watch them overnight. But by the time the twins were eighteen months old, we needed to get away. We arranged to have our regular caregiver stay overnight on Saturday. The trip was wonderful, but it was too short. We left early Saturday morning and came back Sunday at noon, which wasn't enough time to leave all the stresses behind. Dale and I felt pressured, knowing that we only had twenty-four hours to ourselves. Still, it was a romantic twenty-four hours; a wonderful reminder that I married a man whose companionship I treasure.

"Eighteen months later, Dale and I took another trip. This time we 'volunteered' Dale's single sister who lived in town and knew the twins well. I also hired a teenage girl to help out for six hours during the day to give my sister-in-law a break. We still couldn't seem to break away for more than one night, but this time we left *very* early Saturday morning and didn't return until late Sunday evening. The added twelve hours really made it easier to relax. Now that the kids are older, we've decided to give ourselves a yearly weekend retreat at 'our' hotel!"

At the end of their girls' first year, Todd and Linda made plans to get away alone. "Todd had a business trip scheduled to Florida, so I asked my parents if they would like to come and babysit for a week. I flew to meet him in Miami. Then we rented a car and drove to Key West.

"This second honeymoon turned out to be as enjoyable as our first. Key West, with its sunny beaches, stimulating nightclubs, and colorful people, was just what we needed. We left refreshed, with our love revitalized, ready to return to parenting. This worked so well that we had a third honeymoon at the end of the boys' first year as well!"

## *Our Thoughts and Reflections*

LINDA: I realize that a relationship is a series of ups and downs. Working together as a couple, even before children, was a constant endeavor. Yet each of our children has added a whole new dimension to our relationship. Our lives have more humor, love, and bonding. Todd and I have given each other the support needed to grow, not only as a couple, but as a family.

FLORIEN: For me, being a mother has been easy. It is being a partner in a marriage with children that has been hard. Parenthood has required a dedication that comes only in relationships where love and respect are present and where there is a high value on the family unit. Max and Otto have provided the impetus for our marriage to grow and for Devin and me to reach new depths of understanding about each other and how we function as a family.

DEBBIE:   Adding children to a marriage makes a family, which is wonderful, but it also dilutes the marital relationship. Dale and I have fought hard to remain friends and lovers, because it is the essence of our relationship. Having children, especially twins, offset the balance for a while, but we reset the equilibrium because it was important to both of us.

DEBRA:   All of our children bring us treasured moments of pride and joy, but the twins brought us a special gift. Their coming became a catalyst for positive change that has benefitted the entire family, starting with our marital relationship. As we worked through our problems and learned how to let those negative emotions actually help us understand each other, the good, loving feelings returned even stronger than before.

SHERI:   I think what helped Steve and me most was that we were already experienced parents. Everything was much, much easier the second time around, even though we now had two infants and an older child. It was a very difficult time that could have torn us apart; instead, the twins' infancy resulted in making us an even stronger family.

# Chapter 12

# "Do you find time to do anything else?"

## *Our Other Selves*

Soon after our sets of twins came home from the hospital, each of us was mired in minute-to-minute care of them. All we could imagine in our future were mountains of diapers and hour after hour of feeding, cuddling, and consoling. We wondered if we would ever have lives of our own again. Although these thoughts were very real at the time, they did not realistically represent the future. There did come a time in each of our lives when we were able to readdress old dreams or pursue new ones.

This chapter chronicles our personal journeys of self-discovery and how we found ways to mesh motherhood with old and new parts of ourselves. Undoubtedly, you will experience your own metamorphosis, too. It is likely at first that when friends ask you, "Do you find time to do anything else?" your answer will probably be "No!" As the months pass and the timing is right, you will have much to say in answer to this question.

### *Who Am I?*
. . . . . . . . . . . .

For the first few months after our twins were born, we were all so busy being mothers that we gave little thought to who else we were. It took some time to chisel a new identity of ourselves, for mothering twins had added several more facets to the persons we were before. At first, we yearned for just a few precious moments to be alone and ask, "Who am I?" It seemed to Linda that there was little time for anything besides fulfilling her babies' needs.

"Every day, especially on the difficult ones, I looked forward to finding a few moments just for myself. Yet, my only chances to be alone were when I shopped, ran errands, or made a rare trip to the library. Even then, the clock ceaselessly ticked, and it was no time at all before I needed to hurry home to nurse the babies. I often wondered if all mothers craved time to just think and do absolutely nothing constructive. Some days I simply wanted to sit down long enough to count my fingers and toes to make sure I was still me."

Debra experienced this same phenomenon in the first few weeks after Aislynn and Ricky arrived. "I can't describe how lost I felt. It was like waking up and finding myself alone on an island, struggling to survive, and feeling disconnected to the rest of the world. Beyond being a mom, a role I had easily assimilated into my life in the past, I didn't know who I was anymore. Maybe that was because I felt out of touch with the other things I had formerly been attached to."

Mothering newborn twins may mean feeling disoriented at first, especially if, in the past, you have defined yourself by a combination of roles. The opposite was true for Florien, however. She more quickly integrated her other roles into motherhood as her previous employment, volunteer work, and educational background complemented her parenting role well. "From the beginning, I did not see my other roles as separate parts of me, but as pieces that, when joined, made up all of who I am. Instead, what was different for me was the realization that every decision I made as an individual would have a direct impact on Devin and the boys. It certainly has been a challenge to keep my individuality while simultaneously being a wife and mother; but it is a challenge that is important to me, for it brings to my life many smiles, newfound truths, security, and a sense of comfort."

Debbie had been working as a pediatric nurse prior to having her twins, and she felt a need to keep this part of her identity intact while being a mom of twins. She returned to work for one day a week when Michael and Joanna were six months old. "I kept asking myself why I was doing this; the money was minimal and the stress was immense. The answer was simple. I needed to have an identity beyond being Mom. It was important to my sense of self-worth."

Debbie's feelings are not uncommon. It is curious that we, as women, so often define ourselves by what we are doing or in reference to others. Yet little credit is given for our mothering work by ourselves or by others. On the other hand, there is more to a woman who has children than her role as mother. She needs opportunities to do things that are both unrelated to mothering and a reflection of her own dreams and desires. In the first few months of our twins' lives, when breaks ranged from a few minutes to a few hours at a time, we had to be content with short-term pleasures. Resuming favorite pastimes was a wonderful way to start reclaiming our individuality. We had to figure out which of these would personally benefit us most while fitting into our present life-style.

## Personal Interests

Shortly after her girls were born, Linda resumed her jogging. "I managed to schedule a half hour of running alone, even on the most frantic days. No matter how stressful my day has been, the release of tension from sustained exercise revitalizes me.

"Another thing I had always enjoyed was gardening. After the twins were born, I found a great solitude in tending my flowers, herbs, and vegetables. Even the monotonous job of weeding seemed relaxing and fulfilling. After the boys were born, Todd built a beautiful greenhouse with long rows of shelves for plants, tools, and potting soil for me. I loved it. I could put all the children down for a nap and go out (with my intercom) to the greenhouse and putter around. Even if the kids were awake and underfoot, they could play on the floor while my plants were safely out of reach. I was especially proud of my vegetables and herbs because I could use them for my other hobby, cooking."

Debra had been an avid organic gardener and an imaginative cook for several years before Aislynn and Ricky were born. Though she resumed those interests when her twins were about six months old, they no longer held the same satisfaction for her. "I was so tired and there was so little time that my large garden got out of control and became more of a chore for me. Evenings were too hectic for doing something besides throwing together a basic meal. I preferred to spend the little personal time I had doing mentally stimulating activities like reading science books and magazines, going for nature walks, or listening to music. I also craved adult company and would haul the children over to a friend's house for short visits. I really missed having a social life."

Debbie had purposely dropped many of her outside activities once she became pregnant with her tiwns. She felt that this would simplify her life once the babies were born, as she anticipated having little free time and even less energy. "Taking a leisurely bath or sipping a cup of tea while reading a magazine were the only things I could fit into my life for quite a while. Except for rented movies, lunches with friends, and occasional evenings out with Dale, my social life was fairly restricted. Later on, I increased my social engagements to include fun times with the friends I had made in the twin parents support group."

Florien, Sheri, and Debbie belonged to Birth to Three support groups when their twins were young. Not only did they rely on these groups for support, but also for having plain old fun. Going out to breakfast or dinner, relaxing in hot tubs, going bowling or skating, and having parties were some of the adult pleasures they enjoyed together, while at the same time sharing their common experiences of mothering twins. Sheri says the social events with her twin group were her main escape, except for an occasional couple of hours she and Steve found to steal away together. "Even though I had fun times with my twins group and time alone when my family members watched the girls, Steve and I had little time together to relax and have fun. I can't tell you how many times we just went to a fast food restaurant and sat out in the parking lot, eating and talking."

When Linda's girls were a few months old, she and Todd started going out to parties or other social gatherings. Her reentry into the adult world from the world of infant twins was not always smooth. "Attending these functions took on a whole new meaning for me—all of a sudden I felt threatened by dinner conversation! Before we had twins, I had had time to read newspapers, listen to the news, and discuss issues with Todd. But since their births, I had lost all contact with matters outside our limited circle. The major issues of my day were feeding schedules, dirty diapers, and getting enough sleep. Luckily, most of the other parents were interested in hearing about the twins."

Our world did feel smaller during our twins' infancy, and these activities had to suffice until something changed in our lives that allowed time and freedom for other pursuits. The choices we made required an evaluation of where we had been up to that point in our lives and contemplation about where we wanted to go. For some of us, a major issue was whether to work outside the home.

## To Work or Not To Work?
· · · · · · · · · · · · · · · · · · · · · · · ·

For mothers of young twins, thoughts about combining motherhood and employment are braves ones indeed. Of course, financial considerations often make it necessary to work, although a careful appraisal of the actual costs of working should be made. The cost of child care for two children may be prohibitive. Hidden costs, including hiring household help or eating out more often should be part of the calculations when making a decison based on economic considerations. Another point to ponder is the potential stress that will result from working weighed against the amount of support and cooperation that can be expected from the partner and employer. For this reason, many mothers of twins opt for part-time rather than full-time work, when there is a choice. Most importantly, each woman has to factor her personal needs, values, and feelings into her decision to return to work.

As we wrestled with these matters, we were surprised to find that having twins had not only altered our lives, but had changed us as persons, and that fact colored the decisions we made about our former jobs. Our feelings, plans, and priorities about working were either modified or solidified by our experience of mothering twins; in some cases, our careers took different paths altogether.

During her pregnancy, Florien began thinking about what she might do for employment after her twins were born. She knew she would not want to return to her job as a classroom assistant/ interpreter in a special education class, with its time restrictions and schedule inflexibility. She also took into consideration that Devin was working part-time and they would need the additional money. She decided to approach the City of Eugene Specialized Recreation Department about reinstating a recreation program for deaf teens that she had been involved with a few years earlier but had since dissolved. "The recreation department liked the proposal and hired me. The job was ideal; it gave me recreational opportunities as well as income that we needed, while leaving plenty of time for Devin and me to share the care of our twins.

"When Otto and Max were 10 months old, this job led to a temporary position as an international exchange leader on a four-week trip to England. When I returned, I felt motivated to find ways that future work could take the whole family abroad.

"I also took another part-time job during the summer that Max and Otto turned one year old, teaching a parenting class for parents under stress one night a week for eight weeks. It was a great opportunity to reaffirm my parenting skills and it was fun for the boys, who could play in the children's room while I was busy with the group. For me, working and parenting were very compatible."

Sheri felt it would be wise to wait until her twins were toddlers before finding other work outside the home. "Early in our marriage, Steve and I had considered the options and agreed that I would stay home with the children while they were small. I didn't have any misgivings about putting my career on hold for a few years while raising a family because I knew I would have time for that after our children were in school.

"When Kallie was a year old, I began to realize that I needed to be involved in something else. I opened a small used toy and baby equipment business in our home. It was very successful and lots of fun because Kallie and I ran it together. After the first year, my mother became my business partner, and when I found out I was pregnant with twins, she bought my share of the business. At that point I felt a renewed dedication to my commitment of being a stay-at-home mom. I was certain that I would not be able to handle the business and parent three children in my chosen style at the same time.

"I was right, and the loss of income was offset by less stress for me. I felt really good about my decision."

Debra and Linda concur that the primary motive for staying home full-time was feeling a desire to provide consistent, nurturing care. They believed this was important to the healthy development of their children and their relationships with them. Their partners held full-time jobs that provided sufficient income to support that choice, and both they and their partners agreed that the added stress of the two working parents life-style would be too much pressure for their families.

Just after Maiah and Sarah reached one year of age, Linda felt a need to return to work for the social contact. "At that time I felt as if I were emerging from my role as the mother of twins to a more suitable role of mother/individual. After twelve months of being effectively housebound, I was eager to rejoin society, so I decided to go back to work. My former job awaited me, but I went back on a part-time basis. After a long and difficult search, I located a day-care residence for the girls. The first few mornings were tough on all of us but my worries were apparently unfounded; after several days the girls eagerly waved good-bye when I left them there."

When her twins were a year old, Debbie increased the number of hours she worked as a pediatric nurse. "My employer required that I either quit or increase my hours, so I chose the latter. I felt ambivalent about this decision because we could have survived without my income. For a year I worked the additional hours, but during that time the work grew less satisfying and more stressful. More and more often my work schedule conflicted with family outings on the weekend or some fun community activity scheduled during the week. Although I didn't quit working, I decided that quitting my job was an option if the negative aspects of my work consistently outweighed the positive ones. I had finally come to realize that I was worthwhile and still 'me,' whether I worked outside the home or not."

## New Horizons
· · · · · · · · · · · · · · ·

*Volunteer Work:*   Work does not have to result in monetary gain to be satisfying and fulfilling. Volunteer work can be a terrific way to meet one's own needs as well as benefit the community, as Sheri discovered when her twins were nine months old. "My commitment to helping other parents was stronger than ever, as it had grown out of my experience of caring for my colicky infants. Already a participant in our local support group for parents of twins, I took over as facilitator of the group when Florien left. Throughout the year that followed, membership continued to grow, and two new groups were formed. I volunteered to be the coordinator for all the twin groups and added that to my role as facilitator. I also put in place a series of classes on infant care for the new mothers of twins. Much to my surprise, my extensive efforts were rewarded with Birth to Three's Volunteer of the Year award. My greatest satisfaction, however, was knowing how much these parents needed and appreciated the support they received in these groups.

"When Emmy and Tessa turned two, I began focusing on another area that was important to me, supporting the work of Planned Parenthood. I had been involved briefly with a program for teen parents and was concerned by the challenges they faced becoming parents so young. I believed some of my volunteer effort should be directed toward a prevention program. My volunteer work suited my needs for outside activities and balanced well with mothering."

Florien had voluntarily initiated Birth to Three's Twins or More group and stayed with the group for two and a half years. Once she decided to return to graduate school when Max and Otto were two and half years old, she became involved in two projects at the neonatal intensive care unit at her local hospital. "Initially, I compiled a community resource and information packet which was given to all new parents of multiples born at the hospital.

The second part of the project meant volunteering one evening a week to help provide support to families with an infant (or infants) in the NICU. I knew the power of support when one is in need, and I gladly helped out. I also learned about the special needs of the babies who spent time there and their families. This work satisfied my personal commitment to helping families, especially ones with multiples."

*Back to School:*  Because having twins significantly changed our self-images, many of us reevaluated our life goals in light of that experience, and changed the direction of our lives. In some cases, that meant returning to school to accomplish our goals, whether it was one class at a time or a full-time endeavor.

Debra's experience of mothering twins completely changed the course of her career: "Just two months after having my twins, in the quiet hours of the night, I received brilliant insight as to what I might do for a career. While trying to get a baby back to sleep, I had been thinking of the special people who had taken care of me during my pregnancy and the twins' birth—the midwives, the doctor, the nurses—and how I would miss them in my life, for I knew I would not be having any more children. I also thought about our childbirth preparation teacher and how much we had enjoyed the classes. I remembered that she had just moved to Alaska, leaving a vacuum in the community for the service she provided. Instantly, I realized that I wanted to fill that vacancy.

"The more I thought about it, the more excited I became. Within two weeks I had contacted a certification program and started the process. Most of it was home study that I squeezed in whenever I could, and the rest required attendance at seminars and workshops that I put off until the babies' second year.

"When it came time to student teach, the babies were one and a half and could be comfortably left with Rick or Jason. Shortly thereafter, I became involved with the Birth to Three support group and gained skills that helped me both personally and professionally and expanded my contacts with other community resources.

"The best thing about this choice was that, as my children grew older and more time became available, many more opportunities related to my work opened up for me. What began as an eight-hour-per-week commitment evolved at a comfortable pace into a part-time business partnership in a birth and parenting education center."

Florien's career goals also changed after her trip to England late in the first year of Max and Otto's life. After she returned, she and Devin discussed their future family goals and immediate necessities. "One thing was very apparent: we needed more income. Although Devin returned to working full-time after I returned from my overseas employment, my salary still only contributed to our day-to-day expenses. There was not enough left over for extras or to put aside toward our new long-range goals of home ownership and recreational travel. Devin and I felt that I could get more professional work, with higher pay, if I had a master's degree.

"I began to research master-level programs at the local university, and was excited to learn that there were two programs that I could take simultaneously: a program in early childhood special education and an endorsement program in teaching children with severe disabilities.

"When the boys were two and a half, I applied for both programs. I began slowly, going to school part-time in the evenings at first; then, when the boys were three, I quit my two part-time jobs to attend school full-time. I did that so my family wouldn't suffer from my absence (or from my stressed-out presence). It took me three years to complete what should have been a two-year course of study, but taking the longer time was worth it."

Debbie was also tempted to return to college once she had some free time to reevaluate her career goals. Her self-exploration and final determination were quite different than Florien's, however. "When I was an adolescent, I knew exactly what I wanted out of life: I would go to college and get a master's degree or a Ph.D. in an area of study that would result in a high-powered career, then find and marry the perfect man and be the mother of his children. But real life turned out to be more complicated. Twenty years older and wiser, I did have the happy marriage and great kids, but my educational and career goals had fallen short. I had only a bachelor's degree in nursing, and my career had become a very, very part-time job that involved a lot of hard work but offered little respect and even less power.

"Could I get back on track at age 37? Perhaps more importantly, did I want to get back on track? Coming up with solutions required six months of serious, thoughtful, and occasionally painful soul-searching. As I sorted out my hopes and dreams and balanced them against the obligations that I now had toward others, I made a sobering discovery. As the mother of three I had very real emotional and financial responsibilities that tempered the choices I could make about my immediate future. I realized that a master's degree and a full-time career were not my number one priorities at this time. I was not one of those individuals who could successfully balance the stresses and time constraints of a career or graduate studies with raising young children.

"While I did choose motherhood above all other endeavors for the next few years, I refused to let my life stagnate as I waited for my children to grow up. I was still working part-time as a pediatric nurse. I also planned to research various graduate programs at the local university to see if one suited me and I started taking classes to obtain my school nurse certificate. School nursing had been an area of interest for some time and I wanted to ready myself for a possible job change in the future."

*New Challenges:*  In many ways, the strength and courage we gained from mothering twins spurred us to expand our boundaries, for we have gone beyond our own perceived limits and set higher expectations for ourselves. At the least, we have joked that now we are all chronic overachievers. We are more open to learning new things, facing up to our fears, dropping excess baggage, and chasing long-forgotten desires.

In the summer that Maiah and Sarah turned one year old, Linda and Todd purchased a small sailboat, and Linda immediately enrolled in sailing class at a nearby recreational lake. "Every week I faithfully attended the course, my classmates never suspecting that I was a fugitive from mothering twins. Though I never mastered sailing, Todd and I have enjoyed many quiet evenings alone together on our sailboat. I also signed up for piano lessons, just for me, and attended a writing class at our local community college. Todd cared for Sarah and Maiah while I went to class, and always had them in bed by the time I returned home. Over a cup of tea, we discussed the class and my own writing. It was so nice to have some leisurely time for such things; in fact, I learned to schedule some quiet time and solitude just for writing in the evenings after the girls went to bed."

Debbie had a few unmet goals from childhood that she wanted to address after deciding to put her career change on hold for a little longer. "Since I was a young girl I had wanted to learn to play the piano, and this was the perfect time to fulfill my dream. Dale and I saved the money; before long, I had a piano and was embarking on the long, tedious process of learning to play it well. Another of my goals was to conquer my fear of deep water by taking swimming lessons until I was a confident, relaxed swimmer. I knew that if I could do this, I would feel capable of diving into almost any future challenge life could offer."

While at times it has been difficult for our families, writing this book has been a source of personal growth for all of us. And we can proudly add yet another role to our repertoires! Through both our experiences of mothering twins and our involvement with this writing project, we learned the arts of perseverance and patience. Most of all, we have worked hard to be friends and a source of support to each other even when our personal beliefs and opinions differed. That is what we hope comes through in our stories and that is what we wish for all parents: to be understood and supported while parenting their children the best they can.

# Chapter 13

# "Double trouble"

## Toddlers, Years One to Two

Although two active toddlers running in two different directions can be double trouble, they can also provide their parents with double joy. It helps to keep this in mind as you face the day-to-day challenges with your one-year-old twins. During this time period, our twins changed in many ways. With their abilities to rapidly move about and explore their environment came the need for us to be ever-watchful in overseeing their safety and to begin using consistent, simple discipline. As our twins grew more independent, baby foods, bottles, and breast-feeding were left behind. Personality differences and individual preferences began to emerge.

### Changes in Our Toddlers

*Motor Skills:* During this period in children's lives, they experience rapid motor development. Some start the year still crawling, but all of them are running by the time they turn two.

Maiah and Sarah's first birthday party was the prelude to a big event at Linda's house. "Only a week separated Sarah and Maiah's first wobbly attempts at upright locomotion. They immediately started following each other, often falling over like little dominoes when the leader stopped abruptly. Laughing, they would try to pull up on each other, only to end up back on the floor in a pile.

"I began to feel like a mother duck with her brood close behind. Until I got used to their following me, I sometimes accidentally knocked them down when I turned around too quickly. I sometimes imagined that our pediatrician would suspect child abuse when presented with the bruises from their many bumps and scrapes."

At about 18 months, most toddlers start climbing. They climb out of their strollers, their car seats, and their cribs. They may even begin pushing chairs around the kitchen to climb up on for a better view of the countertops. Some will even go farther, and climb onto the countertops! And remember, twins will undoubtedly be working together on these capers.

Florien noticed that her boys encouraged and stimulated each other to try new things. "This was a blessing in that they were always challenging each other in positive ways, but also frustrating because they were apt to get into trouble or get hurt."

Debra vividly remembers that, "Since Aislynn and Ricky had been walking for a few months, they were now into death-defying feats. They were as agile as monkeys, and I don't know how many times I came into a room to find one of them happily perched on a table or a shelf. I swore that they had suction cups on their fingers and toes!"

*Play:* Play is the natural extension of a child's developing motor skills. As our toddlers passed through their second 12 months, they channeled nearly all their physical, verbal, and mental abilities into playing. Their goal was to try out the things that they'd learned about their world and to explore all uncharted territory.

Florien's boys continually kept up their high level of physical energy. "Max and Otto loved to go to parks where they would run from one play structure to another, often spending only minutes at each. They craved thrills and excitement. Playing on the pretend fire truck was only fun if they could be at the steering wheel. The merry-go-round was not going fast enough unless they wobbled from dizziness when they got off. They eagerly joined older boys on the rock sculptures, content to contribute sound effects as the older kids played cowboys, army, and rock-etship. At 18 months, the twins learned to kick balls with a young friend who played soccer. They enjoyed watching their friend's games, although their attention spans lasted only 10 minutes be-fore they wanted to join the game and kick the ball, too."

Debra's children also loved active play. "Ricky especially liked climbing on Jason, who gave endless horsie rides to all three of his younger siblings. The twins liked spinning or swinging sen-sations, and a Sit 'n Spin toy became a much vied-for favorite. The most popular toys at our house were pots and pans, balls to throw or chase, and large empty boxes. An empty appliance box could become a tunnel or a fort that they played with for hours. Aislynn participated in these wild pursuits, but preferred more controlled activities like dancing or circle games."

Sheri's twins were also starting to prefer cooperative games. "Singleton children at this age will play near each other, but don't usually have social interchanges. At 16 months, the twins, on the other hand, had learned how to take turns, and it was natural for them to wait for each other's responses. They spoke mostly non-sense to each other, but all their tones and pauses sounded just like normal speech. At our mealtimes the two played copycat games in their high chairs, imitating and building on each other's actions and then dissolving into giggles.

"Emmy and Tessa would often wait for each other and say, 'Mon, ode ands' (c'mon, hold hands), then join hands and toddle off. The favorite group activity was to dress up, with Kallie de-ciding who wore what and starring in the subsequent dance shows. At this age, Emmy and Tessa didn't care that Kallie hogged the spotlight. They were just happy to be wearing my high-heeled shoes."

During this second year, Florien's boys also played in a more interactive and social style, as they developed a love of music and pretend play. "When Max and Otto were 14 months old, they started to use crayons, and accompanyed their picture-making with occasional 'zips' and 'whees.' The twins were delighted by children's music, at home and in the car. They started to imitate musicians from television and from children's concerts they had attended. They mimicked the singers' movements as they attempted to sing songs. Often they would climb to the top of their indoor play slide and use the platform as a stage for impromptu concerts."

The favorite activity for Linda's girls was listening to music tapes while the whole family danced and clapped. "Ring-around-a-rosy was the favorite. They enjoyed going around and around, but never fell down at the end of the song. They also loved to play 'the word game.' I would sit on the couch and ask each girl to bring me an object: a block, teddy bear, dolly, or shoe. They happily toddled off to fetch the item, and we all clapped and laughed as each thing was brought to me, until my lap and the couch were covered. They weren't as motivated to put everything back, but I tried to make a game of that, too. They also loved their books and spent a lot of time together on the couch looking at the pictures. I suspect that the many hours I spent reading to them piqued their interest.

"Later, when the boys were this age, the girls played many of these same games with their younger brothers. Their favorite pastime became playing house; there were always two moms (Sarah and Maiah) and the boys played the role of babies. The girls wrapped them in blankets and gave them their doll bottles to suck. After only a few minutes, the boys would get up and run around. The result was a mad chase through the house by all four children, which the boys loved even more!"

Some of Michael's and Joanna's favorite toys were blocks. Debbie remembers, "The twins were gradually able to stack them higher and higher as they gained fine motor control. At 13 months they could stack two; by two years old they could stack whole towers. Over the year they learned to manipulate Play-Doh, scribble with crayons, and turn pages in books by themselves.

"Occasionally, Michael would try to roughhouse with Joanna, but she didn't tolerate it for long. Their play sometimes erupted into a fight if I let Joanna and him play together too long without direction from me. When I intervened and played quietly with both of them for 15 minutes or so, Michael would immediately calm down and play well with Joanna."

As our children approached their second birthdays, they were leaving toddlerhood behind. Sheri reflects, "Our little girls now sat glued to the TV, watching 'Cinderella' in the same happy trance as their big sister. They clomped around in my shoes, pushing their little grocery carts past me with announcements of 'Doe tore, dit apow' (Go to the store, get apples). I always waved good-bye and reminded them to get milk, too."

*Language:* During their first year, children communicate very well by crying, smiling, cooing, and gesturing. When they reach 12 months, their vocabularies vary widely. Some say no words at all, while others speak two-word phrases. Between 12 and 24 months, however, verbal language comes more quickly. By age two, many toddlers can speak in three-word phrases. These newfound words begin to make parenting easier because children can finally express some of their basic needs. It also makes for some of the most delightful conversation you can imagine.

Linda was amazed at how rapidly Sarah and Maiah's vocabularies expanded after their first birthday. "Their favorite word was *Mama,* which they used constantly, especially when I went into the bathroom. They had also mastered *no, don't,* and *mine.* At 16 months, they started using each other's names: *Sar-rah* and *May-ya.* By two, they spoke in short sentences."

Florien remembers that Max and Otto chattered constantly. "As their abilities to vocalize their interests and needs increased, so did their volume. They became frustrated when both tried to get an adult's attention at the same time, and it sometimes seemed that they intentionally tried to outtalk each other to see who could get our attention first. The ensuing uproar nearly cost us our sanity. Finally, when the boys were almost two years old, we taught them to raise their hands at the dinner table to give everyone a chance to talk."

Debbie's twins also had a good command of language at this age. "Ever since Michael and Joanna were babies Dale and I talked to them constantly, hoping it would help them develop language skills. I guess it worked, because they both spoke short phrases by 18 months. First one would learn a new word; days later, the other would be using it, too. Their only difference in speech was in their individual enunciation. They both had certain sounds that they couldn't say at all, while the opposite twin spoke them clearly. Dale and I never made an issue of this or compared them negatively to each other. We simply said the word correctly and hoped that with time their enunciaton would improve. It did about a year later."

Debra observed that language development clearly reflected Aislynn's and Ricky's personalities. "Family names and 'yes' and 'no' had been among their first utterings, but from there they differed markedly. Aislynn learned the names of things she wanted and how to ask for them or to do them herself. Ricky still gestured for what he wanted but used words for going places, toys, and animals. At first, he called all animals *doggies,* but imitated their sounds correctly. Then he put the sounds and 'doggie' together to identify the animal, as in 'moo-doggie' or 'oink-doggie.' He used this method until he was just over two years old."

*Temperamental Differences:*   Our twins gained their physical and verbal skills within fairly short time spans of each other. The identical sets tended to develop very similarly, and the fraternals a bit further apart. But even the most marked differences were separated by only a few weeks, so our twins seemed very "twinlike" to strangers. Those close to them, however, knew differently. Our toddlers' individual personalities had been blossoming ever since their births.

Gaining independence was part of everything Aislynn and Ricky did between their first and second birthdays. However, Debra says, they focused their energy in two entirely different arenas. "Aislynn concentrated on learning how to care for herself: She was very motivated to learn how to dress herself and to use personal hygiene, like brushing her teeth and combing her hair. Ricky directed himself to manipulating playthings and getting into everything. They both worked to establish identities separate from me more than from each other. I think this is because boy/girl twins don't have as much need to separate from each other as same-sex twins do. An experience in the week after the twins' first birthday highlighted these changes.

"The twins and I attended a week-long workshop where on-site child care was provided. I was concerned about how the twins would do in child care; they had never been away from me for very long periods. What actually happened was the very opposite of what I had imagined. Aislynn adapted very quickly and was content to let strangers hold or comfort her, while Ricky didn't respond to anyone and remained upset until he could be with me. I realized then that Aislynn, who I sometimes had thought to be more impatient and demanding, was simply more capable of making her needs known; Ricky really depended on me to anticipate or interpret his. I had mistaken his passivity for independence. After that I asked Ricky what he needed more often and let Aislynn learn to wait a bit."

*Separation Anxiety:* Debra's experience with clingy babies was still commonplace for all of us until our twins neared one and a half years old. By then, our toddlers had gained some ability to express themselves, and they started to gain confidence. Many of our twins shed their fear of strangers and some were even transformed into social butterflies.

Sheri and her family visited Disneyland when Emmy and Tessa were 18 months old. "I was afraid that the twins would be unnerved by the crowds of people, but the babies' stranger anxiety was practically nil. They were happy riding in their strollers, loved the rides and the petting zoo, and were fascinated, instead of frightened, by the Disney characters who mingled with the public."

Although most toddlers grow more outgoing at this age, inherent shyness can restrain this tendency. Debbie explains, "Neither Dale nor I are particularly extroverted so it didn't surprise me that Michael and Joanna were cautious in new situations. Joanna was particularly frightened by people in costumes. Santa Claus and the Easter Bunny terrified her. Michael was not so fearful of pretend characters, but unfamiliar people scared him."

*Twin Identity:* At 12 months, most singleton toddlers have a fairly clear idea of who they are. They know when their name is spoken and they respond accordingly. Twin toddlers, though, often have difficulty establishing a clear identity. They may need some careful direction from those whom they trust.

Linda notes that Maiah and Sarah were still confused about their own identities and used each other's names interchangeably. "Even though they looked quite different, when they looked in the mirror each pointed to herself and used the other's name. I was alarmed by this until I learned that it was a normal response for twins at this age. To encourage their own identity formation, I tied long, different-colored ribbons in their hair, then sat them in front of a mirror together. We talked about which girl was which as we matched up the ribbon they could each see on their head with the one in the mirror."

Max and Otto learned that they needed to identify themselves to other people because they looked so similar. Florien says, "I aways tried to dress the boys dissimilarly, so others could tell them apart and call them by their correct name. By pointing to themselves and saying their names along with a one-word description of their clothing, they could tell others who was who. Midway through a horse and buggy ride with their grandparents, Otto turned to find the carriage loaded with passengers. He pointed to Max, saying, 'Max, blue' (Max was wearing blue shorts) and then pointed to himself, saying, 'Otto, frog' (he was wearing shorts with a frog on them)."

*Twin Individuality:* At this age, it was hard for us to tell what our twins thought of themselves. They were so alike in so many ways that their individuality was often overlooked. Even the boy/girl sets of twins had many similarities in their mannerisms and expressions, and the identical sets were sometimes so alike it was astounding. We did our best to support and promote whatever differences they had.

Little by little, Florien and Devin started to notice a few small differences in Max's and Otto's personalities. "We valued this uniqueness and tried to build on it.

"We noticed that Max was more verbal than Otto during their early language development. He would chatter on and on, even if he didn't know how to say what he really wanted to say, trying out new combinations of sounds. Otto didn't babble quite as much as Max did when they were first learning to talk. He watched as Max struggled with the pronunciation of a new word, then would suddenly say it clearly himself. It seemed Otto preferred to wait until he was sure he could say it correctly.

"At this age, Max also enjoyed animals more than Otto did. He had no hesitation or fear of animals and was disappointed if one didn't come to him when he wanted it to.

"Otto showed a special interest in clothing, and preferred to choose his own outfits. Looking good seemed to be important to him, even at such a young age. On the other hand, Max would wear whatever I put out for him. In some ways, Otto's temperament seemed more balanced than Max's. He didn't frustrate as easily and could be talked out of a bad mood if it was dealt with immediately."

As Emmy and Tessa grew, Sheri noticed their individualities blossoming, too. "Each twin had her own special style of waving good-bye. Emmy held her hand flat, waving up and down from her wrist, while Tessa held her hand up, scrunching her fingers in and out. They also used different words when fighting over toys. Locked in a tug-of-war, Emmy would yell 'no-no!' to counter Tessa's 'mine, mine!' I loved these changes. Our identical twins had been so similar for so long that it was really fun to see signs of separateness."

To complement their new independence, our twins were making all kinds of discoveries about themselves and each other. As they grew closer to their second birthdays, they all became very aware of their gender. This was most apparent in boy/girl twins.

Debra's twins, Aislynn and Ricky, had played with the same kinds of toys for most of their first year, but things changed as they approached their second birthday. "Ricky started to prefer small toys like little cars and miniature animals or people. He liked to organize and arrange them, parking his cars in rows or posing the people or animals in order. Up to that point I had purchased unisex educational toys, because I was concerned about role stereotyping. Then I noticed that Aislynn had started babying the stuffed animals: feeding, dressing, and attempting to bathe them. I wondered how much of this was nurturing instinct and how much was being modeled to her. I didn't want to discourage her behavior, but I also didn't want to implant the idea that only girls can do this. In concession to her desires and my concerns,

I bought washable girl and boy dolls with bathtubs. Ricky named his Michael, and Aislynn named hers Amy, but they played with both dolls interchangeably. I knew I'd accomplished my goal when I walked into their room and they were both breast-feeding their babies!

"Most of the time, though, both twins played with trucks and cars, tool and building sets, adventure toys, and lots of dirt and mud. I felt they were well-rounded, but that I had also respected their preferences."

Debbie's twins, Michael and Joanna, started showing gender differences in their play at about 20 months of age. She recounts an incident that involved television, and caught her totally by surprise. "The problem was that I wasn't monitoring closely enough what Michael and Joanna were watching. Along with Mr. Rogers, Sesame Street and Winnie-the-Pooh, they were eavesdropping on Chris's favorite shows, which were filled with violent images and scary sequences that they couldn't begin to understand. While these programs seemed to have no direct effect on Chris or Joanna, they obviously did on Michael. One day Michael was playfully jabbing and hitting at the rest of the family. I chalked this up to typical boy behavior, even though Chris had never been as physical at this age. Then one morning, I noticed Michael intently watching one of Chris's cartoons just as the characters battled with their fists and swords. As soon as the show ended, Michael grabbed an old plastic popsicle holder and chortled as he proceeded to stab everyone in the family. When I told Michael that we don't do this sort of thing because it could hurt someone, his response was, 'Man on TV do it!' From that moment on, Chris watched his programs on a little TV in his bedroom. Within a week of instituting this rule, Michael's aggressive behavior decreased markedly."

Linda didn't notice as much difference between each individual within her twin sets as she did between the girl and boy sets. "Because our yard is partly landscaped with small pebbles, rocks always held a fascination for all our children. However, I saw a big difference at this age in how Sarah and Maiah, and then later Keegan and Colin, played with the rocks. At eighteen months, Sarah and Maiah collected the stones to put in their pockets or their buckets. The girls carried them around the yard, made neat little piles with them, or put them in play cookware to make pretend meals. On the other hand, Keegan and Colin threw them at each other, pitched them into the grass, put them in the dog's food dish, or pushed them through the fence into the neighbor's lawn.

"I had a hard time understanding this gender gap, since I had always treated my children the same regardless of their sex. From infancy, they had all the same toys, from trucks to dolls, to play with, but by 18 months, the boys were clearly boys."

*Twin Bonds:* All our twins had differences as well as similarities. Sometimes they got angry at each other, but they never stayed angry for long. Most of their time was spent as best friends. Boy or girl, fraternal or identical, their bonds to each other were very strong.

Linda was amazed at the special connection between Keegan and Colin. "We didn't take the boys on separate outings until after their first birthday, although this was something that Todd and I had often done with Maiah and Sarah. As a result, the boys were disturbed by their first separation.

"One day, Todd went shopping and took only Keegan along. Colin cried the whole time they were gone; when they returned, he followed his brother around for the rest of the afternoon. Todd said that Keegan had cried, too, but had become distracted once he was in the store.

"I also noticed this form of separation anxiety during naptime. If one twin woke up early, I would take him from their bedroom and leave the other twin sleeping. If I didn't keep the awake twin occupied, though, he would run back into the bedroom to snuggle with his sleeping brother."

Debra's twins displayed their special closeness in an incident when they were 18 months old. "Their DPT immunizations were scheduled a week apart and Aislynn had gotten hers first. She was hesitant to walk the next day because her leg was sore. As she lay on the couch, Ricky kept coming over and patting her. When he received his shot the next week, their roles were reversed. Aislynn kept asking him, 'Owie?' and Ricky would nod his head so she would kiss him."

Sheri was fascinated by Emmy's and Tessa's relationship. "When the twins were 18 months old, we joined an indoor playground limited to children under five years old. Emmy and Tessa rode around, climbed, and played in the playhouse together, in complete harmony. They didn't exclude other children, they just didn't need to include them. I realized that the twins didn't need me constantly entertaining them anymore, and honestly, it was a huge relief."

*Discipline:*  As toddlers, our twins were very active. As they picked up speed and moved in opposite directions, we struggled to keep their behavior in check. Some of our efforts at discipline were successful and others were not. We all agree that we were most effective when we reinforced to them that they had choices, and that there were logical, positive and negative consequences for their actions. The positive consequences lead to greater independence, which they craved. The negative consequences usually led to a "time-out."

Debbie's sweet, compliant twosome became wild toddlers who began to act before thinking. "Impluse became the driving force in Michael's and Joanna's behavior. As a result, they hit in anger, threw toys just to see them fly, ran freely in parking lots, and did countless other things to express their will, while not incidentally endangering themselves and others around them.

"Dale and I knew that we had to set limits on their behavior for three main reasons: to keep them safe, to help them develop self-control, and to teach them a healthy consideration of others. And we had to do it soon! After a few discussions, Dale and I agreed that behaviors that involved intentionally hitting or hurting someone would result in a brief, clear reprimand of the aggressor, followed by a one- to two-minute time-out in the corner of their bedroom. Usually this necessitated my sitting with the child who was being disciplined and silently holding him or her still without making eye contact until the time had elapsed. Then I matter-of-factly reported, 'You're done. You can play now. No more hitting.' After a few minutes, when he or she was happily involved in play,

I would give him or her a reassuring hug and compliment the twins' friendly behavior toward each other.

"We chose to use time-out in these instances because nothing else seemed to have an effect on Michael, and we didn't want to spank him. We were concerned that if we told him not to hit others and then hit him ourselves, he would be one very confused little boy. Joanna was very obedient at this age (so obedient, in fact, that she often snitched on Michael when he misbehaved) and really didn't require time-out to modify her behavior. Speaking firmly to her was always enough. However, when Dale and I noticed that Joanna was halfheartedly disobeying us just to make sure that we disciplined her too, we realized that at this age both twins needed to receive the same punishment for the same wrongdoing.

"Other issues, such as holding Dale's or my hand in a parking lot or throwing toys, were also dealt with firmly, but Dale and I felt they really didn't require measures as severe as time-out. Thrown toys were confiscated. We explained the reasons for our rules and stood our ground, ignoring the inevitable wails of anger. We found that if we were consistent and the rules were reasonable, Michael and Joanna quickly learned to follow them."

When Linda's girls misbehaved she usually got results with a firm "*no,*" but if that didn't work she also used time-out. "I set up their unused playpen in our bedroom where they could be isolated for a few minutes. I put the offender in the playpen, set the timer for one or two minutes, and closed the door halfway. No toys were permitted in the playpen during time-out. There were tears, but neither Sarah nor Maiah climbed out of the playpen. Frequently, however, one twin sneaked into the bedroom to offer the other comfort.

"Maiah even went through a phase of asking for a time-out. She seemed to realize that she needed a break and wanted the solitude of the bedroom. I allowed her to use the playpen for her desired periods of isolation, but continued to use it for discipline as well. Her requests for time-out taught me to take notice of some of the differences between their personalities as they grew, and to treat them accordingly."

As you can see from our examples, the key to effective time-out is not so much where or how you do it, but that the spot you pick provides brief isolation from the other twin or the aggravating situation. The only limits are common-sense ones: The spot you choose for time-out shouldn't be scary or potentially dangerous, and every year of the child's age should equal a maximum of one time-out minute.

Florien and Devin laid some ground rules during this period. "They were: (a) people are not for hurting; (b) toys and other objects are not to be thrown; (c) toys need to be shared; and (d) after the tension of a tantrum is gone, we talk about what happened. While sharing toys is difficult at this age for any child, Devin and I felt it was an area we needed to address with the boys as soon as possible since they were twins and had to share just about everything. Setting a timer for one-minute turns with toys helped immensely.

"When they hurt each other, threw things, or refused to share, we started using time-out. There were times, however, I couldn't use it. While I was attempting to get one boy to stay in the corner or on the couch, the second child could be found doing such things as peeling off all the stickie tabs on my sanitary pads or climbing up onto a counter, and I would soon be trying to give two boys time-outs. They had learned how to use the 'power in numbers' concept to their advantage and sometimes there was no way I could manage the two of them and use time-out at the same time.

"On those occasions, what did work was simply getting down to their level and telling them directly whatever needed to be said. I also found that preventing behaviors from getting out of control really helped a lot. When I saw trouble brewing I could easily step in and distract at least one of the boys, steering him to a new activity and eliminating a potentially tense situation for all of us.

"I also happened on another way to use the principle of time-out. One time when Max and Otto were about 20 months old I got so stressed by their behavior I felt like yelling at them, which I did not want to do. I had tried talking to them, getting them involved in a new activity, and separating them, but nothing seemed to work. Devin and I didn't believe in spanking our children, so I was out of answers. I considered locking myself in my bedroom or the bathroom until I calmed down, but didn't trust the boys in the house without supervison for even five minutes. So I put them in their room where I knew they couldn't get hurt and held their door shut for a few minutes, while I took a few deep breaths and thought of a new plan. Then I took them outside (both boys still screaming), put them in their stroller, and took them for a walk up a nearby hill. A simple change of environment helped to quiet them down, and it proved to be an excellent way for me to physically work off my frustration. We went to the top of the hill and then returned home, calm and re-energized enough to start fresh."

For Linda's boys, the only thing that calmed a tense situation was to remove the object that was causing the discipline problem. "At eighteen months, Keegan and Colin started a terrible ritual of emptying their dresser drawers, throwing their clothes all over the room, and then tipping the dresser over. They did this nearly every morning when they got up, and by the time I heard them it was too late. Telling them 'no' didn't help at all, and time-out wasn't a logical consequence. Finally, I decided to put their dresser inside the closet where they couldn't get at it behind the sliding doors and I stripped their room of everything but a basket of toys and their two cribs. This worked beautifully and demonstrated that I was serious about them playing with their toys, not their furniture."

Debra noticed that Aislynn and Ricky started to show signs of the "No" phase at about twenty months. "At first they simply resisted my requests, but when they were saying 'no' to things that they usually liked to do, it dawned on me that we were beginning the trying period that I had experienced with my two older children. Somewhat dismayed at the prospect of rebellion in tandem, I happened to share my thoughts with a good friend who was a preschool teacher.

"She pointed out that it was also painful and scary for children to risk incurring the wrath of their parents in order to search for independence. She commented that if parents allowed the children to exercise their right to say no in safe ways, without making them feel unloved for doing so, everyone would come through this phase relatively happy. She gave me examples of giving a child choices: 'The red or green shirt today?' or 'Peanut butter with strawberry or raspberry jam for lunch?'—things they could say no to without everything coming to a full stop. Then when the child said no to other things, the parent had energy left to cope; otherwise there would be constant battles of will. I told her I'd give it a try and soon found it to be effective."

*Fighting between Twins:* At this age, the misbehavior and/or lack of cooperation that calls for a time-out is often a conflict between one parent and one child. Fighting between the twins themselves is a slightly different phenomenon. Time-outs may curb squabbles between them, but sometimes the battle resumes as soon as the twins are together again. The most common conflicts center around toys.

Debra agrees. "In order to minimize fighting, we bought two each of the twins' most favorite toys. With the ones that weren't duplicated and had to be shared it was important to let the current owner establish possession first; then this twin could sometimes be persuaded to share with the other twin. I tried to let them settle the disagreements themselves, unless the situation required intervention."

For Debbie, the problems began when Michael and Joanna were fourteen months old. It wasn't fighting over toys that caused the trouble; it was a resurfacing of the once-resolved issue of Michael's greater strength and dominance over Joanna. "Michael would push Joanna down or wrestle her to the ground just for fun. Because Michael's pushing, pulling, and tackling behavior was usually good-natured, I did my best to intervene only when Joanna's physical safety was threatened. One scene I grew familiar with was Michael sitting cross-legged on Joanna's back, laughing gleefully as she screamed in terror and frustration. I simply would pull them apart, take Michael aside, and look him in the eye as I said firmly, 'We don't sit on other children. It hurts.' Then I would go to Joanna and look into her eyes as I told her that she needed to say *no* and get away if Michael was bothering her. Having done this, I tried to distract both of them by involving them in an activity with me.

"I had begun to think they would never enjoy each other's company again when they began to play nicely together for longer periods of time. In large part this was due to the increase in their vocabularies and their understanding of each other's words. Joanna often would say to Michael, 'Go away,' 'No more,' and 'All done,' which greatly reduced his physical assaults. Both of them learned and used the phrases 'my turn,' 'Joanna's turn,' and 'Michael's turn,' leading to increased cooperation and the sharing of toys."

*Temper Tantrums:* By the time toddlers are eighteen months old, many of them experience temper tantrums. Small frustrations turn into huge eruptions as their emotions take over and get the better of them. Some children have daily outbursts of temper, while others go weeks between tantrums.

Experts recommend ignoring these outbursts. As difficult as that sounds, the situation will get worse if parents respond or give in. If parents can calmly walk away, demonstrating that this behavior does not rattle them or change their minds, the tantrum usually stops. Still, we all had moments when the experts' advice didn't work.

Between eighteen and twenty-four months, Florien's boys began to have their share of temper tantrums. "Devin and I tried everything we could do to help them (and ourselves) get through this period of growing up. There were a couple of times when Otto got so worked up over something that I was unable to calm him down. He didn't want me to leave him alone while he cried, nor did he want me to hold him. The only thing that helped was for me to lie on the rug a short distance away and let him cry it out. Sometimes it lasted five minutes and other times it took him a half-hour."

Sheri's girls also reached the tantrum stage in the latter part of the year. "The outbursts weren't all that terrible, and I realized that Emmy and Tessa were just voicing frustrations. Often they were upset at having to take turns with toys. Of course, one twin wanted exactly what the other twin had.

"I finally went to some shops that sold used toys and found some to match up with Kallie's hand-me-downs that were causing the tantrums. Owning two of everything was definitely a compromise on my part; it went against everything I believed about the twins being individuals. Emmy and Tessa were happy, though, and the tantrums all but stopped."

## *Everyday Issues*
. . . . . . . . . . . . . . . . .

*Eating and Weaning:*   During the second year of life, children don't grow as much as they did in their first year, so they don't want or need to eat as much food. Many toddlers also become picky eaters. This can cause parents much frustration as they try to balance nutrition with respect for their children's instincts.

Some of a parent's headaches can be lessened by offering toddlers three meals and three healthy snacks each day. Little tummies fill fast and empty quickly, so this meal schedule provides toddlers with a chance to choose their favorite foods while filling their stomachs with nutritious food. Pasteurized milk can be introduced at this age and foods that are colorful, crunchy, smooth, and/or warm may intrigue a toddler enough that he or she will eat them. It's important to remember that the parents' example at mealtime has by far the most influence on a toddler's attitudes about food. If parents have poor eating habits, their children are likely to follow.

Linda's girls devoted more of mealtime to playing than to eating. "At all their meals, Sarah and Maiah sat in high chairs. Todd and I were trying to introduce them to new foods and get them accustomed to plates, cups, and utensils, but they wanted to eat from their high chair trays with their fingers and use their cups to pour milk on the floor. I pondered the possibility that they might never learn to eat in polite society.

"When one child didn't like something on her tray, she handed it to her sister. If neither one liked the food, they dropped it to the floor. I tried to discourage this latter practice, but if food ended up on the floor I let Bart, our seventy-pound standard poodle, in the house. He cleaned up all the scraps, then sat patiently waiting for the girls to throw him something else. This system worked for us: The girls were happy, Bart was happy, and I was happy to have less vacumming to do!

"When Keegan and Colin were toddlers, they wanted to taste everything that Sarah and Maiah were eating. Getting them to eat was never the problem; the difficulty came in their feeding schedule. The boys were ready to eat at 5:00 P.M., and not a minute later. Many days I ended up preparing two separate dinners, one at 4:30 and the other at 6:30. First I would feed the boys; then later while Sarah and Maiah and one parent ate, the other would give the boys a bath. For a while this was the only way we could schedule a peaceful meal."

Sheri's girls refused to be spoon-fed so their diets consisted mainly of finger foods. "Canned yams turned out to be a much-requested favorite. Next came canned carrots, peas, and green beans. For breakfast they okayed plain pieces of French toast and frozen blueberries. Throughout the day the girls had combinations of saltines, Cheerios, graham crackers, pasta, and plain toast; at 15 months they were eating pizza. The twins drank milk with their meals and usually had juice with snacks. They often threw their Tommee-Tippee cups at me, demanding more; I bought bigger, eight-ounce Tupperware bell tumblers with sipper seals and spouted lids that snap securely on top of the plastic cups."

Debra waited until her twins were almost fifteen months old before she introduced them to self-feeding with utensils and cups. "Aislynn picked up this skill more readily than Ricky did, mostly because he was disinterested and seemed to need more time than she did to adapt to changes. Sometimes Aislynn even spoon-fed Ricky when she finished eating first, and he seemed to like being catered to."

Still intertwined with feeding and sleeping is the issue of weaning. The five of us continued to differ greatly in our handling of this subject.

When Linda's girls were seventeen months old, they were still drinking one bottle of milk before bed. "I made up my mind to wean away the bottles. I knew the task wouldn't get any easier if I waited longer, and our pediatrician had recommended eliminating bottles at sixteen months. Todd and I discussed several methods before we decided that cold turkey was the best alternative.

"One night I put all their bottles away and offered the girls some milk in cups, but Maiah threw her cup at me while Sarah refused to touch hers. They stood at the refrigerator door, pulling on the handle and crying. I felt terrible, but I finally got them out of the kitchen and calmed down. I tried to explain, but I doubt they understood a single word; however, at my urging they took back their cups to drink a little milk as a peace offering before they went to bed. The next night was easier. I offered them their cups nightly, and a few weeks later *they* decided to quit drinking milk before bedtime."

Debbie's twins were still bottle- and breast-feeding. "Neither twin was particularly attached to a bottle, so they responded well at fourteen months when the bottles simply disappeared. By this time they both drank well from covered unbreakable cups, so they really did not need to continue nursing; however, I was still breast-feeding them in the morning and at bedtime because the three of us enjoyed the experience. I had originally planned to stop nursing them at one year, then decided to extend it for six more months. I did this for two reasons: They still wanted to nurse, and nursing them in the morning and before bedtime made me feel closer to them and relieved the guilt I felt for leaving them all day when I worked. My six-month extension passed, then two more months. Although I had reduced the feeding to once a day (each morning), emotionally I was no closer to weaning them than I had been eight months earlier.

"I felt self-conscious about nursing Michael and Joanna at twenty months. Some of my friends were supportive, but others bluntly asked what was wrong with me. Realizing that the decision to continue nursing was partly selfish, I felt defensive. I began to wonder what my real motivatons were, and a quick bit of soul-searching gave me the answers. One answer was practicality— Michael and Joanna were often ill with colds and minor viral illnesses, and nursing them soothed and comforted their irritability. The other was purely selfish—Michael and Joanna would be my last babies. I would never again nurse any other children.

When I finally was able to acknowledge not only my enjoyment of the experience, but also the fact that it infanticized the twins and kept them my cuddly little babies, I knew enough was enough.

"In early December, I made a resolution to wean Michael and Joanna the first day of January; the twins were twenty-one months old. We had a few rough days at first, but nothing that couldn't be handled with some extra cuddling and reading first thing in the morning. Within a week or two, nursing was a distant memory for the twins, and I felt satisfied that I had done the right thing."

Debra intended to breast-feed her twins past their second birthday, but at eighteen months Aislynn weaned herself from nursing. "I think this was primarily due to the fact that my let-down reflex had slowed, so it took longer for her to get milk from my breast than from the bottle. Aislynn began showing a preference for the bottle, but Ricky was still content to nurse. This was helpful because he had begun resisting going to sleep. The twins were sleeping in separate beds now, but they still woke up once or twice a night to be comforted. I didn't mind the interrupted sleep so much now, because their daytime nap routine had changed and they were going to bed earlier."

*Napping and Bedtime:* During their second year, most children decrease their naps from two per day to one. The transition isn't always easy. It's a gradual process and the road can be a bit bumpy for toddlers and parents alike.

Just after Aislynn and Ricky's first birthday, it became apparent to Debra that two naps during the day was too much sleep. "The twins were staying up until ten or eleven o'clock, so I started delaying their morning nap until after noon, but they would become cranky and just pick at their lunch. I tried giving them a later morning snack, putting them down for a nap, then giving them another snack when they woke up. This worked much better, though at dinner they became sleepy again, and sometimes fell asleep in their high chairs if we didn't keep them amused. I found that giving them dinner earlier helped, and we used up a little more time by bathing them before tucking them into bed.

"The nap transition was difficult for the twins, so I let them have two naps every few days to let them catch up on their sleep.

Once they grew accustomed to the change, an eight o'clock bed-time became something I could count on. I finally had a few hours of kid-free time, which were reserved for my pleasure and relaxation."

Napping also developed into a challenge for Linda. "Sarah and Maiah suddenly decided to give up their morning naps in favor of one-hour afternoon naps. I had to adjust to their new schedule and soon found it necessary to put them in separate rooms or they never would have quieted down long enough to fall asleep.

"With my second set of twins, nothing short of staying in their room worked at naptime. I would simply lie down for my much needed rest with the boys, and we would all fall asleep."

Getting our children to sleep at bedtime was an area that im-proved for some of us after our twins passed twelve months of age. Because the twins ran around all day and wore themselves out, they were ready for sleep at night because many had dropped their morning nap, and we had all developed consistent family bedtime rituals. This was not to say that everything was perfect, though.

Linda describes their bedtime routine. "Sarah and Maiah each picked out a book to be read to them on the couch, then Todd and I brushed their teeth, and finally I carried them downstairs to their cribs. The minute I left the room, they stood up in their cribs and demanded attention. First Sarah wanted a drink of water, then Maiah wanted another hug and kiss, then they yelled for their teddy bears. Some evenings they let me get back upstairs and settled into a chair before the shouting started again. Before long, I got tired of this game, and was determined to make only one trip per night. From then on, each night I asked both girls what they needed for bedtime. I fulfilled their requests and said a brief goodnight, then left. There was a lot of crying at first, but within a week the girls accepted the new rules.

"The only nightime problem that remained for us was that pacifiers were still a bedtime habit for Sarah and Maiah. At first, I wasn't anxious to get rid of them because they hadn't been a problem. Then, at twenty-three months, the girls started a game of throwing the pacifiers out of their cribs and yelling for me to come back and pick them up. I took this as a signal that they had become more of toy than a comfort object, so I threw them away. The next evening when the girls asked for their "pacies," I told them they were gone; neither Sarah nor Maiah said anything more. They asked for them at bedtime a few more times, then the pacifiers were forgotten. I realize that getting rid of a pacifier is not usually this easy at this age, so I felt lucky to be spared a potential traumatic experience for all of us.

"Bedtimes with Keegan and Colin went smoothly until the boys turned eighteen months old. I had unthinkingly encouraged Sarah and Maiah to climb into the boys' cribs every morning to entertain them until I cooked breakfast. Keegan and Colin had observed the girls doing this for months, and they finally decided to try it on their own. One morning Colin climbed out of his crib and by that afternoon they both climbed out at naptime. They were proud of their accomplishment; I was completely appalled. From then on, naps and bedtimes turned into a nightmare!

"Anytime I put them in their cribs they would immediately hop up, swing one leg over, and slide down the corner rail. Attempting to thwart them, I lowered their matresses to the lowest rung, but it didn't slow them down at all. Next I tried waiting outside their door until they appeared in the hall, then I'd firmly put them back to bed. I soon realized that the two of them could outlast me. Finally, I gave in and sat on the floor in between their cribs. Every afternoon at naptime, and then again every evening until they fell asleep, I sat on the floor. Sometimes I would sit in the hall, outside their door, where they could hear me while I read the girls their bedtime story. Soon I realized that they depended on me to be present every time they went to sleep, so I decided to change my technique.

"Todd and I took the front pieces off their cribs; they weren't doing any good anyway and the boys could at least get in and out safely. I tucked them into bed, read a story, kissed them goodnight and then walked out, shutting the door behind me. The first few nights I did this, they got out of bed and started crying when they realized they couldn't turn the door handle to get out. I remained in the hall and listened, and after several minutes they stopped crying and got back into bed. After those initial episodes, they never cried again. After I closed their door, I went across the hall to the girls' room to read or talk to Maiah and Sarah. By the time we finished, the boys were usually asleep; I then opened their door and left it ajar for the rest of the night. Of course some nights they laughed and ran around the room, but they'd eventually fall asleep on the floor or in each other's beds.

"For a while, Colin started waking up in the middle of the night. Realizing that the door was open, he came upstairs to find me. He stopped after two nights of me sleeping outside his door, taking him back to bed when he got up, and shutting his door."

Nighttime was going smoothly for Sheri, because Emmy and Tessa continued their attachment to a particular type of receiving blanket. "We had a whole stack of them, all made from the same T-shirt fabric, so the twins could pick a blanket on the way to bed. Then they'd bunch it up and use it for a pillow. If we were away from home, the babies knew that when I pulled out a blanket it meant time to go 'night-night.' The blankets were a wonderful piece of home for them no matter where we were."

Sheri and Florien both had opportunities to move their twins from cribs into real beds when they neared two years old. Florien remembers: "The transition was easy; the boys were excited and proud. I'll never forget their first night in the new beds—Devin and I were sure they would roll out so we put pillows on the floor to soften any falls. They seemed so little in their new beds, and so much bigger than just the day before. That night they slept peacefully, but to be safe, the next day we bought side rails for the beds, which kept the boys from falling out until they learned to feel the edge of the bed a couple of months later."

*Toilet Training:* Debbie, Debra, and Sheri all had older children with whom they had success potty training when the children were near two years of age. Toddlers may show an interest at this age; however, girls generally become potty trained near two and a half years of age, and boys often wait until after they've turned three. Regardless of our twins' gender, none of us even attempted to toilet train them until well after their second birthday. By that age they were not only interested, but motivated.

Linda was new at the game of toilet training, and didn't see any reason to wait until Maiah and Sarah turned two years old.

"Taking a relaxed, nonpressuring approach to this big event, I started by placing their two potty chairs in our bathroom. Sarah and Maiah were excited by these new toys, especially when I showed them they could sit on the potty chairs without wearing diapers. When occasional 'accidents' into the potty occurred, they jumped up in surprise. I never forced or coerced them into using their potty chairs, but on the rare occasion that one twin used it successfully, I praised her and gave her a bear sticker to put on her hand.

"Their initial interest lasted only a short while; then they wanted to stand on the stools or sit down wearing their underclothes. As the end of their second year drew close, the girls seemed content to stay in diapers forever, but they did finally potty train when they were almost three.

"I had learned my lesson, and didn't even attempt to potty train Keegan and Colin at this age. Although they constantly ran into the bathroom to watch their big sisters use the toilet, they had no intention of learning to potty train and I had no intention of teaching them."

## Our Evolving Families

*Enjoying Our Twins:* The realm of activities we could enjoy with our twins grew considerably during their second year. Our toddlers were very happy out and about, as they could be entertained for longer periods of time by what they saw and heard. They loved walks, brief shopping trips, and short rides in the car. On the other hand, they were often frustrated at their inability to do things as well as the older children and adults that they saw when we were out. This sometimes resulted in tantrums and fighting. The possibilities for family activities had grown, but we had to carefully consider our choices.

As Florien's boys became more mobile, they began to take notice of the outdoors. "One of our family's favorite activities was to walk in the neighboring woods to visit a stream and explore the surrounding foliage. Even though Devin and I ended up carrying them for much of the walk, Max and Otto's delight made it worth our effort. They became more aware of the sky and their environment, and pointed out birds, airplanes, or squirrels in trees."

Debbie's twins also loved watching animals, but from a safe distance. "Trips to the zoo were fantastically successful at this age, as long as we took along the stroller and lots of snacks. Michael and Joanna were in awe of every animal and found the variety of human visitors fascinating, too. After a trip there, my twins' vocabularies grew as they proudly identified in their picture books the animals they'd seen."

Todd and Linda took their twins on several camping trips. "We had taken the girls on their first camp-out when they were fourteen months old. We spent one horrible night in a two-man tent, at a wilderness campground, in the rain. I swore I would never try camping with small children again. But when the boys were seventeen months old, we decided to go camping on the Oregon coast. This time we had a two-room tent, and our campground had bathrooms, showers, a playground, and a beach nearby. All these 'luxuries' made for a great trip."

Debra and her family took a vacation to the coast when the twins were eighteen months old. "Rick and I agreed that the whole family deserved a fun, relaxing trip. We spent hours walking along the beach, pulling the twins in a large red wagon, stopping often to explore. Aislynn and Ricky were fascinated, but true to form the twins explored this novel environment in entirely different ways. Aislynn flitted around, picking up one thing after another, while Ricky sat in one place, totally absorbed in every detail of his immediate surroundings."

*Safety:*   Twelve to twenty-four months is a dangerous age for children. Parents tend to relax a bit, as their toddlers entertain themselves more and more. But curiosity and a desire to be independent are the brew for serious safety hazards. This is the age when parents begin to say, "It's been quiet too long," as they realize that their toddlers have gone somewhere, or are doing something, unsupervised.

As her boys neared their second birthday, Florien found it very frustrating and potentially dangerous to take them out by herself.

"Max and Otto were no longer satisfied to sit in the stroller as we went about our errands. They would climb out and wander off in different directions. I was always chasing them, steering them away from water fountains, cigarette butts, and old wads of gum."

Rick and Debra had to invoke safety rules to curb Aislynn and Ricky's daring stunts. "The children accepted 'It's safer to walk down the stairs' better than 'Don't jump—you'll get hurt,' which was taken as a challenge. It was hard to be consistent about using more positive, proactive words because I was just learning about them, but they worked great with the kids when I did use them."

Debbie had a scary evening when her twins were almost two years old. "Both Michael and Joanna had very curious natures which Dale and I had always respected and enjoyed, but which presented us with serious dangers on several occasions. As the twins grew closer to two, Joanna consistently tempered her curiosity with timidity and was less of a problem to control than Michael, who was curious, clever, and fearless, a worrisome combination. The house had been childproofed since the twins' infancy. We watched them closely when they were in the house, and when we were outdoors Dale or I was always close by. When we were near streets or in parking lots, we held their hands firmly and were especially careful.

"But despite our best efforts, an incident occurred that could have had a tragic end. It happened late in a hectic day, when I was very tired. With all the dinner dishes washed and Michael, Joanna, and Chris playing happily, I was looking forward to putting my feet up and reading. Everything seemed under control. Dale decided to take the opportunity to run a quick errand. He announced he was leaving and rushed out the door as Michael yelled, 'I go with Daddy! I go with Daddy!' I responded with a brusque 'No, you stay with Mommy. Daddy will be right back.' I returned to my book as Michael, crying, toddled down the hall toward his room.

"Fewer than five minutes later I noticed that Michael had not yet returned from his room, and I assumed he was looking out the window while he waited for Dale's return. I had a fleeting impulse to check on him but told myself that, with the entire house childproofed and all the outside doors locked securely as usual, he couldn't get into trouble in just a few minutes. Reassured, I smiled down at Joanna, who was playing at my feet, and promised myself that I would look in on Michael in a little while.

"Another minute or two had passed when I heard knocking at the back door and a familiar voice calling my name. When I got up to answer, I found Chris's friend Matt standing in the open doorway, holding Michael's hand. He said, 'I found him outside by your garage; he was watching me play basketball. I thought you wouldn't want him out there alone.' Aghast, I knelt to Michael's level as he announced, smiling, 'I go find Daddy.'

"I felt relief, then shame, then thankfulness as I gathered Michael into my arms and held him close. But how had he slipped out? One look at the back door gave me my answer: We each had assumed that someone else would deadbolt the door, but no one had. Michael had only to turn the knob, open the door, and walk outside in his search for Daddy. I couldn't put Michael down for half an hour, and several days went by before I could see Matt without profusely thanking him. I also thanked God that I had learned an important lesson without anyone getting hurt: No matter how hectic the circumstances were or how tired I felt, I could never let up on the supervison of my children."

## *Our Thoughts and Reflections*

SHERI:     Busy as they were, pushing chairs to the counter for a better vantage point and figuring out how to undo the cupboard latches, Emmy and Tessa were really fun to have around. They were very friendly and social among people, and because each had a playmate who was usually in the same mood as herself, they constantly entertained each other. It was heaven. For the first time in two years I actually had some time for myself.

LINDA:     The twins' enormous leaps in development were amazing, but their daily antics dismayed me. I wiped up more spilt milk, rerolled more toilet paper, fixed more toys, and dried more tears than I ever thought possible. My sense of humor helped me make it through.

DEBBIE: At one year Michael and Joanna could barely walk, said only a few words, and were still nursing; Michael wasn't even eating table foods yet. By two years, they ran with confidence, spoke in short sentences, and were weaned from bottle- and breast-feeding. High on the list of joys were hearing Michael and Joanna say, 'I love you' to Dale and me for the first time, teaching and exposing them to the wonders of life, and watching them develop special relationships with each other and with Chris.

FLORIEN: The first six months of Max's and Otto's second year, they were always happy and only sometimes testy. The latter six months were filled with days when their emotions seemed to easily take over, and doing things their way was the only way. Fortunately, the emotional upheavals diminished near their second birthday, and they became a little more independent and less testy. They were comfortable with the rules that had been established, and seemed almost to like the security of the limitations we set for them.

DEBRA: Like Aislynn and Ricky, I, too, had focused on regaining some of my own independence that year, so my growth paralleled the twins'. As we approached the twins' second birthday, clearer identities emerged for all of us.

# Chapter 14

# "What one doesn't think of, the other one will!"

## *Preschool Twins*

O ther mothers of twins used to tell us, "When your twins turn two, watch out, because what one doesn't think of, the other will!" These words made us wonder just how horrible life could be with two children in the "terrible twos." The idea of toilet training two obstinate toddlers who were screaming "No!" or disciplining two angry children who were striving for independence was cause for anxious anticipation.

We are not prepared to say that life during this year was a breeze and that all our worries were unfounded, but honestly, it wasn't so bad. In fact, twins at the age of two can be the cutest, most curious, and most loving people on the face of the earth. We have all learned much about handling twin two-year-olds, and although the end of the chapter marks the end of our writing about our children's lives, it certainly doesn't mark the end of our efforts to be the best mothers we can be. This will be a lifelong endeavor.

### Changes in Our Twins

A two-year-old is approximately two inches shorter and three pounds lighter than a three-year-old. At a glance, you might not be able to tell them apart. However, if you were given a few minutes for closer observation, differences would be obvious—the speech, play, activity, and demeanor of the two-year-old are much less sophisticated. He is still clinging to infancy, while the three-year-old is on the brink of childhood.

*Developing Motor Skills:* Between two and three years of age, children learn to control their bodies in many ways. They may enjoy using their hands to put together simple puzzles, scribble or make circles with crayons, string wooden beads to make necklaces, and stack up to ten blocks to build towers. They become more independent in their daily activities as they begin to learn to dress themselves, feed themselves with forks and spoons, and try to brush their teeth. By three years of age, most children can walk up and down the stairs, jump forward with their feet together, climb up and down play equipment, kick and throw a ball, and ride a bicycle. This all translates into active young children with independent ideas and personalities who are constantly on the move, looking for new and fun things to do.

*Play:* Play evolves in exciting ways throughout this year. At age two, they are just beginning to cooperate by sharing toys and ideas, but by the time they reach three, they enjoy playing together and are more capable of taking turns, following rules, and building on each other's imagination. Of course, there will be times when each twin wants to play alone or prefers the company of another child, but by and and large, they are best buddies jumping from one activity to the next throughout the day.

Playtime for our twins was most enjoyable when they had a variety of toys and activities to explore, which encouraged cooperation and creativity. Debra explains, "Toys that could be shared turned out to be our most worthwhile investments. Blocks, interlocking building toys, dolls, puzzles, a miniature kitchen center with kid-size dishes, dress-up clothes, and pretend grocery store items provided for many hours of fun."

Playing store, with one twin being the cashier and one being the customer, is just one type of role-playing activity they can enjoy. They may also play house as each takes turn being the mommy, daddy, and baby brother or sister, or they may get their ideas from the media, as Florien's boys Max and Otto did.

Florien remembers, "The boys loved Superman and Spiderman videos, comic books, cassette tapes, and records. Anything related to stories about their favorite characters was a popular form of entertainment, but their most favorite thing was dressing up as a superhero. They would put on their Superman pajamas, add red underwear, red socks, yellow belts, and pretend capes, and become *Superman*! Soon Spiderman came along to balance out the action, since they both couldn't be Superman at the same time. I got a kick out of watching them play in this way. Plus, I finally got a few minutes of rest as this was the first activity that kept their attention for more than ten or fifteen minutes at a time."

Sheri's girls also developed an interest in television and movie characters, but their attachment grew too strong, which made Sheri uncomfortable. "Emmy and Tessa loved to watch videotapes. They picked up this habit from their big sister, who hadn't been interested in television as a small child, but had grown into a six-year-old who could stare blankly at a program for an hour and become completely oblivious to everything else around her. I didn't worry about Kallie watching too much TV because she always preferred to spend her time doing other things.

"Emmy and Tessa were another matter, though. Without realizing it, I was encouraging them to quietly sit and watch television instead of playing with their toys. It was so nice to leave the twins in front of the television, slip quietly to my desk to balance the checkbook in peace, and return thirty minutes later to find them sitting where I left them. When their videotape ended, they'd beg to watch it again, and I happily complied. Then one day when our babysitter, Sara, was playing with the girls, Emmy raised her arms, and loudly sang, 'Ahhh-ahhh-ahhh!' She'd been singing this song constantly, and I thought it was cute until that day, when Sara pointed out that Emmy was imitating Disney's Little Mermaid, Ariel, giving her voice to the sea witch. At that moment, I made up my mind that Emmy and Tessa were being too strongly influenced by television, so I limited their viewing privileges and sent them off to play with their toys."

No matter how many interesting toys or playthings we had for our twins, there came a time when they all needed variety in their play life. During the winter months preschool, indoor play-grounds, and going to other children's houses offered them a release from boredom. During warmer weather, the outdoors supplied them with a whole new set of adventures that used up their abundant energy and offered them chances to practice some of their new physical abilities.

Debra has particularly fond memories of the summer her twins were two. "That summer we had picnic lunches together and spent sultry days drifting on a floating dock at a neighbor's private lake. Jason captured salamanders for the smaller kids to play with. He and I took turns swimming and watching the little ones, who were in life jackets. I was in heaven! With a swing set, wading pool, sandbox and three-wheeled riding toys to entertain the children we spent many carefree hours together."

Sheri, too, had a relaxing summer with her two-year-old twins. "At two and a half, Emmy and Tessa could play without my con-stant supervision. They climbed on the swing set, picked straw-berries, and rode trikes. I learned that they could climb trees, too. To my dismay, our small, thickly-branched cherry tree soon became their favorite summer playground. Whenever I lost track of them, I'd walk to the tree to find them giggling and chattering in its limbs."

*Language:* The burst in vocabulary that occurs during this year is impressive. Most children start the year uttering one- or two-word phrases, identifying basic thoughts or desires, and they end the year speaking in three-word phrases. Some children even speak in four- to five-word sentences, revealing more complex ideas and feelings. Of course, as in everything else, each child progresses at his or her own rate.

Debra's set of twins provides a good example: "There were vast differences in Aislynn's and Ricky's ability to speak. At twenty months of age, Aislynn was already speaking in four- or five-word sentences, while Ricky could only say one or two words at a time. I didn't worry about this difference because I knew from books I'd read that their variations were within normal ranges of development.

"However, I did encourage Ricky's development of language by responding positively to his attempts to talk and not criticizing or comparing his jumbled grammar to Aislynn's more advanced ability. I also tried to be a good role model by not using baby talk. Finally, when Ricky was two and a half, he surprised me by rattling off several sentences in a row. Once this happened, Aislynn and Ricky communicated on the same level."

Sometimes the delay in language acquisition that was apparent at a younger age persists. Linda's boys, Keegan and Colin, who had little expressive language at a year old, continued to lag behind. At two and a half, Keegan and Colin understood language well, but continued to struggle to speak in simple phrases. Again, Linda consulted her pediatrician, who felt that the boys' language skills were within normal limits but suggested they undergo a language and hearing evaluation to be sure. The results of the evaluation showed Keegan and Colin to have an expressive language delay of one year. Linda was glad to have their problems identified at such a young age. Soon afterward they began speech therapy to improve their language skills.

Another speech problem that may occur at this age is stuttering, which happened with Florien's boys. "When Max and Otto were about two and a half, they began stuttering whenever they were excited. The behavior rotated between the boys, with Max stuttering one month and Otto the next. Devin and I weren't alarmed, but we talked to our doctor. He felt that the stuttering was a result of the twins' inability to verbalize all their thoughts, and that they would grow out of it when their vocabularies increased. If it persisted, we should let him know. Fortunately, by the time Max and Otto were three and in command of many new words, the stuttering lessened quite a bit. By five years of age, it stopped completely."

Our twins' increased ability to communicate made life easier for all of us. Debbie sums it up: "By the time Michael and Joanna were three, their speech had matured to the point that day-to-day events went more smoothly. They got along better with me and with each other because they could talk to each other, communicate their needs, and work out minor differences."

*Twin Identity and Individuality:* As twins grow capable of expressing their wants and desires, their temperamental differences and personal strengths and weaknesses all become clearer. Our twins' manifestations of individuality came in many forms.

Debbie describes Michael and Joanna's relationship: "At about age two, Joanna emerged as the boss of the duo and consistently tried to manage Michael by telling him what to do or how to play. Naturally, this caused some friction, but there were also many occasions when one twin's strengths smoothed the way for the other twin. For example, Joanna was afraid of almost every animal, even small ones, but she loved people. Michael loved animals, but was quite shy with adults. Instinctively, they seemed to know each other's weaknesses, and each came to the other's aid in those circumstances that one found frightening.

"These protective roles seemed healthy, but I realized that as Michael and Joanna got older, they would each need to face their fears on their own to avoid becoming too dependent on each other."

Debra's twins showed their personality differences in other ways. "Ricky and Aislynn's individuality was most evident in how they chose to play, which evolved along traditional male/female orientations. This surprised me because Rick and I had tried to expose both of them to similar toys and experiences.

"Nevertheless, Ricky became enthralled with real trucks, boats, and construction equipment like he had seen on the highway. When he played, he imitated what he had seen, building roads and hauling freight. Aislynn, who played dress-up and hairstylist with her older girl cousins, wanted me to do this with her, too. She beamed when she and I spent special time doing this. It made me realize that I needed to share more individual time with each of my twins, which they thoroughly enjoyed."

Identical twins will also search for their special interests and talents, but they may be more subtle, as Florien points out. "I must admit that Devin and I have always felt that in many ways Max and Otto are very similar. It has been important for us to look for those subtle differences that do exist and then support them.

"Max and Otto had some temperamental differences in infancy, but when they became toddlers these differences leveled out. It wasn't until they were almost three that each began to express special interests.

"Max adored music; he sang all day long. Sometimes he sang a song exactly as he heard it; at other times, he changed the words. He liked all kinds of music: children's, rock, new wave, classical, and country and western.

"At the same time Max was discovering music, Otto was becoming fascinated with clothes. He loved to dress up in make-believe clothing during play. If he couldn't find an entire cowboy outfit, he would design a 'good-guy' outfit, wearing all white clothes, including white covers for his hands and head. He also liked to choose his own clothing each day, being careful to pick items that matched or went together as a set. He loved to wear fancy clothes with a bow tie and suspenders. He basked in the attention he got for being well-dressed."

As twins begin to identify who they are as individuals, they sometimes become competitive with each other. "Otto had a desire to practice new skills until he could do them well, while Max preferred to watch and learn from Otto's mistakes. This set up mild competition between them. Eventually, Otto would acquire the skill a bit earlier than Max. Then Otto would claim he could do it better because he had conquered the task first, while Max felt he was better because he learned it with fewer attempts. Devin and I had to continually point out that neither boy was better for learning something first or for learning it more quickly. They had learned differently, but both had the same end result."

Competition between twins can be healthy as it gives them the opportunity to face and overcome challenges they may not have been inclined to consider if they were singletons. Unfortunately, if a twin does not feel approval from his parents or he is made to feel that he is "less than" his twin sibling, his self-esteem will suffer.

We tried to avoid unhealthy competition between our sets of twins while still acknowledging their differences, by praising their successes, showing a sincere interest in their special interests, and allowing them to have close friendships with other children. Their

birthdays were excellent opportunities to celebrate their uniqueness. We felt it was important to make or buy each of our twins
their own small cake; we sang "Happy Birthday" twice, so they
both had a special moment in the limelight. Whenever possible,
we avoided giving them combined gifts and instead chose separate
presents that reflected each twin's wants and desires.

Another significant factor that influenced our twins' ability to
gain a healthy sense of self-identity was whether we presented
them to the world dressed alike, enhancing their "twinness," or
dressed differently, expressing their individuality. When our twins
were infants we all dressed them alike or in complementary outfits
at least some of the time. It was fun; and it drew positive attention
to us, which we badly needed at the time. Of course, as infants
our twins didn't mind what they had on as long as it was comfortable and suitable for the weather.

However, as the identical twins got older, it became more
important for people to tell them apart. Florien and Sheri both
grew concerned that most people, even their preschool teachers,
couldn't tell who was who. They both found similar solutions to
the problem.

Florien encouraged Max and Otto to dress differently so that
others could tell them apart more easily. "Despite my suggestions,
there were a few days that Otto and Max insisted on dressing
alike, which was fine on occasion. Overall, though, they followed
my wishes. At their day-care, I suggested that Max and Otto be
given name tags so the staff members could distinguish who was
who and call them by the correct name. This worked very well
at first, but then Max and Otto decided it would be fun to switch
their name tags to confuse everyone. We solved that problem by
putting their name tags on their backs where they couldn't reach
them easily. There was one added benefit to this: People were
forced to at least try to tell them apart by their features when
addressing them face to face.

"After the name tag switching incident, I also bought Max and
Otto shoes and coats of the same style, but different colors. I
really felt this was important to their sense of self and I continued
doing it until they were able to choose their own clothes."

Whether or not to dress twins alike is not only an issue for parents of identical twins. It is an issue for all parents of twins because by the time twins reach two, they have preferences for certain clothes and some are already uncomfortable dressing alike. In any case, parents should be sensitive to their twins' feelings on the matter.

Debbie came face-to-face with Michael's desires in this regard when he was almost three. "When Michael and Joanna were infants, I often dressed them alike or in complementary outfits. As they grew older, I continued to do this on special occasions when I knew photos would be taken, but I stopped when my shy Michael told me how he felt one evening. He saw me lay out the male version of the clothes Joanna was to wear. He said, 'I don't wanna wear that. Everyone will notice me.' He was genuinely distressed. He wore some nondescript outfit that night, which wasn't nearly as cute, but I had respected his feelings. That was the important thing."

We do not want to give the impression that twins over age two should never be dressed alike or in similar outfits. There are occasions when it is fun and appropriate and some twins love it. Our recommendation is to balance your twins' need for individuality with any desire you may have to dress them alike.

*The Struggle for Independence:* When a twin starts to distinguish himself from his twin sibling, he also recognizes the need to separate himself from his parents. The fight for independence begins as he challenges his parents' every act and request by asserting, "No!" or "I don't want to!" Imagine these adamantly spoken remarks in stereo and you begin to understand the challenge facing the parents of all two-year-old twins.

Linda remembers, "As Sarah and Maiah grew into two independent toddlers, 'No, I don't hafta!' echoed through our house. Todd and I previously had been confronted with brief periods of newfound assertiveness, but now the girls jumped into their individuality with all four feet. They desperately struggled for control of their emotions, environment, and other people. I felt I could do nothing right as they rejected any sort of intervention from me. They didn't know what they wanted. In the morning, they refused to get dressed; at night, they refused to get undressed. They didn't want to wear diapers. They didn't want to eat their dinners. The list of negatives grew and grew. Meals were stressful as the girls became picky about what foods they ate, and even where the food was placed on their plates.

"I read books on developmental stages of childhood as I strove to be patient and supportive. I knew that understanding was the key to coping, but often I was left intimidated, exasperated, and exhausted from our struggles. Until my twins passed this phase of the terrible twos times two, I chose to spend most of our time at home."

Debbie also had difficulty. "I swear that a genie whispered in Michael and Joanna's ears, 'You're almost two; act terrible,' because by the time Michael and Joanna's second birthdays arrived, they were willful, argumentative, sneaky, and, (dare I say it?) Monsters. The height of this period lasted about two months. During this time, Michael's favorite phrases were 'I don't want to' and 'I don't have to.' He spoke these words clearly and calmly, more as a statement of fact than as an act of open defiance. Not to be outdone, our formerly compliant Joanna just quietly did what she wanted to when she wanted to, and ignored Dale's and my rules in the process. Gone was the sweet toddler who once helped me keep tabs on Michael's misadventures; in her place was a sly little girl ready to link arms with him in creating all sorts of mischief.

"To help Michael and Joanna express their need for independence, Dale and I decided to give them some control over the daily events in their lives. For example, Joanna and Michael both enjoyed making leisurely good-byes and slowly walking to the car when I picked them up from preschool; I simply scheduled dawdling time into our day so they could have their fun and I wouldn't feel rushed. On the rare occasions when I was in an unavoidable hurry, Michael and Joanna seemed to understand and tolerate it well.

"I also set up simple choices of foods to eat and clothes to wear, from which they could pick their preferences. Whenever possible, I allowed them to do as much as they could for themselves. I am convinced that, because Michael and Joanna felt control over the smaller items in their lives, they were able to relinquish, without undue anguish, the big decisions to Dale and me."

Debra's twins had their own ways of expressing their need for autonomy, and she created solutions suited to these needs. "Aislynn and Ricky had very different ways of acting out their need to separate from me. Aislynn plainly and flatly responded negatively to any request. When given a choice, she'd change her mind again and again until we both were frustrated. I finally had to say that the third choice was final. She had a right to change her mind, but I had a right to my sanity! She also was very whiny, which truly aggravated me. Unfortunately, my response to her whining was inconsistent. Ignoring it worked, but was hard to do. If I yelled at her to stop, it only made her whine more. The most effective reaction was to say, 'I can only hear you when you use your talking voice.' Gradually the habit diminished, but it was tough while it lasted.

"In contrast, Ricky was quietly stubborn and sometimes would hide if he were playing with or doing something he wasn't supposed to. I gave him until the count of three to respond, with a consequence if he didn't. Many times he'd do as requested, but very slowly. He was especially uncooperative when it was time to help pick up toys. Two things alleviated this problem. One was to comment that I appreciated Aislynn's and Muggy's willingness to help, instead of berating Ricky for his refusal. He soon caught on to the idea that he got more attention by joining in. The other tactic was to make a game of cleaning up by 'shopping for toys' with toy shopping baskets that the kids had received for Christmas."

As two-year-old twins strive for independence, they test limits and scale new heights of misbehavior. They may not always intend to be naughty, but they will be in trouble—a lot! When the mischief is innocent play, a sense of humor will hold you in good stead.

Linda has one memory that she won't soon forget. "One morning Sarah and Maiah took Todd's gourmet cooking pots into the living room. They put all their puzzle pieces into the pots pretending to cook breakfast. I listened from the other room as they played. Distracted, I stopped listening until I heard Maiah exclaim, 'You go potty, Sar-rah.' By the time I reached them, both Sarah and Maiah were sitting naked on the pots, urinating on their puzzle pieces. The girls were having a great time. I felt like screaming, but couldn't help laughing because I knew they meant no harm. Still, I had them help me clean up as I explained that they needed to use their potty chairs when they had to urinate."

Although two-year-olds need to test limits to find the boundaries of acceptable behavior, they also need reasonable rules to reestablish order. Sheri describes a recurring problem in their home and the rule she set to meet her twins' needs and her own.

"Emmy and Tessa were very confident about their climbing abilities, and they loved pulling Kallie's stool up to our kitchen cupboards, so they could climb up on the counter. The twins knew they weren't supposed to do this, but by age two, they simply stopped following that rule.

"Almost daily, I would find a trail of smashed Cheerios which led me through several rooms before I found the culprit contentedly eating cereal out of the box and sharing it with her twin sister.

"To save my floors and my sanity, I insisted that the twins ask me for snacks, so I could supervise as they got them out. Because the twins were partially motivated by the sheer delight of finding out what lay behind the cupboard doors, I also let them fetch ingredients and kitchen utensils for me during the early, unhurried stages of our meal preparations. This substantially reduced the number of cupboard raids and half-eaten apples that I found under the coffee table!"

For several weeks, Linda had her hands full keeping Maiah in clothes. "As fast as I dressed Maiah, she took her clothes off. "Eventually, I came to the realization that fighting her every minute of the day about wearing clothes served no real purpose. Instead, I made up a house rule. When we stayed indoors at home Maiah could be naked. When we went out, she had to be dressed. This alleviated the problem at home, though she still had some problems at her play group. I'd drop her off fully dressed, and return to find her in a diaper. I took some solace in knowing that I was not the only person having trouble keeping her dressed! Finally I decided that even though I would continue to dress her for her play group, I would ignore it completely (weather permitting) if she were nude when I went to pick her up. This decreased the tension we all felt and before long the behavior stopped."

Florien's twins had their own style of limit-testing as they lived up to the reputation of "double trouble." She remembers, "Max and Otto were simply not listening and following our directions or those of other adults. They attempted and got away with plans that one child alone would never consider, much less act upon. To make matters worse, other children often followed them in their misadventures. It is one thing to have your own children acting silly and not following directions, but it concerned us when we saw other children emulating Otto's and Max's behaviors.

"To work on this problem, Devin and I decided to have family meetings over dinner. The meetings were brief and simple, and the boys looked forward to them. Devin and I would tell about our day and ask about the boys' days as we modeled appropriate kinds of conversation. Usually, the twins listened when we discussed topics that involved them, such as not obeying rules or sharing toys. At two years old, they were too young to be a part of these conversations, but by the time they were three they were able to actively participate. As a result, we noticed an improvement in their ability to judge what they should and should not be doing. Devin and I finally felt they were beginning to learn the value of rules and the importance of good judgment, not merely complying with our demands."

Despite our best efforts, there were still times that our twins' behavior was so dangerous, persistently mischievous, or blatantly against the rules that using time-out was our best option. The only problem with time-out was that we had to do it differently than the way we did it when our twins were eighteen months old, as described in Chapter 13, if it were to be effective.

Just after Michael and Joanna turned two, Debbie says, "If I were home alone with Michael and Joanna when they both needed time-outs, I would try my best to sit on the floor and hold them still for thirty to sixty seconds, but they never took it seriously. Disciplining one twin at a time didn't work either; seconds after I sat down in the corner of the room with the offender, the other twin would burst in on us. Time-out simply wasn't working any-more, either as brief social isolation or as an incentive for the twins to change their behavior.

"Frustrated, Dale and I decided to place them in their cribs for a minute or two. At first I resisted this solution, because associating discipline with their cribs seemed unwise, but I had to agree with Dale that it was our best option, with the under-standing that neither Dale nor I would ever, ever say that Michael and Joanna had to go to bed because they were naughty."

A crib may not be the best time-out spot for all children. Sheri's twins, who no longer slept in cribs, were sat on the floor in a quiet hallway. Linda's boys, Keegan and Colin, never cooperated with sitting still or staying in bed for time-out. She responded by simply taking the offender to his room and shutting the door, asking him not to come out until he was ready to behave appro-priately. She says, "By the time I got up to the stairs from the downstairs bedroom, he would already be out the door. Never-theless, when he returned his behavior was improved."

Florien devised an entirely different sort of time-out proce-dure. "No matter what I did, I still couldn't get Max and Otto to cooperate with time-out. In an attempt to come up with a solution, I spoke to other parents. Through my inquiries, I began to see that time-out wasn't meant to punish a child, but is supposed to provide him or her with an opportunity to calm down and refocus his attention. Then, when the episode is past, the parent and child can talk about the misbehavior and come up with alternative ways to act.

"Devin and I were excited about the prospect of turning our twins' battle of wills into something positive. Instead of having to sit perfectly still during time-out, one boy was directed to play quietly in his room for a few minutes, while the other had the same options in the living room. Later, at our dinnertime dis-cussions, we addressed their misbehavior, and discussed what had happened and how we all could have done things differently. This form of time-out worked so well for limit testing that before long I began using it with equal success when the boys fought with each other."

There is one complicating factor that must be considered when managing the mischief of two-year-old twins—determining who is the guilty party. Linda remembers, "When the girls were younger, they both had proudly exclaimed, 'I did it!' whenever they were asked about some wrongdoing. Neither one was concerned about the consequences involved or the fact that a guilty plea wasn't the best response. After the 'I did it!' stage, there came a time when the guilty person was 'Sarahmaiah,' with neither one taking the blame singly. For a while Sarahmaiah got into a lot of trouble at our house.

"When the girls turned two, they began to strive for control and express their individual desires. This was when they started placing the blame on each other. Suddenly everything was the other twin's fault."

In determining the origin of your twins' rebellious activities, we also caution you never to make assumptions. Debbie explains, "One of Michael's and Joanna's favorite disobedient pastimes was to sneak outside unsupervised. They always waited to make their move until I was home alone with them and then, when I went to the bathroom or answered the phone, they would race to the family room and let themselves out through the sliding glass door into our fenced backyard. When I returned minutes later and found them outside, I would give them a verbal reprimand and bring them back into the house. Most often I aimed my words at Michael, because only he was strong and tall enough to unlatch the lock and push open the heavy glass door and I assumed that he had led their escape to freedom.

"I learned how wrong this assumption was one afternoon, while eavesdropping on their conversation. Joanna said to Michael, 'Open door. Let's go outtide.' Initially he resisted her suggestion, but she persisted and he finally agreed to open the door. Just as Joanna started to rush outside, I intervened. After this incident, I never came to a conclusion without having all the facts. And when the facts weren't readily available, I often made both of them accountable for their mischievous misdeeds."

*Fighting between Twins:* Although two-year-old twins are a tight twosome who delight in being cohorts, there will be times during every day when they fight. The fighting is different from the types of battles they had a year ago. Less and less are the arguments punctuated with "That's mine!" as the twins bite or pull each other's hair. Instead, it is more likely a refusal to co-operate. As the disagreement escalates, there is pushing and shoving, with threats of lifelong hatred. While such disagreements are to be expected, they do present a challenge to parents as they come to grips with how to handle them.

As much as safety and reason would allow, we ignored our twins' squabbles to give them an opportunity to resolve problems by themselves. However, when disagreements grew too intense for them to handle, we stepped in. Time-out was often effective in managing fights, because it gave both twins the chance to be alone and get control of their emotions, but it was only one method we used to keep fighting to a minimum.

Debbie tried to help her twins understand the reason for their fighting. "Even though Michael and Joanna got along pretty well, there were still lots of times when one or the other of them lost control. The usual scenario was that Joanna bossed Michael and directed their play until he couldn't take it anymore. Instead of using words, he'd just haul off and push her down. Of course, she'd come screaming 'My-toe hit me, My-toe hit me!' Having seen their interaction escalate, I usually just reminded Michael that hitting hurts people and it was not okay to do that. I'd also ask him to use words to let Joanna know he was angry. I'd then explain to Joanna that when she bossed Michael it wasn't fun for him to play with her. In the short run, this kind of conversation wasn't effective, but by the time my twins turned three, I began to see results as Michael and Joanna got better at talking things over, and stopped hitting each other so much. They also developed an awareness that each had feelings that should be respected.

"I also found another way to curb their aggressive impulses, which was to allow rough, but safe, play. I never let them break toys or threaten to hurt anyone, but when I let them play games where they had imaginary powers to fight evil or they expended lots of energy running and climbing, they had fewer angry outbursts during the day."

Florien agrees that it was helpful to give Max and Otto time each day to burn off excess energy by playing actively, but she also found a way for the boys to monitor their own behavior. "It seemed like I was always breaking up fights that started over whose turn it was—who got to use the rocking horse, who got to wear the red Superman cape, etc., etc., etc.

"A friend suggested that I buy the boys a timer and teach them how to set it for five or ten minutes. I followed her advice; before I knew it, whenever they both wanted to do something at the same time, they would set the alarm and then take turns nicely. I think the reason it worked so well was that it gave them equal control over the situation and they didn't have to come crying to me for help."

Debra also got some good advice from a friend. "I know that some of Ricky and Aislynn's fighting was really an issue of power; each wanted it and struggled to have more than his twin. My friend, who had four-year-old twins, was using something called the *table technique*. Ricky and Aislynn were not quite three, but I decided to give a try. In the middle of a fight, you have the two parties involved sit across from each other at a table. The children may not get up until each gives the other permission to do so, or until they have worked out a solution that is satisfactory to both. If the fight is over a toy, it is placed in the middle of the table, and they have to come to a mutual agreement about how it is to be shared.

"When the disagreement was minor, my twins got up right away. Very upset twins could force one another to sit a while, which reflected the seriousness of the crime. If either twin abused his or her power by refusing to come to an agreement, he or she soon learned that doing so was counterproductive, as they both had to stay put until mutual permission to leave was granted."

Blaming and tattle-telling is a common result of twin fights. This occurred often in Debra's household: "By the time my twins were three, Aislynn had gotten into the habit of running to me constantly with reports of Ricky's wrongdoing. I started to observe the children more carefully and discovered that Aislynn was provoking fights so she could tell on Ricky and get him in trouble. One friend suggested I make them *both* responsible for the fighting. If either twin came to me to report on the other, they both got a time-out. That took away both the incentive for fighting and tattle-telling and the good guy-bad guy scenario, and reminded them that they both had a part in getting along."

The methods we used to manage our twins' squabbles were effective, but they didn't eliminate fighting entirely. This is to be expected since a certain amount of sibling discord is normal. However, we did notice that disagreements between our sets of twins occurred more frequently when there was increased stress in the family. A job change for one of the parents, a move to a new house, the twins getting a different baby-sitter, or family members being ill often stressed our twins, making them irritable and prone to fighting. In these situations, time and attention were our best allies as we took one day at a time.

*Temper Tantrums:* Temper tantrums are without a doubt one of the most unpleasant behaviors of this age. These outbursts of sheer rage and frustration usually stop when a toddler reaches his or her third birthday. Some children have only rare fits of temper, while it is a daily occurrence for others.

Many tantrums can be avoided by keeping children well-rested and well-fed and intervening *before* they reach their breaking point. Florien found this to be successful. "If I supervised Max and Otto closely, I could almost always predict when one of them was ready to lose control over their behavior. If I gently interrupted what they were doing and engaged them in a new activity in another part of the house, I usually could prevent a tantrum from happening. While this sounds very simple, it isn't. I had to be constantly aware of what the boys were doing and be able to read their signals before the temper tantrum took place, and I couldn't do this 100 percent of the time."

When a temper tantrum does occur in a two-year-old, the adult response is in many ways the same as the response for a toddler. The same rules apply: Be calm, but firm, and give the child no undue attention. As children grow more verbal, an additional technique can be used that eases the intensity of the tantrum. Sheri explains, "I attended a panel discussion on child-rearing where the consensus was that the most important factor in the parent-child relationship was open communication. They recommended that the best way to facilitate such communication was through the acknowledgment of feelings.

"Emmy's and Tessa's attempts to communicate were often frustrated by their inability to describe how they were feeling. When I squatted down to their level during a tantrum and said, 'You look like you feel really angry!' they were then able to talk about the problem, and the remedy, which was usually quite simple. Often the girls even forgot they were angry. Whining and complaining could also be transformed into conversation by acknowledging their feelings and saying, 'You seem pretty frustrated right now.' I realize this sounds almost too simple to be true, but it really worked to defuse emotionally charged situations with my twins."

## Everyday Issues

*Napping:* When twins reach two years of age, most of them will be taking just one nap a day of one to two hours in the midafternoon. This pattern may persist until age five when they go to kindergarten, but quite often twins give up this nap by age three.

When Emmy and Tessa were a year and a half old, they started to keep each other awake at naptimes. Sheri solved this problem easily enough: "I put the girls down to sleep in separate bedrooms, which worked well until they were two and a half. Then they started to test the limits by getting up and down, up and down. Even when I gave them books or small toys to look at, they wouldn't rest quietly. They weren't getting any sleep and I certainly wasn't getting a break, so I decided to stop putting them down for naps. Sometimes they were a little sleepy in the afternoon, so I read books to them or had them watch a calm video for an hour or so, but that was it. It wasn't long before I noticed that they were having better sleeping patterns at night after they'd had a full day of play."

Sheri's experience with her twins is not unusual. While we could exert our influence on our singleton children to nap, or at least rest quietly, it never worked quite so easily with our twins.

Florien, on the other hand, found that Max and Otto were grumpy and fussy in the late afternoon and evening when they didn't nap. She found a pleasant way to help her boys fall asleep. "Besides doing quiet activities with the boys before naptime, I also consistently started rubbing their backs and singing them to sleep. If I had found this to be bothersome to me, I wouldn't have done it, but I used it as an opportunity to get a short nap and reenergize myself. I would fall asleep on one of the boys' beds for half an hour or so and then wake up before they did, with enough time left to relax by myself. Boy, did it feel good. I've never had a better excuse for taking a nap in the middle of the day."

Linda was also highly motivated to have Keegan and Colin nap. "The only break I had from my two sets of twins during the day was when the girls were at school and the boys were napping. Getting them to fall asleep wasn't easy. I laid a large quilt down on the floor in their bedroom. The three of us rested on it until they finally fell asleep about thirty to forty-five minutes later. I was then free for an hour before they awakened. I know this may sound like a ridiculous amount of work for one hour of peace and quiet, but it was important to me and worth the struggle."

*Falling Asleep at Night:*  The goofing around and silliness that makes napping nearly impossible for two-year-old twins can make falling asleep at night equally difficult. Of course, as we mentioned earlier, if your twins stop napping, they will be so sleepy at bedtime that this won't be a problem.

Debra found this to be so true of Ricky and Aislynn that she went to great lengths to be sure they didn't nap during the day. "When Ricky and Aislynn were two and a half, their bedroom addition was complete. They made the transition to their own beds easily and Ricky voluntarily ended his early morning habit of climbing into my bed for nursing. About this time, both twins also gave up their naps. They went to bed a little earlier and slept through the whole night. With my sleep no longer interrupted every night, I started feeling truly normal again. I tried to encourage this new situation, which was easy to do. Car rides into town inevitably put Ricky and Aislynn to sleep, but I soon came up with a solution. They loved to sing and recite the ABCs so I just started a few songs while we were driving and left the rest up to them. It almost always worked."

Not all sleeping problems of this age are handled so easily. If consistent bedtime routines have not been used and parents have not been firm in getting twins to bed when they were younger, now that the twins are older and more rebellious the struggle will be greater. This sort of problem is as much an issue of discipline as it is of sleep. It should be addressed by starting satisfying bedtime activities, and setting and following through with a specific bedtime. Allowing twins to repeatedly get out of bed for one more drink or one more hug doesn't serve any real purpose except to stall sleep. This sort of continual nagging on the part of the child should be met with a firm "no" after the child has had every opportunity to settle down.

When twins encourage each other's negative behavior, making bedtime unbearable, it may be helpful to temporarily institute separate bedtimes. Arbitrarily pick one child to go to bed first, telling both that this is happening because they cannot settle down. Go through the bedtime routines with one child; thirty minutes later get the other twin ready for bed. One night of this will turn things around if the twins are tightly bonded and dislike going to sleep without each other's company. However, if Mom and Dad's attention is a big treat, this approach could backfire.

*Scary Thoughts:* Another common nighttime problem in children this age is scary thoughts that intensify when all is quiet and the child is nearly asleep. These are not nightmares, which occur when children are fast asleep. These are the leftover thoughts of the day—things the child has seen or heard, either on television or in his environment, which resurface as he relaxes before sleep. It is almost impossible to predict what a child will find frightening. It may be the obvious scary movie, or it could be an offhand remark that sets a child's mind racing.

Twins present an interesting angle on this nighttime problem, as they have the potential to either calm or escalate the fear that is present in the other. When both twins are very verbal and highly imaginative, one child may "infect" the other child with his fears and soon both are too frightened to sleep. On the other hand, when one twin likes to play the role of protector, he or she may have such a strong calming influence that parental intervention may not even be necessary.

Debbie remembers, "Michael is a very sensitive child who magnifies and worries about what he has seen or heard during the day. Many nights I put Michael and Joanna down to sleep, happy as clams. When I walked past their room a few minutes later, I could hear them talking. Michael was sharing his fears and Joanna was saying, 'It's okay, Michael, I'm here.' Soon they were both asleep."

When twins are unable to comfort each other, the parent must respond with loving reassurance. The best treatment for nighttime worries, though, is prevention; this underscores the importance of having a predictable nighttime routine, including pleasant stories or songs just before sleep. It is also important to consider the temperament of your twins; restrict their access to those movies, television shows, books, and games that you know could upset them and carefully consider the types of topics discussed within their earshot.

*Nightmares:* Nightmares are similar to scary thoughts in that their genesis is often fear or stress that accumulates during the daytime. However, nightmares occur during sleep and may not even fully awaken children when they cry out. Nightmares are a normal part of a person's dreaming life. They start in infancy, increase at about age two and persist throughout childhood and adulthood.

A parent's response to nightmares in a child this age will be quite similar to the comforting measures given to an infant experiencing nightfrights. Quick reassurance is the first line of action. If the child is still asleep, there is no need to fully awaken him. Soothing words alone may put him back to sleep. However, if his screaming has gotten him (and perhaps his twin) up, you need to talk about the dream and the feelings it evoked. To what depth you discuss this will depend on the reaction of the child. Follow his cues. Usually a brief talk is enough to calm most children. If this is not the case, and your child is particularly

346 *"What One Doesn't Think Of, The Other One Will!"*

frightened, you might consider letting him sleep in your bed or a sleeping bag in your room, or you can stay in the twin's room until he falls asleep.

Florien suggests another possibility Devin and she created for Max and Otto. "The first time one of the boys awakened with a nightmare, Devin and I devised a plan. Each boy was given a secret, imaginary ladder to keep in his pocket or under his pillow. We instructed Max and Otto that their secret ladders were always available to them and could be used to climb out of a bad dream or escape a nightmare. Every once in a while at breakfast, one of them says that he had a scary dream the night before and that he used his ladder to get out of it and go somewhere nice!"

Although nightmares are a normal occurrence, if they occur to a particular child on many nights in succession, you should look at the stresses in his life and consider if they are part of the problem. For example, if your child is in the midst of potty training, be sure you are not working on it too intensely. If there is a new baby in the home or some other change in the household equilibrium, he may need more attention during the day.

*Night Terrors:* The most frightening (particularly to the parent) and rarest of all nighttime waking is night terrors. These can begin occurring as early as age two and usually stop by age five. Night terrors are distinct from nightmares. Nightmares occur during the dreaming stages of sleep, while night terrors are believed to be caused by an interference with a person's physical arousal system. During a night terror, a child looks awake: His eyes are open, and he may even be talking or moving about, but he is not awake. What he is seeing, hearing, or talking about has nothing to do with reality, and he probably will not respond in a sensible way to attempts to talk with him.

A parent will become aware of the child's night terrors when he is awakened by frightened screams. If twins are sharing a room, it is wise to have both parents help with the comforting, as night terrors are more intense and more prolonged than nightmares and it is quite likely that the other twin will be awakened and need attention, too.

The adult comforting the twin with night terrors should first try to quietly settle him down by speaking his name and helping him lie down. However, don't force him to lay down or try to converse with him because he is not truly awake. If he doesn't quickly settle down, stay with him. Do not attempt to awaken him, as he will probably go back to sleep himself, having no memory of this incident in the morning.

It is not known why some children have night terrors and others do not. It is known that they are more likely to occur when a child is ill with a fever, has experienced a traumatic event, or has taken a sedative. Although a night terror can be disconcerting to watch, they are self-limiting. Children outgrow them and develop normally.

*Toilet Training:* Teaching twins to use the toilet appropriately is perhaps the biggest challenge of this age. A philosophy we all shared in toilet training our twins was: Don't rush it! If at all possible, don't even start until your twins are past the obstinate, rebellious, "I don't want to" phase of their development. We are convinced that if you wait until both twins show signs of readiness, it will go smoothly and be far from the ordeal you might have anticipated.

One of the keys to successful toilet training is readiness. This comes at different times for each child, although girls tend to show readiness six to twelve months before boys. Physical readiness is fairly easily determined. When a child wakes up dry in the morning or after naps and stays dry for three or more hours during the day, he probably has the bladder capacity and control to begin toilet training. Some children will show this kind of readiness by eighteen months of age, but very few will be emotionally prepared for the challenge. Emotional readiness is shown when a child asks about the toilet, is curious about his own ability to urinate and defecate, is willing to learn, and is finished having daily power struggles with his parents.

To proceed before twins are ready invites trouble, as Debbie can tell you. "When Michael and Joanna were two and a half, I decided to introduce them to the world of potty chairs and 'big boy' and 'big girl' underpants. They enjoyed looking at their new underwear, talking about toilet training, and sitting, fully clothed, on their potty chairs, but that was as far as it went. As soon as I tried to actually initiate their urinating into the potty chair, Michael adamantly refused. Joanna showed more interest and actually used the potty chair a few days later after her bath, but as Michael's disinterest grew more apparent, she grew less enthusiastic. I decided to hold off for a few more months, but I left the potty chairs in the bathroom where they could see them. Once in a while we talked about how to use them and occasionally Michael and Joanna would put their dolls on them, but pretty much we just dropped the subject."

Although Debbie felt like she had dropped the topic of toilet training for the time being, she really hadn't. Because the potty chairs were still out, her twins were getting the benefit of exploring and growing comfortable with the concept which is part of the emotional preparation. Experts believe it is important to give a child a few weeks to scrutinize his potty chair as he adjusts to the idea of toilet training.

For twins it is nice, but not essential to have potty chairs that each can call his own. Debra had a small bathroom and did very well with one potty seat that fit over the toilet and had a step attached so Ricky and Aislynn could securely climb up onto the seat. Her twins thought the whole idea was great and couldn't wait to use it.

Some experts recommend that a child be successful at bowel training before starting bladder training. Children have good control of their bowel movements by age two and have only one or two bowel movements a day, which makes bowel training relatively easy. However, this also makes the entire process of toilet training slower and more drawn out. When twins are involved, bowel and bladder training of both children at the same time is preferred by mothers, because it is the quickest, most efficient method for them.

We all followed this last plan of action. Debra tells of her experience with Ricky and Aislynn. "I waited to start toilet training until the twins were twenty-seven months old. By this time they had outgrown their need to challenge everything I said. I started during winter, which suited me just fine because I thought that their being indoors would make it easier for me to observe when they needed to use the toilet.

"Ricky and Aislynn liked the idea of toilet training and were fascinated with flushing the toilet. Every two hours I accompanied each child in turn to the bathroom, going through the steps appropriate to his or her sex. Before long both twins knew the words to use for their bodily functions, were aware of the feelings associated with them, and simply came and told me they had to go. By the end of the week, I didn't even need to come in with them. There were a few misses, but after two months the twins only wore diapers at night."

As Debra discovered, sometimes twins toilet train easier than singletons, because they have each other to learn from. Florien remembers Max and Otto's toilet training experience just before they turned three. "True to form, Otto was the first to 'take the risk' and practice using the toilet. He learned to control his bladder and use the toilet effectively about one week before Max did. As Otto practiced, Max watched him and discussed how it was going. Max still preferred to wear his diaper, which I let him do without admonishment. Once summer arrived and Max had fewer clothes to manage when he went to the bathroom, he decided on his own to try potty training. Within a few days, he was successful."

Unfortunately, the course of potty training does not always run this smoothly. Debbie and Sheri both had trouble getting their twins fully trained as they vacillated between good days and bad days for weeks on end. Debbie recalls her struggles: "I waited a few months after Michael and Joanna first refused to potty train. I tried again and the same thing happened—Michael refused, so Joanna lost interest. I really wanted to avoid a power struggle, so I backed off again. Their birthday was approaching and I told them that when they were three I was going to start potty training. As the weeks passed, I occasionally reminded them and true to my word, the day after their third birthday, we started serious potty training. To my surprise, Michael took it very well, and within a week they were trained during the daytime. They still had accidents, especially at night, but I didn't complain about them because I knew this was to be expected.

"By three and a half, Michael and Joanna were fully trained during the day but still had occasional nighttime accidents. To deal with this, I kept them both in diapers at night until they had about two months of consecutive dry nights. Then I let them go to bed without diapers, but I continued to have them sleep in their cribs, because when the rare nighttime accidents did occur, I knew the crib linens would be much easier to change and launder than full-sized sheets. By age four, diapers were a mere memory."

Sheri's girls were quite independent, but not very interested in toilet training. "When they were two and a half, they were quite happy to urinate in the toilet as long as they had bare bottoms. But if they wore a diaper, training pants, or panties they would use them instead. So they ran around our house with bare bottoms, wearing only a dress or sweatshirt. Obviously, this dress code wasn't feasible when we were out and about, so Emmy and Tessa continued to wear diapers on those occasions.

"Finally, when they were just about to turn three, and as I was wondering if I'd ever quit changing diapers, the girls took over the situation and simply did it."

Sheri's experience highlights an important concept. When toilet training children, it helps to be supportive, informative, and patient, but in the end it is they who will decide when they are going to do it. To ridicule, demean, or force the process does not necessarily quicken it—it only makes it unpleasant for everyone involved.

## Our Evolving Families
. . . . . . . . . . . . . . . . . . . . .

*Enjoying Our Twins:* As our twins matured, learning to command their bodies and express themselves in words, their older siblings looked at them with renewed interest and discovered their potential as friends and playmates. Sheri's daughter, Kallie, at first reluctantly, but later with pride, played Barbie dolls with Emmy and Tessa. Kallie provided most of the story lines and changes of clothes, while Emmy and Tessa provided the enthusiasm.

Debbie and Debra soon noticed that their older children also developed an interest in spending more time with the twins. Muggy especially loved to play school. He was the teacher while his willing younger siblings colored, cut, pasted, and painted as he directed. He also loved to be the leader in taking Ricky and Aislynn on nature walks, identifying plants and animals on their country property.

Debbie's son, Chris, then aged ten, loved active games where chasing and wrestling were involved. "The twins loved it and so did he," she says, "although I had to keep a careful eye on things because if I didn't, eventually Chris would get too physically active or emotionally intense and one of the twins would get scared or hurt. Of course, after a few minutes of comforting, the mildly traumatized twin was pleading for more and off he went."

Knowing that our families were evolving in positive ways was satisfying for all of us. This was never more evident than at the holidays. Linda recalls holiday celebrations at her house, when Keegan and Colin were two. "The boys started to understand our holiday traditions and for the first time were able to participate. They displayed uninhibited delight and wonder.

"When the Christmas season arrived, we drove to the country, cut down our own tree, then spent one whole day decorating it. The boys sat in their high chairs munching on holiday cookies as the girls carefully handed Todd ornaments to be hung on the tree. When we took all four kids to see Santa Claus, they happily climbed up onto his lap for a candy cane and coloring book. Christmas morning was pure chaos as they all laughed excitedly and tore their packages open, but it was a wonderful sort of chaos, like Christmas morning with children should be."

*Safety:* The same curious, spontaneous, and energetic qualities that make two-year-old children so much fun to be with can also put them at risk. Occasionally our children got themselves into dangerous situations, and we were reminded that you can never be too cautious when supervising twins.

Even when a potential danger is known you may find yourself unable to prevent it from happening. Linda recalls a horrible moment in her life the summer Keegan and Colin were two years old. "When I think about it, I still feel panicked and sick to my stomach as if it were yesterday. I put the boys down for their afternoon nap. While they were sleeping, a friend came over to

352 "What One Doesn't Think Of, The Other One Will!"

pick up an upright freezer from our back porch. It had been outside all summer, securely turned with the door against the house. Before my friend loaded the freezer, he decided to clean it out. While it was airing out in the sun, he realized that he had forgotten the rope he needed to transport the freezer and he went home to get it.

"I was in my office writing, and on his way past my door he told me that he had left the freezer door open. At the time I thought to myself that leaving the freezer door propped open, even for a few minutes, was dangerous, but I knew it was behind a latched gate and the boys were asleep in the house.

"I made a point of going out to tell five-year-old Sarah and Maiah, who were playing in the backyard with an older friend, not to play near the freezer. I stopped by the boys' bedroom; they were still napping in their cribs, so I went back to my writing. Fifteen minutes later I heard the back door slam, but thinking it was one of the girls on the way to the bathroom, I didn't make too much of it at first. After a few minutes, I decided to go check on the boys. Their cribs were empty and they weren't anywhere in the house. I headed for the backyard calling their names. Getting no response, I looked toward the side gate and saw that it was open and the freezer door was shut. I raced toward the freezer, screaming, and yanked open the door. There they were, happily sitting side by side. They didn't start to cry, until I grabbed them both in my arms and hugged them tightly to my chest. All I could think of was that my two-year-old twins were possibly minutes from suffocating in a freezer.

"I'm still not sure how they got there so quickly. They had to climb out of their cribs, go through the back door, unlatch the gate (something I thought they were incapable of doing), go immediately to the freezer, and move the two heavy lawn chairs that were holding the freezer door open. It seemed too complex a set of events to have happened in only a few minutes. Now I realize that's how tragedies happen."

Florien also had an unforgettable experience with her twins when they were two and a half. "One day I overheard Max tell Otto that if you ate a lot of their vitamins, they tasted just like candy. My heart skipped a beat as I calmly told them that vitamins are like medicine and can hurt you if you take too many or if you take some that belong to someone else. Max calmly told me that their vitamins were different, because he had just eaten some and they didn't hurt him at all. I took a deep breath and asked him how he reached them on top of our refrigerator.

"Max showed me how Otto and he had moved a sturdy chair to the counter, and how he had climbed up onto the counter and tiptoed to get to the vitamins. By this time, I knew he was telling me the truth. My heart sank as I looked at the recently purchased bottle of vitamins with fluoride and found it half empty. I couldn't tell exactly how many were gone. Max wasn't much help; he said he had eaten more than two and that 'they fit in my hand.'

"I called my pediatrician's office. Since I suspected that Max could have taken as many as twenty tablets, she suggested I induce vomiting with syrup of Ipecac. Fortunately, I had two bottles locked in our medicine cabinet (where the vitamins should also have been stored). I gave the prescribed dose to Max. Within fifteen minutes, he was retching and vomiting. Ever since that day, all medicines are always locked away at our house. Max and Otto have never again touched vitamins or medicine without my permission."

Debbie's twins presented her with a different, but also dangerous, situation. "When Michael and Joanna were two, one of their favorite forms of rebellion was to break away from my hand-grasp whenever we went outdoors and run in opposite directions. I spent some time thinking about how I could prevent this and came up with the twin-grip, a special handhold I created. First, I caught the more rambunctious of the twins (usually, but not always, Michael). Once I had him within grabbing distance, I quickly placed the thumb of one of my hands in between the thumb and first finger of his opposite hand and into his palm. It was essential that I placed my thumb in between his thumb and index finger, so that I could then wrap my index finger on one side of his wrist and curl the rest of my fingers around the opposite side of his wrist. In this way, my index and second fingers formed a 'V' on the back of his hand, which stabilized the grip. I only had to squeeze firmly to keep him confidently within my grasp. I simply repeated the process with my other hand with Joanna, and my two toddlers were in safe and inescapable handholds. My twins are now four years old and I still use this method.

"I decided that the best way to handle getting the kids into the car was to open one door and put them both inside the car before I started putting them in their car seats. They loved to go wild in the car, climbing over the seats and making a mess, but at least they were contained safely. When I got them out of the car, I took one twin out of his car seat and quickly belted that child in the twin stroller or held him in my arms, before I tended to the other child. If for some reason I couldn't use the stroller when we were out, then I used the twin-grip."

## Our Thoughts and Reflections

SHERI:   I constantly marvel at Emmy's and Tessa's close relationship; my only regret is that Steve and I didn't separate them more often and spend individual time with each twin. Now that Emmy and Tessa can tell us what they want, I've realized that one-on-one time with a parent is a treat for all children, especially twins.

LINDA:   When each of my twins was two he or she had the first real taste of life. Since then, they have continued to learn, explore, and experience many new things. Some days it is sour and not so good, but many days it is sweet and wonderful. Both Todd and I feel very grateful to savor life with them.

DEBBIE:   Despite the toilet training, the negativity, and the double trouble of twins at two, my job as a mother got easier and more manageable at this age. In fact, when I kept my life child-centered with predictable routines and fun activities for the kids, life went very smoothly. Of course, that would be just about the time I'd decide I could handle more commitments in my own life, which would then send everything off balance. I start each day over with new possibilities, realizing that although the first three years in a child's life are important ones, they are just the beginning.

FLORIEN:   During the summer of Max and Otto's third year, I took them on a trip to Connecticut. The boys were now fairly independent and it made me realize how far we had come in three short years. I learned to relax that summer and truly enjoy my silly, active, lovable children.

DEBRA:    At the end of Ricky and Aislynn's third summer, they grew more self-sufficient and desired additional freedom. The twins repeatedly tested my limits on riding their wheelers down the steep part of our long, rocky driveway. I was worried that they would lose control and tumble onto the rocks, but I finally gave them permission to try it. It was one of those things you let your children do with your eyes closed. They took off, gathering speed and squealing with excitement, then safely landed on the flat runway. I'd finally let my fledglings fly on their own!

That simple act generated ambivalent feelings for me. I was sad that my babies were growing up so fast, and promised myself that I would make the best of the years we had together before they really left the nest. I honestly was thankful that we were at the point where constant parental attention was no longer necessary. I was grateful for the enlightenment that having children brought me. But most of all, I appreciated the unconditional love that existed between us, no matter how many mistakes were made.

# Chapter 15

# "It's your turn"

## *A Father's Perspective*

**W**hen our twins were young, the words "It's your turn!" were often heard in our households. Sometimes these words were spoken in love and sometimes they were barked in frustration; in either case they served as cues to our husbands that we were on the brink of exhaustion and needed relief from caring for the twins. And they would return the phrase when they were equally drained.

It is to our able helpmates that we turn over this last chapter. This is their opportunity to share those impressions or experiences they feel are most important or will be most helpful in revealing what it is like to be the father of twins. Since the greatest portion of this book was written from the mothers' perspectives, we suppose it is only fair to give our husbands the last word!

### *Todd Albi (Linda's Husband)*
. . . . . . . . . . . . . . . . . . . . . . . . . . . . .

I can't adequately express the joy of parenting two sets of twins; I love it. I'm always moved upon entering either set of twins' bedroom in the morning and being greeted with opposing sets of smiles and twinkling eyes. This alone makes life worth living.

Creating twins (or any child) takes no experience, expertise, or special training. Being a father, however, demands an incredible combination of time, energy, love, and understanding. Twins, of course, are going to require much more of the above. I suppose I held many preconceived ideas of what being a father would be all about. There seems to be plenty of advice and myths on how to parent. So far, from what I can tell, there's no right way, ideal age, sum of money, status, or appropriate time to begin a family. What parenting really takes is giving of oneself, as with any endeavor in life. Of course, being flexible and relaxed helps.

Expect chaos. There will be trying moments, but there are supposed to be. I found becoming a parent quite enlightening; you now wear your own parents' shoes. It helps to give you a glimpse of what raising you must have been like. I don't think you can really appreciate your parents until you experience parenting yourself.

I enjoy being a father—at least someone thinks I'm important! I don't have the time to do everything I'd like to do, but who honestly does? When you are part of a family, there has to be give-and-take or resentment can build. I know. I've been caught more than once in the garage with the tablesaw roaring, drowning out the children's noise, when I should have been inside helping Linda. Activities must be prioritized and creative solutions applied to maximize your time with your family.

Incorporating your children in the family's activities can be rewarding. I haven't taken my twins rock climbing (not yet), but short hikes are great. I enjoy including all four twins during my runs by pushing them in a twin racing stroller; the girls hold the boys in their laps, seat-belted in. When we ride our bikes, I use a bike trailer to pull Keegan and Colin along behind, while the girls ride their bikes with training wheels. They love it!

A good friend once offered his theory on good parenting—of course, he doesn't have any children himself. He contended that if you get your children involved and allow them to tag along they'll turn out all right. On the other hand, if you overprotect, coerce, ignore, or abuse them, you'll create goons, thugs, or worse. His theory is a bit simplistic, but overall I have to agree.

I often end up very frustrated about not spending enough time with my family, the most important thing in my life. There are always endless projects that I feel I must accomplish—build a fence, sandbox, deck, etc. Although these projects are appreciated (I hope), I often think that the end doesn't justify the means, and my family suffers due to the lack of attention and love they deserve.

The most important thing a husband and father can do is spend time and grow with his family. Doing this is much more important than completing any project or participating in any activity. I recently took our family to catch crayfish in a nearby river. Our children shrieked with glee as they watched Linda and me scurry after our dinner in the shallow riverbed. They had a lot of fun dumping our nets of crayfish into their buckets. And I felt myself swelling with pride as I later watched Sarah and Maiah catch some themselves, which I never would have thought possible. My children's spirit, unconditional love, and development awe me.

In summary, I wish I had some profound advice to give but I don't. What I do know is that, if you give your children love and time, for the most part everything will work out fine. Good luck!

## Devin Willard
## (Donna Florien's Husband)

Raising twins; raising children and living.

What can I say that hasn't already been said? I don't have any amusing anecdotes to share, although Otto and Max do things every day that make me laugh and smile. I don't have many tips to make your job easier. My only words of advice are, just don't let yourself get too hungry or too tired (easier said than done)!

When I think about parenting, I consider the big picture. What's the driving force, the compelling reason to keep on keeping on with life's hardest, most physically and emotionally draining, most rewarding, and possibly most disappointing job in the world? Well, as I said to Florien when we first found out she was pregnant, "I haven't got anything better to do." She's thrown that one back at me a few times, but it's still the way I feel.

I'm sure there are a lot of people with more important things to do than raising children. Perhaps they would be better off without children, and that's fine. We don't need everyone in the world raising kids (it's not like there's a big people shortage out there). But for me, I really haven't got anything better to do. I mean, like, what would I trade this for—a mansion and a yacht? Naw. How about a mansion and a yacht and 200 motorcycles and a harem? Getting warmer, but no. Sure, there are a lot of self-indulgent pleasures I would have much more time and money to partake of if we didn't have kids, but that wouldn't get me or us anywhere. The world seems as if it's ready to take a dive these days, and one way we have of recovering is the chance that we can replace ourselves with people who are better than we are. So, when I think of life that way . . . naw, I haven't got anything better or more important to do.

In a way, survival is what raising kids is all about. On one level it's about getting by in the day-to-day existence of providing for a family, and on another level it's about getting by as a rare biological occurrence in the universe. Raising a family and settling down: There's nothing hip about it. It's hard work. Before Otto and Max were born, I didn't have any real plans for my life. Now Florien and I constantly have to plan, follow routines, provide stability, and ensure a sense of trust, love, and happiness in our children. On the one hand, raising children seems so mundane. On the other hand, it's the riskiest and hardest thing I've ever done.

Okay, I've said a couple of times that it's hard, but what's hard? Sure, there's the constant work of maintaining a family, and perhaps one has to give up a few of life's pleasures just to get along once in a while, but for me the absolute hardest part of raising twins has been the emotional aspects involved. Yes, there are the everyday stresses of getting along, but who hasn't got that already? The unique thing about having children is the love that comes along with them.

The love I have for them is so strong it's like nothing else I've ever had before. I'm not even sure I could have this kind of love for anyone else. I know it sounds kinda corny, but that's how I feel. And it's a very big risk, because if anything bad happens to them it hurts me; if anything *really* bad ever happened to them it could devastate me. And that's one hell of a risk. But it has also given me a reason to exist at my highest potential. It's this love that makes the day-to-day business of getting along worthwhile.

That's the hook. That is what makes raising children the hardest job I've ever had, the biggest accomplishment, and the greatest achievement of my life—and it's still got a long way to go. Almost everyone wants to *be somebody*, create something important, have a lasting achievement and obtain fame, wealth, and power along with it. We are given a dangled carrot, and told that if we try hard enough we can have these things. But the truth is that most of us won't get all the power, fame, and fortune that we desire and seek. And those who do might still be quite unsatisfied with their lives.

I remember reading in a magazine article recently that 75 percent of the people in the United States regret not having spent more time with their children. I do not care to be part of that 75 percent. One of the most satisfying days I've ever spent was the first time I took care of Max and Otto for the entire day, from morning to night, with no one else around. They were ten and a half months old and needed a lot of nurturing, care, and attention. When that day was over and the boys were in bed sleeping, I felt really good about myself, about them, about life, and about the world.

Yeah, it sounds corny. But I haven't got anything better to do.

## Dale Johnson (Debbie's Husband)

I had always dreamt of being a father, but never the father of twins. For the past few years, I've been learning the job and enjoying the blessings.

Whenever I'm asked what it's like to be the father of twins the response that immediately comes to mind is that I'm involved. From the moment the doctor asked me if I wanted to cut Michael's umbilical cord to this instant, I've been the willing captive of our twins. There is so much to do that one parent cannot do it all and still enjoy the experience. Debbie and I have always shared the household chores; the children increased the list of things to be done. Fortunately, we already had learned how to communicate our needs, share our feelings, and plan ways to deal with problems together. With that foundation, we were well prepared to meet the challenge of raising twins.

While raising twins is much like having a second job for me, it's a job I truly look forward to each day. There always has been one baby for me to hold, so I've never felt left out. The kids come to me as often as they do to Debbie for comforting and other needs. I'm pleased to know that I'm a big part of their day and someone they miss when I'm at work. I've gotten back from them as much as I've given and more.

One thing I've never regretted doing was spending the time and money necessary to document Michael and Joanna's rapidly changing lives. Before the babies were born, we saved enough money to buy a video camcorder. Since their births, we've also purchased a good autofocus camera. Our parents live in Wisconsin and Hawaii, and they and our siblings have enjoyed watching the twins grow up on video. I've tried to use the camcorder each week, even if it's just to record five minutes of the usual routines. I've also tried to take a lot of snapshots, from varying distances and angles, of the twins together and alone, posed or candid. I figured no one could have too many photos of their kids, and if we do, we can always send some to relatives. After all, could grandparents ever have too many pictures of their grandchildren?

Being the husband of a mother of twins is probably the task I was best prepared for. Patience is my strong suit, and patience is needed in large amounts. There are a number of doubts, fears, frustrations, resentments, and anxious moments that come with the responsibility of being the mother of twins. Sometimes I was the target of these highly charged emotions; other times, I was just in the attack zone. After a weekend alone with the children, I came to realize exactly *why* Debbie was often irritable and exhausted at the end of the day. It was then that I accepted that Debbie's job at home, caring for the kids, was just as stressful in its own way as my demanding job at the office. Debbie, as does any mother of twins, needed a lot of cooperation, understanding, and comforting. She needed a sounding board for all the day's events, good and bad. She needed time away from the children just as I did, to be with her friends and family, or by herself. With patience and understanding, many problems were solved, while others simply ceased to be important.

One thing I haven't done well since the twins were born is to make sure that Debbie and I take enough time out for ourselves. I could come up with an impressive list of excuses, including but not limited to lack of time, not enough money, access to video rentals, general fatigue, and being a homebody. But the sad truth is that we should have found more time, money, and energy to go out by ourselves.

Being the father of a big brother of twins was the role I was most worried about. My stepson, Chris, and I have been very close since Debbie and I decided to get married. He was eighteen months old at the time. Since then, he has been a focal point in our family activities—soccer, basketball, baseball, hiking, and church. When Debbie became pregnant in 1987, Chris was seven and a half and very excited about becoming a big brother. He was used to getting all our attention and didn't seem to realize what a time commitment the babies would be for us. He found out shortly after they were born.

I learned that my worries were justified, but fortunately Chris adapted well to being a brother and to sharing our time and attention. Three things that helped were involving him in the raising of the babies, continuing to support him in all his school and sports activities, and making special time for us to do things as a threesome, "like in the old days."

Debbie and I felt that eight-year-old Chris should have chores to do at home, and he had assumed responsibility for the upkeep of his room, taking out the trash, and setting the table. As the twins grew from infancy to age three, Chris's list of chores increased; they included putting away Michael and Joanna's toys and helping them get ready for bed every evening. He seemed to understand our directives about setting a good example for the twins. Having younger twin siblings taught Chris a lot about responsibility and nurturing. At age twelve he is their hero, and he has earned the title.

We decided before Michael and Joanna were born that we would try to keep Chris's life-style, essentially school and sports activities, as status quo as possible. That meant taking the twins to places and events that weren't particularly interesting to them and didn't allow them to move around without constant supervision. We weathered those sessions because Chris is just as important to us as the twins are. I know he has appreciated our efforts.

My last bit of advice on helping older siblings to find their place in the family is to take time to listen. I would need a calculator to tabulate the number of times Debbie or I told Chris that we couldn't answer his questions immediately, or that he was interrupting our conversation about the twins, or that he would have to wait until after we completed an activity with, or chore for, Michael and Joanna.

To ensure that Chris got his share of our parental attention, Debbie and I learned to put the twins' needs on hold occasionally. We also discovered that if we set aside a special time after the twins were asleep for Chris to be with us, to talk or play a game, he responded in a positive way. Through these evenings together, we rediscovered what a great kid we have who now also happens to be a wonderful big brother.

Just as becoming a big brother taught Chris the importance of being unselfish, patient, and responsible, becoming the father of twins instantly enrolled me in a refresher course in the same virtues. I like to think I'm making the grade so far.

### Rick Blair (Debra's Husband)

Much of what I have to say about fathering twins comes from hindsight. It also has more to do with being a parent in general than with any topic specific to twins.

I thought I had home plate pretty well covered by providing my family with financial support and a roof over their heads. That I mean literally, for I was trying to build more spacious and permanent living quarters for all of us when the twins were born. I just should have covered the other bases better, under the circumstances. If I had it all to do over again, I'd be sure to direct more attention to three areas.

To begin with, first base would have involved getting more education about marriage and children. Never in my life did I receive any training in being a husband or parent. Even the prenatal class we took focused mainly on the woman and the birth. I think there should be classes that emphasize the changes that can occur *after* a baby is born, and also include how the father can help his partner. At least doctors, nurses, or midwives could yank us aside and tell us what we should be doing. (I know I'm going to eat these words the next time I complain about Deb's running off to teach one of her classes or support groups on these very subjects!) This is definitely one impact having twins has had on my life. But I must honestly say that, had there been a class on this subject then, I might not have gone anyway. Remember, we're talking about hindsight here. I just know that being informed might have at least prevented me from making the assumptions that I did.

Second base, then, would have been to speak with my wife ahead of time about setting priorities. My focus was more future-oriented. I turned forty years old one day before Aislynn and Ricky were born, and I felt an urgency to get my family better situated while I still had plenty of drive left. I was actually thinking about the fact that the twins would graduate in the year 2000 and how much they would require as teenagers, rather than about them as little babies. Also, putting in time and energy at work was of foremost importance. I had just started my job and was striving to gain recognition for my managerial abilities, which I hoped would lead to a better-paying position. There just wasn't room for compromise in that area. The majority of my time after work was devoted to our building project. Some of the troubles we've had in our marriage have occasionally caused me to lose interest in completing the house, especially when it looked as if we were going to break up. Most of the time, though, I was motivated to get it into a livable condition, which actually took several years. My wife needed more support from me than she was getting, but I really didn't know that at the time.

I assumed that, because Deb had handled Muggy so competently, she would also manage well with the two babies. She did appear to be in control of everything, except when she lost her temper. And that I just chalked up to her being tired and having hormonal imbalances. I had no idea about the other things she was feeling, nor did I know she thought I was letting her down. Believe me, she has made a point of letting me know since then! If we'd just talked about our priorities beforehand, I'd have known that the months (or even a year) spent giving Deb more support would have been a wiser investment of my time and energy. Still, talking about these things up front would have been only a partial solution—which leads me to third base.

I think the thing that would really help the mother most would be to keep asking her what she needs. That gets right to the point. You might think that running the vacuum over the floor is helping, but she may be fuming, "I could care less about that damn floor! I just want to get out of here!" Deb is a strong woman, and I used to think she didn't have any needs that weren't being satisfied. She didn't ask for help, so I thought she didn't need any. Boy, was I wrong. Now I'm aware that I need to ask her and keep asking. I think that dads need to help care for their babies when they can, but I really believe that supporting the mother is the father's main job when the babies are young, especially if the mother is breast-feeding.

A stark reality of trying to care for young babies is that fathers are missing some very important equipment that seemed to be the cure-all when our babies fussed. I used to get so frustrated because I didn't have a teat to stick in their mouths when Deb was gone, especially when there were two to comfort. When they began to walk and talk, the kids appreciated what I had to offer. They responded to me in ways that encouraged me to interact with them more. My saving grace has been that I've learned from my mistakes and consciously choose to interact with my family now in the ways they need me to. So even if I didn't cover my bases well in the past, I've been able to do some repair work, which has really paid off.

One of the unexpected bonuses of fathering is the enjoyment I get from watching the kids learn new things and develop into little persons. As I observe them climbing, building things, and pretending, I purposely recall myself at their age. When I compare my children's capabilities with mine at the same age, I am amazed at how much earlier they have mastered everything. I can see that they will know at twenty what I knew at forty.

These personal recollections do have an ulterior motive, though. With them, I can anticipate the next logical step the kids will take in many things that they do. I was a very adventuresome and creative child, attempting things I surely will never tell my children about. This gives me an edge in keeping them out of harm's way. For example, when the three kids were digging fire pits and stacking twigs in them, I knew what their next thoughts would be and headed them off at the pass. I can walk around the property and tell what they did while playing. They think I have spies lurking in the woods to report to me each night when I come home. Hopefully, by the time they figure out that I don't have any, they will be thinking for themselves. I'm glad we have provided them with a country environment in which their imaginations flourish.

Our children play more with rocks, sticks, and dirt than any of the store-bought lumps of plastic that just end up being teething biscuits for the dog. I feel a need to clarify that these lumps of plastic do not include warrior or horror figures! One of the most important things I've learned about having children is that they are entertained by the simplest things, and that their needs are very basic and uncomplicated.

I used to think that children should only come into the world when their parents were settled, established in a nice house, and financially secure. If you didn't have those things when they arrived, you'd better try hard to get them as soon as possible. Well, those things are nice if you have them, but I've learned that they are not a prerequisite for healthy, happy children. Once children are here, the main focus should be on giving them love, attention, and understanding. I think these are the key ingredients in yielding decent, productive, and caring adults.

## Steve Greatwood (Sheri's Husband)

I suppose there are two ends of the spectrum with regard to paternal involvement while raising children. One end would be total involvement, sharing all responsibilities equally with the mother, and the other end would be total noninvolvement. Obviously there are factors limiting how much either parent can immerse him- or herself in bringing up their children, and I can only write about my experiences. I am not an authority on the subject, nor am I passing any judgments on others. I have thought long and hard about where I would fall on the scale, and I think it would be somewhere in the middle.

I feel a need to help Sheri with the kids, and often do. However, my attitude about child-rearing is still pretty chauvinistic. I feel that it's primarily her responsibility and that I have the role of "relief pitcher," coming in from the bullpen. When the twins were born, I gained a new understanding of just how much work it is to care for children, and I have a greater respect for the job that Sheri does. I think it's very easy for a man to come home from work and expect to find the house clean, dinner minutes away, and his wife waiting to lovingly soothe away the tensions of his long day. To be honest, I would love it to be like that but it just doesn't work that way. Usually, when I walk in our front door, I enter a world that would make the roughest day at work seem like sitting on a warm, sunny beach watching the waves lap at my feet.

For a long time, it was hard for me to empathize with Sheri and understand why things weren't perfect around the house. It really got to me when I'd come home to find the kids still napping and Sheri sitting on the couch staring blankly at the television, a magazine, or maybe even the wall. Sometimes she was just getting the chance to finish lunch at five o'clock. And the last thing wafting from the kitchen would be the aroma of a gourmet dinner in its finishing stages. Occasionally, I'd give her an accusing stare and mumble some sarcastic remark about how easy she had it, lounging around the house all day. This immediately would put her on the defensive, which led to my blowing up and reducing Sheri to tears. The babies would wake up crying, and then I'd have one hell of a mess! The worst part of the whole situation was that I truly believed I had a tougher time of it at work than she did at home. I'm not saying that my job is easier than hers, but I've come to realize that her day is every bit as demanding and important as mine.

The single event that put me on the road to enlightenment occurred when the twins were fifteen months old. One Friday afternoon, Sheri walked out the door. Bags packed, she jumped in the car, smiled and waved, and took off for the coast with the other mothers in her twins group. Sure, I had taken care of the kids before—a few hours here and there, but never for an entire weekend.

First off, I did what any self-respecting father would do: I packed up the kids and took them out for pizza. Not just any pizza parlor would do, either. It had to be one with a playground where hard-working fathers could sit, have a cold beer, and let their kids work off steam before they ate. Much to my amusement, two other babysitting fathers from the twins group showed up with their kids, and we all had fun. But after that hiatus, I never found time to relax. As soon as I got the breakfast dishes cleaned up, it was time to start fixing lunch. At 11:45 in the morning, I realized that I hadn't found time to dress the kids, let alone brush their teeth or hair. Two days went by in a blur as I lived for their naps and bedtimes.

I won't divulge all the gory details of the weekend; suffice it to say we survived. And at the end of each day, when the kids were in bed, I was surprised to discover in myself a real feeling of accomplishment. That weekend taught me just how tough it is to run a household on a day-to-day basis. I must say that I was never so happy to see my wife come walking through the door, even if I didn't admit it to her at the time.

After that weekend I became more realistic in my expectations of what one person can accomplish. I also realized how much the time off with her group rejuvenated Sheri, and how valuable it was for her to get out of the house by herself. Having the kids on my own still is a challenge for me, but I've definitely become more at ease with them. I really enjoy taking the kids out and about; it's great for my ego, because whatever extra attention a mother of twins gets, a lone father with twins gets double! I also recognize in myself a certain smugness derived from showing the world that dads are perfectly capable of taking care of their children.

The births of my older daughter and then the twins forced me to realize that my golf game can wait to improve, and there will still be fish in the river when I have more time for fishing. Early on, these ideas were tough to swallow. But raising a family calls for some sacrifices, so I've learned to modify my outside activities to fit in with my family's schedule. Sometimes I tie flies at home instead of going out fishing, and I've learned that playing nine holes of golf gets me home before Sheri gets too stressed. When I do get to play golf for an entire afternoon, I make sure that Sheri gets reciprocal time off, and everyone stays happy.

Having twins guarantees that your life will change in many ways, and the experience definitely will be hard on you and your wife. My advice is: Do the most you can for your relationship and your children. Be with them as much as possible, and you will all benefit in ways you never imagined.

# Epilogue:

## *Our Final Thoughts and Reflections*

Although we are at the end of this book our journeys as the mothers of twins have really just begun. To be honest, we are pleased that the physically demanding first years are behind us, and yet we look back fondly because those years hold many special memories for each of us. This is the irony of the twin experience: The most difficult phases are often filled with the dearest moments. An uncomfortable twin pregnancy ceases to be bothersome and instead feels miraculous to the expectant mother when both babies fill her uterus with movement. Fussy newborn twins are a handful and yet when they finally quiet down and their mother holds them close, the love and tenderness that she feels is boundless. Even obstinate two-year-old twins will melt their mother's heart when they place their soft little arms around her, give her sticky kisses, and say, "I wuv you."

In this book we have struggled to balance the hard times with the joyous ones, the mistakes with the successes, the medical and expert information with our personal experiences. Within that context, we have all sought to include those issues that were dearest to us. And now we are at the end of this project. Here are our final thoughts and reflections about having twins.

*Linda Albi:* The arrival of my second set of twins has kept me completely immersed in the day-to-day challenges of young children. Diapers, temper tantrums, naps, and uncommunicative language continue to be very much a part of my life. However overwhelming my days become, I am encouraged by the fact that I've gone through this before and I know, with a little tenacity and a whole lot of love and understanding, I will make it through again. In addition, the advice and support given me by my co-authors and my constant involvement in writing about twins has given me added encouragement.

In order to endure, I have learned to keep an open mind and not fight against the many changes that have assailed me. I continue to grow along with my twins; ever so slowly the patience and understanding have seeped into my stubborn self. Many former plans have been abandoned or laid aside, but none of that matters for the moment. The future is too far away; I want to concentrate on the days at hand rather than think about what our life will be like with four children simultaneously in grade school, junior high, and high school. Inevitably, I have finally accepted the fact that I'm never going to get caught up! I'm not even sure what I was trying to catch up with, but I know now it isn't important. I will always have laundry to fold, dishes to wash, and floors to sweep. My focus is no longer on chores to do but rather on my children, to enjoy.

*Florien Deurloo:* Since becoming a mother of twins, I have discovered that being a parent can bring many joys to life and can also teach one many valuable lessons. Overall I have been comfortable in my role as mother; learning to have patience, to slow down, to not be perfect, and to have a good sense of humor. I have worked hard to give my children a happy and safe childhood and to help them feel good about themselves, each other, and being identical twins. I have found that decisions that were once easy to make on my own or with Devin are now more complex, for we have two young children we need to take into consideration. I have also learned that being a good parent is not always easy. I've made some mistakes, but have tried to learn from them so things may go better the next time I am in a similar situation.

As Max and Otto have grown into preschool-aged boys, I have continued to be in awe at the love, warmth, sense of humor, and compassion they share with one another and with their friends and family. So many times, I try to have the correct perspective on their relationship to one another. Is it the same as any siblings' or is it special because they are twins; and identical twins at that? Have I done my best at fostering their independence as individuals while still respecting their twinness? Will their closeness continue to be a positive influence for them as they grow into youth or will they drift apart, striving to be independent of one another? The truth is that I find it very difficult to answer any of these questions with any sense of certainty. I can only assure myself that Devin and I have done our best at helping them to like who they are as individuals as well as to treasure the fact that they are indeed special because they are identical twins.

One final thought is that simply being a parent of twins has given me an unforeseen gift. I believe strongly that all families of multiple birth children are somehow united, joined into a "family" of their own. We provide support and information to one another that cannot be found elsewhere. I hope that this book is a gift to at least a few of you, our readers; that you may find understanding and support within it that will in turn make your day-to-day living easier and happier as parents of twins.

*Debbie Johnson:* It has been nearly five years since Michael and Joanna were born. Although these five years have been very busy ones, they have also been the most productive years of my life. I have learned a lot during this time, including practical mothering skills: how to feed and comfort infant twins, how to discipline and travel with twin toddlers, how to deal with the very real, but sometimes subordinated, needs of my older son, Chris, and how to make time for my husband, Dale.

Other things I have learned promoted personal growth. Over the years I've come to see that although my perfectionist, compulsive, and impatient tendencies make me a great nurse, they are not necessarily good qualities for a mother. So as much as possible I've tackled these traits and tried (notice I said *tried*) to soften them.

Of all the discoveries I have made, perhaps the most important ones are those that have forever changed how I see myself, motherhood, and life in general. Expressions like "Patience is a virtue" came alive to me when I tried to teach Michael and Joanna potty training and Michael's response until age three was to play the pretend potty game—he ran around the house buck naked, screaming with glee, "I 'tend to go potty on floor, I 'tend to go potty on couch, I 'tend to go potty outtide!" Just before Michael ran outside, I'd catch him and spare the neighbors the view of Michael 'tending to go potty on the flowers!

"Do everything in moderation" hit home when I took the kids on errands or outings and realized that I couldn't see everything or do everything without stressing them and me to the limit. And I was familiar with 'This too shall pass,' but it became my daily battle cry throughout my twins' infancy as I waited for life to grow easier. Lately, I learned what people who have faced great challenges in life already know: When dealing with stressful events in life (and raising twins is one of those events), it makes the going easier to share the daily struggles with others in a similar situation. I regularly attended my bimonthly twin group meetings for years for the invaluable support it gave me. Only recently have I started going just for the fun of it.

This book was written to provide an extension of the support that mothers of twins give to each other every day on a face-to-face basis. Look for this support. Seek it out. You and your family will benefit from it. It will allow you to see that raising young twins can be more than a challenge; it can be a wonderful opportunity for personal growth as well as one of the greatest adventures of a lifetime. But don't just take my word for it, find out for yourself. Good luck!

*Debra Catlin:* In writing my part of this book, my inner self has found expression, so this has been a coming-out of sorts for me. I'm okay sharing what I feel because I believe that what connects us to each other as human beings is the capacity to share our joy and pain; only the source of these is different for each of us. I may not have liked going through the changes I did, but they made me face up to areas of my life that I needed to grow in. I would not have wanted to be deprived of the opportunity to learn so much about myself through my experience of mothering twins.

The most significant thing I have learned is that the events that occur and the people I come across in my life can be viewed as messengers, bringing with them something I need to know. I can choose to heed the message or not. I now find it is easier if I approach them, instead of waiting for the messengers to beat me over the head to get their point across. With this attitude, I can find lessons throughout all areas of my life, both past and present.

My twins, Aislynn and Ricky, have sprouted up into two young trees, true to the distinctly different seeds they came from. Aislynn is tall, graceful, and ever-changing, much like the beautiful birch. She is still a high-need, sensitive child, and she has taught me that I must give attention according to individual need. I am still learning how to feel deserving of this child's unlimited and frequently expressed love for me.

Ricky is like the strong, compact, and silent oak. He could easily slip into the background if I let him. He has had to be drawn out and reminded to express his wants, needs, and feelings. His presence in my life constantly reflects the similar child still inside me.

Muggy has always been very expressive of his feelings and I can count on him to be the barometer of the family atmosphere. He has kept me honest about how I really can affect the children if I don't own up to the origin of my feelings. As I learned myself, I must continue to teach the children that they are responsible only for their own feelings and actions.

My oldest son, Jason, helps me to remember that parenting is truly a lifelong career! He had a late teenage rebellion after he left home that gave us the opportunity to refocus attention on some of the unfinished business between us. He is a young man to be truly proud of for the way in which he has handled his own challenges.

Rick and I learned to create an entirely different comfort level between us, based on acceptance of each other and recognition that honesty is less painful and energy-consuming.

My own work has led to an expansion of the birth and parenting education service into a full-fledged nonprofit community education center. Every day the childbearing families we serve affirm that validation, adequate physical resources, and emotional support help create a climate in which parents feel connected and will thrive, even in difficult times. While it is neither possible nor desirable to make everything right for them, I am content to know that we exchange messages during the time that our paths cross. Participating in this book project has given me great satisfaction; it provided an opportunity to send out messages that could be meaningful to someone open to receiving them.

*Sheri Greatwood:* I am not a religious person, nor do I believe in fate. I think we get one shot at life and we make our own breaks. My best friend always says, "This isn't a practice life," and I know she's right.

Thousands of twins are born every day to people who have the potential to be good parents. Whether they are, or are not, is up to them. Parenting skills are not inbred and instinctive to humans, they are learned. We learn them first from our own parents, but then we fly solo. Whether or not we choose to enrich our parenting skills with education is a choice that we have.

Parenting involves children, and they teach us as much as we teach them, so I believe that we must look at parenting as a continuing education program for us and for our children. We have chosen to enroll in it and we have a responsibility to finish what we start.

This teaching and learning process happens from the very beginning because our children love us and want to learn from us the moment they are born. We have a few special years when they want us around. After that, we have to run after them for attention. It's so fast, just a few years and it's over. So be careful, don't miss it.

# Resource Directory

*Pregnancy and Childbirth*

American Academy of Husband-Coached Childbirth
(the "Bradley Method")
P.O. Box 5224
Sherman Oaks, CA 91413
1-800-423-2397; in California (818) 788-6662

Write or call for information on the Bradley childbirth method
and for a list of affiliated teachers in your area.

American Society for Psychoprophylaxis in Obstetrics, Inc.
(ASPO/Lamaze)
Dept. 3197
Washington, DC 20042-3197
1-800-368-4404

Provides information to expectant parents on the Lamaze (psy-
choprophylactic) method of childbirth and on family-centered
maternity care. The organization, which publishes *Lamaze Parents'*

*Magazine,* also operates a free referral service to provide names of local, ASPO-certified childbirth educators to expectant parents.

> C/SEC, Inc. (Caesareans/Support, Education, and Concern)
> 22 Forest Road
> Framingham, MA 01701
> (508) 877-8266

Gives emotional support to cesarean parents and provides information and education on cesarean childbirth, cesarean prevention, and vaginal birth after a cesarean. Published *Frankly Speaking, A Book for Cesarean Couples.* Ask for referral to a support group in your area. Send a stamped, self-addressed business envelope for a free copy of the organization's brochure.

> Depression After Delivery
> P. O. Box 1282
> Morrisville, PA 19067
> (215) 295-3994

Provides information and support about postpartum adjustments, difficulties, and depression. Mutual self-help support groups are held throughout the United States.

> Foundation for Hospice and Home Care
> 519 C St., N.E.
> Washington, DC 20002
> (202) 547-7424

Can provide a list of home health care agencies near you for qualified medical help in your home.

> InterNational Association of Parents and Professionals for Safe Alternatives in Childbirth (NAPSAC)
> P. O. Box 646
> Marble Hill, MO 63764
> (314) 238-2010

Dedicated to exploring, examining, implementing, and establishing childbirth programs that meet the needs of families while also promoting safe medical care of the mother and babies. Be sure to indicate that you are expecting twins when you write or call.

ICAN (International Cesarean Awareness Network, Inc.)
Dept. C
P. O. Box 152
Syracuse, NY 13210
(315) 424-1942

(Formerly, Cesarean Prevention Movement, Inc.) Support network for those healing from cesarean birth. Encouragement and information for those wanting vaginal birth after cesarean. Quarterly newsletter.

International Childbirth Education Association (ICEA)
P. O. Box 20048
Minneapolis, MN 55420
(612) 854-8660

*and*

% Barbara Hanrahan, International Coordinator
57 Carisbrook St.
Sydenham, South Africa 2192

Provides referrals to local childbirth educators and family-centered facilities. Also publishes and distributes pamphlets, books, and periodicals relating to childbearing. The association has a mail order book center. Send for catalog, *ICEA Bookmarks*.

March of Dimes Birth Defects Foundation
1275 Mamaroneck Avenue
White Plains, NY 10605
(914) 428-7100

Provides information, research, and direct service pertaining to the prevention, treatment, and diagnosis of prenatal problems.

Write for their extensive catalog of written material, films, and audiovisuals on perinatal problems, birth defects, and prenatal care.

National Center for Education in Maternal and Child Health (NCE MCH)
2000 15th St. N. #701
Arlington, VA 22201-2617
(703) 524-7802

Provides information about maternal and child health.

National Childbirth Trust of Great Britain
9 Queensborough Terrace
London W2 3TB
England
(01) 221-3833

Services England, Wales, and Scotland, by offering prenatal classes, postpartum support, and breastfeeding counseling through its branches nationwide. In Britain send a stamped, self-addressed envelope for a catalog, price lists, and an events list.

National Genetics Foundation, Inc.
555 West 57th Street
New York, NY 10019
(212) 586-5800

A voluntary health agency serving individuals and families with known or suspected genetic problems. Provides information about genetic evaluation, counseling, and treatment, as available. The foundation can also arrange referrals to genetic centers for these genetic services. Write for copies of their pamphlets *Can Genetic Counseling Help You?* and *How Genetic Disease Can Affect You and Your Family,* and *For the Concerned Couple Planning a Family* (single copies free). Also write for details about their new computerized "Family Health History Analysis," in which both members of a couple complete family history questionnaires. The analysis can pinpoint genetic risks to yourselves as well as to your future children. The analysis should take place before the tenth week of a pregnancy, or preferably before a pregnancy is attempted, and the results are sent to your physician. There is a charge for this analysis.

National Health Information Clearinghouse
P. O. Box 1133
Washington, DC 20013
1-800-336-4797; in Virginia (703) 522-2590

This organization provides information to help consumers locate required health care services.

National Perinatal Information Center
1 State St.
#102
Providence, RI 02908
(401) 274-0650

Provides information and support to families experiencing high-risk pregnancies.

Read Natural Childbirth Foundation, Inc.
P. O. Box 150956
San Rafael, CA 94915
(415) 456-8462

Provides information on the method of childbirth preparation developed by English physician Grantly Dick-Read. Write for a free information packet describing their philosophy and for information on the annotated bibliography and class manual available for purchase.

Sidelines National Support Network
P.O. Box 10808
Laguna Beach, CA 92652
(714) 497-2265 (Candace Hurley)

A support service for women with complicated pregnancies.

## *Prematurity*

Parent Care, Inc.
9041 Colgate St.
Indianapolis, IN 46268
(317) 872-9913

Offers information, referrals, and other services to families, parent support groups, and health care professionals concerned with infants who require intensive or special care after birth. Has a directory listing parent support groups in the United States, Canada, and abroad, and other resources and products, such as breast pumps, preemie diapers, and preemie clothing. The directory is a benefit of membership in this nonprofit organization, along with the quarterly newsletter *Parent Care . . . News Brief.*

Parents of Premature and High Risk Infants International, Inc.
Maureen Lynch, Executive Director
% The National Self-Help Clearinghouse
25 West 43rd St. Room #620
New York, NY 10036
(212) 642-2944

A source of information, referrals, and support for those concerned with infants who require special care. Parents of premature multiples will find useful material through this clearinghouse.

## *Miscarriage/Death of a Child*

Bittersweet Beginnings
% Terri Koelling
5700 E. Greenwood Place
Denver, CO 80222
(303) 759-3979

A support network for parents experiencing loss of a multiple.

Center for Loss in Multiple Birth
% Jean Kollaantai
P. O. Box 1064
Palmer, AK 99645-1064
(907) 745-2706

Publishes "Our Newsletter" monthly. Offers support and information for parents who have experienced loss of one, both, or all of their children during a twin pregnancy, higher order multiple pregnancy, at birth or during infancy.

The Compassionate Friends, Inc. (TCF)
National Headquarters
P. O. Box 3696
Oak Brook, IL 60522-3696
(708) 990-0010

*and*

In Canada:

The Compassionate Friends National Center
685 Williams Ave.
Winnipeg, Manitoba R3E 0Z2
(204) 787-2460

In England:

53 North St.
Bristol BS3 1EN
England
0272-655-202

In Australia:

> Lower Parish Hall
> 300 Camberwell Rd.
> Camberwell 3124
> Victoria, Australia
> 03-882-3355

In New Zealand:

> % Bereaved Parents Group
> P.O. Box 4422
> Christ Church
> New Zealand

Provides understanding and support to bereaved families after miscarriage or death of a child. An international organization, TCF offers assistance through 300 support groups, telephone friends, and a quarterly newsletter. Write for brochures, a book list, and referral to a local chapter. Two booklets available for purchase from TCF are *The Grief of Parents . . . When a Child Dies,* by Margaret S. Miles, and *When a Baby Dies,* by Martha Jo Church, Helen Chazin, and Faith Ewald.

> National Council of Guilds for Infant Survival
> 9178 Nadine River Circle
> Fountain Valley, CA 92708
> 1-800-247-4370

Support and education for parents who experience sudden infant death syndrome (SIDS) and for families using in-home monitors for high-risk infants. Quarterly newsletter, group development guidelines, correspondence.

> Pregnancy and Infant Loss Center
> 1421 E. Wayzata Blvd.
> Wayzata, MN 55391
> (612) 473-9372

Offers families, friends, and professional care providers information on education, counseling services, and local, national, and international support groups. Publishes a newsletter.

SIDS Alliance
10500 Little Patuxent Pkwy. #420
Columbia, MD 21044

The foundation has a network of volunteer chapters throughout the United States that can be helpful to parents of victims of SIDS and to families with high-risk infants. Write for a list of their publications and for referral to a local chapter.

Support After Neonatal Death (SAND)
Alta Bates Hospital
3001 Colby Street at Ashby
Berkeley, CA 94705
(510) 540-0337 (Janet Kirksey, R.N.); or (510) 540-1571 (for recorded message or to leave a message)

Offers support, consultation, and educational services to parents who have lost a baby through miscarriage, abortion, or stillbirth, or whose infant has died during or after birth. These services are provided by trained parents and professionals who have also lost an infant.

Twinless Twins Support Group International
Dr. Raymond W. Brandt, Ph.D.
11220 St. Joe Road
Fort Wayne, IN 46835-9737
(219) 627-5414

A group for those persons whose multiple-birth sibling is deceased or in a terminal state.

## Child Health and Safety

American Academy of Pediatrics
Publications Department
141 N.W. Point Blvd.
Elk Grove Village, IL 60009
(708) 228-5005 or 1-800-433-9016

Write for a price list of publications on first aid and poisoning
prevention, nutrition, breast-feeding, automobile safety, car seats,
car seat loan programs, and other subjects concerning child health.

American Dental Association
Department of Public Information and Education
211 East Chicago Avenue
Chicago, IL 60611
(312) 440-2500

Ask for a copy of *Your Child's Teeth,* free to parents.

Association for the Care of Children's Health (ACCH)
7910 Woodmont Avenue
Suite 300
Bethesda, MD 20814
(301) 654-6549

An international organization that provides resources to parents
and professionals to humanize the health care environment
through education, research, advocacy, and networking. ACCH
publishes and disseminates information on such topics as infant
care, chronic illness, and developmental disabilities. Write for a
list of their publications.

Children in Hospitals (CIH)
% The Federation for Children with Special Needs
95 Berkeley St.
Boston, MA 02116
(617) 482-2915

Offers support and education to parents who wish to keep in close touch with their children during a hospital stay. Offers counseling, a newsletter, information sheets, and meetings.

Consumer Product Safety Commission
Washington, DC 20207
1-800-638-CPSC (2772)

Ask for free fact sheets and information on toy and baby equipment safety and on poison prevention. Two helpful free publications are "The Safe Nursery" and "The Super Sitter."

Foundation for Hospice and Home Care
519 C St., N.E.
Washington, DC 20002
(202) 547-7424

Can provide a list of home health care agencies near you for qualified medical help in your home.

National Genetics Foundation, Inc.
555 West 57 Street
New York, NY 10019
(212) 586-5800

Provides information and referrals regarding genetic problems.

National Health Information Clearinghouse
P. O. Box 1138
Washington, DC 20013
1-800-336-4797; in Virginia, (703) 522-2590

Provides information to help consumers locate required health care services.

National Highway Traffic Safety Administration
Office of Occupant Protection (NTS-10)
U.S. Department of Transportation
Room 5118
400 7th Street, S.W.
Washington, DC 20590
(202) 366-0123

Write for free information on automobile safety seats and for the address of your state's highway safety office.

## *Breast-feeding*

Association of Breast-feeding Mothers
10 Hershell Road
London SE 23 1 EG
England

IBFAN North American/INFANT Canada
10 Trinity Square
Toronto, Ontario
Canada

International Breastfeeding Affiliation
13 Glen Street
Hawthorne, Victoria 3122
Australia

International Lactation Consultants Associations (ILCA)
201 Brown Ave.
Evanston, IL 60202
(708) 260-8874

Parents can write for referrals to lactation consultants in your area.

La Leche League International, Inc. (ILL)
P. O. Box 1209
Franklin Park, IL 60131-8209
(708) 455-7730 (24-hour referrals, office hours Monday
through Friday, 8 to 3)

*and*

La Leche League
BM 3424
London WCIV6XX
England

Secrétariat Général de La Leche League
CF. P. 874
Ville St. Laurent, Québec H4L 4W3
Canada

Promotes the mother-infant relationship through breast-feeding.
ILL groups are located throughout the United States and in Canada and in countries throughout the world. Check your library or local phone books, or write or call the international headquarters to find the ILL leader nearest you. Send a self-addressed, stamped envelope for information or to request a copy of the *La Leche League International Catalogue.* Publications of particular interest include *Mothering Multiples* (no. 267), a book by Karen Kerkhoff Gromada, and the La Leche League handbook, *The Womanly Art of Breastfeeding* (no. 250), both listed separately under "Books"; the information sheet "Breastfeeding Your Premature Baby" (no. 13) by Sandy Countryman, and *Nighttime Parenting,* by William Sears, M.D. (no. 276). Also available free or at a nominal cost: "Breastfeeding Your Premature Baby," "Breastfeeding After a Cesarean Section," "A Mother's Guide to Breastfeeding and Mothering the Premature or Hospitalized Infant," and "Managing Nipple Problems."

Nursing Mothers of Australia
5 Glendale Street
Nunawaiting 3131
Australia


Nursing Mothers Counsel, Inc.
P. O. Box 50063
Palo Alto, CA 94303
(415) 591-6688

Counseling on breast-feeding is available through this organization. Publications include "Maintaining a Milk Supply While Separated from the Infant," "The Newborn Who Wouldn't Nurse," "Treatment of Mastitis," "Detection and Correction of Inverted Nipples," and "Working and Nursing."


## *Twin Information and Services*

Australian Multiple Birth Association (AMBA)
% Helen Green
76 Scotsborn Way
Endeavor Hills
Australia

This voluntary, self-help organization is concerned with the care and management of multiple-birth children and with the well-being of their parents and families. Write for information on membership and for a list of leaflets, publications, and sound or slide programs.

The Center for Study of Multiple Birth
Suite 476
333 Superior Street
Chicago, IL 60611
(312) 266-9093

A nonprofit organization. Conducts medical research on the subject of multiple birth with findings published in medical and clinical journals. The center conducts research at the Twinsburg Festival in Twinsburg, Ohio during the first week of August each year.

International Twins Association (ITA)
% Lynn Long or Lori Stewart
6898 Channel Rd.
Minneapolis, MN 55432
(612) 571-3022
(612) 517-8910

A nonprofit organization promoting the spiritual, intellectual, and social welfare of multiples throughout the world. A twin convention is held each year in a different city over the Labor Day weekend.

Multiple Births Foundation
Institute of Obstetrics and Gynecology Trust
Queen Charlotte's and Chelsea Hospital
Goldhawk Road
London, England W6oXG
(01) 748-4666, ext. 6201

New Zealand Multiple Birth Association
P. O. Box 1258
Wellington
New Zealand

Offers help, support, and advice to parents of multiples, acts as a liaison between New Zealand clubs and overseas organizations with similar objectives, and publishes a quarterly. Write for information on how to order . . . *and One Makes Two: A Practical Guide for New Parents of Twins,* by Jo Broad (Wellington, New Zealand; Wellington Gemini Club, 1980).

National Organization of Mothers of Twins Clubs, Inc.
(NOMOTC)
P. O. Box 23188
Albuquerque, NM 87192-1188
(505) 275-0955

A network of clubs devoted to research and education with chapters throughout the United States. Call or write for referral to a local club. Fathers, grandparents, adoptive or foster parents, and parents of supertwins (i.e., triplets or more) are also welcome to join. The *MOTC's Notebook* is the organization's official quarterly newspaper, available free to members and to nonmembers for a fee. New and expectant parents can send for a copy of *Your Twins and You,* which gives helpful hints for twin care and facts about twins. Purchase the booklet *How to Organize a Mothers of Twins Club* if there is no club in your area and you would like to start one.

Parents of Multiple Births Association (POMBA)
4981 Highway #7—East
Unit 12A; Suite 16
Markham, Ontario L3R 1N1
Canada
(416) 513-7506

Provides referrals to local clubs or helps parents start one. The organization also conducts scientific, social, and consumer-oriented research on multiple births. Reports are available. A mail-order book service offers books, booklets, and pamphlets on multiple births, pregnancy through school age, and includes materials on twins, triplets, and quads. Write for a price list and for information about the quarterly news magazine, *Double Feature,* and the organization's other publications.

Supertwin Statistician
"Miss Helen" Kirk
P. O. Box 254
Galveston, TX 77553
(409) 762-4792

"Miss Helen," as she is fondly known, has historical and current records and a wealth of information on twins and supertwins (triplets or more) throughout the world.

The Triplet Connection
8900 Thornton Rd.
P.O. Box 99571
Stockton, CA 95209
(209) 474-0885

Provides help and encouragement to expectant mothers and fathers of supertwins, offers ideas and support to parents after the birth of the children and as they grow, and helps connect families and supertwins themselves who are looking for others in a similar situation. Members receive the organization's monthly newsletter.

Twin Services
P. O. Box 10066
Berkeley, CA 94709
(510) 524-0863 (TWINLINE counseling and referral service, Monday–Friday, 10–4 Pacific time)

Services and publications for parents of multiples on pregnancy, care, development, disabilities, and loss. A network of resources and training for health and family service providers and self-help organizations.

The Twins Foundation
P. O. Box 6043
Providence, RI 02940-9487
(401) 274-TWIN (8946)

This nonprofit organization established by twins has three major programs: the research library, the museum and traveling exhibits, and the hall of fame. The research library houses educational, historical, sociological, and scientific information about multiples and helps pilot new research through seminars and conferences. The organization is developing a museum and traveling exhibits that will offer displays on the education, historical, and humanistic aspects of multiples. Through its hall of fame, the foundation recognizes major achievements of accomplished twins and is in the process of establishing scholarships for twins and developing a bureau of speakers, films, and other audiovisual materials. Write for membership information.

Twins and Multiple Births Association (TAMBA)
59 Sunnyside
Worksop, Notts 581 7LN
England
732-868-000

This self-help organization, founded in 1978, has local chapters throughout Great Britain. TAMBA provides encouragement and support to parents of multiples and attempts to create greater public awareness of the needs of multiple-birth children and their families. Please send a self-addressed envelope with inquiries.

International Society for Twin Studies
% The Mendel Institute
Piazza Galeno, 500161
Rome, Italy

An international multidisciplinary organization that furthers research and social action in all fields related to twin studies, for the mutual benefit of twins and their families. Publishes *Acta Geneticae Medicae et Gemellologiae*. For more information in the United States, contact:

Adam P. Matheny, Jr.
% The Louisville Twin Study
Child Development Unit
2301 S. 3rd St.
Louisville, KY 40208


## Twin Equipment

Gemini Baby Carrier for Twins
Tot Tenders, Inc.
712 S.W. 3rd
Corvallis, OR 97333
1-800-634-6870; or (503) 758-5458

Carry babies together up to approximately 14 pounds each; then separate and continue using as a single carrier.

Huffy
% T.R.I. Industries, Inc.
7401 Washington Ave. S.
Edina, MN 55439
(612) 944-5198

Double Easy Strider to take your twins jogging.

Kid-Kuffs, Inc.
5608 N. Roosevelt
Loveland, CO 80538
(308) 669-4568

Leash systems for children, including the Kid-Kuff Single, Kid-Kuff Double, and Kart-Kuff safety belt for shopping carts.

Nurse Mate
Four Dee Products
Dept. TW
6014 Lattimer
Houston, TX 77035
1-800-526-2594

The Nurse Mate pillow gives Mom free hands during the simultaneous breast feeding of her twins. Babies rest on a pillow, relieving Mom's arm- and back-muscle stress. The pillow has a washable zippered cover in a nursery print with eyelet lace that fits over soft foam.

## *Parenting*

Birth To Three and Beyond
3411 Willamette Street
Eugene, OR 97405
(503) 484-4401

Parent education/support services to parents of infants and toddlers, parents of multiples, teenaged parents, parents experiencing high levels of stress, and pregnant and parenting mothers in recovery from substance abuse. Please write for information on how to start your own support groups, to subscribe to monthly newsletter, or to order these publications: "Birth to Three: Support for New Parents," "Educational Materials for New Parents," "Make Parenting a Pleasure: A Curriculum Guide for Parents Under Stress," "Teen Parent Manual," and "Fundraising for Non-Profits."

Family Resource Coalition
200 South Michigan Avenue
Chicago, IL 60604
(312) 341-0900

This organization represents family resource programs in the United States and Canada and maintains a clearinghouse for information about these programs. The coalition provides a national referral service to parents. It also publishes the *FRC Report* and produces publications on family resource programs.

National Self-Help Clearinghouse
25 West 43rd Street Room 620
New York, NY 10036
(212) 840-1259

Contact the clearinghouse for a list of self-help (nonprofessional) parent support groups in your area.

Parents Anonymous
520 S. Lafayette Park #316
Los Angeles, CA 90057
1-800-421-0353; in California, 1-800-352-0386

This organization provides help for parents under stress. If you are having trouble coping and are hurting your children or afraid you might hurt them, give PA a call.

Parents Without Partners (PWP)
8807 Colesville Road
Silver Spring, MD 20910
1-800-637-7974; or (301) 588-9354

This national organization has local chapters that provide various activities for single parents and their children. In the United States and Canada, write for chapter referral and for a list of their available materials aimed at the problems faced by single parents.

Stepfamily Association of America (SAA)
215 Centennial Mall South
Suite 212
Lincoln, NE 68508
(402) 477-7837

This national association offers workshops and support groups, provides professional referrals, and acts as a national advocate for stepparents, remarried parents, and their children. SAA publishes a quarterly newsletter for stepfamilies and has a national conference each year. Write or call for information about the chapter nearest you and for a list of publications and their prices.

## Special Needs Children

Clearinghouse on the Handicapped
U.S. Department of Education
Switzer Building, Room 3132
Washington, DC 20202
(202) 732-1245


A *Pocket Guide for the Disabled Person* and a newsletter called *O.S.E.R.'s\* News in Print*. Both publications are free. (\*Office of Special Education and Rehabilitation)


Federation for Children with Special Needs
95 BerkeleySt. #104
Boston, MA 02116
(617) 482-2915


A center in which parents and parent organizations work together to better serve children with special needs. The federation publishes a newsletter, *Newsline*. All services are provided free of charge.


Let's Play to Grow
8610 Contee Rd.
Laurel, MD 20708
(301) 776-8054
(202) 673-7166

Develops small clubs for families of children with special needs. Parent training, education for child through recreation. Newsletter, guidelines, and technical assistance in starting clubs.

March of Dimes Birth Defects Foundation
1275 Mamaroneck Avenue
White Plains, NY 10605
(914) 428-7100

Fights birth defects by funding research, medical services, and education programs. Write the organization's community services department or call the chapter listed in your local telephone directory. Ask for a list of free materials on the subject of maternal and child health, genetic counseling, birth defects, and parenting. Two useful pamphlets are *Be Good to Your Baby Before It Is Born,* and *Data: Drugs, Alcohol, Tobacco Abuse During Pregnancy.*

National Association for Hearing and Speech Action (NAHSA)
10801 Rockville Pike
Rockville, MD 20852
(800) 638-TALK (8255) (Monday–Friday, 8–4)

Provides information on all communicative disorders through its Helpline (the number listed above). Write for a price list of their brochures.

National Health Information Clearinghouse
P. O. Box 1133
Washington, DC 20013
1-800-336-4797; in Virginia, (703) 522-2590

Provides information to help consumers locate required health care services.

National Information Center for Handicapped Children and
Youth (NICHCY)
P. O. Box 1492
Washington, DC 20013
1-800-999-5599

A free information service that helps parents, educators, care-
givers, advocates, and others to improve the lives of children and
youth with disabilities. The organization answers questions, develops and shares new information through fact sheets and news-
letters, provides advice to people working in groups, and connects
people across the country who are solving similar problems.

Parentele
8331 Kimball Ave.
Skokie, IL 60076
(301) 654-6549

Information and support for parents of children with disabilities.
Quarterly newsletter, resource guide, bibliography.

Parents Helping Parents
535 Race St., #140
San Jose, CA 95126
(408) 288-5010

Support and information to help families cope with having a special child, with mental or physical disabilities. Newsletter, how-
to manuals, telephone support.

Pilot Parents Program
3610 Dodge St.
Omaha, NE 68131
(402) 346-5220

Support to parents of children with developmental disabilities (mental retardation, cerebral palsy, epilepsy, autism, and others). Handbook to develop chapters, pen-pal program; established 1971.

# Suggested Reading

## On Multiples

Alexander, Terry Pink. *Make Room for Twins.* New York: Bantam, 1987.

Clegg, Averil, and Anne Wodett. *Twins: From Conception to Five Years.* New York: Ballantine, 1991

Noble, Elizabeth. *Having Twins.* Boston: Houghton-Mifflin, 1991.

Novotny, Pamela. *The Joy of Twins.* New York: Crown, 1988.

## Nutrition During Pregnancy

Brewer, Gail Sforza, and Tom Brewer, M.D. *The Brewer Medical Diet for Normal and High Risk Pregnancy.* New York: Simon & Schuster, 1983.

Eisenberg, Arlene, et al. *What to Eat When You're Expecting.* New York: Workman, 1986.

Suggested Reading

## Pregnancy and Birth

Eisenberg, Arlene. *What to Expect When You're Expecting.* New York: Workman, 1991.

Johnston, Susan, and Deborah Kraut. *Pregnancy Bedrest: A Guide for the Pregnant Woman and Her Family.* New York: Holt, 1990.

Rich, Laurie. *When Pregnancy Isn't Perfect: A Layperson's Guide to Complications in Pregnancy.* New York: Dutton, 1991.

Simkin, Penny. *The Birth Partner: Everything You Need to Know to Help a Woman Through Childbirth.* Boston: Harvard Common Press, 1989.

## Prematurity

Flushman, Bette, Gary Gale, et al. at Children's Hospital in Oakland. *My Special Start: A Guide to Help Parents in the Neonatal Intensive Care Unit.* Palo Alto, CA: VORT.

Harrison, Helen. *The Premature Baby Book: A Parent's Guide to Coping and Caring in the First Years.* New York: St. Martin's, 1984.

## Breast-feeding

Eiger, Marvin, and Sally Wendkos Olds. *The Complete Book of Breastfeeding.* New York: Bantam, 1987.

Walker, Marsha, and Jeanne Driscoll. *Breastfeeding Your Premature or Special Care Baby.* 1989.

*The Womanly Art of Breastfeeding.* Franklin Park, IL: La Leche League International, 1991.

## Families with Children Who Require Special Care

Finston, Peggy, M.D. *Parenting Plus: Raising Children with Special Health Needs.* New York: Viking Penguin, 1990.

Powers, Michael D., Psy. D., ed. *The Special Needs Collection: Chil-*

*dren with Autism: A Parents' Guide.* Rockville, MD: Woodbine
House, 1989. (Woodbine House publishes a series of books
that come highly recommended as "first books" for parents
with children with disabilities.)

Pueschel, Siegfried M., M.D., James C. Bernier, M.S.W., and
Leslie E. Weidenman, Ph.D. *The Special Child: A Source Book
for Parents of Children with Developmental Disabilities.* Balti-
more: Paul H. Brooks, 1988.

## Grief/Loss

Borg, Susan. *When Pregnancy Fails.* Boston: Beacon, 1988.
Ilse, Sherokee. *Empty Arms: Coping After Miscarriage, Stillbirth,
and Infant Loss.* Long Lake, MN: S.L. Ilse, 1990.

## Infant and Child Care and Development

Leach, Penelope. *Your Baby and Child, From Birth to Age Five.*
New York: Knopf, 1989.
Samuels, Michael, and Nancy Samuels. *The Well Baby Book.* New
York: Summit Books, 1991.

## Adjusting to Parenthood

Brazelton, T. Berry. *On Becoming a Family.* New York: Dell, 1981.
Briggs, Dorothy. *Your Child's Self-Esteem.* New York: Dolphin
Doubleday, 1975.
Dix, Carol. *New Mother Syndrome.* New York: Doubleday, 1985.
Faber, Adele, and Elaine Mazlich. *How to Talk So Kids Will Listen
and Listen So Kids Will Talk.* New York: Avon, 1975.
Lim, Robin. *After the Baby's Birth: A Woman's Way to Wellness.*
Berkeley, CA: Celestial Arts, 1991.
Muir, John. "Being a Father: Family, Work, and Self." *Mothering,*
1990.

Turecki, Stanley, M.D. *The Difficult Child.* New York: Bantam, 1989.

## Periodicals and Magazines

*Double Talk.* P.O. Box 412, Amelia, OH 45102. (513) 753-7117.
*Twins.* P.O. Box 12045, Overland Park, KS 66212. (913) 722-1090.

# Index

Disciplining
  of preschoolers, 336–38
  of toddlers, 306–10
Disposable diapers, 65, 141
Doula services, 161, 62
DPT injection, 140
Dreams
  bad, 252, 253
  during pregnancy, 32
Dressing
  babies, 142–43
  alike, 331, 32
Dyzygotic twins, *see* Fraternal
  twins

Eclampsia, 57–59
Effacement, 79
Electronic fetal monitors, 77
Employment, *see* Work
Epidural anesthesia, 83
Equipment, resources on, 394–95
Exercise during pregnancy, 41–42
Exhaustion, parental, 144–46

Family-centered birth, 83
Family history of twins, 21, 22
Family Resource Coalition, 396
Fatigue during pregnancy, 36
Fathers, 356–69
  at cesarean births, 83, 84
  and emotional changes in preg-
    nancy, 31–33
  relationship with, *see* Couple re-
    lationships
  support from, 154–56
Federation for Children with Special Needs, 398
Feeding, 120–31, 243–45
  burping and, 127
  coordinating, 123–25
  growth and, 127–28
  positions for, 125–27
  schedule for, 121–23
  solid food, 130–31, 245–48

  of toddlers, 312–15
  *See also* Bottle-feeding; Breast-
    feeding
Feelings, acknowledgment of, 342
Feet, swollen, 38
Fetal distress, 87
Fetal movement, 23
Fighting
  by preschoolers, 338–41
  by toddlers, 310–11
Formula, 120–21
Foundation for Hospice and
  Home Care, 378, 387
Fraternal twins, 20–21
  genetic abnormalities in, 53, 54
  predisposition to having, 21–22
  temperamental differences of,
    239
  as toddlers, 300
Friends
  exchanging child care with,
    210–11
  support from, 156–60

Gas pains, 37
Gemini Baby Carrier for Twins,
  394–95
Gender differences
  of preschoolers, 329
  of toddlers, 303–5
General anesthesia, 83
Genetic disorders
  resources on, 380–81, 387
  testing for, 53
Gestational diabetes, 51, 56–57
Glucose tolerance test, 51, 56, 57
Grandparents
  as overnight babysitters, 212
  support from, 156–60
Grief, anticipatory, 113
Grocery store, trips to, 182–83
Growth
  feeding and, 127–28
  during first year, 235

Napping, 251–52
of preschoolers, 342–43
of toddlers, 315–18
Nausea during pregnancy, 34–35
Neonatal intensive care unit
(NICU), 69–70, 80, 82, 84,
86–87, 93, 100–14
bonding with infants in, 98, 112
breastfeeding in, 108–10
discharge from, 113–14
participating in care of infants
in, 102–3
postpartum period and, 95–96
sibling visits to, 219
Newborns, 117–49
bathing and dressing, 142–43
comforting, 132–35
coming home with, 117–20
diapering, 141
enjoying time with, 143–44
feeding, 120–31
illness in, 139–41
pacifiers for, 142
siblings and, 219–26
sleep of, 135–39
New Zealand Multiple Births Association, 391
Nightmares, 252, 253
Night terrors, 346–47
Night-waking, 137–39, 252–54
Non-stress tests, 55, 73
"No" phase, 309
Nurse Mate, 395
Nurse midwives, 43–44
Nursing, *see* Breast-feeding
Nursing Mothers of Australia, 389
Nursing Mothers Counsel, Inc.,
389–90
Nutrition during pregnancy, 40–
41

Obstetricians, 43–44
birth plans and, 68
Outings, 175–94, 258

attention from strangers during,
192–93
equipment for, 176–80
short, 181–87
Overnight trips, 187–92
babysitters for, 211–12, 280–
281
Oxytocin, 88

Pacifiers, 142, 250
at bedtime, 316–17
Packs, 178
Parental leave acts, 155
Parent Care, Inc., 382
Parentele, 399
Parenting resources, 395–97
Parents Anonymous, 396–97
Parents Helping Parents, 399–400
Parents of Multiple Births Associ-
ation (POMBA), 392
Parents Without Partners, 397
Parents of Premature and High
Risk Infants International,
Inc., 382
Partners, *see* Fathers
Part-time jobs, 288
Pediatricians
at cesarean births, 84
choosing, 66
and illnesses in infancy, 139–40
visits to, 186–87
Personal interests, 285–87
Pertussis, 140
Pets, 259
Phenobarbitol, 92
Phototherapy, 104–5
Pilot Parents Program, 400
Pitocin, 88, 91, 96
Placenta, 21
expulsion of, 79
Placenta previa, 59–60
Plane trips, *see* Air travel
Play
with newborns, 143–44
of older babies, 237–38

Recreational day trips, 184–85
Relatives
  babysitting by, 197–98
  support from, 156–60
Respiratory distress syndrome, 71,
  106–7
Restaurants, 183
Rubella, 140

Safety
  babyproofing and, 191–92,
    259–61
  for preschoolers, 351–54
  resources on, 385–88
  for toddlers, 320–22
Scary thoughts, 344–45
Schedules, 121–23
  outings and, 81
School, returning to, 291–93
Self, sense of, 283–85
Self-care during pregnancy, 39–42
Senior citizen babysitters, 199
Separation anxiety, 241–43
  nighttime, 249–50
  of toddlers, 301
Sexual abstinence during pregnancy, 49–50
Sexual intimacy, 271–73
Shortness of breath, 38
Siblings, 214–33
  bonds between twins and, 226–
    228
  fathers and, 362–63
  fighting among, 228–32
  and homecoming of twins, 219–
    26
  illnesses and, 139
  during pregnancy, 32, 214–19
Sidelines National Support Network, 381–82
Single parents, resources for, 397
Sleep
  deprivation in parents, 144–46
  disturbed, during pregnancy, 38

getting babies to, 135–39, 248–
  252
  lack of, in postpartum period,
    95
  *See also* Bedtime; Napping
Social service organizations, 161
Solid food, 130–31, 245–48
Sonogram, *see* Ultrasound
Special needs children, resources
  for, 397–400
Spinal anesthesia, 83, 89
Stepfamily Association of America
  (SAA), 397
Steroids, 71, 72
Stranger anxiety, 243
Stress, 167–72
  postpartum depression and, 147
  during pregnancy, 32
Strollers, 177–78
Sudden infant death syndrome
  (SIDS), 384, 385
SIDS Alliance, 385
Supertwin Statistician, 392
Support, 150–74
  community, 162–65
  hired, 160–62
  from husband/partners, 154–56
  inner, 171–72
  need for, 150–51
  during pregnancy, 151–54
  from relatives and friends, 156–
    160
  self-, 165–67
Support After Neonatal Death
  (SAND), 385
Surfactant, 107
Swimming, 258

Table technique, 340
Talking, *see* Language development
Tantrums, 311–12, 341–42
Tattle-telling, 340–41
Teenage babysitters, 198–99
Teething, 235–36
Television, 326